The Pocket Cengage Handbook

KIRSZNER
& MANDELL

2016 MLA Update Edition

The Pocket Cengage Handbook

KIRSZNER & MANDELL

Seventh Edition

2016 MLA Update Edition

Laurie G. Kirszner
University of the Sciences, Emeritus

Stephen R. Mandell
Drexel University

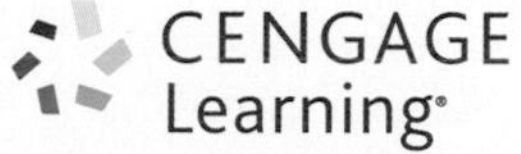

Australia • Brazil • Mexico • Singapore • United Kingdom • United States

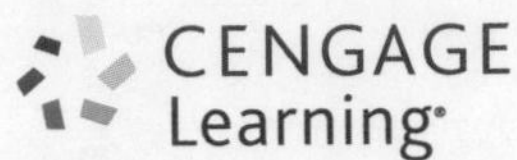

The Pocket Cengage Handbook, Seventh Edition
2016 MLA Update Edition
Laurie G. Kirszner, Stephen R. Mandell

Product Director: Monica Eckman

Product Team Manager: Nicole Morinon

Product Manager: Laura Ross

Senior Content Developer: Leslie Taggart

Content Developer: Karen Mauk

Associate Content Developer: Karolina Kiwak

Associate Content Developer: Rachel Smith

Product Assistant: Claire Branman

Senior Managing Content Developer: Cara Douglass-Graff

Marketing Director: Stacey Purviance

Senior Content Project Manager: Jennifer K. Feltri-George

Senior Art Director: Marissa Falco

Manufacturing Planner: Betsy Donaghey

IP Analyst: Ann Hoffman

IP Project Manager: Farah Fard

Production Service: Karen Stocz, Cenveo® Publisher Services

Compositor: Cenveo® Publisher Services

Text and Cover Designer: Cenveo® Publisher Services

Cover Image: James Weinberg

WCN: 01-100-101

Library of Congress Control Number: On file

Student Edition:
ISBN: 978-1-337-27993-2

Cengage Learning
20 Channel Center Street
Boston, MA 02210
USA

Cengage Learning is a leading provider of customized learning solutions with employees residing in nearly 40 different countries and sales in more than 125 countries around the world. Find your local representative at **www.cengage.com.**

Cengage Learning products are represented in Canada by Nelson Education, Ltd.

To learn more about Cengage Learning Solutions, visit **www.cengage.com.** Purchase any of our products at your local college store or at our preferred online store **www.cengagebrain.com.**

Printed in China
Print Number: 01 Print Year: 2016

How to Use This Book

We would like to introduce you to *The Pocket Cengage Handbook*, Seventh Edition, a quick reference guide for college students. This book was designed to be a truly portable handbook that can fit easily in a backpack or pocket. Despite its compact size, *The Pocket Cengage Handbook* covers all the topics you'd expect to find in a much longer book: the writing process (illustrated by a model student essay); sentence grammar and style; punctuation and mechanics; the research process (illustrated by four model student research papers); and MLA, APA, Chicago, and CSE documentation styles. In addition, the book devotes a full chapter to writing an argumentative essay—and a full section to practical assignments (including composing in digital environments, document design, writing in the workplace, presentations, and composing in the disciplines). Finally, it includes a chapter that addresses the concerns of multilingual writers.

The explanations and examples of writing in *The Pocket Cengage Handbook* can guide you not just in first-year courses but throughout your college career and beyond. Our goal throughout is to make the book clear, accessible, useful, and—most of all—easy to navigate. To achieve this goal, we incorporated distinctive design features throughout to make information easy to find and easy to use.

Design Features

- **New planning guides** throughout the text help you plan and organize a range of documents in various genres.
- **Numerous checklists** summarize key information that you can quickly access as needed.
- **Close-up boxes** provide an in-depth look at some of the more perplexing writing-related issues you will encounter.
- **Part 3 (easily identified with a "Documenting Sources" tab)** includes the most up-to-date documentation and format guidelines from the Modern Language Association, the American Psychological Association, the University of Chicago Press, and the Council of Science Editors.

- Chapter 10 includes the updated documentation guidelines put forth in the eighth edition of the *MLA Handbook* (2016). The style has been simplified to emphasize a common approach to a wide variety of source types, and the updated chapter introduces the new approach while continuing to offer numerous citation examples for students.
- **Specially designed documentation directories** make it easy to locate models for various kinds of sources, including those found in online databases such as *Academic Search Premier* and *LexisNexis*. In addition, annotated diagrams of sample works-cited entries clearly illustrate the elements of proper documentation.
- **Marginal cross-references** throughout the book allow you to flip directly to other sections that treat topics in more detail.
- **Marginal multilingual cross-references** throughout the book direct you to sections of Part 9, "Composing for Multilingual Writers," where concepts are presented as they apply specifically to multilingual writers.
- **Multilingual tips** are woven throughout the text to explain concepts in relation to the unique experiences of multilingual students.
- **A new "Ten Habits of Successful Students" foldout** illustrates and helps you apply the strategies of successful students both in and out of college.

Acknowledgments

We would like to take this opportunity to thank Anne Stameshkin for her work on the new "Ten Habits of Successful Students" foldout and on the documentation updates; Kelly Cannon, Muhlenberg College, for his research advice; and Sherry Rankins-Robertson, University of Arkansas at Little Rock, for her digital writing advice.

We also thank the following reviewers for their advice, which helped us develop the seventh edition:

Negussie Abebe, *Lone Star College, University Park*
Christine Barr, *Lone Star College, University Park*
Christina Bisirri, *Seminole State College of Florida*
Woodward Bousquet, *Shenandoah University*
William Carney, *Cameron University*
James Crooks, *Shasta College*
Michael Duffy, *Moorpark College*
Christopher Ervin, *Western Kentucky University*

Daniel Fitzstephens, *University of Colorado Boulder*
Ginger Fray, *Lone Star College, Greenspoint Center*
Hillary Gallego, *North Lake College*
Andrew Green, *University of Miami*
Rebecca Hoff, *West Virginia University Parkersburg*
John Hyman, *American University*
Parmita Kapadia, *Northern Kentucky University*
Laura Knight, *Mercer County Community College*
Bobby Kuechenmeister, *University of Toledo*
Laura La Flair, *Belmont Abbey College*
Angela Laflen, *Marist College*
Meredith Love-Steinmetz, *Francis Marion University*
Walter Lowe, *Green River Community College*
Cassie Plott, *Rowan-Cabarrus Community College*
Chrishawn Speller, *Seminole State College of Florida*
Mary Tripp, *University of Central Florida*
Isera Tyson-Miller, *State College of Florida*
Martha Vertreace-Doody, *Kennedy-King College*
Alex Vuilleumier, *Portland Community College*
Ann Westrick, *Bowling Green State University*
Karen Wilson, *Lakeland Community College*

As we have worked to develop a book that would give you the guidance you need to become a self-reliant writer and to succeed in college and beyond, we have had the support of an outstanding team of creative professionals at Cengage Learning: Product Team Manager Nicole Morinon; Product Manager Laura Ross; Senior Content Developer Leslie Taggart; Associate Content Developer Rachel Smith; Product Assistant Claire Branman; and Senior Content Project Manager Rosemary Winfield.

We have also had the good fortune to work with an equally strong team outside Cengage Learning: our outstanding Content Developer Karen Mauk; the staff of Cenveo; our very talented Project Manager and Copyeditor, Karen Stocz; and James Weinberg, whose cover image is the icing on the cake. To these people, and to all the others who worked with us on this project, we are very grateful.

Laurie Kirszner
Steve Mandell
January 2016

Teaching and Learning Resources

Online Instructor's Manual

The Online Instructor's Manual contains an abundance of instructor materials, including sample syllabi and activities. To download or print the manual, log on to <https://login.cengage.com> with your faculty account.

MindTap

MindTap® English for Kirszner and Mandell's *The Pocket Cengage Handbook*, seventh edition, engages your students to become better thinkers, communicators, and writers by blending your course materials with content that supports every aspect of the writing process.

- Interactive activities on grammar and mechanics promote application in student writing
- Easy-to-use paper management system helps prevent plagiarism and allows for electronic submission, grading, and peer review
- A vast database of scholarly sources with video tutorials and examples supports every step of the research process
- Professional tutoring guides students from rough drafts to polished writing
- Visual analytics track student progress and engagement
- Seamless integration into your campus learning management system keeps all your course materials in one place

MindTap lets you compose your course, your way.

PART 1

Approaching Texts

1 Reading to Write 2

1a Previewing a Text 2
1b Highlighting a Text 3
1c Annotating a Text 4
1d Reading Electronic Texts 6
1e Writing a Critical Response 8

2 Understanding the Rhetorical Situation 9

2a Considering the Rhetorical Situation 10
2b Determining Your Purpose 10
2c Identifying Your Audience 12
2d Selecting a Genre 14

3 Developing Essay Projects 15

3a Planning 15
3b Shaping 17
3c Constructing a Scratch Outline 20
3d Drafting and Revising 20
3e Editing and Proofreading 23
3f Model Student Essay 25
3g Creating a Writing Portfolio 30

4 Writing an Argumentative Essay 32

4a Organizing an Argumentative Essay 32
4b Model Argumentative Essay 34

CHAPTER 1

Reading to Write

Reading is an essential part of learning. Before you can become an effective writer and a successful student, you need to know how to get the most out of the texts you read.

Central to developing strong reading skills is learning the techniques of **active reading**: marking the text in order to identify parallels, question ambiguities, distinguish important points from not-so-important ones, and connect causes with effects and generalizations with specific examples. The understanding you gain from active reading prepares you to think (and write) critically about a text.

MULTILINGUAL TIP

When you read a text for the first time, don't worry about understanding every word. Instead, just try to get a general idea of what the text is about and how it is organized. Later on, you can use a dictionary to look up any unfamiliar words.

1a Previewing a Text

Before you begin reading a text, you should **preview** it—that is, skim it to get a general sense of its content and emphasis.

When you preview a **periodical article**, scan the introductory and concluding paragraphs for summaries of the author's main points. (Journal articles in the sciences and social sciences often begin with summaries called **abstracts**.) Thesis statements, topic sentences, repeated key terms, transitional words and phrases, and transitional paragraphs can also help you to identify the key points a writer is making. In addition, look for the visual cues—such as headings and lists—that writers use to emphasize ideas.

See 39b–c

When you preview a **book**, start by looking at its table of contents, especially at the sections that pertain to your topic. Then, turn to its index to see how much coverage the book gives to subjects that may be important to you. As you leaf through the chapters, look at any pictures, graphs, and tables, and read the captions that appear with them.

CHECKLIST

Previewing a Text

When you preview a text, try to answer these questions:

- ❑ What is the text's general subject?
- ❑ What are the writer's main points?
- ❑ How much space does the writer devote to topics relevant to your interests or research?
- ❑ What other topics are covered?
- ❑ Who is the author of the text? What do you know about this writer?
- ❑ Is the text current? Is its information up to date?
- ❑ Does the text strike you as interesting, accessible, and useful?

Close-Up VISUAL CUES

When you preview a text, don't forget to note its use of color and of various typographical elements—such as typeface and type size, boldface and italics—to emphasize ideas.

1b Highlighting a Text

When you have finished previewing a work, you should **highlight** it—that is, use a system of symbols and underlining to identify the writer's key points and their relationships to one another. (If you are working with library material, photocopy the pages you need before you highlight them.)

CHECKLIST

Using Highlighting Symbols

- ❑ Underline to indicate information you should read again.
- ❑ Box or circle key words or important phrases.
- ❑ Put question marks next to confusing passages, unclear points, or words you need to look up.
- ❑ Draw lines or arrows to show connections between ideas.
- ❑ Number points that appear in sequence.
- ❑ Draw a vertical line in the margin to set off an important section of text.
- ❑ Star especially important ideas.

1c Annotating a Text

After you have read through a text once, read it again—this time, more critically. At this stage, you should **annotate** the pages, recording your responses to what you read. This process of recording notes in the margins or between the lines will help you understand the writer's ideas and your own reactions to those ideas.

MULTILINGUAL TIP

You may find it useful to use your native language when you annotate a text.

Some of your annotations may be relatively straightforward. For example, you may define new words, identify unfamiliar references, or jot down brief summaries. Other annotations may reflect your personal reactions to the text. For example, you may identify a parallel between your own experience and one described in the text, or you may record your opinion of the writer's position.

As you start to **think critically** about a text, your annotations may identify points that confirm (or dispute) your own ideas, question the appropriateness or accuracy of the writer's support, uncover the writer's biases, or even question (or challenge) the writer's conclusion.

The following passage illustrates a student's highlighting and annotations of a passage from Michael Pollan's book *The Omnivore's Dilemma.*

In the early years of the nineteenth century, Americans began drinking more than they ever had before or since, embarking on a collective bender that confronted the young republic with its first major public health crisis—the obesity epidemic of its day. Corn whiskey, suddenly superabundant and cheap, became the drink of choice, and in 1820 the typical American was putting away half a pint of the stuff every day. That comes to more than five gallons of spirits a year for every man, woman, and child in America. The figure today is less than one.

People drank 5x as much as they do today

As the historian W. J. Rorabaugh tells the story in *The Alcoholic Republic,* we drank the hard stuff at breakfast, lunch, and dinner, before work and after and very often during.

!!

Employers were expected to supply spirits over the course of the workday; in fact, the modern coffee break began as a late-morning whiskey break called "the elevenses." (Just to pronounce it makes you sound tipsy.) Except for a brief respite Sunday morning in church, Americans simply did not gather—whether for a barn raising or quilting bee, corn husking or political rally—without passing the whiskey jug. Visitors from Europe—hardly models of sobriety themselves—marveled at the free flow of American spirits. "Come on then, if you love toping," the journalist William Cobbett wrote his fellow Englishmen in a dispatch from America. "For here you may drink yourself blind at the price of sixpence."

?

The results of all this toping were entirely predictable: a rising tide of public drunkenness, violence, and family abandonment, and a spike in alcohol-related diseases. Several of the Founding Fathers—including George Washington, Thomas Jefferson, and John Adams—denounced the excesses of "the Alcoholic Republic," inaugurating an American quarrel over drinking that would culminate a century later in Prohibition.

*

Did the gov't take action?

But the outcome of our national drinking binge is not nearly as relevant to our own situation as its underlying cause. Which, put simply, was this: American farmers were producing far too much corn. This was particularly true in the newly settled regions west of the Appalachians, where fertile, virgin soils yielded one bumper crop after another. A mountain of surplus corn piled up in the Ohio River Valley. Much as today, the astounding productivity of American farmers proved to be their own worst enemy, as well as a threat to public health. For when yields rise, the market is flooded with grain, and its price collapses. What happens next? The excess biomass works like a vacuum in reverse: Sooner or later, clever marketers will figure out a way to induce the human omnivore to consume the surfeit of cheap calories.

Why?

*

Examples from contemporary US farming?

This is his point

CHECKLIST

Reading Texts

As you read a text, keep the following questions in mind:

- ❑ Does the writer provide any information about his or her background? If so, how does this information affect your reading of the text?
- ❑ What is the writer's purpose? How can you tell?
- ❑ What audience is the text aimed at? How can you tell?
- ❑ What genre is the writer using? What are the genre's specific features?
- ❑ What is the most important idea? What support does the writer provide for that idea?
- ❑ What information can you learn from the introduction and conclusion?
- ❑ What information can you learn from the thesis statement and topic sentences?
- ❑ What key words are repeated? What does this repetition tell you about the writer's purpose and emphasis?
- ❑ How would you characterize the writer's tone?
- ❑ Where do you agree with the writer? Where do you disagree?
- ❑ What, if anything, is not clear to you?

See Ch. 2
See 2d
See 3b

1d Reading Electronic Texts

Even when electronic documents physically resemble print documents (as they do in online newspaper articles), the way they present information can be very different. Print documents are **linear**; that is, readers move in a straight line from the beginning of a document to the end. Print documents are also self-contained, including all the background information, explanations, supporting details, and visuals necessary to make their point.

Electronic documents, however, are usually not linear. They often include advertising, marginal commentary, and graphics, and they may also include sound and video. In addition, links embedded in the text encourage readers to go to other sites for facts, statistical data, visuals, or additional articles that supplement the discussion. For example, readers of the electronic discussion of gun control pictured in Figure 1.1 could link to FBI data about the connection between "concealed carry laws" and violent crime. Once they access this material, they can choose to read it carefully, skim it, or ignore it.

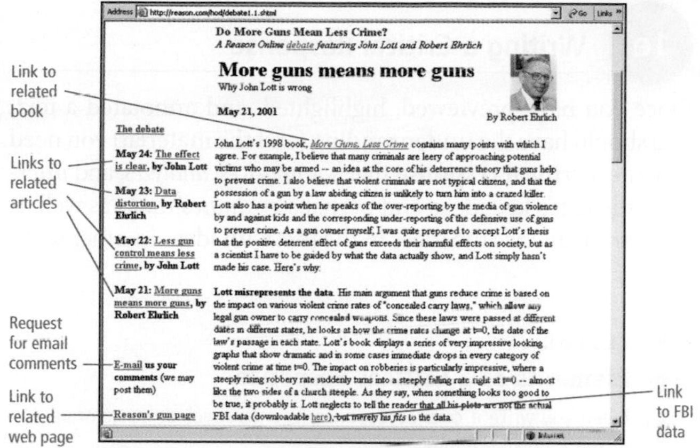

Address http://reason.com/hod/debate1.1.shtml

Do More Guns Mean Less Crime?
A Reason Online debate featuring John Lott and Robert Ehrlich

More guns means more guns

Why John Lott is wrong

May 21, 2001

By Robert Ehrlich

The debate

May 24: The effect is clear, **by John Lott**

May 23: Data distortion, **by Robert Ehrlich**

May 22: Less gun control means less crime, **by John Lott**

May 21: More guns means more guns, **by Robert Ehrlich**

E-mail **us your comments** (we may post them)

Reason's gun page

John Lott's 1998 book, *More Guns, Less Crime* contains many points with which I agree. For example, I believe that many criminals are leery of approaching potential victims who may be armed -- an idea at the core of his deterrence theory that guns help to prevent crime. I also believe that violent criminals are not typical citizens, and that the possession of a gun by a law abiding citizen is unlikely to turn him into a crazed killer. Lott also has a point when he speaks of the over-reporting by the media of gun violence by and against kids and the corresponding under-reporting of the defensive use of guns to prevent crime. As a gun owner myself, I was quite prepared to accept Lott's thesis that the positive deterrent effect of guns exceeds their harmful effects on society, but as a scientist I have to be guided by what the data actually show, and Lott simply hasn't made his case. Here's why:

Lott misrepresents the data. His main argument that guns reduce crime is based on the impact on various violent crime rates of "concealed carry laws," which allow any legal gun owner to carry concealed weapons. Since these laws were passed at different dates in different states, he looks at how the crime rates change at t=0, the date of the law's passage in each state. Lott's book displays a series of very impressive looking graphs that show dramatic and in some cases immediate drops in every category of violent crime at time t=0. The impact on robberies is particularly impressive, where a steeply rising robbery rate suddenly turns into a steeply falling rate right at t=0 -- almost like the two sides of a church steeple. As they say, when something looks too good to be true, it probably is. Lott neglects to tell the reader that all his plots are not the actual FBI data (downloadable here), but merely his *fits* to the data.

FIGURE 1.1 Excerpt from "Do More Guns Mean Less Crime?" A *Reason Online* Debate. Reprinted by permission of Reason.

The format of electronic texts presents challenges to readers. First, because links to other material interrupt the document's flow, it may be hard for readers to focus on a writer's main idea and key points or to follow an argument's logic. In addition, pages may be very busy, crowded with distracting marginalia, visuals, and advertisements. For these reasons, it makes sense to use a slightly different process when you apply active reading strategies to an electronic text.

Previewing During the previewing stage, you will probably want to skim the text online, doing your best to ignore visuals, marginal commentary, advertising, and links. If the text looks like something you will want to read more closely, you should print it out (taking care to choose the "printer-friendly" version, which will usually omit the distracting material and enable you to focus on the text's content).

Highlighting and Annotating Once you have hard copy of an electronic text, you can proceed to highlight and annotate it just as you would a print text. Reading on hard copy will enable you to follow the writer's main idea instead of clicking on every link. However, you should be sure to circle any links that look promising so you can explore them later on.

Note: You can also highlight and annotate web-based texts by using a program such as *Diigo*, which makes it possible for you to highlight and write self-stick notes on electronic documents.

1e Writing a Critical Response

Once you have previewed, highlighted, and annotated a text, you should have the understanding (and the material) you need to write a **critical response** that *summarizes, analyzes,* and *interprets* the text's key ideas and perhaps *evaluates* them as well. It can also *synthesize* the ideas in the text with ideas in other texts.

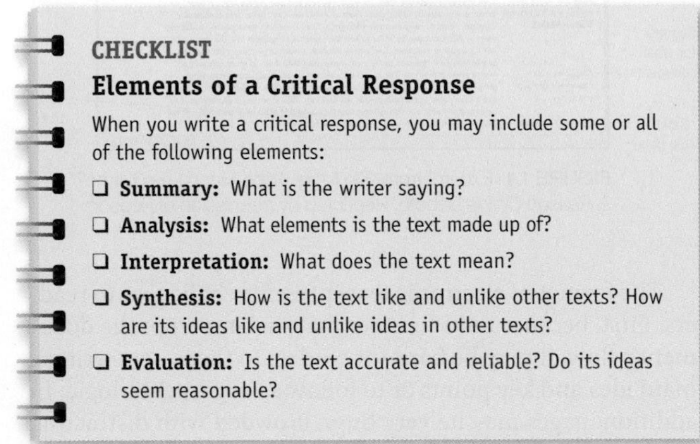

CHECKLIST

Elements of a Critical Response

When you write a critical response, you may include some or all of the following elements:

- ❑ **Summary:** What is the writer saying?
- ❑ **Analysis:** What elements is the text made up of?
- ❑ **Interpretation:** What does the text mean?
- ❑ **Synthesis:** How is the text like and unlike other texts? How are its ideas like and unlike ideas in other texts?
- ❑ **Evaluation:** Is the text accurate and reliable? Do its ideas seem reasonable?

The following is a student's critical response to the passage from *The Omnivore's Dilemma* on pages 4–5.

Author and title identified

Summary

Analysis and interpretation

Evaluation

In an excerpt from his book *The Omnivore's Dilemma*, Michael Pollan discusses the drinking habits of nineteenth-century Americans and makes a connection between the cause of this "national drinking binge" and the factors behind our twenty-first-century unhealthy diets. In both cases, he blames the overproduction of grain by American farmers. He links nineteenth-century overproduction of corn with "a rising tide of public drunkenness, violence, and family abandonment, and a spike in alcohol-related deaths," and he also links the current overproduction of grain with a "threat to public health." Although there are certainly other causes of our current problems with obesity, particularly among young children, Pollan's analogy makes sense. As long as farmers need to sell their overabundant crops, consumers will be presented with a "surfeit of cheap calories"—with potentially disastrous results.

CHECKLIST

Writing a Critical Response

As you first read a text, keep the following questions in mind:

- ❑ Does the text provide any information about the writer's background? If so, how does this information affect your reading of the text?
- ❑ What is the writer's purpose? How can you tell?
- ❑ What audience is the text aimed at? How can you tell?
- ❑ What is the text's most important idea? What support does the writer provide for that idea?

Then, as you look more closely at the text, think about these questions:

- ❑ What information can you learn from the text's introduction and conclusion?
- ❑ What information can you learn from the thesis statement and topic sentences?
- ❑ Does the writer make any statements that suggest a particular bias?
- ❑ How would you characterize the writer's tone?
- ❑ Are there parallels between the writer's experiences and your own?
- ❑ Where do you agree with the writer? Where do you disagree?

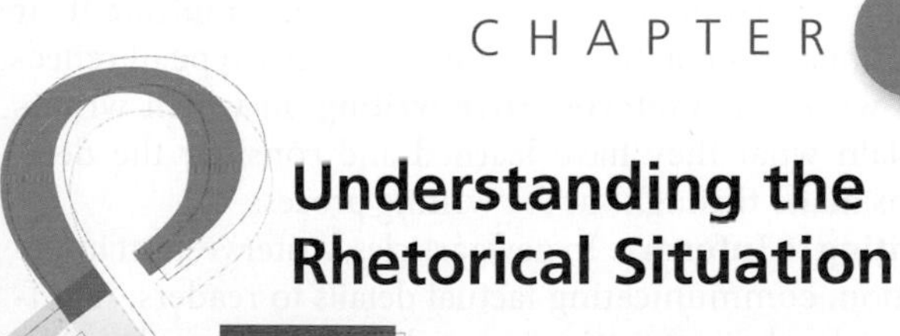

CHAPTER 2

Understanding the Rhetorical Situation

Everyone who sets out to write confronts a series of choices. In the writing that you do in school, on the job, and in your personal life, your understanding of the rhetorical situation is essential, influencing the choices you make about content, emphasis, organization, format, style, and tone.

Before you begin to write, you should try to answer the following questions:

- What is my **rhetorical situation**, or context for writing?
- What is my **purpose** for writing?
- Who is my **audience**?
- See 2d What genre should I use in this situation?

2a Considering the Rhetorical Situation

Begin by considering the **rhetorical situation**, the set of conventions that are associated with a particular writing assignment. By keeping this rhetorical situation in mind throughout the writing process, you make sure that your writing keeps its focus.

In college, the rhetorical situation is often identified by your assignment prompt. In personal, civic, and professional writing, the rhetorical situation is often determined by a particular event, interest, or concern that creates the need for this writing.

2b Determining Your Purpose

In simple terms, your **purpose** for writing is what you want to accomplish:

- **Writing to Reflect** In journals, writers are often introspective, exploring private ideas and feelings to make sense of their experiences; in autobiographical memoirs and personal blog posts, writers communicate their emotions and reactions to others. Another type of reflective writing is **metacognitive writing**, in which writers explain what they have learned and consider the decisions made throughout the writing process.
- **Writing to Inform** In news articles, writers report information, communicating factual details to readers; in reference books, instruction manuals, textbooks, and the like (as well as on websites sponsored by government agencies or nonprofit organizations), writers provide definitions and explain concepts or processes, trying to help readers see relationships and understand ideas.

Note: In your personal writing, you may convey information informally in *Facebook* updates, text messages, tweets, and instant messages.

- **Writing to Persuade** In proposals and editorials, as well as in advertising and on political websites and blogs, writers try to convince readers to accept their positions on various issues.
- **Writing to Evaluate** In reviews of books, films, or performances and in reports, critiques, and program evaluations, writers assess the validity, accuracy, and quality of information, ideas, techniques, products, procedures, or services, perhaps assessing the relative merits of two or more things.

Although writers write to reflect, to inform, to persuade, and to evaluate, these purposes are not mutually exclusive, and writers may have other purposes as well. And, of course, in any piece of writing, a writer may have a primary aim and one or more secondary purposes; in fact, a writer may even have different purposes in different sections—or different drafts—of a single document. The checklist below lists some specific purposes for writing.

CHECKLIST

Determining Your Purpose

In any piece of writing, you can have one or more of the following purposes:

- ❑ to express emotions
- ❑ to inform
- ❑ to persuade
- ❑ to explain
- ❑ to amuse or entertain
- ❑ to evaluate
- ❑ to discover
- ❑ to analyze
- ❑ to debunk
- ❑ to draw comparisons
- ❑ to make an analogy
- ❑ to define
- ❑ to criticize
- ❑ to motivate
- ❑ to satirize
- ❑ to speculate
- ❑ to warn
- ❑ to reassure
- ❑ to take a stand
- ❑ to identify problems
- ❑ to propose solutions
- ❑ to identify causes
- ❑ to predict effects
- ❑ to reflect
- ❑ to interpret
- ❑ to instruct
- ❑ to inspire

As you begin to write, determining your purpose for writing is critical. As you consider the requirements of your genre, your rhetorical situation and purpose work together. Later, identifying and considering the needs of your audience will shape the content, organization, tone, and style of your writing.

2c Identifying Your Audience

Most of the writing you compose is directed at a specific **audience**, a particular reader or group of readers.

1 Writing for an Audience

At different times, in different roles, you address a variety of audiences. Before you write, you should think about the characteristics of the audience (or audiences) that you will be addressing.

- **In your personal life**, you may write notes, emails, or texts to friends and family members. You may find yourself writing on social media and for special occasions in a variety of formats or genres. See 2d
- **As a citizen**, a consumer, or a member of a community, you may respond to social, economic, or political issues by writing emails or letters to a newspaper, a public official, or a representative of a special interest group.
- **As an employee**, you may write letters, memos, and reports to your superiors, to staff members you supervise, or to coworkers; you may also be asked to address customers or critics, board members or stockholders, funding agencies, or the general public.
- **As a student**, you will likely write reflective statements and responses as well as essays, reports, and exams in various academic disciplines. See Ch. 43 You may also participate in peer review See 2c3 sessions, writing evaluations of classmates' drafts as well as written responses to classmates' comments about your own work-in-progress.

As you write, you shape your writing in terms of what you think your audience needs and expects. Your assessment of your readers' interests, educational level, biases, and expectations determines what information you include, what you emphasize, and how you arrange your material.

2 The College Writer's Audience

As a student, you may be asked to write for a specific audience, or you may be asked to select an audience. Often, college writers assume they are writing for an audience of one: the instructor who assigns the essay; however, this is not always the case because many instructors want students to address real-life rhetorical situations.

When writing for your instructors, you need to demonstrate your knowledge of the subject; instructors want to see whether you can express your ideas clearly and accurately. They assign written work to encourage you to use **critical thinking** skills—to ask questions and form judgments—so the way you organize and express your ideas can be as important as the ideas themselves.

Instructors expect accurate information, standard grammar and correct spelling, logically presented ideas, and a reasonable degree of stylistic sophistication. They also expect you to define your terms and to support your generalizations with specific examples. Finally, instructors also expect you to draw your own conclusions and to provide full and accurate **documentation** for ideas that are not your own. See Pt. 3

3 Writing for Other Students

Before you submit an essay to an instructor, you may have an opportunity to participate in **peer review**, sharing your work with your fellow students and responding in writing to their work.

- **Writing Drafts** If you know that other students will read a draft of your essay, consider how they might react to your ideas. For example, are they likely to agree with you? To challenge your ideas? To be confused, or even mystified, by any of your references? To be shocked or offended by your essay's language or content? You should not assume that your fellow students will automatically share your values or your cultural frame of reference. For this reason, it is important to maintain a neutral tone and use moderate language in your essay and to explain any historical, geographical, or cultural references that you think might be unfamiliar to your audience.
- **Making Comments** When you respond to another student's writing, you should take into account how he

or she will react to your comments. Your tone is important. You want to be encouraging and polite, offering insightful comments that can help your classmate write a stronger essay. Remember, when you respond to another student's essay, your goal is to be constructive, not critical or negative.

CHECKLIST

Audience Concerns for Peer-Review Participants

To get the most out of a peer-review session, keep the following guidelines in mind:

- ❑ **Know the material.** To be sure you understand what kind of comments will be most helpful, read the essay several times before you begin writing your response.
- ❑ **Focus on the big picture.** Try not to get bogged down by minor problems with punctuation or mechanics or become distracted by an essay's proofreading errors.
- ❑ **Look for the strongest feature.** Try to zero in on what you think is the essay's greatest strength.
- ❑ **Be positive throughout.** Try to avoid words such as *weak, poor,* and *bad;* instead, try using a compliment before delivering the "bad news": "Paragraph 2 is really well developed; can you add this kind of support in paragraph 4?"
- ❑ **Show respect.** It is perfectly acceptable to tell a writer that something is confusing or inaccurate, but don't go on the attack.
- ❑ **Be specific.** Avoid generalizations such as "needs more examples" or "could be more interesting"; instead, try to offer helpful, focused suggestions: "You could add an example after the second sentence in paragraph 2"; "Explaining how this process operates would make your discussion more interesting."
- ❑ **Don't give orders.** Ask questions, and make suggestions.
- ❑ **Include a few words of encouragement.** In your summary, try to emphasize the essay's strong points.

2d Selecting a Genre

In your college courses, you will compose many different kinds of texts—for example, academic essays, book reviews, research reports, proposals, lab reports, and case studies.

These different types of texts—with their distinctive characteristics and conventions—are referred to as **genres**. In simple terms, a genre is a way of classifying a text according to its style, structure, and format.

A writer's choice of a genre, structure, and medium for writing is based on the message he or she wants to send and the audience he or she intends to reach. Most college writing assignments specify a particular genre. For example, your composition instructor might ask you to write an essay about a personal experience, to evaluate a novel or a film, or to take a position on an issue that you feel strongly about. In these cases, your familiarity with the conventions of the narrative essay, the book or film review, and argumentative writing, respectively, would help you decide how to approach and develop the assignment. Your knowledge of the requirements and features of a specific genre would also be essential if you were going to complete a literature review for your psychology class, a lab report for your chemistry class, or a business proposal for your management class. (For detailed discussions of the genres most frequently used in various disciplines, **see Part 8**.)

CHAPTER 3

Developing Essay Projects

Writing is a constant process of decision making—of selecting, reconsidering, deleting, and rearranging material as you plan, shape, draft and revise, and edit and proofread your work.

3a Planning

Once you understand the **rhetorical situation** you are ready to begin planning your essay—thinking about what you want to say and how you want to say it. See Ch. 2

1 Understanding Your Assignment

Before you start writing, be sure you understand the exact requirements of your **assignment**, and keep those guidelines in mind as you write and revise. Don't assume anything; ask questions, and be sure you understand the answers.

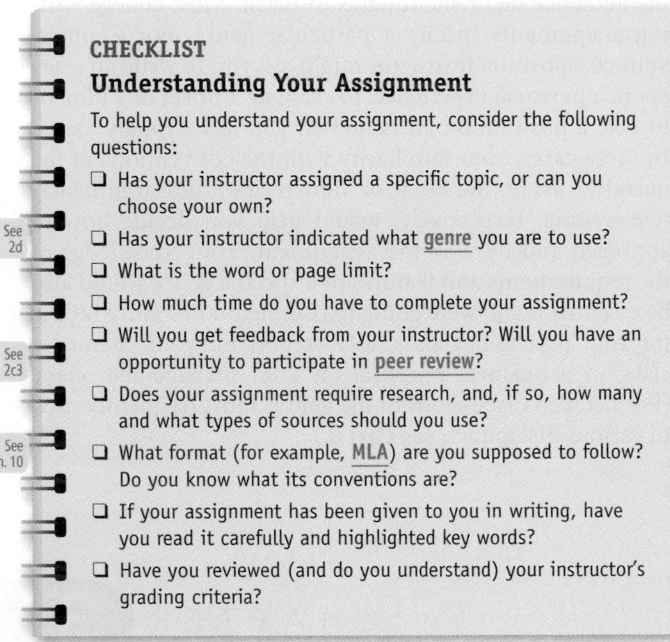

CHECKLIST

Understanding Your Assignment

To help you understand your assignment, consider the following questions:

- ❑ Has your instructor assigned a specific topic, or can you choose your own?
- ❑ Has your instructor indicated what genre you are to use? See 2d
- ❑ What is the word or page limit?
- ❑ How much time do you have to complete your assignment?
- ❑ Will you get feedback from your instructor? Will you have an opportunity to participate in peer review? See 2c3
- ❑ Does your assignment require research, and, if so, how many and what types of sources should you use?
- ❑ What format (for example, MLA) are you supposed to follow? Do you know what its conventions are? See Ch. 10
- ❑ If your assignment has been given to you in writing, have you read it carefully and highlighted key words?
- ❑ Have you reviewed (and do you understand) your instructor's grading criteria?

2 Finding a Topic

Sometimes your instructor will assign a specific topic, but most of the time you will be given a general, structured assignment, which you will have to narrow to a **topic** that suits your purpose, audience, and page limit.

Finding a Topic

Course	Assignment	Topic
Composition	Write an essay about a challenge students face in their college classes	Learning how to evaluate research sources

3 Finding Something to Say

Once you have a topic, you can begin to collect ideas for your essay, using one (or several) of the strategies listed below:

- **Reading and Observing** As you read textbooks, magazines, and newspapers and explore the Internet, as you engage in conversation with friends and family, and as you watch films and TV shows, look for ideas you can use.
- **Keeping a Journal** Try recording your thoughts about your topic in a print or electronic journal, where you can explore ideas, ask questions, reflect on your thinking and the information you are processing, and draw tentative conclusions.
- **Freewriting** Try doing timed, unstructured writing. Writing informally for five to ten minutes without stopping may unlock ideas and encourage you to make free associations about your topic.
- **Brainstorming** On an unlined sheet of paper, record everything you can think of about your topic—comments, questions, lists, single words, and even symbols and diagrams.
- **Asking Questions** If you prefer an orderly, systematic strategy for finding material to write about, apply the basic journalistic questions—*who? what? why? where? when?* and *how?*—to your topic.
- **Doing Research** Many college assignments require you to do library or Internet research. **See Part 2** for information on composing with sources.

MULTILINGUAL TIP

Don't waste time worrying about writing grammatically correct sentences. Remember, the purpose of writing is to communicate ideas. If you want to write an interesting, well-developed essay, you will need to devote plenty of time to the planning activities described in this section. You can then edit your work once you have determined and refined your ideas.

3b Shaping

Once you have collected material for your essay, your next step is to **shape** your material into a thesis-and-support structure.

A **thesis-and-support essay** includes a **thesis statement** (which expresses the **thesis**, or main idea, of the essay) and the specific information that explains and develops that thesis.

PLANNING GUIDE

THESIS-AND-SUPPORT ESSAY

Your **assignment** will ask you to write an essay that supports a thesis.

Your **purpose** will be to present ideas and support them with specific reasons, examples, and so on.

Your **audience** will usually be your instructor or other students in your class.

INTRODUCTION

Thesis statement templates:
- Although…,…
- Because…, it seems likely that…
- Many people believe…; however,…

- Begin by introducing readers to your subject.
- Use a specific introductory strategy to create interest.
- State your essay's thesis.

BODY PARAGRAPHS

Topic sentence templates:
- The first (second, third) cause is…
- One (another, the final) example is…

Templates for introducing support:
- For example,…
- As…points out,…
- According to…,…

- Begin each paragraph with a topic sentence that states the paragraph's main idea.
- In each paragraph, support the topic sentence with facts, details, reasons, examples, and so on.
- Arrange material in each paragraph according to a specific pattern of development: narration, cause and effect, comparison and contrast, and so on.
- Include transitional words and phrases to connect ideas within and between paragraphs.

CONCLUSION

Closing statement templates:
- All in all,…
- All things considered,…
- For all these reasons,…

- Begin with a restatement of your thesis (in different words) or a review of your essay's main points.
- Use a specific concluding strategy to sum up your ideas.
- Try to close with a memorable sentence.

Close-Up WRITING EFFECTIVE THESIS STATEMENTS

An effective thesis statement has four characteristics:

1. **An effective thesis statement clearly communicates your essay's main idea.** It tells your readers not only what your essay's topic is but also how you will approach that topic and what you will say about it. Thus, your thesis statement reflects your essay's purpose. See 2b
2. **An effective thesis statement is more than a general subject, a statement of fact, or an announcement of your intent.**

   Subject: *Wikipedia*

   Statement of Fact: Many college students rely on *Wikipedia* for basic information.

   Announcement: The essay that follows will show why *Wikipedia* is not a trustworthy source for a research paper.

   Thesis Statement: For college-level research, *Wikipedia* is most valuable not as an end in itself but as a gateway to more reliable research sources.
3. **An effective thesis statement is carefully worded.** Your thesis statement—usually expressed in a single concise sentence—should be direct and straightforward. Avoid vague phrases, such as *centers on*, *deals with*, *involves*, *revolves around*, or *is concerned with*. Do not include phrases such as *As I will show*, *I plan to demonstrate*, and *It seems to me*, which weaken your credibility by suggesting that your conclusions are based on opinion rather than on reading, observation, and experience.
4. **Finally, an effective thesis statement suggests your essay's direction, emphasis, and scope.** Your thesis statement should not make promises that your essay will not fulfill. It should suggest the major points you will cover and the order in which you will introduce them.

Note: As you write and rewrite, you may modify your essay's direction, emphasis, and scope; if you do so, you must also reword your thesis statement.

3c Constructing a Scratch Outline

Once you have a thesis statement, you may want to construct a scratch outline to guide you as you write. A **scratch outline** is a brief, informal organizational plan that arranges your essay's main points (and perhaps its major supporting ideas) in an orderly way.

The following is a scratch outline for the model student essay in **3f**.

Scratch Outline

Thesis statement: For college-level research, *Wikipedia* is most valuable not as an end in itself but as a gateway to more reliable research sources.

- Definition of wiki and explanation of *Wikipedia*
- *Wikipedia*'s benefits
  - Links
  - Comprehensive abstracts
  - Current and popular culture topics
  - "Stub" articles
- *Wikipedia*'s potential
- *Wikipedia*'s drawbacks
  - Not accurate
  - Bias
  - Vandalism
  - Not enough citations
- Financial accounting example: benefits
- Financial accounting example: drawbacks

3d Drafting and Revising

1 Writing a Rough Draft

When you write a rough draft, your goal is to get ideas down so you can react to them. You will generally do several drafts of your essay, and you should expect to add or delete words, reword sentences, rethink ideas, and reorder paragraphs as you write. You should also be open to discovering new ideas—or even to taking an unexpected detour.

At this point, concentrate on the body of your essay, and don't waste time writing the "perfect" introduction and conclusion. To make revision easier, leave extra space between lines. You may want to print out your draft and edit by hand on hard copy, typing in your changes on subsequent drafts.

MULTILINGUAL TIP

Using your native language occasionally as you draft your essay may keep you from losing your train of thought. However, writing most or all of your draft in your native language and then translating it into English is generally not a good idea. This process will take a long time, and the translation into English may sound awkward, especially if it comes from a translation tool located online or in your word-processing program.

2 Revising Your Drafts

When you revise, you "re-see" what you have written and write additional drafts. Everyone's revision process is different, but the following specific strategies can be helpful at this stage of the process:

- **Outline your draft.** A formal outline can help you check the logic of your essay's structure. See 5i1
- **Use word-processing tools.** Use tools such as *Microsoft Word*'s **Track Changes** and **Compare Documents** to help you see how your revisions change your work-in-progress.
- **Participate in peer review.** Ask a classmate for feedback on your draft.
- **Use instructors' comments.** Study your instructor's comments on your draft, and arrange a conference if necessary.
- **Schedule a writing center conference.** A writing center tutor can give you additional feedback on your draft.
- **Use a revision checklist.** Revise in stages, first looking at the whole essay and then turning your attention to the individual paragraphs, sentences, and words. You can use the revision checklists on the next page to guide you through the process.

CHECKLISTS FOR REVISING YOUR ESSAY

The Whole Essay

- ❑ Are your thesis and support logically related, with each body paragraph supporting your thesis statement? **(See 3b.)**
- ❑ Is your thesis statement clearly and specifically worded? **(See 3b.)**
- ❑ Have you discussed everything promised in your thesis statement? **(See 3b.)**

Paragraphs

- ❑ Does each body paragraph focus on one main idea, expressed in a clearly worded topic sentence? **(See 20a.)**
- ❑ Are the relationships of sentences within paragraphs clear? **(See 20b.)**
- ❑ Are your body paragraphs fully developed? **(See 20c.)**
- ❑ Does your introductory paragraph arouse interest and prepare readers for what is to come? **(See 20d1.)**
- ❑ Does your concluding paragraph sum up your essay's main idea? **(See 20d2.)**

Sentences

- ❑ Have you used correct sentence structure? **(See Chapters 14 and 15.)**
- ❑ Are your sentences varied? **(See Chapter 21.)**
- ❑ Have you eliminated wordiness and unnecessary repetition? **(See 22a–b.)**
- ❑ Have you avoided overloading your sentences with too many words, phrases, and clauses? **(See 22c.)**
- ❑ Have you avoided potentially confusing shifts in tense, voice, mood, person, or number? **(See 23a.)**
- ❑ Are your sentences constructed logically? **(See 23b–c.)**
- ❑ Have you strengthened your sentences by using parallel words, phrases, and clauses? **(See 24a.)**
- ❑ Have you placed modifiers clearly and logically? **(See Chapter 25.)**

Words

- ❑ Have you eliminated jargon, pretentious diction, clichés, and offensive language from your writing? **(See 26b–c.)**

Close-Up CHOOSING A TITLE

When you are ready to decide on a title for your essay, keep these criteria in mind:

- A title should convey your essay's focus, perhaps using key words and phrases from your essay or echoing the wording of your assignment.
- A title should arouse interest, perhaps with a provocative question, a quotation, or a controversial position.

Assignment: Write an essay about a challenge students face in their college classes.

Topic: Learning how to evaluate research sources.

Possible Titles:

Evaluating Research Sources: A Challenge for College Students (echoes wording of assignment and uses key words from essay)

Wikipedia: "Making Life Easier" (quotation)

Blocking *Wikipedia* on Campus: The Only Solution to a Growing Problem (controversial position)

Wikipedia: Friend or Foe? (provocative question)

3e Editing and Proofreading

When you **edit**, you concentrate on grammar, spelling, punctuation, and mechanics. When you **proofread**, you reread every word carefully to make sure you did not introduce any errors as you typed.

Close-Up PROOFREADING STRATEGIES

To help you proofread more effectively, try using these strategies:

- Read your essay aloud, listening for places where you stumble or hesitate.
- Have a friend read your essay aloud to you.
- Read silently, word by word, using your finger or a sheet of paper to help you keep your place.
- Read your essay's sentences in reverse order, beginning with the last sentence.

As you edit, use the Search or Find command to look for usage errors you commonly make—for instance, confusing *it's* with *its*, *lay* with *lie*, *effect* with *affect*, *their* with *there*, or *too* with *to*. You can also uncover **sexist language** by searching for words such as *he*, *his*, *him*, or *man*.

See 26c2

Keep in mind that neatness does not equal correctness. The clean text that your computer produces can mask flaws that might otherwise be apparent; for this reason, it is up to you to make sure no spelling errors or typos slip by. When you have finished proofreading, check to make sure the final typed copy of your essay conforms to your instructor's format requirements.

Close-Up USING SPELL CHECKERS AND GRAMMAR CHECKERS

Although spell checkers and grammar checkers can make the process of editing and proofreading your work easier, they have limitations. Remember, spell checkers and grammar checkers are no substitutes for careful editing and proofreading.

- **Spell Checkers** A spell checker simply identifies strings of letters it does not recognize; it does not distinguish between homophones or spot every typographical error. For example, it does not recognize *there* in "They forgot there books" as incorrect, nor does it identify a typo that produces a correctly spelled word, such as *word* for *work* or *thing* for *think*. Moreover, a spell checker may not recognize every technical term, proper noun, or foreign word you may use.
- **Grammar Checkers** A grammar checker scans documents for certain features (the number of words in a sentence, for example); however, it is not able to read a document to see if it makes sense. As a result, a grammar checker is not always accurate. For example, it may identify a long sentence as a run-on when it is, in fact, grammatically correct, and it generally advises against using passive voice—even in contexts where it is appropriate. Moreover, a grammar checker does not always supply answers; often, it asks questions—for example, whether *which* should be *that* or whether *which* should be preceded by a comma—that you must answer. In short, a grammar checker can guide your editing and proofreading, but you must be the one who decides when a sentence is (or is not) correct.

3f Model Student Essay

James 1

Rebecca James

Professor Burks

English 101

14 March 2016

Wikipedia: Friend or Foe?

When given a research assignment, students often turn first to *Wikipedia*, the popular free online encyclopedia. With over 26,000,000 articles, *Wikipedia* is a valuable source for anyone seeking general information on a topic. For college-level research, however, *Wikipedia* is most valuable when it is used not as an authoritative source but as a gateway to more reliable research sources.

Introduction

Thesis statement

A wiki is an open-source website that allows users to edit and add to its content. Derived from a Hawaiian word meaning "quick," the term *wiki* conveys the swiftness and ease with which users can access information on such sites as well as contribute content ("Wiki"). Since its creation in 2001 by Jimmy Wales, *Wikipedia* has grown into a huge database of articles on topics ranging from contemporary rock bands to obscure scientific and technical concepts. In accordance with the site's policies, users can edit existing articles and add new articles using *Wikipedia*'s editing tools, which do not require specialized programming knowledge or expertise.

Background on wikis and *Wikipedia*

Wikipedia offers several benefits to researchers seeking information on a topic. Longer *Wikipedia* articles often include comprehensive abstracts that summarize their content. Articles

Benefits of *Wikipedia*

James 2

also often include links to other *Wikipedia* articles. In fact, *Wikipedia*'s internal links, or "wikilinks," are so prevalent that they significantly increase *Wikipedia*'s web presence. According to Alison J. Head and Michael B. Eisenberg, college students conducting a *Google* search often click first on the *Wikipedia* link, which usually appears on the first page of *Google*'s list of search results. Head and Eisenberg quote a student from their study as saying, "I don't really start with *Wikipedia*; I *Google* something and then a *Wikipedia* entry usually comes up early on, so I guess I use both in kind of a two-step process." In addition, many *Wikipedia* articles contain external links to other online and print sources, including reliable peer-reviewed sources. Finally, because its online format allows users to update its content at any time from any location, *Wikipedia* offers up-to-the-minute coverage of political and cultural events as well as information on popular culture topics that receive little or no attention in other reference sources. Even when the available information on a particular topic is limited, *Wikipedia* allows users to create "stub" articles, which provide basic information that other users can expand over time. In this way, *Wikipedia* offers an online forum for a developing bank of information on a range of topics.

Benefits of *Wikipedia*

Another benefit of *Wikipedia* is that it has the potential to become a reliable and comprehensive database of information. As *Wikipedia*'s "About" page explains, the site's articles "are never

James 3

considered complete and may be continually edited and improved." This ongoing editing improves quality and helps to ensure "a neutral representation of information." Using the criteria of accuracy, neutrality, completeness, and style, *Wikipedia* classifies its best articles as "featured" and its second-best articles as "good." In addition, *Wikipedia*'s policy statements indicate that the information in its articles must be verifiable and must be based on documented, preexisting research. Although no professional editorial board oversees the development of content within *Wikipedia*, experienced users may become editors, and this role allows them to monitor the process by which content is added and updated. Users may also use the "Talk" page to discuss an article's content and make suggestions for improvement. With these control measures in place, some *Wikipedia* articles are comparable to articles in professionally edited online resources.

Limitations of *Wikipedia*

Despite its numerous benefits and its enormous potential, *Wikipedia* is not an authoritative research source. As the site's "Researching with *Wikipedia*" page concedes, "not everything in *Wikipedia* is accurate, comprehensive, or unbiased." Because anyone can create or edit *Wikipedia* articles, they can be factually inaccurate or biased—and they can even be vandalized. Many *Wikipedia* articles, especially those that are underdeveloped, do not supply citations to the sources that support their claims. This absence of source information should lead users to question the articles' reliability. Of course, many underdeveloped *Wikipedia* articles include labels to identify their particular shortcomings—for example, poor grammar or missing documentation. Still, users cannot always determine the legitimacy of information contained in the *Wikipedia* articles they consult.

Strengths of "Financial Accounting" *Wikipedia* article

For college students, *Wikipedia* can provide useful general information and links to helpful resources. For example, accounting students will find that the *Wikipedia* article "Financial Accounting" defines this field in relation to basic accounting concepts and offers a visual breakdown of the key terms within the discipline. This article can help students in accounting classes to understand the basic differences between this and other types of accounting. The article contains several internal links to related *Wikipedia* articles and some external links to additional resources and references. In comparison, the wiki *Citizendium* does not contain an article on financial accounting, and the "Financial Accounting" article in the professionally edited *Encyclopaedia Britannica* consists only of a link to a related *EB* article.

Weaknesses of "Financial Accounting" *Wikipedia* article

Although the *Wikipedia* article on financial accounting provides helpful general information about this accounting field, it is limited in terms of its reliability and scope. The top of the article displays a warning label that identifies the article's shortcomings. As fig. 1 illustrates, the article's

James 5

problems include a lack of cited sources. The limitations of the financial accounting article reinforce the sense that *Wikipedia* is best used not as a source but as a path to more reliable and comprehensive research sources.

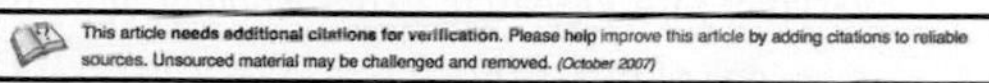
This article needs additional citations for verification. Please help improve this article by adding citations to reliable sources. Unsourced material may be challenged and removed. *(October 2007)*

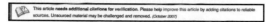

Fig. 1. "Financial Accounting." *Wikipedia*. 14 Mar. 2016, 15:04, en.wikipedia.org/wiki/Financial_accounting.

Conclusion

Like other encyclopedia articles, *Wikipedia* articles should be used only as a starting point for research and as a link to more in-depth sources. Moreover, users should keep in mind that *Wikipedia* articles can include more factual errors, bias, and inconsistencies than professionally edited encyclopedia articles. Although future enhancements to the site may make it more reliable, *Wikipedia* users should understand the current shortcomings of this popular online tool.

James 6

Works Cited

"About *Wikipedia*." *Wikipedia,* 8 Mar. 2016, 15:07, en.wikipedia.org/wiki/Wikipedia:About.

Head, Alison J., and Michael B. Eisenberg. "How College Students Use the Web to Conduct Everyday Life Research." *First Monday,* vol. 16, no. 4, 2011. *Google Scholar,* papers.ssrn.com/sol3/papers.cfm?abstract_id=2281533.

"Wiki." *Encyclopaedia Britannica,* 2014, www.britannica.com/topic/wiki.

"Researching with *Wikipedia*." *Wikipedia,* 8 Mar. 2016, 15:25, en.wikipedia.org/wiki/Wikipedia:Researching_with_Wikipedia.

3g Creating a Writing Portfolio

A **writing portfolio**, a collection of written work in print or electronic form, offers a unique opportunity for you to present your intellectual track record, showing how you have developed as a writer in response to the **learning outcomes** (what you are expected to learn) set by your instructor or your school. Increasingly, colleges have been using portfolios as a way not only to assess individual students' performance but also to see if the student body as a whole is meeting the school's standards.

While compiling individual items (usually called **artifacts**) to include in their portfolios, students reflect on their work and measure their progress; as they do so, they may improve their ability to evaluate their own work.

1 Assembling Your Portfolio

Many academic disciplines are moving toward electronic portfolios because, when posted on the Internet, they are immediately accessible to peers and instructors (as well as to prospective employers).

CHECKLIST

Suggested Content for Portfolios

The following material might be included in a portfolio:

- ❑ **Internal hyperlinks within a table of contents or home page** to help readers navigate artifacts in the portfolio
- ❑ A reflective statement in the form of a cover memo, letter, or essay, with internal hyperlinks to portfolio content See 3g2
- ❑ **Writing prompts** that provide context for portfolio content
- ❑ **Planning material**, such as journal or blog entries and brainstorming notes
- ❑ **Shaping material**, such as thesis statements and outlines
- ❑ **Rough drafts with comments** made by peer reviewers, instructors, and writing center tutors
- ❑ **Revised drafts**, showing revisions made with Track Changes
- ❑ **Photocopies of source material**
- ❑ **Final drafts**
- ❑ **External hyperlinks** to online source material and other websites that support the portfolio
- ❑ **Visuals** that enhance your documents
- ❑ **Audio and video clips of presentations**
- ❑ ***PowerPoint*** slides
- ❑ **Collaborative work**, with your own contributions clearly marked
- ❑ **A résumé,** if the portfolio will be submitted to a prospective employer

2 Writing a Reflective Statement

Instructors usually require students to introduce their portfolios with a **reflective statement**—a memo, letter, or essay in which students assess their writing improvement and achievements over a period of time.

Excerpt from Reflective Statement

What has always scared me even more than staring at a blank computer screen is working hard on an essay only to have it returned full of red comments. The step-by-step *Wikipedia* essay assignment helped me to confront my fear of revision and realize that revision—including outside feedback—is essential to writing.

Comments I received in peer review showed me that feedback could be constructive. I was relieved to see my classmates' comments were tactful and not too critical of my essay's flaws. I think the electronic format was easier for me than face-to-face discussions would have been because I tend to get discouraged and start apologizing when I hear negative comments.

CHAPTER 4

Writing an Argumentative Essay

4a Organizing an Argumentative Essay

An **argumentative essay** takes a stand on an issue and uses logic and evidence to change the way readers think or to move them to action. When you write an argumentative essay, you follow the same process you use when you write any essay. However, argumentative essays use special strategies to win audience approval and to overcome potential opposition.

See Ch. 3

PLANNING GUIDE

ARGUMENTATIVE ESSAY

Your **assignment** will ask you to take a stand on an issue.

Your **purpose** will be to convince readers to accept your position on the issue.

Your **audience** will be your instructor or other students in your class or school.

INTRODUCTION

- Begin by presenting a brief overview of your subject.
- Show readers how your subject concerns them.
- State your thesis. (If your thesis is very controversial, you may want to delay stating it until later in the essay.)

Thesis statement templates:
- The idea that…is popular, but…
- Recent studies, however, suggest that…
- The following actions are necessary because…
- In my opinion,…

BACKGROUND

- Briefly review the basic facts of the controversy.
- Provide definitions of key terms or an overview of others' opinions on the issue.

Topic sentence templates:
- One (another) way is…
- The first (second, third) reason is…
- One advantage (another advantage) is…

ARGUMENTS IN SUPPORT OF THE THESIS

- Begin with your weakest argument and work up to the strongest.
- If your arguments are equally strong, begin with the one with which your readers are most familiar and most likely to accept.
- Support your arguments with evidence—facts, examples, and expert opinion.

Templates for introducing support:
- As…mentions in his/her article, "…"
- According to…,…
- In his/her book,…says, "…"

REFUTATION OF OPPOSING ARGUMENTS

- Refute opposing arguments by demonstrating that they are untrue, unfair, illogical, or inaccurate.
- If an opposing argument is particularly strong, concede its strength, and point out its limitations.

Refutation templates:
- Of course, not everyone agrees that…; however, …
- Although it is true that…, it is not necessarily true that…
- On the one hand,…; on the other hand,…

CONCLUSION

- Reinforce the stand you are taking.
- Remind readers of the weaknesses of opposing arguments, or underscore the logic of your position.
- End with a strong concluding statement, such as a memorable quotation or a call to action.

Closing statement templates:
- For these reasons,…
- The current situation can be improved by…
- Let us hope that…
- In conclusion,…

4b Model Argumentative Essay

The following argumentative essay includes many of the elements outlined in the Planning Guide. The student, Samantha Masterton, was asked to write an argumentative essay on a topic of her choice, drawing her supporting evidence from her own knowledge and experience as well as from other sources.

Masterton 1

Samantha Masterton

Professor Egler

English 102

14 April 2016

The Returning Student: Older Is Definitely Better

After graduating from high school, young people must decide what they want to do with the rest of their lives. Many graduates (often without much thought) decide to continue their education uninterrupted, and they go on to college. This group of teenagers makes up what many see as typical first-year college students. Recently, however, this stereotype has been challenged by an influx of older students, including myself, into American colleges and universities (Holland). Not only do these students make a valuable contribution to the schools they attend, but they also offer an alternative to young people who go to college simply because they do not know what else to do. A few years off between high school and college can give many students the life experience they need to appreciate the value of higher education and to gain more from it.

Introduction

Thesis statement

The college experience of an eighteen-year-old is quite different from that of an older "nontraditional" student. The typical high school graduate is often concerned with things other than studying—for example, going to parties, dating, and testing personal limits. However, older students—those who are twenty-five years

Background

Masterton 2

of age or older—are serious about the idea of returning to college. Although many high school students do not think twice about whether or not to attend college, older students have much more to consider when they think about returning to college. For example, they must decide how much time they can spend getting their degree and consider the impact that attending college will have on their family and their finances.

Background (continued)

In the United States, the makeup of college students is changing. According to the US Department of Education report *Pathways to Success*, the percentage of students who could be classified as "nontraditional" is continually increasing (2-3). So, despite the challenges that older students face when they return to school, more and more are choosing to make the effort.

Argument in support of thesis

Most older students return to school with clear goals. Getting a college degree is often a requirement for professional advancement, and older students are therefore more likely to take college seriously. In general, older students enroll in college with a definite course of study in mind. For older students, college is an extension of work rather than a place to discover what they want to be when they graduate. An influential study by psychologists R. Eric Landrum, Je T'aime Hood, and Jerry M. McAdams concluded, "Nontraditional students seemed to be more appreciative of their opportunities, as indicated by their higher

Masterton 3

enjoyment of school and appreciation of professors' efforts in the classroom" (744).

Argument in support of thesis

Older students also understand the actual benefits of doing well in school; as a result, they take school seriously. The older students I know rarely cut classes or put off studying. This is because older students are often balancing the demands of home and work and because they know how important it is to do well. The difficulties of juggling school, family, and work force older students to be disciplined and focused—especially concerning their schoolwork. This pays off: older students tend to spend more hours per week studying and tend to have a higher GPA than younger students do (Landrum et al. 742-43).

Argument in support of thesis

My observations of older students have convinced me that many students would benefit from delaying entry into college. Eighteen-year-olds are often immature and inexperienced. They cannot be expected to have formulated definite goals or developed firm ideas about themselves or about the world in which they live. In contrast, older students have generally had a variety of real-life experiences. Most have worked for several years, and many have started families. Their years in the "real world" have helped them become more focused and more responsible than they were when they graduated from high school. As a result, they are better prepared for college than they would have been when they were younger.

Masterton 4

Refutation of opposing argument

Of course, postponing college for a few years is not for everyone. Certainly some teenagers have a definite sense of purpose and these individuals would benefit from an early college experience. Charles Woodward, a law librarian, went to college directly after high school, and for him the experience was positive. "I was serious about learning, and I loved my subject," he said. "I felt fortunate that I knew what I wanted from college and from life." Many younger students, however, are not like Woodward; they graduate from high school without any clear sense of purpose. For this reason, it makes sense for them to postpone college until they are mature enough to benefit from the experience.

Refutation of opposing argument

Granted, some older students have difficulties when they return to college. Because they have been out of school so long, these students may have problems studying and adapting to academic life. As I have seen, though, most of these problems disappear after a period of adjustment. Of course, it is true that many older students find it difficult to balance the needs of their family with college and to deal with the financial burden of tuition. However, this challenge is becoming easier with the growing number of online courses, the availability of distance education, and the introduction of governmental programs, such as educational tax credits (Agbo 164-65).

Masterton 5

Conclusion

It is clear that in many cases, higher education is often wasted on the young, who are either too immature or too unfocused to take advantage of it. Taking a few years off between high school and college would give these students the time they need to make the most of a college education. The increasing number of older students returning to college seems to indicate that many students are taking this path. According to a US Department of Education website, *Fast Facts,* eight million students enrolled in American colleges in 2012 were twenty-five years of age or older. Older students such as these have taken time off to serve in the military, to gain valuable work experience, or to raise a family. In short, they have taken the time to mature. By the time they get to college, these students have defined their goals and made a firm commitment to achieve them.

Concluding statement

Masterton 6

Works Cited

Works-cited list begins new page

Agbo, Seth. "The United States: Heterogeneity of the Student Body and the Meaning of 'Nontraditional' in U.S. Higher Education." *Higher Education and Lifelong Learners: International Perspectives on Change*, edited by Hans G. Schuetze and Maria Slowey, Routledge, 2000, pp. 149-69.

Holland, Kelley. "Back to School: Older Students on the Rise in College Classrooms." *NBCNews.com*, 28 Aug. 2014, www.nbcnews.com/business/business-news/back-school-older-students-rise-college-classrooms-n191246.

Landrum, R. Eric, et al. "Satisfaction with College by Traditional and Nontraditional College Students." *Psychological Reports*, vol. 89, no. 3, 2001, pp. 740-46.

United States, Department of Education, Institute of Educational Sciences. *Fast Facts*, 2014.

---. ---. *Pathways to Success: Integrating Learning with Life and Work to Increase National College Completion*. By the Advisory Committee on Student Financial Assistance, 2012.

Woodward, Charles B. Interview. 8 Mar. 2016.

Two sets of three unspaced hyphens indicate that *United States* and *Dept. of Educ.* are repeated from the previous entry

PART 2

Conducting Research

5 Developing a Research Project 42

5a Moving from Assignment to Topic 43
5b Doing Exploratory Research and Formulating a Research Question 43
5c Assembling a Working Bibliography 44
5d Developing a Tentative Thesis 45
5e Doing Focused Research 46
5f Managing Photocopies, Scans, and Downloaded Material 48
5g Taking Notes 50
5h Fine-Tuning Your Thesis 57
5i Outlining, Drafting, and Revising 57
5j Preparing a Final Draft 70

6 Finding Information 70

6a Finding Information in the Library 70
6b Finding Information on the Internet 81
6c Doing Field Research 87

7 Evaluating Sources 89

7a Evaluating Library Sources 89
7b Evaluating Internet Sources 91

8 Integrating Source Material into Your Writing 95

8a Integrating Quotations 95
8b Integrating Paraphrases and Summaries 98

9 Using Sources Ethically 99

9a Defining Plagiarism 99
9b Avoiding Unintentional Plagiarism 100
9c Avoiding Intentional Plagiarism 101
9d Avoiding Other Kinds of Plagiarism 101
9e Revising to Eliminate Plagiarism 102
9f Understanding Plagiarism in the Disciplines 105

CHAPTER 5

Developing a Research Project

Research is the systematic investigation of a topic outside your own knowledge and experience. However, doing research means more than just reading about other people's ideas. When you undertake a research project, you become involved in a process that requires you to **think critically**: to evaluate and interpret the ideas explored in your sources and to formulate ideas of your own. Whether you are working with print sources (journals, magazines, books) or electronic sources (online catalogs or discovery services, databases, the Internet), in the library or on your own computer, your research will be most efficient if you follow a systematic process. (As an added benefit, such a process will help you avoid unintentional **plagiarism**.)

See Ch. 9

CHECKLIST

The Research Process

- ❑ Move from an assignment to a topic. **(See 5a.)**
- ❑ Do exploratory research and formulate a research question. **(See 5b.)**
- ❑ Assemble a working bibliography. **(See 5c.)**
- ❑ Develop a tentative thesis. **(See 5d.)**
- ❑ Do focused research. **(See 5e.)**
- ❑ Manage photocopies, scans, and downloaded material. **(See 5f.)**
- ❑ Take notes. **(See 5g.)**
- ❑ Fine-tune your thesis. **(See 5h.)**
- ❑ Construct an outline. **(See 5i1.)**
- ❑ Write a rough draft. **(See 5i2.)**
- ❑ Revise your work. **(See 5i3.)**
- ❑ Prepare a final draft. **(See 5j.)**

5a Moving from Assignment to Topic

The first step in the research process is to make sure you understand your assignment: when your paper is due, how long it should be, and what manuscript guidelines and documentation style you are to follow. Once you understand the basic requirements and scope of your assignment, you need to find a topic to write about.

In many cases, your instructor will help you to choose a topic, either by providing a list of suitable topics or by suggesting a general subject area—for example, a famous trial, an event that happened on the day you were born, a social problem on college campuses, or an issue related to the Internet. Even in these cases, you will still need to choose one of the topics or narrow the subject area—deciding, for example, on one trial, one event, one problem, or one issue.

If your instructor prefers that you select a topic on your own, you should consider a number of possible topics and weigh both their suitability for research and your interest in them. You decide on a topic for your research paper in much the same way as you decide on a topic for a short essay: you read, brainstorm, talk to people, and ask questions.

Specifically, you talk to friends and family members, coworkers, and perhaps your instructor; you attend a library orientation session with your class; read online magazines and news sources, blogs, and *Wikipedia* entries (*Wikipedia* can be a great resource for brainstorming, though it would not typically be referenced as a scholarly source in an academic research project); browse the library's online databases (especially those relevant to the discipline); take stock of your interests; and consider possible topics suggested by your other courses (historical events, scientific developments, and so on).

5b Doing Exploratory Research and Formulating a Research Question

Doing **exploratory research**—searching the Internet and looking through the library's online reference collections, such as *Credo Reference* and the *Gale Virtual Reference Library*—helps you to get an overview of your topic. Your goal at this stage is to formulate a **research question**, the question you want your research paper to answer. A research question helps you to decide which sources to seek out, which to examine first, which to examine in depth, and which to skip entirely. (The answer to your research question will be your paper's thesis statement.)

See 3b

5c Assembling a Working Bibliography

During your exploratory research, you begin to assemble a **working bibliography** of the sources you consult. (This working bibliography will be the basis for your works-cited list, which will include all the sources you cite in your paper.)

See 10a2

1 Keeping Track of Your Sources

Keep records of interviews (including telephone and email interviews), meetings, lectures, films, blogs, and websites as well as print and electronic articles and books. For each source, include basic identifying details—such as the date of an interview, the call number of a hard-copy library book, and the URL of an Internet source. (Make sure the URL is not unique to the search session. Some databases provide what is called a permalink. Such a durable or permanent URL is always preferable to the URL provided by a browser.) Also, record the date you downloaded the source (and perhaps the search engine you used to find it as well), or the author of an article accessed from a library's subscription database. Also, write up a brief **evaluation** that includes comments about the kind of information the source contains, the amount of information offered, its relevance to your topic, and its limitations.

You can record this information in a digital file designated "Bibliography."

Information for Working Bibliography

Author	Bauerlein, Mark
Title	*The Dumbest Generation: How the Digital Age Stupefies Young Americans and Jeopardizes Our Future (or, Don't Trust Anyone Under 30)*
Publication information	Penguin, 2008.
Evaluation	Book is several years old, so information may be dated. Chapter 4, "Online Learning and Non-Learning," includes useful discussion of poor writing in *Wikipedia* articles.

As you go about collecting sources and building your working bibliography, monitor the quality and relevance of all the materials you examine, and download or print all the sources you plan to use. Making informed choices early in the research process will save you a lot of time in the long run. (For information on evaluating sources, **see Chapter 7.**)

2 Preparing an Annotated Bibliography

Some instructors require an **annotated bibliography**, a list of all your sources accompanied by a brief summary and evaluation of each source.

Annotated Bibliography (Excerpt)

Wilson, Jodi L. "Proceed with Extreme Caution: Citation to *Wikipedia* in Light of Contributor Demographics and Content Policies." *Vanderbilt Journal of Entertainment & Technology Law*, vol. 16, no. 4, 2014, pp. 857-908. *Academic Search Complete*, web.a.ebscohost.com.ezproxy.cul.columbia.edu/ehost/detail/detail?vid=4&sid=14afe0c2-3351-4754-93dc-2371d2724d5d.

This academic journal article discusses the kinds of people who most commonly consult *Wikipedia*, considering factors such as age and education level. It includes charts that give percentages of *Wikipedia* users within these categories.

This article is a primary source that contains original research and has been peer-reviewed. It provides important data on *Wikipedia* users, arguing that, although the majority of *Wikipedia* users are educated adults, researchers should be careful to consider the credibility of the *Wikipedia* contributors to articles they use in their research.

5d Developing a Tentative Thesis

Your **tentative thesis** is a preliminary statement of the main point you think your research will support. This statement, which you will eventually refine into a thesis statement, should be the tentative answer to your research question. See 5h

Developing a Tentative Thesis

Subject Area

Issue related to the Internet

Topic

Using *Wikipedia* for college-level research

Research Question

What effect has *Wikipedia* had on academic research?

Tentative Thesis

The debate surrounding *Wikipedia* has helped people in the academic community to consider how college-level research has changed in recent years.

Because your tentative thesis suggests the specific direction your research will take as well as the scope and emphasis of your paper, it can help you generate a list of the key points you plan to develop in your paper. This list can help you narrow the focus of your research so you can zero in on a few specific areas to explore as you read and take notes.

Listing Your Key Points

Tentative thesis: The debate surrounding *Wikipedia* has helped people in the academic community to consider how college-level research has changed in recent years.

- Give background about *Wikipedia*; explain its benefits and drawbacks.
- Talk about who uses *Wikipedia* and for what purposes.
- Explain possible future enhancements to the site.
- Explain college instructors' resistance to *Wikipedia*.
- Talk about efforts made by librarians and others to incorporate *Wikipedia* into academic research.

5e Doing Focused Research

Once you have decided on a tentative thesis and made a list of the main points you plan to discuss in your paper, you are ready to begin your focused research. During exploratory research, you look at reference works to get an overview of your topic. During **focused research**, however, you look for the specific information—facts, examples, statistics, definitions, quotations—you need to support your points.

1 Reading Sources

As you look for information, try to explore as many sources and as many different viewpoints as possible. It makes sense to examine more sources than you actually intend to use. This strategy will enable you to proceed even if one or more of your sources turns out to be biased, outdated, unreliable, superficial, or irrelevant—in other words, not suitable. Exploring different viewpoints is just as important. After all, if you read only those sources that agree on a particular issue, you will have difficulty understanding the full range of opinions about your topic.

As you explore various sources, try to evaluate their potential usefulness to you as quickly as possible. For example, if your source is a book, skim the table of contents and the index; if your source is a journal article, read the abstract. Then, if an article or a section of a book seems useful, photocopy it for future reference. Similarly, when you find an online source that looks promising, send yourself the link (or print the pages you need) so that you can evaluate the material further later on.

See Ch. 7

2 Balancing Primary and Secondary Sources

During your focused research, you will encounter both **primary sources** (original documents and observations) and **secondary sources** (interpretations of original documents and observations).

Primary and Secondary Sources

Primary Source in the Humanities	Secondary Source in the Humanities
Novel, poem, play, film	Scholarly analysis and criticism
Diary, autobiography	Biography
Letter, historical document, speech, oral history	Review

continued

Primary and Secondary Sources *(continued)*

Primary Source in the Humanities	Secondary Source in the Humanities
Newspaper or magazine article from the time period being discussed	
Interview	

Primary Source in the Social Sciences and Sciences	Secondary Source in the Social Sciences and Sciences
Raw data from questionnaires or interviews	Literature review
Observation/experiment	
Scientific (empirical) article containing original research	
Case study	

For some research projects, primary sources are essential; however, most research projects in the humanities rely heavily on secondary sources, which provide scholars' insights and interpretations. Remember, though, that the further you get from the primary source, the more chances exist for inaccuracies caused by misinterpretations or distortions.

5f Managing Photocopies, Scans, and Downloaded Material

Much of the information you gather will be in the form of photocopies or scanned pages saved as PDFs (of articles, book pages, and so on) and material downloaded from the Internet or from a library database. Learning to manage this source information efficiently will save you a lot of time.

First, do not use the ease of copying and downloading as an excuse to postpone decisions about the usefulness of your material. If you download or copy every possible source, you can easily accumulate so much information that it will be almost impossible for you to keep track of it.

Also keep in mind that the sources you find are just raw material. You will still have to interpret and evaluate your sources and make connections among their ideas.

Moreover, photocopies, scans, and downloaded material do not give you much flexibility: after all, a single page may include information that could be earmarked for several different sections of your paper. This lack of flexibility makes it almost impossible for you to arrange source material into any meaningful order. Just as you would with any source, you will have to take notes on the information you read. These notes will give you the flexibility you need to organize and write your paper.

Close-Up AVOIDING PLAGIARISM

To avoid the possibility of accidental plagiarism, never paste source material directly into your paper. Instead, keep all downloaded material in a separate file—not in your Notes file. After you read this material and decide how to use it, you can move the information you use into your Notes file (along with full source information).

See Ch. 9

CHECKLIST

Working with Photocopies, Scans, and Downloaded Material

To get the most out of photocopies, scans, and material downloaded from the Internet, follow these guidelines:

- ❑ Be sure you have recorded full and accurate source information, including the inclusive page numbers, electronic address (URL), and any other relevant information, in your working bibliography file.
- ❑ Do not photocopy or scan a source without reminding yourself—*in writing*—why you are doing so. In pencil or on removable self-stick notes, record your initial responses to the source's ideas, jot down cross-references to other sources or to your notes, and highlight important sections.
- ❑ Photocopying can be time-consuming and expensive, so try to avoid copying material that is only marginally relevant to your paper.
- ❑ Keep all hard copies of source material together in a separate file so you will be able to find them when you need them. Keep all electronic copies of source material together in one clearly labeled file.

5g Taking Notes

As you locate information in the library and on the Internet, take notes to create a record of exactly what you found and where you found it. These notes will help you to fine-tune your thesis and decide how to develop your paper.

1 Recording Source Information

See 5g2

Each piece of information you record in your notes (whether summarized, paraphrased, or quoted from your sources) should be accompanied by a short descriptive heading that indicates its relevance to one of the points you will develop in your paper. Because you will use these headings to guide you as you organize your notes, you should make them as specific as possible. For example, labeling every note for a paper on *Wikipedia* ***Wikipedia*** or **Internet** will not prove very helpful later on. More focused headings—for instance, ***Wikipedia*'s popularity** or **college instructors' objections**—will be much more useful.

Also include brief comments that make clear your reasons for recording the information. These comments (enclosed in brackets so you will know they are your own ideas, not those of your source) should establish the purpose of your note—what you think it can explain, support, clarify, describe, or contradict—and perhaps suggest its relationship to other notes or to other sources. Any questions you have about the information (or its source) can also be included in your comment.

Finally, be sure each note fully and accurately identifies the source of the information you are recording. You do not have to write out the complete citation, but you do have to include enough information to identify your source. For example, **Wilson** would be enough to send you back to your working bibliography, where you would be able to find the complete documentation for the author's article.

Close-Up TAKING NOTES

When you take notes, your goal is flexibility: you want to be able to arrange and rearrange information easily and efficiently as your paper takes shape.

Type each individual note (accompanied by source information) under a specific heading rather than listing all information from a single source under the same heading, and be sure to divide notes from one another with extra space or horizontal lines. (As you revise, you can move notes around so notes on the same topic are grouped together.)

Notes

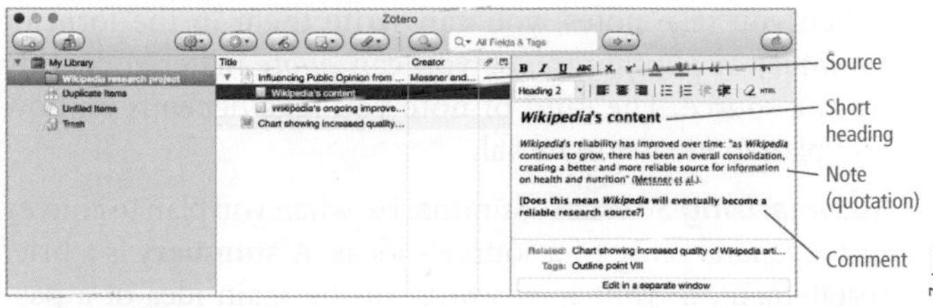

Zotero

CHECKLIST
Taking Notes

- ❑ **Identify the source of each piece of information,** including the page numbers of quotations from paginated sources.
- ❑ **Include everything now that you will need later** to understand your note—names, dates, places, connections with other notes—and to remember why you recorded it.
- ❑ **Distinguish quotations from paraphrases and summaries and your own ideas from those of your sources.** If you copy a source's words, place them in quotation marks (and boldface the quotation marks). If you record your own ideas, enclose them in brackets and boldface them as well. These techniques will help you avoid accidental **plagiarism** in your paper. See Ch. 9
- ❑ **Put an author's ideas into your own words whenever possible,** summarizing and paraphrasing material as well as adding your own observations and analyses.
- ❑ **Copy quoted material accurately,** using the exact words, spelling, punctuation marks, and capitalization of the original.
- ❑ **Never paste information from a source directly into your paper.** This practice can lead to plagiarism.

MULTILINGUAL TIP

Taking notes in English (rather than in your native language) will make it easier for you to transfer the notes into a draft of your paper. However, you may find it faster and more effective to use your native language when writing your own comments about each note.

2 Summarizing, Paraphrasing, and Quoting

When you take notes, you can write them in the form of *summary or paraphrase*, or you can *quote* material directly from a source. The kind of note you take depends on how you plan to use the material.

Summarizing Sources Summarize when you plan to convey just a general sense of a source's ideas. A **summary** is a brief restatement, *in your own words*, of the main idea of a passage or an article. A summary is always much shorter than the original because it omits the examples, asides, analogies, and rhetorical strategies that writers use to add emphasis and interest.

When you summarize, be very careful not to use the exact language or phrasing of your source. Remember that your summary should include only your source's ideas, not your interpretations or opinions. Finally, be sure to document the summary.

Original Source

Today, the First Amendment faces challenges from groups who seek to limit expressions of racism and bigotry. A growing number of legislatures have passed rules against "hate speech"—[speech] that is offensive on the basis of race, ethnicity, gender, or sexual orientation. The rules are intended to promote respect for all people and protect the targets of hurtful words, gestures, or actions.

Legal experts fear these rules may wind up diminishing the rights of all citizens. "The bedrock principle [of our society] is that government may never suppress free speech simply because it goes against what the community would like to hear," says Nadine Strossen, president of the American Civil Liberties Union and professor of constitutional law at New York University Law School. In recent years, for example, the courts have upheld the right of neo-Nazis to march in Jewish neighborhoods; protected cross-burning as a form of free expression; and allowed protesters to burn the

American flag. The offensive, ugly, distasteful, or repugnant nature of expression is not reason enough to ban it, courts have said.

But advocates of limits on hate speech note that certain kinds of expression fall outside of First Amendment protection. Courts have ruled that "fighting words"—words intended to provoke immediate violence—or speech that creates a clear and present danger are not protected forms of expression. As the classic argument goes, freedom of speech does not give you the right to yell "Fire!" in a crowded theater. (Sudo, Phil. "Freedom of Hate Speech?")

Summary

Some people think stronger laws against the use of hate speech weaken the First Amendment, but others argue that some kinds of speech remain exempt from this protection (Sudo 17).

Close-Up SUMMARIZING

- **A summary is original.** It should use your own language and phrasing, not the language and phrasing of your source.
- **A summary is concise.** It should always be much shorter than the original—sometimes just a single sentence.
- **A summary is accurate.** It should precisely and accurately express the main idea of your source.
- **A summary is objective.** It should not include your opinions.
- **A summary is complete.** It should convey a sense of the entire passage, not just part of it.

Paraphrasing Sources A summary conveys just the main idea of a source; a **paraphrase**, however, is a *detailed* restatement, in your own words, of a source's key ideas—but not your opinions or interpretations of those ideas. A paraphrase not only indicates the source's main points but also reflects its tone and emphasis. For this reason, a paraphrase can sometimes be as long as—or even longer than—the source itself. (If you quote distinctive words or expressions from your source, be sure to put them in quotation marks.) Finally, be sure to document the paraphrase.

Compare the following paraphrase with the summary of the same source above.

Paraphrase

Many groups want to limit the right of free speech guaranteed by the First Amendment to the Constitution. They believe this is necessary to protect certain groups of people from "hate speech." Women, people of color, and gay men and lesbians, for example, may find that hate speech is used to intimidate them. Legal scholars are afraid that even though the rules against hate speech are well intentioned, such rules undermine our freedom of speech. As Nadine Strossen, president of the American Civil Liberties Union, says, "The bedrock principle [of our society] is that government may never suppress free speech simply because it goes against what the community would like to hear" (qtd. in Sudo 17). People who support speech codes point out, however, that certain types of speech are not protected by the First Amendment—for example, words that create a "clear and present danger" or that would lead directly to violence (Sudo 17).

Close-Up PARAPHRASING

- **A paraphrase is original.** It should use your own language and phrasing, not the language and phrasing of your source.
- **A paraphrase is accurate.** It should reflect both the ideas and the emphasis of your source.
- **A paraphrase is objective.** It should not include your own opinions or interpretations.
- **A paraphrase is complete.** It should include all the important ideas in your source.

MULTILINGUAL TIP

If you find yourself imitating a writer's sentence structure and vocabulary, try reading the passage you want to paraphrase and then putting it aside and thinking about it. Then, try to write down the ideas you remember without looking at the original text.

Quoting Sources Quote when you want to use a source's unique wording. When you **quote**, you copy a writer's statements exactly as they appear in a source, word for word and punctuation mark for punctuation mark, enclosing the borrowed words in quotation marks.

As a rule, you should not quote extensively in a research paper. Numerous quotations interrupt the flow of your discussion and give readers the impression that your essay is just an unassimilated collection of other people's ideas.

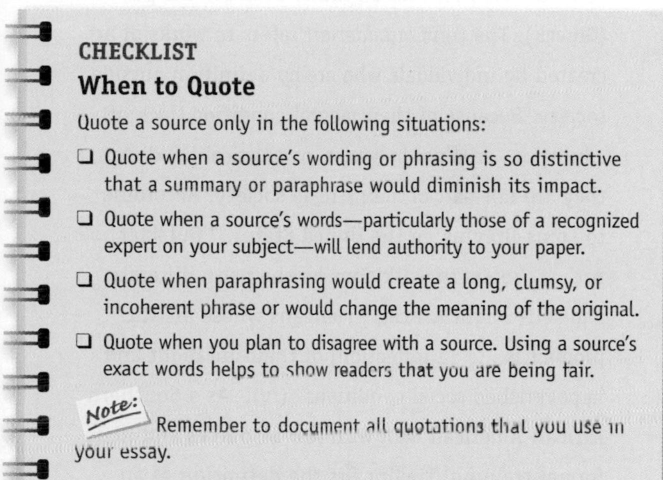

CHECKLIST

When to Quote

Quote a source only in the following situations:

- ❑ Quote when a source's wording or phrasing is so distinctive that a summary or paraphrase would diminish its impact.
- ❑ Quote when a source's words—particularly those of a recognized expert on your subject—will lend authority to your paper.
- ❑ Quote when paraphrasing would create a long, clumsy, or incoherent phrase or would change the meaning of the original.
- ❑ Quote when you plan to disagree with a source. Using a source's exact words helps to show readers that you are being fair.

Note: Remember to document all quotations that you use in your essay.

❸ Synthesizing Sources

Summaries and paraphrases rephrase a source's main ideas, and quotations reproduce a source's exact language. Synthesis combines summary, paraphrase, and quotation to create a paragraph or essay that expresses your original viewpoint about a topic.

A **synthesis** integrates information from two or more sources. In a synthesis, you weave ideas from your sources together and show how these ideas are similar or different. In the process, you try to make sense of your sources and help readers understand them in some meaningful way. For this reason, knowing how to write a synthesis is an important skill.

The following synthesis, written by a student as part of a research paper, effectively uses summary, paraphrase, and quotation to define the term *outsider art* and to explain it in relation to a particular artist's life and work.

Sample Student Synthesis

Topic sentence states main point

Summary of online Karlins article

Paraphrase from one-page Glueck article

Quotation from introduction to exhibit pamphlet

Conclusion summarizes main point

Bill Traylor is one of America's leading outsider artists. According to *Raw Vision* magazine, Traylor is one of the foremost artists of the twentieth century (Karlins). Born on a cotton plantation as a slave in the 1850s and illiterate all his life, Traylor was self-taught and did not consider himself an artist. He created works for himself rather than for the public (Glueck). The term *outsider art* refers to works of art created by individuals who are by definition outside society. Because of their mental condition, lack of education, criminal behavior, or physical handicaps, they are not part of mainstream society. According to Louis-Dreyfus, in the United States, "'Outsider Art' . . . refers to work done by the poor, illiterate, and self-taught African Americans whose artistic product is . . . [a reflection] of their untaught and impoverished social conditions" (iv). As a Southern African American man with few resources and little formal training, Traylor fits the definition of an outsider artist whose works are largely defined by the hardships he faced.

As this example demonstrates, an effective synthesis weaves information from different sources into the discussion, establishing relationships between sources and the writer's own ideas.

PLANNING GUIDE

SYNTHESIS

- Analyze and interpret your source material.
- Begin with a statement that sums up the main idea you want your synthesis to convey.
- Blend sources carefully, identifying each source and naming its author(s) and title.
- Identify key similarities and differences among your sources.

- Use identifying tags and transitional words and phrases to help readers follow your discussion.
- Be sure to clearly differentiate your ideas from those of your sources.
- Document all paraphrased and summarized material as well as all quotations.
- Proofread to make sure that you have not inadvertently plagiarized.

5h Fine-Tuning Your Thesis

After you have finished your focused research and note-taking, you are ready to refine your tentative thesis into a carefully worded statement that expresses a conclusion that your research can support. This **thesis statement** should be more detailed than your tentative thesis, accurately conveying the direction, emphasis, and scope of your paper. See 3b

Fine-Tuning Your Thesis

Tentative Thesis

The debate surrounding *Wikipedia* has helped people in the academic community to consider how college-level research has changed in recent years.

Thesis Statement

All in all, the debate over *Wikipedia* has been a positive development because it has led the academic community to confront the challenges of open, collaborative software on the web.

5i Outlining, Drafting, and Revising

Once you have a thesis statement, you are ready to construct an outline to guide you as you draft your paper.

1 Outlining

Before you can write your rough draft, you need to make some sense out of all the notes you have accumulated, and you do this by sorting and organizing them. A **formal outline** includes all the ideas you will develop in your paper, indicating not only the exact order in which you will present these ideas but also the relationship between main points and supporting details. It may also be helpful to list sources by author name or by a brief description of where you plan to use them in your paper.

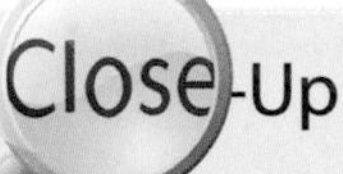

CONSTRUCTING A FORMAL OUTLINE

When you construct a formal outline for your research project, follow these guidelines:

Structure

- Outline format should be followed strictly.

    I. First major point
        A. First subpoint
        B. Next subpoint
            1. First supporting example
            2. Next supporting example
                a. First specific detail
                b. Next specific detail
    II. Second major point

- Headings should not overlap.
- No heading should have a single subheading. (A category cannot be subdivided into one part.)
- Each entry should be preceded by an appropriate letter or number, followed by a period.
- The first word of each entry should be capitalized.

Content

- The outline should include your thesis statement.
- The outline should cover only the body of the essay, not the introductory or concluding paragraphs.
- Headings should be concise and specific.

Style

- Headings of the same rank should be grammatically parallel.
- A **topic outline** should use words or short phrases, with all headings of the same rank using the same parts of speech.
- In a topic outline, entries should not end with periods.
- A **sentence outline** should use complete sentences, with all sentences in the same tense.
- In a sentence outline, each entry should end with a period.

The following is a **topic outline** for the model student research paper in **10c**.

Topic Outline

Thesis statement: All in all, the debate over *Wikipedia* has been a positive development because it has led the academic community to confront the challenges of open, collaborative software on the web.

I. Definition of wiki and explanation of *Wikipedia*
   A. Fast and easy
   B. Range of topics

II. Introduction to *Wikipedia*'s drawbacks
   A. Warnings on "Researching with *Wikipedia*" page
   B. Criticisms in "Reliability of *Wikipedia*" article
   C. Criticisms by academics
      1. Villanova University
      2. Middlebury College history department

III. *Wikipedia*'s unreliability
   A. Lack of citations
   B. Factual inaccuracy and bias
   C. Vandalism

IV. *Wikipedia*'s poor writing
   A. *Wikipedia*'s coding system
   B. *Wikipedia*'s influence on students' writing (Bauerlein)

V. *Wikipedia*'s popularity and benefits
   A. Wilson's findings (charts)
   B. Comprehensive abstracts, links to other sources, and current and comprehensive bibliographies

VI. *Wikipedia*'s advantages over other online encyclopedias
   A. Very current information
   B. More coverage of popular culture topics
   C. "Stub" articles

VII. *Wikipedia*'s ongoing improvements
   A. Control measures
   B. Users as editors
   C. "Talk" page

VIII. *Wikipedia*'s content
   A. View of Messner et al.
   B. Chart showing increased quality of *Wikipedia* articles over time

IX. Academic community's reservations about *Wikipedia*
   A. Academics' failure to keep up with technology
   B. Academics' qualifications to improve *Wikipedia*

X. Instructors' and librarians' efforts to use and improve *Wikipedia*
   A. Snyder's and Power's support for *Wikipedia*
   B. Responsibility of academic community

XI. *Wikipedia* in the classroom
   A. *Wikipedia*'s education program
   B. Collaborative and critical thinking assignments

XII. Academics' changing view of *Wikipedia*
   A. Academics' increasing acceptance
   B. Academics' increasing involvement
   C. *Wikipedia*'s best practices

The following is an excerpt from a **sentence outline** for the model student research paper in **10c**.

Sentence Outline (Excerpt)

Thesis statement: All in all, the debate over *Wikipedia* has been a positive development because it has led the academic community to confront the challenges of open, collaborative software on the web.

I. *Wikipedia* is the most popular wiki.
   A. Users can edit existing articles and add new articles using *Wikipedia*'s editing tools.
   B. *Wikipedia* has grown into a huge database.

II. *Wikipedia* has several shortcomings that limit its trustworthiness.
  A. *Wikipedia*'s "Researching with *Wikipedia*" page acknowledges existing problems.
  B. *Wikipedia*'s "Reliability of *Wikipedia*" page presents criticisms.
  C. Academics have objections.

III. *Wikipedia* is not always reliable or accurate.
  A. Many *Wikipedia* articles do not include citations.
  B. *Wikipedia* articles can be inaccurate or biased.
  C. *Wikipedia* articles can be targets for vandalism.

2 Drafting

When you write your **rough draft**, follow your outline, using your notes as needed. As you draft, jot down questions to yourself, and identify points that need further clarification (you can bracket your comments and print them in boldface on your draft, or you can write them on self-stick notes). You can also use *Microsoft Word*'s Comment tool to add notes. Finally, leave space for material you plan to add, and bracket phrases or whole sections that you think you may later decide to move or delete. In other words, lay the groundwork for revision. See 3d1

As your draft takes shape, be sure to supply transitions between sentences and paragraphs to show how your points are related. Also be careful to copy source information fully and accurately on this and every subsequent draft, placing documentation as close as possible to the material it identifies.

Close-Up DRAFTING

You can use a split screen or multiple windows to view your notes as you draft your essay. You can also copy the material that you need from your notes and then insert it into the text of your essay. (As you copy, be especially careful that you do not unintentionally commit **plagiarism**.) See 9b

Like any other essay, a research paper has an introduction, a body, and a conclusion. In your rough draft, as in your outline, you focus on the body of your paper. You should not spend time planning an introduction or a conclusion at this stage; your ideas will change as you write, and you will want to develop your opening and closing paragraphs later to reflect those changes.

PLANNING GUIDE

RESEARCH PROJECT

Your **assignment** will be to read a variety of sources to help you explore a subject that you want to learn more about.

Your **purpose** will be to interpret and evaluate your sources' ideas and to develop an original idea about your topic.

Your **audience** will usually be your instructor.

INTRODUCTION

Thesis statement templates:
- Despite…, the evidence suggests that…
- Although many people believe…, it seems more likely that…is actually the case.

- Begin by introducing readers to your subject and suggesting how you will approach it.
- Provide background to help readers understand the context for your discussion, perhaps briefly summarizing research already done on your topic.
- State your thesis, the position your research will support.

BODY PARAGRAPHS

Topic sentence templates:
- The first (second, final) point/example is…
- Another point that supports this position is…

Templates for introducing support:
- As many scholars observe,…
- Several sources make the case that…
- Another study demonstrates that…
- According to…,…

- Begin each paragraph with a topic sentence that corresponds to a section of your outline.
- In each body paragraph, provide support for your thesis, synthesizing source information with ideas of your own.
- Use summary, paraphrase, and quoted material from your sources to support your statements.
- Use different patterns of development to shape the individual paragraphs of your essay.
- Connect sentences and paragraphs with clear transitions, including transitional paragraphs where necessary.
- Be careful to keep track of your sources and to avoid plagiarism.

- Consider including visuals where appropriate.
- Include parenthetical documentation where necessary.

CONCLUSION

- Restate your thesis (in different words).
- Summarize your key points.
- End with a strong concluding statement.

Concluding statement templates:
- As the ongoing debate around this issue suggests, . . .
- For all the reasons summarized above, . . .
- Given the supporting evidence outlined here, it seems likely that . . .

Close-Up USING TOPIC SENTENCES AND HEADINGS

Clear, specific topic sentences will help readers follow your discussion.

> Without a professional editorial board to oversee its development, *Wikipedia* has several shortcomings that limit its trustworthiness.

You can also use headings if they are a convention of the discipline in which you are writing. See 39b

> *Wikipedia's Advantages*
>
> *Wikipedia* has advantages over other online encyclopedias.

In the body of your paper, you evaluate and interpret your sources, comparing different ideas and assessing various points of view. As a writer, your job is to draw your own conclusions, blending information from your sources into a paper that coherently and forcefully presents your own original viewpoint to your readers.

Be sure to **integrate source material** smoothly into your paper, clearly and accurately identifying the relationships among various sources (and between those sources' ideas and your own). If two sources present conflicting interpretations, you should be especially careful to use precise language and accurate transitions to make the contrast apparent (for instance, **Although some academics** See Ch. 8

believe that *Wikipedia* should not be a part of college-level research, Snyder argues . . .). When two sources agree, you should make this clear (for example, **Like Snyder, Power claims . . .** or **The findings of Messner et al. support Snyder's point**). Such phrasing will provide a context for your own comments and conclusions. If different sources present complementary information about a subject, blend details from the sources carefully, keeping track of which details come from which source.

Close-Up INTEGRATING VISUALS

See 39d

Photographs, diagrams, graphs, tables, and other visuals can be very useful in your research paper because they can provide additional support for the points you make. You may be able to create a visual on your own (for example, by taking a photograph or creating a bar graph). You may also be able to scan an appropriate visual from a book or magazine or access an image database, such as *Google Images* or *Creative Commons*.

3 Revising

Using Outlines and Checklists A good way to begin revising is to make an outline of your draft to check the logic of its organization and the relationships among sections of the paper. As you continue to revise, the checklists in **3d2** can help you assess your paper's overall structure and its individual paragraphs, sentences, and words.

Using Instructor Comments Your instructor's revision suggestions, which can come in a conference or in handwritten comments on your paper, can also help you revise. Alternatively, your instructor may use *Microsoft Word*'s Comment tool to make comments electronically on a draft that you have emailed to him or her. When you revise, you can incorporate these suggestions into your paper.

Draft with Instructor's Comments (Excerpt)

Comment [JB1]: You need a transition sentence before this one to show that this ¶ is about a new idea. See 20b.

Emory University English professor Mark Bauerlein asserts that *Wikipedia* articles are written in a "flat, featureless, factual style" (153). Even though *Wikipedia* has instituted a coding system in which it labels the shortcomings of its less-developed articles, a warning about an article's poor writing style is likely to go unnoticed by the typical user.

Comment [JB2]: Wordy. See 22a.

Revision Incorporating Instructor's Suggestions

Because they can be edited by anyone, *Wikipedia* articles are often poorly written. Emory University English professor Mark Bauerlein asserts that *Wikipedia* articles are written in a "flat, featureless, factual style" (153). Even though *Wikipedia* has instituted a coding system to label the shortcomings of its less-developed articles, a warning about an article's poor writing style is likely to go unnoticed by the typical user.

Using Peer Review Feedback you get from **peer review**—other students' comments, handwritten or electronic—can also help you revise. As you incorporate your classmates' suggestions, as well as your own changes and any suggested by your instructor, you can use *Microsoft Word*'s Track Changes tool to help you keep track of the revisions you make on your draft.

Draft with Peer Reviewers' Comments (Excerpt)

Because users can update articles in real time from any location, *Wikipedia* offers up-to-the-minute coverage of political and cultural events as well as timely information on popular culture topics that receive little or no attention in other reference sources. In addition, because *Wikipedia* has such a broad user base, more topics are covered in *Wikipedia* than in other online resources. Even when there is little information on a particular topic, *Wikipedia* allows users to create "stub" articles, which provide minimal information that users can expand over time. Thus, *Wikipedia* can be a valuable first step in finding reliable research sources.

Comment [RS1]: I think you need a better transition here.

Comment [TG2]: I think some examples here would really help.

Comment [DL3]: I agree. Maybe talk about a useful *Wikipedia* article you found recently.

Comment [RS4]: Why?

Revision with Track Changes

Wikipedia has advantages over other online encyclopedias. Because users can update articles in real time from any location, *Wikipedia* offers up-to-the-minute coverage of political and cultural events as well as timely information on popular culture topics that receive little or no attention in other reference sources. In addition, because *Wikipedia* has such a broad user base, more topics are covered in *Wikipedia* than in other online resources. For example, a student researching the history of video gaming would find *Wikipedia*'s "Wii U" article, with its numerous pages of information and nearly two hundred references, to be a valuable resource. *Encyclopedia Britannica* does not contain a comparable article on this popular game console. Even when there is little information on a particular topic, *Wikipedia* allows users to create "stub" articles, which provide minimal information that users can expand over time. Thus, by offering immediate access to information on relatively obscure topics, *Wikipedia* can be a valuable first step in finding reliable research sources on such topics.

Keep in mind that you will probably take your paper through several drafts, changing different parts of it each time or working on one part over and over again. After revising each draft thoroughly, print out a corrected version and label it *First draft, Second draft*, and so on. Then, make additional corrections by hand on that draft before typing in changes for the next version. You should also save and clearly label every electronic draft.

When you finish revising your paper, copy the file that contains your working bibliography and insert it at the end of your paper. Keep the original file for your working bibliography as a backup in case any data is lost in the process. Delete any irrelevant entries, and then create your works-cited list. (Make sure the format of the entries in your works-cited list conforms to the documentation style you are using.)

If you save multiple drafts of your works-cited list, be sure to name each file with the date or some other label so that it is readily identifiable. Keep all files pertaining to a single project in a folder dedicated to that paper or assignment.

Close-Up USING CITATION TOOLS

Use citation tools such as the following to create your bibliography and to make sure all the sources you used—and only those sources—appear in your works-cited list.

BibMe

- Free and easy to use: made for quick copying and pasting of citations anywhere; allows saving for later use
- Entirely web-based
- Supports MLA, APA, and Chicago documentation styles

EasyBib

- Free and easy to use: made for quick copying and pasting of citations anywhere; allows saving for later use
- Entirely web-based
- Supports MLA, APA, and Chicago documentation styles

EndNote

- Purchase required (consult with your college library or bookstore for free institutional access or student discounts; if you access through your institution's license, you may not be able to access your citations after graduation)
- Easy to use: allows you to collect citations and add notes with unlimited storage. Cite While You Write feature allows you to cite within a document. Compatible with *Microsoft Office*, *OpenOffice*, and *iWork Pages*.
- Works on both Mac and PC either offline or online, but more robust when used on a local computer. Syncs with *EndNote Basic* for web access.
- Supports MLA, APA, Chicago, CSE, and many other documentation styles

(continued)

USING CITATION TOOLS *(continued)*

EndNote Basic/EndNote Web

- Free and easy to use: allows sharing of citations with others, as in group projects. Compatible with *Microsoft Word*.
- Entirely web-based (Internet connection needed to access citations). Syncs with *EndNote* (on a local computer).

Mendeley

- Free (unless large-capacity online storage space is needed)
- Easy to use: allows you to collect citations and add notes. Citations can be shared privately with up to two additional users or open to public viewing. Retains PDFs alongside citations with easy organization and retrieval. Compatible with *Microsoft Word, OpenOffice*, and *LaTeX*.
- Works on both Mac and PC either offline or online, but more robust when used on a local computer. Can be synced with multiple devices, allowing access to citations from anywhere.
- Supports MLA, APA, Chicago, and many other documentation styles

Qiqqa

- Free and easy to use: allows you to collect citations and add notes. InCite feature allows you to cite within a document. Retains PDFs alongside citations with easy organization and retrieval.
- PC-compatible only
- Supports MLA, APA, Chicago, and many other documentation styles

RefWorks

- Purchase required (consult with your college library or bookstore for free institutional access or student discounts; if you access through your institution's license, you may not be able to access your citations after graduation)
- Easy to use: allows you to collect citations and add notes. Write-N-Cite feature allows you to cite within a document. *RefShare* (a companion to *RefWorks*) allows you to share citations with others.
- Entirely web-based
- Supports MLA, APA, Chicago, CSE, and many other documentation styles

Zotero

- Free (unless large-capacity online syncing storage space is needed)
- Easy to use: allows you to collect citations and add extensive review notes. Plug-in automatically inserts footnotes or parenthetical citations into a word-processing document. Quick Copy function allows you to drag and drop a citation in any text field in your document. "Scrapes" websites for citation information by taking a snapshot (some data may need to be added if *Zotero* cannot identify a particular field). Allows sharing of citations with others, as in group projects. Retains PDFs alongside citations with easy organization and retrieval. Compatible with *Microsoft Word, OpenOffice*, and *Google Drive*.
- Works on both Mac and PC either offline or online, but more robust when used on a local computer. Can be synced with multiple devices, allowing access to citations from anywhere. Prefers *Firefox* browser.
- Supports MLA, APA, Chicago, CSE, and many other documentation styles

CHECKLIST

Revising a Research Paper

As you revise, keep the following questions in mind:

- ❑ Should you do more research to find support for certain points?
- ❑ Do you need to reorder the major sections of your paper?
- ❑ Should you rearrange the order in which you present your points within those sections?
- ❑ Do you need to add topic sentences? Section headings? Transitional paragraphs?
- ❑ Have you **integrated your notes** smoothly into your paper? See Ch. 8
- ❑ Do you introduce source material with **identifying tags**? See 8a
- ❑ Are quotations blended with paraphrase, summary, and your own observations and reactions?
- ❑ Have you avoided **plagiarism** by carefully documenting all borrowed ideas? See Ch. 9
- ❑ Have you analyzed and interpreted the ideas of others rather than simply stringing those ideas together?
- ❑ Do your own ideas—not those of your sources—establish the focus of your discussion?

5j Preparing a Final Draft

See 3e

Before you hand in the final version of your paper, **edit and proofread** a hard copy of your works-cited list as well as the paper itself. Next, consider (or reconsider) your **title**. It should be descriptive enough to tell your readers what your paper is about, and it should create interest in your subject. Your title should also be consistent with your **purpose** and tone. (You would hardly want a humorous title for an essay about famine in Sub-Saharan Africa or inequities in the American judicial system.) Finally, your title should be engaging and to the point—perhaps even provocative. Often, a quotation from one of your sources will suggest a likely title.

See 2b

When you are satisfied with your title, read your paper through one last time, proofreading for any grammar, spelling, or typing errors you may have missed. Pay particular attention to parenthetical documentation and works-cited entries. (Remember that every error undermines your credibility.) Finally, make sure your paper's format conforms to your instructor's guidelines. Once you are satisfied that your paper is as accurate as you can make it, print out a final copy or email it to your instructor, following his or her guidelines. (For a model MLA-style research paper, **see 10c.**)

CHAPTER 6

Finding Information

6a Finding Information in the Library

When it comes to finding trustworthy, high-quality, and authoritative sources, nothing beats your college library. A modern college library offers you resources that you cannot find anywhere else—even on the Internet.

Close-Up WHY USE THE LIBRARY?

- Many important publications are available only in print or through the library's databases.
- The information in your college library is cataloged and classified.
- Because the library's databases list only published sources, the information you access will always be available, unlike the information on the Internet.
- Because librarians screen the resources in your college library, these resources are likely to meet academic standards of reliability. (Even so, you still have to evaluate any information before you use it in an essay.)
- Bibliographic information for the documents in your college library is easy to determine, unlike that of documents on the Internet.
- The library staff is available to answer your questions and to help you find material.

See 7a

1 Searching the Library's Online Catalog or Discovery Service

The best way to start your research is by visiting your college library's **website**. The website's home page is a gateway to a vast amount of information—for example, the library's catalog or discovery service, the databases the library makes available, special library services, and general information about the library. Figure 6.1 shows the home page of a library's website.

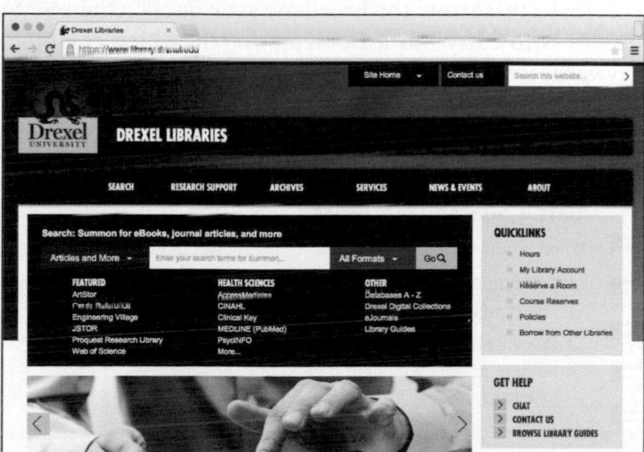

FIGURE 6.1 Home page of an academic library's website. © Drexel University.

Your next step is to search the library's **online catalog**, a comprehensive database that lists the journal titles (but not the articles themselves), books, and multimedia held in the library's collections. When you search the online catalog or discovery service for information, you may do either a *keyword search* or a *subject search*.

Close-Up A DISCOVERY SERVICE

Many libraries have a **discovery service**, which includes not only the physical items held by a library but also e-books and journal articles, including those from electronic databases, as well as articles and books held at other libraries. These items may be obtained through interlibrary loan.

Doing a Keyword Search When you do a **keyword search**, you enter into the search box of the online catalog or discovery service a word (or words) associated with your topic. The computer then displays a list of entries (called **hits**) that contain these words. The more precise your keywords, the more specific and useful the information you retrieve will be. For example, *Civil War* will yield many thousands of hits; *The Wilderness Campaign* will yield far fewer.

Because vague or inaccurate keyword searching can yield an overwhelming number of irrelevant hits, you need to focus your search by using **search operators**, words or symbols that can narrow (or broaden) your query. One way to do this is to carry out a **Boolean search**, which combines keywords with the search operators *and*, *or*, or *not*.

CHECKLIST

Using Search Operators

When you do a keyword search, follow these guidelines:

- ❑ Use **quotation marks** to search for a specific phrase: *"Baltimore Economy."*
- ❑ Use an **asterisk** after a word to retrieve a root word with any ending: *photo** will yield *photograph*, *photographer*, *photojournalist*, *photoactive*, and so on.

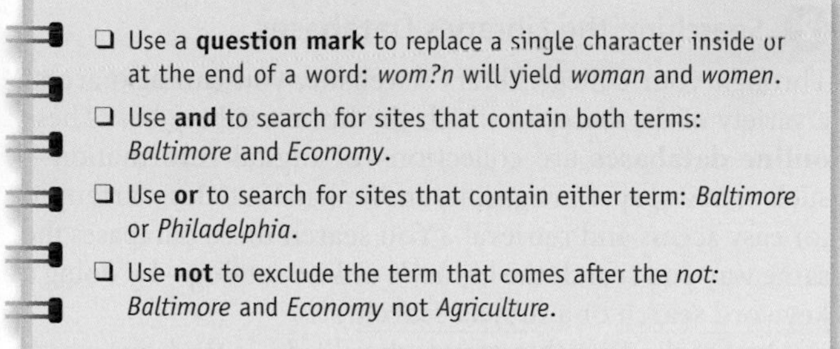

- ❑ Use a **question mark** to replace a single character inside or at the end of a word: *wom?n* will yield *woman* and *women*.
- ❑ Use **and** to search for sites that contain both terms: *Baltimore* and *Economy*.
- ❑ Use **or** to search for sites that contain either term: *Baltimore* or *Philadelphia*.
- ❑ Use **not** to exclude the term that comes after the *not: Baltimore* and *Economy* not *Agriculture*.

Doing a Subject Search When you do a **subject search**, you enter a subject heading into the search box of the online catalog or discovery service. The resources in an academic library are classified under specific subject headings. Many online catalogs list these subject headings to help you identify the exact words that you need for your search. Figure 6.2 below shows the results of a subject search in a university library's discovery service.

Note: *WorldCat and WorldCat Local* are "super" catalogs of millions of items. If your college library provides access to these resources, you can locate books, DVDs, music, photographs, and specialized databases from thousands of participating libraries around the world and in your community. Check with your reference librarian for information about these resources.

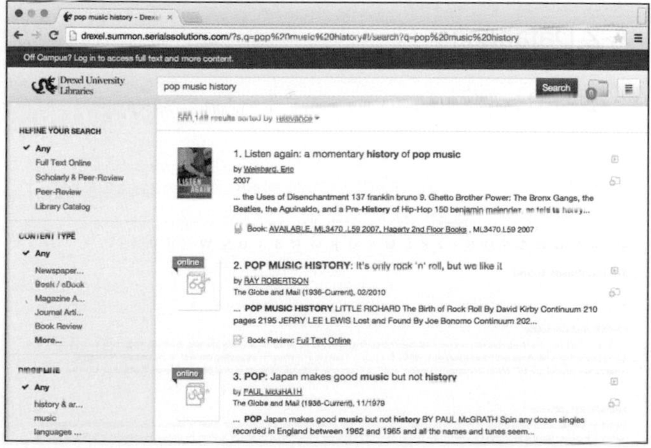

FIGURE 6.2 Discovery service search results for the subject heading *pop music history*. © Drexel University.

2 Searching the Library's Databases

Through your college library's website, you can also access a variety of databases to which the library subscribes. These **online databases** are collections of digital information—such as newspaper, magazine, and journal articles—arranged for easy access and retrieval. (You search these databases the same way you search the library's online catalog—by doing a keyword search or a subject search.)

See 6a1

One of the first things you should do is find out which databases your library subscribes to. You can usually access these databases through the library's website, and if necessary, you can ask a reference librarian for more information. Figure 6.3 shows a partial list of databases to which one library subscribes.

College libraries subscribe to information service companies, such as Gale Cengage Learning, which provide access to hundreds of databases not available for free on the Internet. These databases enable you to access current information from scholarly journals, abstracts, books, reports, case studies, government documents, magazines, and newspapers. Most libraries subscribe to databases that cover many subject

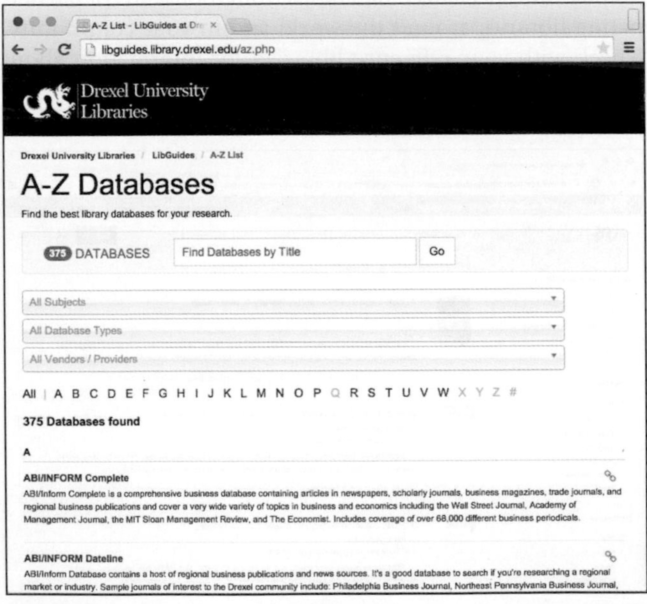

FIGURE 6.3 Excerpt from list of databases to which one academic library subscribes. © Drexel University.

areas (*Expanded Academic ASAP*, EBSCOhost's *Academic Search*, and *LexisNexis Academic Universe*, for example); others cover a single subject area in great detail (*PsycINFO* or *Sociological Abstracts*, for example).

Assuming that your library offers a variety of databases, how do you know which ones will be best for your research? First, you should determine the level of the periodical articles listed in the database. A **periodical** is a scholarly journal, magazine, newspaper, or other publication that appears at regular intervals (weekly, monthly, or quarterly, for example). **Scholarly journals** are often the most reliable sources you can find on a subject. They contain articles written by experts in a field, and because journals focus on a particular subject area, they usually provide in-depth analysis. However, because journal articles are aimed at experts, they can be difficult for general readers to understand. **Popular periodicals** are magazines and newspapers that publish articles aimed at general readers. These periodicals are more accessible, but they are less reliable than scholarly journals because they vary greatly in quality. Some articles might conform to academic standards of reliability, but others may be totally unsuitable as sources.

Close-Up CHOOSING A LIBRARY DATABASE

Consulting with a reference librarian is an excellent way to get connected to the best databases for your topic. You could also ask your instructor if your class will be visiting the library for a research session conducted by a reference librarian. These hands-on sessions will help guide you through the maze of resources to the best ones for your topic.

Next, you should look for a database that is suitable for your topic. Most libraries list databases alphabetically by title or arrange them by subject area. Some offer online study guides (also called research guides or subject guides) that were designed by reference librarians and that list databases (as well as other resources) that are appropriate for research in a given subject area. If you know what database you are looking for, you can find it in the alphabetical listing. If you don't, go to the subject list and locate your general subject area—*History*, *Nursing*, or *Linguistics*, for example. Then, review the databases that are listed under this heading.

You can begin with a multisubject **general database** such as *Expanded Academic ASAP* or EBSCOhost's *Academic Search* that includes thousands of full-text articles. Then, you can move on to more **specialized databases** that examine your specific subject in detail and that include a far greater number of discipline-specific sources than do general-interest databases.

Close-Up USING MULTI SEARCH

Check to see if your library uses EBSCO Discovery Service, which enables you to search many library databases at one time. Libraries often call it "One Search" or "Multi Search," and it typically appears as one search box on the home page, as in this example.

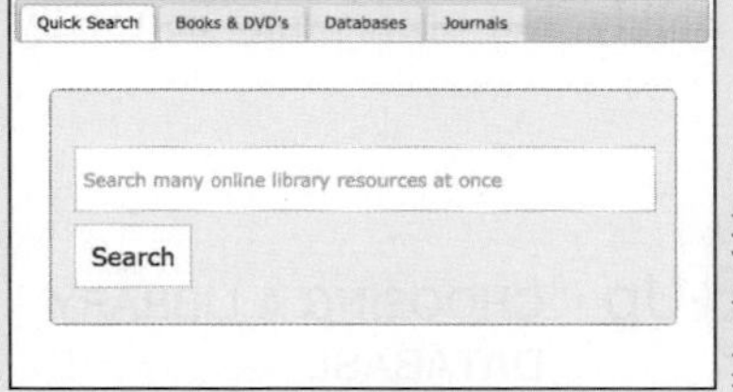

University of Arkansas

Frequently Used General Databases

Database	Description
Academic OneFile	Articles from journals and reference sources in a number of disciplines
Credo Reference	A database of several hundred reference books
EBSCOhost's *Academic Search*	Thousands of periodical articles on many subjects
Expanded Academic ASAP	Articles from journals in the humanities, social sciences, and the natural and applied sciences

JSTOR	Full-text articles from older issues (typically three to five years out) of hundreds of peer-reviewed journals spanning all disciplines from major academic presses, such as Stanford University and University of Chicago
LexisNexis Academic Universe	Full-text articles from national, international, and local news publications as well as legal and business publications
Opposing Viewpoints Resource Center	A library of debates on current topics
Project MUSE	Articles from dozens of major peer-reviewed journals with an emphasis on the humanities
ProQuest Research Library	An index of journal articles in various disciplines, many full text

Specialized Databases

HUMANITIES

Database	Description
Arts	
Art Abstracts	Articles in art magazines and journals
Communication	
Communication & Mass Media Complete	Index and abstracts for more than four hundred journals and coverage of two hundred more
History	
America: History and Life	Articles on North American history
Historical Abstracts	Articles on world history
History Reference Center	Full-text articles and other resources for the study of history
Literature	
MLA International Bibliography	An index for books, articles, and websites focusing on literature, language, and film studies
Gale Literature Criticism Online	Full-text articles on literary criticism and analysis

continued

Specialized Databases *(continued)*

HUMANITIES

Database	Description
Philosophy	
Philosopher's Index	Index and abstracts from over five hundred fifty journals from forty countries
Religion	
ATLA Religion	Articles in religion studies journals

SOCIAL SCIENCES

Database	Description
Business	
ABI/INFORM Global	A ProQuest collection of over eighteen hundred journals and company profiles
Business Source Premier	Indexes more than seventy-eight hundred publications
Economics	
EconLit	Offers a wide range of economics-related resources
Education	
Education Research Complete	The world's largest collection of full-text education journals
Psychology	
PsycINFO	Indexes books and journal articles in the psychological and behavioral sciences
Sociology and Social Work	
Sociological Abstracts	An index of literature in sociology
Social Work Abstracts	An index of current research in social work

NATURAL AND APPLIED SCIENCES

Database	Description
Biology	
Biological Sciences	Abstracts and citations from a wide range of biological research
Chemistry	
American Chemical Society Publications	Articles from over thirty peer-reviewed journals
Computer Science	
ACM Guide to Computing Literature	Over 750,000 citations and abstracts of literature about computing

Engineering	
IEEE Xplore	Full-text access to all IEEE journals, magazines, and conference proceedings
Environmental Science	
Environmental Science Database	Information on environmental subjects
Nursing	
ProQuest Nursing & Allied Health Source	Resources for nursing and the allied health fields

CHECKLIST

Questions for Choosing the Right Database

Before you decide which database to use, ask the following questions:

- ❑ Is the database suited to your subject? Is it too general or too specialized?
- ❑ Does the database include scholarly journals, popular periodicals, or both?
- ❑ Does the database contain the full text of articles or just citations?
- ❑ Are you able to limit your search—for example, to just scholarly publications or to just peer-reviewed publications?
- ❑ How easy (or difficult) is the database to use?
- ❑ Does the database allow you to download and/or email documents?
- ❑ What years does the database cover?

3 Finding Books

The library's online catalog or discovery service also give you the information you need for locating specific books. Entries for books include the author's name, the title, the subject, publication information, and a call number. A **call number** is like a book's address in the library: it tells you exactly where to find the book you are looking for. (Figure 6.4 shows the results of an author search in a university library's online catalog.)

Note: Do not limit yourself to your library's book collection. Ask your reference librarian about the interlibrary loan process. After you submit an interlibrary loan request, you will

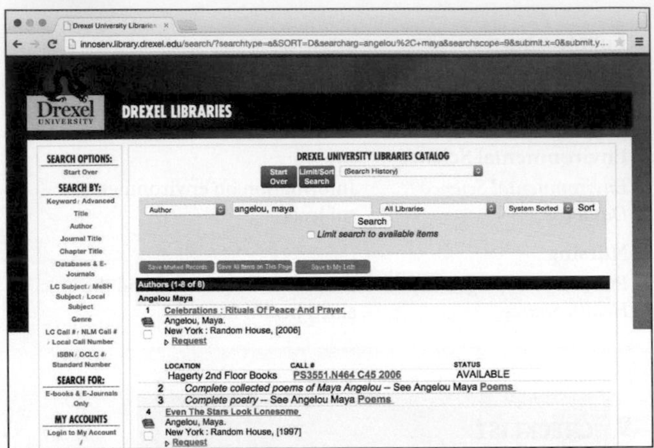

FIGURE 6.4 Online catalog search results for the author *Maya Angelou*. © Drexel University.

receive an email announcement that the book you requested can be picked up at your library's circulation desk.

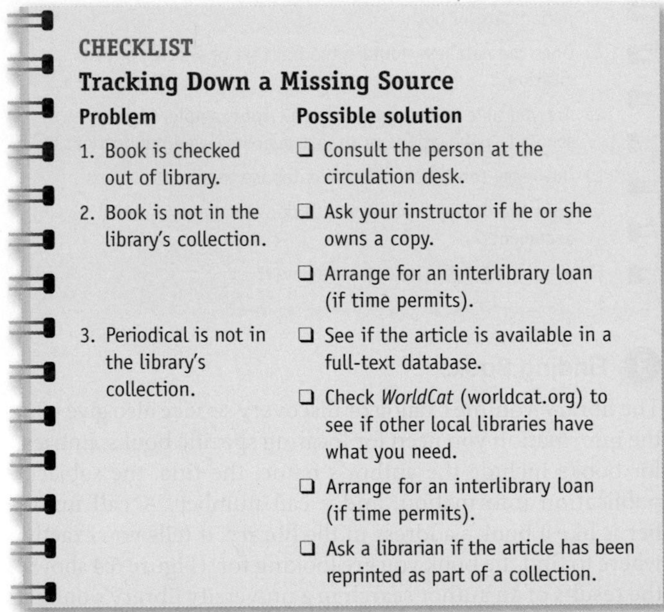

CHECKLIST

Tracking Down a Missing Source

Problem	Possible solution
1. Book is checked out of library.	❑ Consult the person at the circulation desk.
2. Book is not in the library's collection.	❑ Ask your instructor if he or she owns a copy.
	❑ Arrange for an interlibrary loan (if time permits).
3. Periodical is not in the library's collection.	❑ See if the article is available in a full-text database.
	❑ Check *WorldCat* (worldcat.org) to see if other local libraries have what you need.
	❑ Arrange for an interlibrary loan (if time permits).
	❑ Ask a librarian if the article has been reprinted as part of a collection.

4 Consulting Reference Sources

Reference sources—online and print dictionaries, encyclopedias, almanacs, atlases, bibliographies, and so on—can provide an overview of your topic as well as essential background and factual information. Even though they do not discuss your topic in enough depth to be used as research sources, the following reference works can be useful for gathering information and for focusing your research on the specific issues you want to explore in depth.

- **Encyclopedias**—such as the *Encyclopedia Americana* and *The New Encyclopaedia Britannica*—provide an introduction to your topic and give you a sense of the scholarly debates related to it. Individual encyclopedia entries often contain bibliographies that can lead you to works that you can use as research sources.
- **Bibliographies** are lists of sources on a specific topic. For example, the *MLA International Bibliography* lists books and articles published in literature, and the *Bibliographic Guide to Education* lists published sources on all aspects of education. Bibliographic entries often include abstracts.
- **Biographical reference books**—such as *Who's Who in America, Who's Who*, and the *Dictionary of American Biography*—provide information about people's lives as well as bibliographic listings. They can also provide general information about the times in which people lived.
- **Special dictionaries** focus on topics such as synonyms, slang and idioms, rhyming, symbols, proverbs, sign language, and foreign phrases. Other special dictionaries concentrate on specific academic disciplines, such as law, medicine, and computing.

6b Finding Information on the Internet

The **web** (which is part of the Internet) is the research tool of choice for most college students. This strategy is not without its drawbacks, however. Because no one is responsible for checking web documents to make sure they are trustworthy, factually accurate, or current, you have to use them with care.

Of course, there are many trustworthy sources of information on the Internet. You can learn to use the search engine *Google* in ways to better find trustworthy materials, and *Google Scholar* provides links to scholarly and academic sources that can also be found in your college's online library databases. In addition, the *Directory of Open Access Journals* (doaj.org) lists almost ten thousand open-access scientific and scholarly journals—many of which are highly respected—in its directories.

The Internet can be a valuable resource for research, but you must be able to search effectively for, keep track of, and carefully evaluate materials you find. To carry out a web search, you need a **web browser**, an application—such as *Google Chrome, Mozilla Firefox, Microsoft Internet Explorer*, or *Safari*—that enables you to view information on the web.

You access information on the web by either entering a URL into your browser's search field or using your search engine to carry out a keyword search.

1 Pasting a URL

Every page and document on the web has an electronic address called a **URL** (uniform resource locator). When you paste a URL into your browser's location field and click Search, you will be connected to the website you want. (Figure 6.5 shows a location field.)

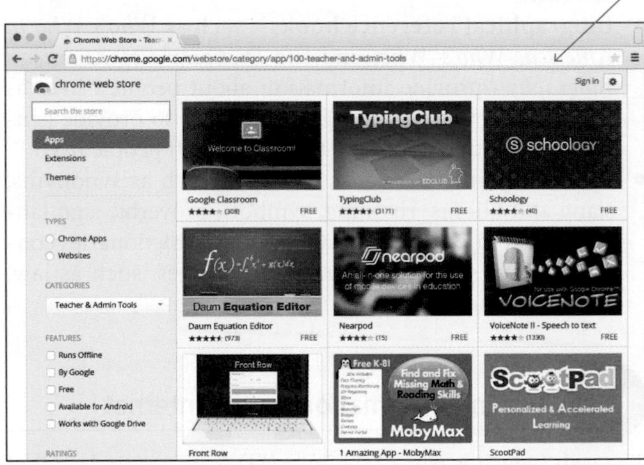

FIGURE 6.5 Where to copy and paste an address (URL) in *Google Chrome*. © Google Chrome

2 Doing a Keyword Search

Once you are connected to the web, use your browser to access a **search engine**, an application such as *Google* or *Google Scholar* that searches for and provides links to documents. You carry out a **keyword search** by entering a keyword (or keywords) into your search engine's search field. (Figure 6.6 shows a search engine's keyword search page.) The search engine will identify any site in its database on which

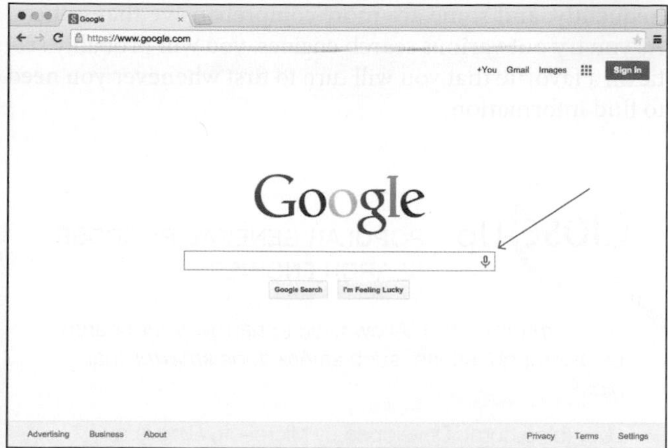

FIGURE 6.6 Google keyword search page. © Google

the keyword (or keywords) you have typed appears. (These are called **hits**.)

You can develop a list of useful keywords by looking at your college library's online catalog or discovery service and using its headings as keywords. You can also find keywords by looking at the list of Library of Congress Subject Headings (id.loc.gov/authorities/subjects.html). Finally, you can access an online general encyclopedia, such as *Wikipedia*, and look at the category list that follows each article. These categories make excellent keywords that you can use as you search. (Keep in mind, however, that articles from general encyclopedias are typically not acceptable for including as sources in your writing for college-level research unless your assignment states otherwise.)

Many search engines have advanced options that enable you to limit the number of irrelevant results. For example, you can tailor your search so that it retrieves only documents from a particular type of site (*.edu* or *.org*, for example) or documents containing certain keywords in the title or URL. For more on *Google* search operators, see (www.googleguide.com/advanced_operators_reference.html).

3 Choosing the Right Search Engine

General-Purpose Search Engines The most widely used search engines are **general-purpose search engines** that focus on a wide variety of topics. Some of these search engines are more user-friendly than others; some allow for more sophisticated searching functions; some are updated more frequently; and some are more comprehensive than others. As you try out various search engines, you will probably settle on a favorite that you will turn to first whenever you need to find information.

POPULAR GENERAL-PURPOSE SEARCH ENGINES

Ask.com (ask.com): Allows you to narrow your search by asking questions, such as *Are dogs smarter than pigs?*

Bing (bing.com): Developed by Microsoft, *Bing* is a solid competitor to *Google*. *Bing* offers suggestions for follow-up searches, called "Also Try" and "Related Searches." *Bing* favors *.edu, .gov*, and *.mil* sites more than *Google*, paying close attention to top-level domain names, while *Google* pays more attention to PageRank (see the *Google* description below). *Bing* has excellent image and video functions.

Google (google.com): Arguably the best search engine available, it accesses a large database that includes both text and graphics. It is easy to navigate, and searches usually yield a high percentage of useful hits. *Google* purportedly ranks its results using an algorithm called PageRank, based on the number of times a page is linked to other sites. The more a page is linked, the higher it will rise to the top of the results list. (See pages 85–86 for more information about *Google* resources.)

Yahoo! (yahoo.com): *Yahoo!* relies heavily on the titles of pages. If your keywords appear in the title of a page, that page is likely to rise to the top of the results list. *Yahoo!* also favors more popular pages, measured by the number of times a page is clicked.

Because even the best search engines search only a fraction of the material available on the web, if you use only one search engine, you will most likely miss much valuable information. In addition, search engines vary widely in the way they rank results; this means that the results displayed on the first few pages of one search engine may be completely different from those displayed in another search engine. It is therefore a good idea to repeat each search with several different search engines or to use a **metasearch** or **metacrawler** engine that uses several search engines simultaneously.

Close-Up METASEARCH ENGINES

Dogpile (dogpile.com)

Ixquick (ixquick.com)

Kartoo (kartoo.com)

Mamma (mamma.com)

SurfWax (surfwax.com)

Yippy (yippy.com)

Zoo (zoo.com)

Specialized Search Engines In addition to general-purpose search engines and metasearch engines, there are also **specialized search engines** devoted entirely to specific subject areas, such as literature, business, sports, and women's issues. Hundreds of specialized search engines are indexed at *listofsearchengines.info*.

Close-Up *GOOGLE* RESOURCES

Google is the most-used search engine on the Internet. Most people who use *Google*, however, do not actually know its full potential. Following are just a few of the resources that *Google* offers:

- ***Blogger*** (blogger.com) A tool for creating and posting blogs online
- ***Book Search*** (books.google.com) A database that allows users to access millions of books that they can either preview or read for free
- ***Google Earth*** (earth.google.com) A downloadable, dynamic global map that enables users to see satellite views of almost any place on the planet

(continued)

GOOGLE RESOURCES *(continued)*

- ***Finance*** (google.com/finance) Business information, news, and interactive charts
- ***News*** (news.google.com) Enables users to search thousands of news stories
- ***Patent Search*** (google.com/patents) Enables users to search the full text of US patents
- ***Google Scholar*** (scholar.google.com) Searches scholarly literature, including peer-reviewed papers, books, and abstracts
- ***Google Translate*** (translate.google.com) A free online language translation service that instantly translates text and web pages

CHECKLIST

Tips for Effective Web Searches

- ❑ **Choose the right search engine.** No single all-purpose search engine exists. Review the list of search engines in the boxes on pages 84–85.
- ❑ **Choose your keywords carefully.** A search engine is only as good as the keywords you use.
- ❑ **Include enough terms.** If you are looking for information on housing, for example, search for several variations of your keyword: *housing, houses, home buyer, buying houses, residential real estate*, and so on.
- ❑ **Use more than one search engine.** Because different search engines index different sites, try several. If one does not yield results after a few tries, try another. Also, don't forget to try a metasearch engine such as *Zoo*.
- ❑ **Use the advanced search features of a search engine.** For example, *Google Advanced Search* (google.com/advanced_search) is a powerful search tool that makes Boolean operators unnecessary. It can limit your search to a specific date range and even limit by domain (such as *.org*, *.edu*, and *harvard.edu*).
- ❑ **Add useful sites to your Bookmark or Favorites list.** Whenever you find a particularly useful website, **bookmark** it by selecting this option on the menu bar of your browser (with some browsers, such as *Microsoft Internet Explorer*, this option is called Favorites).

4 Using *Wikipedia* as a Research Source

Although no encyclopedia—electronic or print—should be used as a research source, *Wikipedia* requires an extra level of scrutiny.

Wikipedia is an open-source, online general encyclopedia created through the collaborative efforts of its users. Anyone (not necessarily experts) registered with the site can write an article, and in most cases, anyone who views the site can edit an article. The theory is that if enough people contribute, over time, entries will become more and more accurate. Many instructors point out, however, that the coverage in *Wikipedia* is uneven; some articles follow acceptable standards of academic research, but many others do not. Because some articles have little or no documentation, it is difficult to judge their merit. In addition, because *Wikipedia* does not have an editorial staff responsible for checking entries for accuracy, it is not necessarily a reliable source of information. Finally, critics point out that there is no foolproof way that *Wikipedia* can guard against **vandalism**—the purposeful addition of false or misleading information into an article.

Still, *Wikipedia* does have its strengths. Because its content is constantly being revised, *Wikipedia* can be more up to date than other reference sources. Also, many articles contain bibliographic citations that enable users to link to reliable sources of information. Still, even though you can use *Wikipedia* to get a general overview of your topic, most instructors do not consider it a trustworthy, let alone authoritative, research source.

6c Doing Field Research

In addition to using information you find in the library or on the Internet, you can find your own information by doing **field research**—making observations, conducting interviews, and conducting surveys.

1 Making Observations

Some writing assignments are based on your own **observations**. For example, an art history essay can include information gathered during a visit to a museum, and an education essay can include an account of a classroom visit.

CHECKLIST

Making Observations

- ❑ Decide what you want to observe and where you want to observe it.
- ❑ Determine in advance what you hope to gain from your observations.
- ❑ Bring a laptop or tablet so that you can record your observations.
- ❑ Make a record of the time, date, and place of your observations.

2 Conducting Interviews

Interviews (conducted in person, by telephone, or by email) can provide material that you cannot find anywhere else—for example, a first-hand account of an event or an opinion of an expert.

CHECKLIST

Conducting Interviews

- ❑ Always make an appointment.
- ❑ Prepare a list of questions tailored to the subject matter.
- ❑ Do background reading about your topic. Do not ask for information that you can easily get elsewhere.
- ❑ Have a pen and paper or laptop with you. If you want to record the interview, get your subject's permission in advance.
- ❑ Send an email thanking the subject of the interview.

3 Conducting Surveys

If your research project is about a contemporary social, political, or economic issue, a **survey** of attitudes or opinions can give you valuable information.

CHECKLIST

Conducting Surveys

- ❑ Determine what you want to know.
- ❑ Generate a list of questions.
- ❑ Decide how to distribute your survey. Will you email it? Post a questionnaire on *Facebook*? Use an online tool such as *SurveyMonkey* or *Google Forms*?
- ❑ Collect and analyze the responses.

CHAPTER 7

Evaluating Sources

The sources that you use in your essays help you to establish credibility. If you use high-quality, reliable sources, your readers are likely to assume that you have more than a superficial knowledge of your subject. If, however, you use questionable sources, readers will begin to doubt your authority, and they may dismiss your ideas. For these reasons, it is very important to **evaluate** your research sources to make sure they are trustworthy and reliable.

7a Evaluating Library Sources

Before you decide to use a library source (print or electronic), you should assess its suitability according to the following criteria:

- **Reliability:** *Is the source trustworthy?* Does the writer support his or her conclusions with facts and expert opinion, or does the source rely on unsupported opinion? Is the information accurate and free of factual errors? Does the writer include documentation and a bibliography?
- **Credibility:** *Is the source respected?* A contemporary review of a source can help you make this assessment. (*UlrichsWeb* is a subject-specific database that your library may subscribe to that includes reviews of books and journals that have received attention in a particular field.) Is the writer well known in his or her field? Can you check the writer's credentials? Is the article **refereed** (that is, chosen by experts in the field)?
- **Currency:** *Is the source up to date?* The date of publication tells you whether the information in a book or article is current. A source's currency is particularly important for scientific and technological subjects, but even in the humanities, new discoveries and new ways of thinking lead scholars to reevaluate and modify their ideas.
- **Objectivity:** *Does the writer strive to present a balanced discussion?* Sometimes a writer has a particular agenda to advance. Compare a few statements from the source

with a neutral source—a textbook or an encyclopedia, for example—to see whether the writer seems to be exhibiting bias or slanting facts.

- **Scope of coverage:** *Does the source treat your topic in enough detail?* To be useful, a source should treat your topic comprehensively. For example, a book should include a section or chapter on your topic, not simply a brief reference or a note. To evaluate an article, either read the abstract or skim the entire article for key facts, looking closely at section headings, information set in boldface type, and topic sentences. An article should have your topic as its central subject (or at least one of its main concerns).

In general, **scholarly publications**—peer-reviewed books and journals aimed at an audience of expert readers—are more reliable than **popular publications**—books, magazines, and newspapers aimed at an audience of general readers. However, assuming they are current, written by reputable authors, and documented, articles from respected popular publications (such as the *Atlantic* and *Scientific American*) may be appropriate for your research. Check with your instructor to be sure.

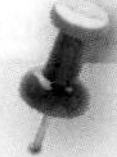

Scholarly versus Popular Publications

American Association for the Advancement of Science

Popular Science

FIGURE 7.1 Scholarly (left) and popular (right) publications.

Scholarly Publications	Popular Publications
Report the results of research	Entertain and inform
Are often published by a university press or have some connection with a university or other academic organization	Are published by commercial presses

Are usually peer reviewed—that is, reviewed by other experts in the author's field before they are published	Are usually not peer reviewed
Are usually written by someone who is a recognized authority in the field	May be written by experts in a particular field but more often are written by freelance or staff writers
Are written for a scholarly audience so often use technical vocabulary and include challenging content	Are written for general readers so tend to use an accessible vocabulary and do not include challenging content
Nearly always contain extensive documentation as well as a bibliography of works consulted	Rarely cite sources or use documentation
Are published primarily because they make a contribution to a particular field of study	Are published primarily to make a profit

7b Evaluating Internet Sources

Because anyone can post anything on the Internet, you can easily be overwhelmed by unreliable material. As you sort through and attempt to evaluate this information, the following general guidelines can help you distinguish between acceptable and unacceptable research sources.

ACCEPTABLE VERSUS UNACCEPTABLE INTERNET SOURCES

Acceptable

- Websites sponsored and maintained by reliable organizations
- Articles in established online encyclopedias, such as (britannica.com)
- Websites sponsored by reputable newspapers and magazines
- Blogs by reputable authors

(continued)

ACCEPTABLE VERSUS UNACCEPTABLE INTERNET SOURCES *(continued)*

Unacceptable

- Information from anonymous sources
- Information found in chat rooms and on discussion boards
- Articles in e-zines and other questionable online publications
- Personal and commercial websites that post no standards for publication

Before you use an Internet source, you should evaluate it for *reliability*, *credibility*, *currency*, *objectivity*, and *scope of coverage*.

Reliability **Reliability** refers to the accuracy of the material itself and to its use of proper documentation.

Factual errors—especially errors in facts that are central to the main idea of the source—should cause you to question the reliability of the material you are reading. To evaluate a site's reliability, ask these questions:

- Is the text free of basic grammatical and mechanical errors?
- Does the site contain factual errors?
- Does the site provide a list of references?
- Are working links available to other sources?
- Can information be verified by print or other sources?

Credibility **Credibility** refers to the credentials of the person or organization responsible for the site.

Websites operated by well-known institutions (the Smithsonian or the Library of Congress, for example) have a high degree of credibility. Those operated by individuals (personal web pages or blogs, for example) are often less reliable. To evaluate a site's credibility, ask these questions:

- Does the site list an author (or authors)? Are credentials (for example, professional or academic affiliations) provided for the author?
- Is the author a recognized authority in his or her field?
- Is the site **refereed**? That is, does an editorial board or a group of experts determine what material appears on the website?
- Can you determine how long the website has existed?

Currency **Currency** refers to how up to date the website is.

The easiest way to assess a site's currency is to see when it was last updated. Keep in mind, however, that even if the date on the site is current, the information that the site contains may not be. To evaluate a site's currency, ask these questions:

- Does the site indicate the date when it was last updated?
- Are all the links to other sites still functioning?
- Is the actual information on the page up to date?
- Does the site clearly identify the date it was created?

Objectivity **Objectivity** refers to the degree of bias that a website exhibits.

Some websites strive for objectivity, but others make no secret of their biases. They openly advocate a particular point of view or action, or they clearly try to sell something. Some websites may try to hide their biases. For example, a website may present itself as a source of factual information when it is actually advocating a political point of view. To evaluate a site's objectivity, ask these questions:

- Does advertising appear in the text?
- Does a business, a political organization, or a special interest group sponsor the site?
- Does the site express a particular viewpoint?
- Does the site contain links to other sites that express a particular viewpoint?

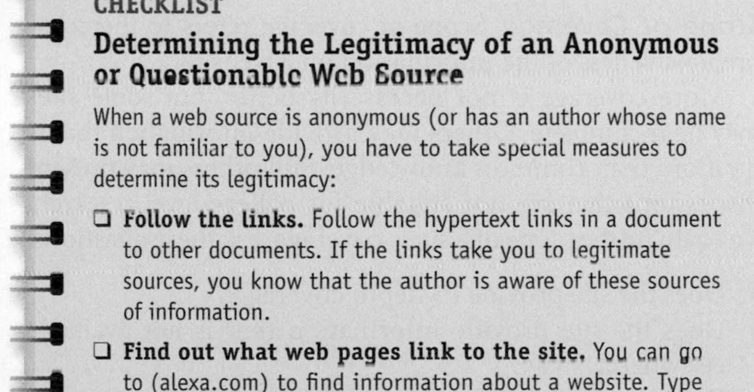

CHECKLIST

Determining the Legitimacy of an Anonymous or Questionable Web Source

When a web source is anonymous (or has an author whose name is not familiar to you), you have to take special measures to determine its legitimacy:

- ❑ **Follow the links.** Follow the hypertext links in a document to other documents. If the links take you to legitimate sources, you know that the author is aware of these sources of information.
- ❑ **Find out what web pages link to the site.** You can go to (alexa.com) to find information about a website. Type the website's URL into *Alexa*'s search box, and you will be given the volume of traffic to the site, the ownership information for the site, and the other sites visited by

continued

Determining the Legitimacy of an Anonymous or Questionable Web Source *(continued)*

people who visited the URL. You will also be given a link to the "Wayback Machine" (archive.org/web/web.php), an archive that shows what the page looked like in the past.

- ❑ **Do a keyword search.** Do a search using the name of the sponsoring organization or the author as keywords. Other documents (or citations in other works) may identify the author.
- ❑ **Verify the information.** Check the information you find against a reliable source—a textbook or a reputable website, for example. Also, see if you can find information that contradicts what you have found.
- ❑ **Check the quality of the writing.** Review the writing on the website to see if there are typos, misspellings, and errors in grammar or word choice. If the writer is careless about these things, he or she has probably not spent much time checking facts.
- ❑ **Look at the URL.** Although a website's URL is not a foolproof guide to the site's purpose, it does give you some useful information. The last part of a website's URL (immediately following the **domain name**) can often tell you whether the site is sponsored by a commercial entity (*.com*), a nonprofit organization (*.org*), an educational institution (*.edu*), the military (*.mil*), or a government agency (*.gov*). Knowing this information can help you assess its legitimacy.

Scope of Coverage **Scope of coverage** refers to the comprehensiveness of the information on a website.

More coverage is not necessarily better, but some sites may be incomplete. Others may provide information that is no more than common knowledge. Still others may present discussions that are not suitable for college-level research. To evaluate the scope of a site's coverage, ask these questions:

- Does the site provide in-depth coverage?
- Does the site provide information that is not available elsewhere?
- Does the site identify a target audience? Does this target audience suggest the site is appropriate for your research needs?

Close-Up EVALUATING MATERIAL FROM ONLINE FORUMS

Be especially careful with material posted on discussion boards, blogs, newsgroups, and other online forums. Unless you can adequately evaluate this material—for example, determine its accuracy and the credibility of the author or authors—you should not use it in your essay. In most cases, online forums are not good sources of high-quality information because they are published without formal review.

CHAPTER 8

Integrating Source Material into Your Writing

Experienced researchers know that copying down the exact words of a source is the least efficient way of taking notes. A better approach is to take notes that combine summaries, paraphrases, and quotations. This strategy ensures that you understand your source material and see its relevance to your research.

See 5g

8a Integrating Quotations

Be sure to work quotations smoothly into your sentences. Quotations should never be awkwardly dropped into your essay, leaving the exact relationship between the quotation and your point unclear. Be sure to provide a context for the quotation, and quote only those words you need to make your point.

Unacceptable: For the Amish, the public school system represents a problem. "A serious problem confronting Amish society from the viewpoint of the Amish themselves is the threat of absorption into mass society through the values promoted in the public school system" (Hostetler 193).

Improved: For the Amish, the public school system is a problem because it represents "the threat of absorption into mass society" (Hostetler 193).

Whenever possible, use an **identifying tag** (a phrase that identifies the source) to introduce the quotation.

As John Hostetler points out, the Amish see the public school system as a problem because it represents "the threat of absorption into mass society" (193).

Close-Up INTEGRATING SOURCE MATERIAL INTO YOUR WRITING

To make sure all your sentences do not sound the same, experiment with different methods of integrating source material into your paper.

- Vary the verbs you use to introduce a source's words or ideas (instead of repeating *says*).

acknowledges	discloses	observes
admits	explains	predicts
affirms	finds	proposes
believes	illustrates	reports
claims	implies	speculates
comments	indicates	suggests
concludes	insists	summarizes
concurs	notes	warns

- Vary the placement of the identifying tag, putting it sometimes in the middle or at the end of the quoted material instead of always at the beginning.

Quotation with Identifying Tag in Middle: "A serious problem confronting Amish society from the viewpoint of the Amish themselves," observes Hostetler, "is the threat of absorption into mass society through the values promoted in the public school system" (193).

Paraphrase with Identifying Tag at End: The Amish are also concerned about their children's exposure to the public school system's values, notes Hostetler (193).

Close-Up PUNCTUATING IDENTIFYING TAGS

Whether or not to use a comma with an identifying tag depends on where you place the tag in the sentence. If the identifying tag immediately precedes a quotation, use a comma.

> As Hostetler points out, "The Amish are successful in maintaining group identity" (56).

If the identifying tag does not immediately precede a quotation, do not use a comma.

> Hostetler points out that the Amish frequently "use severe sanctions to preserve their values" (56).

Note: Never use a comma after *that:* Hostetler says that, Amish society is "defined by religion" (76).

Substitutions or Additions within Quotations Indicate changes or additions that you make to a quotation by enclosing these changes in brackets.

> **Original Quotation:** "Immediately after her wedding, she and her husband followed tradition and went to visit almost everyone who attended the wedding" (Hostetler 122).

> **Quotation Revised to Make Verb Tenses Consistent:** Nowhere is the Amish dedication to tradition more obvious than in the events surrounding marriage. Right after the wedding celebration, the Amish bride and groom "visit almost everyone who [has] attended the wedding" (Hostetler 122).

> **Quotation Revised to Supply an Antecedent for a Pronoun:** "Immediately after her wedding, [Sarah] and her husband followed tradition and went to visit almost everyone who attended the wedding" (Hostetler 122).

Quotation Revised to Change a Capital to a Lowercase Letter: The strength of the Amish community is illustrated by the fact that "[i]mmediately after her wedding, she and her husband followed tradition and went to visit almost everyone who attended the wedding" (Hostetler 122).

Omissions within Quotations When you delete words from a quotation, substitute an **ellipsis** (three spaced periods) for the deleted words.

See 32f

Original: "Not only have the Amish built and staffed their own elementary and vocational schools, but they have gradually organized on local, state, and national levels to cope with the task of educating their children" (Hostetler 206).

Quotation Revised to Eliminate Unnecessary Words: "Not only have the Amish built and staffed their own elementary and vocational schools, but they have gradually organized . . . to cope with the task of educating their children" (Hostetler 206).

Note: If the passage you are quoting already contains ellipses, place brackets around any ellipses that you add.

Close-Up OMISSIONS WITHIN QUOTATIONS

Be sure that you do not misrepresent quoted material when you delete words. For example, do not say, "the Amish have managed to maintain . . . their culture" when the original quotation is "the Amish have managed to maintain *parts* of their culture."

Note: For information on integrating long quotations into your essays, **see 31a3**.

8b Integrating Paraphrases and Summaries

Introduce paraphrases and summaries with identifying tags, and end them with appropriate documentation. By doing so, you enable your readers to differentiate your ideas from those of your sources.

Misleading (Ideas of Source Blend with Ideas of Writer): Art can be used to uncover many problems that children have at home, in school, or with their friends. For this reason, many therapists use art therapy extensively. Children's views of themselves in society are often reflected by their art style. For example, a cramped, crowded art style using only a portion of the paper shows their limited role (Alschuler 260).

Correct (Identifying Tag Differentiates Ideas of Source from Ideas of Writer): Art can be used to uncover many problems that children have at home, in school, or with their friends. For this reason, many therapists use art therapy extensively. According to William Alschuler in *Art and Self-Image,* children's views of themselves in society are often reflected by their art style. For example, a cramped, crowded art style using only a portion of the paper shows their limited role (260).

CHAPTER 

Using Sources Ethically

9a Defining Plagiarism

When you do a research project, you use information from your sources. It is your ethical responsibility to present this material fairly and to make sure that you document it appropriately.

Plagiarism occurs when a writer (intentionally or unintentionally) uses the words, ideas, or distinctive style of others without acknowledging the source. For example, you plagiarize when you submit someone else's work as your own or fail to document appropriately.

Most plagiarism is **unintentional plagiarism**—for example, inadvertently pasting a quoted passage into a paper and forgetting to include the quotation marks and documentation.

There is a difference, however, between an honest mistake and **intentional plagiarism**—for example, copying a passage word for word from a journal article or submitting a paper that someone else has written. The penalties for unintentional plagiarism may sometimes be severe, but intentional plagiarism is almost always dealt with harshly: students who intentionally plagiarize can receive a failing grade for the paper (or the course) and can even be expelled from school.

Close-Up DETECTING PLAGIARISM

The same technology that has made unintentional plagiarism more common has also made plagiarism easier to detect. By doing a *Google* search, an instructor can quickly find the source of a phrase that has been plagiarized from an Internet source. In addition, plagiarism detection services, such as *Turnitin.com*, can search scholarly databases and identify plagiarized passages in student essays.

9b Avoiding Unintentional Plagiarism

The most common cause of unintentional plagiarism is sloppy research habits. To avoid this problem, start your research paper early. Do not cut and paste text from a website or full-text database directly into your essay. If you paraphrase, do so correctly by following the advice in **5g2**.

See 5c1

In addition, make sure to keep track of your sources—especially those you scan, download, or otherwise save electronically—so that they do not overwhelm you. Unintentional plagiarism often occurs when students use information from a source thinking that it is their own.

See Chs. 10–13

Another cause of unintentional plagiarism is failure to use proper documentation. In general, you must document the following information:

- Direct quotations, summaries, and paraphrases of material in sources (including web sources)
- Images that you borrow from a source (print or electronic)
- Facts and opinions that are another writer's original contributions

- Information that is the product of an author's original research
- Statistics, charts, graphs, or other compilations of data that are not yours

Material that is considered **common knowledge** (information most readers probably know) need not be documented. This includes facts available from a variety of reference sources, familiar sayings, and well-known quotations. Your own original research (interviews and surveys, for example) also does not require documentation.

So, although you do not have to document the fact that John F. Kennedy graduated from Harvard in 1940 or that he was elected president in 1960, you do have to document information from a historian's evaluation of his presidency. The best rule to follow is, if you have doubts, document.

9c Avoiding Intentional Plagiarism

When students plagiarize *intentionally*, they make a decision to misappropriate the ideas or words of others—and this is no small matter. Not only does intentional plagiarism deprive the student of a valuable educational experience (instructors assign research for a reason), it also subverts the educational goals of other students as well as of the institution as a whole. Because academic honesty is absolutely central to any college or university, intentional plagiarism is a very serious breach of trust.

9d Avoiding Other Kinds of Plagiarism

When instructors assign a research paper, they expect it to be your original work and to be written in response to a specific assignment. For this reason, you should not submit an essay that you have written for another course.

Collaborative work is acceptable in the course for which it was assigned. Even so, each member of the group should clearly identify the sections on which he or she worked.

Finally, passages written by a writing center tutor or by a friend or a family member are unacceptable. If you present material contributed by others as if it were your own original work, you are committing plagiarism.

9e Revising to Eliminate Plagiarism

You can avoid plagiarism by using documentation wherever it is required and by following these guidelines.

1 Enclose Borrowed Words in Quotation Marks

Original: DNA profiling begins with the established theory that no two people, except identical twins, have the same genetic makeup. Each cell in the body contains a complete set of genes. (William Tucker, "DNA in Court")

Plagiarism: William Tucker points out that DNA profiling is based on the premise that genetic makeup differs from person to person and that each cell in the body contains a complete set of genes (26).

Even though the student writer documents the source of his information, he uses the source's exact words without placing them in quotation marks.

Correct (Borrowed Words in Quotation Marks): William Tucker points out that DNA profiling is based on the premise that genetic makeup differs from person to person and that "[e]ach cell in the body contains a complete set of genes" (26).

Correct (Paraphrase): William Tucker points out that DNA profiling is based on the premise that genetic makeup differs from person to person and that every cell includes a full set of an individual's genes (26).

CHECKLIST

Plagiarism and Internet Sources

Any time you download text from the Internet, you risk committing plagiarism. To avoid the possibility of unintentional plagiarism, follow these guidelines:

- ❑ Download or otherwise collect information into individual files so that you can keep track of your sources.
- ❑ Do not cut and paste blocks of downloaded text directly into your essay.
- ❑ Whether your information is from emails, online discussion groups, blogs, or websites, always provide appropriate documentation.
- ❑ Always document figures, tables, charts, and graphs obtained from the Internet or from any other electronic source.

2 Do Not Imitate a Source's Syntax and Phrasing

Original: If there is a garbage crisis, it is that we are treating garbage as an environmental threat and not what it is: a manageable—though admittedly complex—civic issue. (Patricia Poore, "America's 'Garbage Crisis'")

Plagiarism: If a garbage crisis does exist, it is that people see garbage as a menace to the environment and not what it actually is: a controllable—if obviously complicated—public problem (Poore 39).

Although this student does not use the exact words of her source, she closely follows the original's syntax and phrasing, simply substituting synonyms for the author's words.

Correct (Paraphrase in Writer's Own Words; One Distinctive Phrase Placed in Quotation Marks): Patricia Poore argues that America's "garbage crisis" is exaggerated; rather than viewing garbage as a serious environmental hazard, she says, we should look at garbage as a public problem that may be complicated but that can be solved (39).

3 Document Statistics Obtained from a Source

Although many people assume that statistics are common knowledge, they are usually the result of original research and must be documented.

Correct (Documentation Provided): According to one study of 303 accidents recorded, almost one-half took place before the drivers were legally allowed to drive at eighteen (Schuman et al. 1027).

4 Differentiate Your Words and Ideas from Those of Your Source

Original: At some colleges and universities traditional survey courses of world and English literature . . . have been scrapped or diluted. . . . What replaces them is sometimes a mere option of electives, sometimes "multicultural" courses introducing material from Third World cultures and thinning out an already thin sampling of Western writings, and sometimes courses geared especially to issues of class, race, and gender. (Irving Howe, "The Value of the Canon")

Plagiarism: At many universities the Western literature survey courses have been edged out by courses that

> emphasize minority concerns. These courses are "thinning out an already thin sampling of Western writings" in favor of courses geared especially to issues of "class, race, and gender" (Howe 40).

Because the student writer does not differentiate her ideas from those of her source, it appears that only the quotation in the last sentence is borrowed when, in fact, the first sentence also owes a debt to the original. The writer should have clearly identified the boundaries of the borrowed material by introducing it with an identifying tag and ending with documentation.

> **Correct:** According to critic Irving Howe, at many universities the Western literature survey courses have been edged out by courses that emphasize minority concerns. These courses, says Howe, are "thinning out an already thin sampling of Western writings" in favor of "courses geared especially to issues of class, race, and gender" (40).

CHECKLIST

Avoiding Plagiarism

- ❑ **Take careful notes.** Be sure you have recorded information from your sources carefully and accurately.
- ❑ **Store downloaded sources in clearly labeled files.** If you are writing a short paper, you can keep your source material in one file. For longer papers, you may find it best to create a separate file for each of your sources.
- ❑ **In your notes, clearly identify borrowed material.** Always enclose your own comments within brackets. In handwritten notes, put all words borrowed from your sources inside *circled* quotation marks. If you are taking notes on a computer, boldface all quotation marks.
- ❑ **In your essay, differentiate your ideas from those of your sources** by clearly introducing borrowed material with an identifying tag and by following it with parenthetical documentation.
- ❑ **Enclose all direct quotations** used in your essay within quotation marks.
- ❑ **Review all paraphrases and summaries** in your essay to make certain that they are in your own words and that any distinctive words and phrases from a source are quoted.

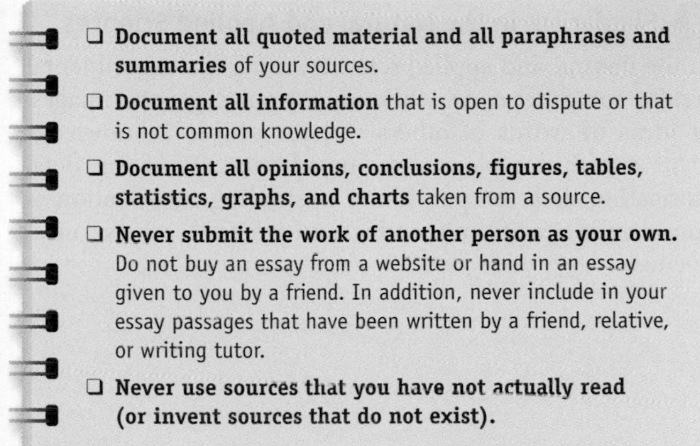

- ❑ **Document all quoted material and all paraphrases and summaries** of your sources.
- ❑ **Document all information** that is open to dispute or that is not common knowledge.
- ❑ **Document all opinions, conclusions, figures, tables, statistics, graphs, and charts** taken from a source.
- ❑ **Never submit the work of another person as your own.** Do not buy an essay from a website or hand in an essay given to you by a friend. In addition, never include in your essay passages that have been written by a friend, relative, or writing tutor.
- ❑ **Never use sources that you have not actually read (or invent sources that do not exist).**

9f Understanding Plagiarism in the Disciplines

Although plagiarism always involves the misappropriation of ideas, words, or research results, different disciplines have different conventions about what constitutes plagiarism. Becoming familiar with the conventions of the discipline in which you are writing will help you avoid the most common causes of plagiarism.

1 Plagiarism in the Humanities

In the humanities, plagiarism is often the result of inaccurate summarizing and paraphrasing, failure to use quotation marks where they are required, and confusion between your ideas and those of your sources. You can eliminate these problems by taking accurate notes, avoiding cutting and pasting sources directly into your papers, and documenting all words and ideas that are not your own.

2 Plagiarism in the Social Sciences

In the social sciences, you can avoid plagiarism by correctly documenting paraphrases, summaries, and quotations as well as all statistics and visuals that are not your own. Keep in mind that the social sciences are bound by ethical considerations regarding the treatment of research subjects and the protection of privacy as well as the granting of credit to all individuals who contribute to a research project.

3 Plagiarism in the Natural and Applied Sciences

In the natural and applied sciences, using the experimental results, computer codes, chemical formulas, graphs, images, or ideas or words of others without proper acknowledgment constitutes plagiarism. In addition, falsifying data, fabricating data, or publishing misleading information is considered scientific misconduct and can have serious consequences.

Directory of MLA Parenthetical References

1. A work by a single author (p. 115)
2. A work by two authors (p. 115)
3. A work by three or more authors (p. 115)
4. A work in multiple volumes (p. 115)
5. A work without a listed author (p. 115)
6. A work that is one page long (p. 115)
7. An indirect source (p. 115)
8. More than one work (p. 116)
9. A literary work (p. 116)
10. Sacred texts (p. 116)
11. An entire work (p. 117)
12. Two or more authors with the same last name (p. 117)
13. A government document or a corporate author (p. 117)
14. A legal source (p. 117)
15. An electronic source (p. 118)

Directory of MLA Works-Cited List Entries

Entries For Periodicals

Scholarly Journals

1. An Article in a Scholarly Journal (p. 122)
2. An Article in a Scholarly Journal from an Online Database (p. 124)
3. An Article with a Title within Its Title (p. 123)

Magazines

4. An Article in a Magazine (p. 124)
5. An Article in a Magazine from an Online Database (p. 124)

Newspapers and News Services

6. An Article in a Newspaper (p. 125)
7. An Article in a Newspaper from an Online Database (p. 125)
8. A News Service (p. 125)
9. An Editorial or Letter to the Editor in a Newspaper (p. 126)

Book Reviews, Newsletters, and Encyclopedias

10. A Book Review (p. 126)
11. An Article in a Newsletter (p. 127)
12. An Article in an Encyclopedia (p. 127)

Entries For Books

Authors

13. A Book by One Author (p. 128)
14. A Book by Two Authors (p. 128)
15. A Book by Three or More Authors (p. 128)
16. Two or More Books by the Same Author (p. 129)
17. A Book by a Corporate Author (p. 129)
18. An Edited Book (p. 129)
19. A Translation (p. 130)
20. A Subsequent Edition of a Book (p. 130)
21. A Republished Book (p. 130)
22. A Book in a Series (p. 130)
23. A Multivolume Work (p. 130)
24. An Illustrated Book or a Graphic Narrative (p. 131)
25. The Foreword, Preface, or Afterword of a Book (p. 131)
26. A Book with a Title within Its Title (p. 131)
27. Sacred Texts (p. 132)
28. A Book Accessed through an E-reader (p. 132)

Parts of Books

29. A Short Story, Play, or Poem in a Collection (p. 132)
30. An Essay in an Anthology or Edited Collection (p. 132)
31. More than One Work from the Same Anthology (p. 132)
32. A Scholarly Article Reprinted in a Collection (p. 133)
33. An Article in a Reference Book (p. 133)

Entries For Internet-Specific Sources

34. An Entire Website (p. 133)
35. A Document within a Website (p. 133)
36. A Home Page for a Course (p. 133)
37. A Podcast or a Radio Program Accessed Online (p. 134)
38. An Online Video (p. 134)
39. A Television Program Streamed via *Netflix* or *Amazon* (p. 134)
40. A Blog, Tweet, or Social Networking Post (p. 135)
41. A Comment on a Blog, Tweet, or Other Online Forum (p. 135)
42. An App (or any Computer Software) (p. 135)
43. A Source Accessed through an App (p. 135)
44. Email (p. 135)

Entries For Other Sources

45. A Photograph or Painting (p. 136)
46. A Cartoon/Comic Strip (p. 136)
47. An Advertisement (p. 136)
48. A Map (p. 136)
49. A Film (p. 137)
50. A Television Program (p. 137)
51. An Audio Recording (p. 137)
52. An Image or Video on a Website (p. 137)
53. A Dissertation (p. 138)
54. A Government Publication (p. 138)
55. A Pamphlet (p. 139)
56. A Lecture (p. 139)
57. A Personal Interview or Letter (p. 139)
58. A Published Interview (p. 139)
59. A Published Letter (p. 139)

CHAPTER 10

MLA Documentation Style

Documentation is the formal acknowledgment of the sources you use in your essay. This chapter explains and illustrates the documentation style recommended by the Modern Language Association (MLA). Chapter 11 discusses the documentation style of the American Psychological Association (APA), Chapter 12 gives an overview of the format recommended by *The Chicago Manual of Style*, and Chapter 13 presents the format recommended by the Council of Science Editors (CSE) and the formats used by organizations in other disciplines.

Note: **See 5i3** for a list and description of useful digital citation tools.

10a Using MLA Style

MLA style* is required by instructors of English and other languages as well as by many instructors in other humanities disciplines. MLA documentation has three parts: *parenthetical references in the body of the essay (also known as in-text citations), a works-cited list,* and *content notes.*

1 Parenthetical References

MLA documentation uses parenthetical references in the body of the essay keyed to a works-cited list at the end of the essay. A typical parenthetical reference consists of the author's last name and a page number.

The colony appealed to many idealists in Europe (Kelley 132).

If you state the author's name or the title of the work in your discussion, do not also include it in the parenthetical reference.

*MLA documentation style follows the guidelines set in the *MLA Handbook*, 8th ed. (MLA, 2016).

Penn's political motivation is discussed by Joseph J. Kelley in *Pennsylvania, The Colonial Years, 1681-1776* (44).

To distinguish two or more sources by the same author, include a shortened title after the author's name. When you shorten a title, begin with the word by which the work is alphabetized in the list of works cited.

Penn emphasized his religious motivation (Kelley, *Pennsylvania* 116).

Close-Up PUNCTUATING WITH MLA PARENTHETICAL REFERENCES

Paraphrases and Summaries Parenthetical references are placed *before* the sentence's end punctuation.

Penn's writings epitomize seventeenth-century religious thought (Dengler and Curtis 72).

Quotations Run In with the Text Parenthetical references are placed *after* the quotation but *before* the end punctuation.

As Ross says, "Penn followed his conscience in all matters" (127).

According to Williams, "Penn's utopian vision was informed by his Quaker beliefs . . ." (72).

Quotations Set Off from the Text When you quote more than four lines of prose or more than three lines of poetry, parenthetical references are placed one space *after* the end punctuation.

See 31a3

According to Arthur Smith, William Penn envisioned a state based on his religious principles:

> Pennsylvania would be a commonwealth in which all individuals would follow God's truth and develop according to God's law. For Penn, this concept of government was self-evident. It would be a mistake to see Pennsylvania as anything but an expression of Penn's religious beliefs. (314)

Sample MLA Parenthetical References

1. A Work by a Single Author

Fairy tales reflect the emotions and fears of children (Bettelheim 23).

2. A Work by Two Authors

The historian's main job is to search for clues and solve mysteries (Davidson and Lytle 6).

3. A Work by Three or More Authors

List only the first author, followed by **et al.** ("and others").

Helping each family reach its goals for healthy child development and overall family well-being was the primary approach of Project EAGLE (Bartle et al. 35).

4. A Work in Multiple Volumes

If you list more than one volume of a multivolume work in your works-cited list, include the appropriate volume and page number (separated by a colon followed by a space) in the parenthetical citation.

Gurney is incorrect when he says that a twelve-hour limit is negotiable (6: 128).

5. A Work without a Listed Author

Use the full title (if brief) or a shortened version of the title (if long), beginning with the word by which it is alphabetized in the works-cited list.

The group later issued an apology ("Satire Lost" 22).

6. A Work That Is One Page Long

Do not include a page reference for a one-page article.

Sixty percent of Arab Americans work in white-collar jobs (El-Badru).

7. An Indirect Source

If you use a statement by one author that is quoted in the work of another author, indicate that the material is from an indirect source with the abbreviation **qtd. in** ("quoted in").

According to Valli and Lucas, "the form of the symbol is an icon or picture of some aspect of the thing or activity being symbolized" (qtd. in Wilcox 120).

8. More Than One Work

Cite each work as you normally would, separating one citation from another with a semicolon.

> The Brooklyn Bridge has been used as a subject by many American artists (McCullough 144; Tashjian 58).

Note: Long parenthetical references distract readers. Whenever possible, present them as **content notes**.

See 10a3

9. A Literary Work

When citing a work of **fiction**, it is often helpful to include more than the author's name and the page number in the parenthetical citation. Follow the page number with a semicolon, and then include any additional information that might be helpful.

> In *Moby-Dick*, Melville refers to a whaling expedition funded by Louis XIV of France (151; ch. 24).

Parenthetical references to **poetry** do not include page numbers. In parenthetical references to *long poems*, cite division and line numbers, separating them with a period.

> In the *Aeneid*, Virgil describes the ships as cleaving the "green woods reflected in the calm water" (8.124).

(In this citation, the reference is to book 8, line 124 of the *Aeneid*.)

When citing *short poems*, identify the poet and the poem in the text of the essay, and use line numbers in the citation.

> In "My mistress' eyes are nothing like the sun," Shakespeare's speaker says, "I have seen roses damasked red and white, / But no such roses see I in her cheeks," (lines 5-6).

Note: When citing lines of a poem, include the word **line** (or **lines**) in the first parenthetical reference; use just the line numbers in subsequent references.

When citing a **play**, include the act, scene, and line numbers (in arabic numerals), separated by periods. Titles of classic literary works (such as Shakespeare's plays) are often abbreviated (**Mac. 2.2.14-16**).

10. Sacred Texts

When citing sacred texts, such as the Bible or the Qur'an, include the version (italicized) and the book (abbreviated if longer than four letters, but not italicized or enclosed in quotation marks), followed by the chapter and verse numbers (separated by a period).

> The cynicism of the speaker is apparent when he says, "All things are wearisome; no man can speak of them all" (*New English Bible*, Eccles. 1.8).

Note: The first time you cite a sacred text, include the version in your parenthetical reference; after that, include only the book. If you are using more than one version of a sacred text, however, include the version in each in-text citation.

11. An Entire Work

When citing an entire work, include the author's name and the work's title in the text of your essay rather than in a parenthetical reference.

> Lois Lowry's *Gathering Blue* is set in a technologically backward village.

12. Two or More Authors with the Same Last Name

To distinguish authors with the same last name, include their initials in your parenthetical references.

> Increases in crime have caused thousands of urban homeowners to install alarms (L. Cooper 115). Some of these alarms use sophisticated sensors that were developed by the army (D. Cooper 76).

13. A Government Document or a Corporate Author

Cite such works using the organization's name followed by the page number (**American Automobile Association 34**). You can avoid long parenthetical references by working the organization's name into your discussion.

> According to the President's Commission for the Study of Ethical Problems in Medicine and Biomedical and Behavioral Research, the issues relating to euthanasia are complicated (76).

14. A Legal Source

Titles of acts or laws that appear in the text of your essay or in the works-cited list should not be italicized or enclosed in quotation marks. In the parenthetical reference, titles are usually abbreviated, and the act or law is referred to by sections. Include the USC (United States Code) and the year the act or law was passed (if relevant).

> Such research should include investigations into the cause, diagnosis, early detection, prevention, control, and treatment of autism (42 USC 284q, 2000).

Names of legal cases are usually abbreviated (**Roe v. Wade**). They are italicized in the text of your essay but not in the works-cited list.

> In *Goodridge v. Department of Public Health*, the court ruled that the Commonwealth of Massachusetts had not adequately provided a reasonable constitutional cause for barring same-sex couples from civil marriages (2003).

15. An Electronic Source

If a reference to an electronic source includes paragraph numbers rather than page numbers, use the abbreviation **par.** or **pars.** followed by the paragraph number or numbers.

> The earliest type of movie censorship came in the form of licensing fees, and in Deer River, Minnesota, "a licensing fee of $200 was deemed not excessive for a town of 1000" (Ernst, par. 20).

If the electronic source has no page or paragraph numbers, cite the work in your discussion rather than in a parenthetical reference. By consulting your works-cited list, readers will be able to determine that the source is electronic and may therefore not have page numbers.

> In her article "Limited Horizons," Lynne Cheney observes that schools do best when students read literature not for practical information but for its insights into the human condition.

2 Works-Cited List

The works-cited list, which appears at the end of your essay, is an alphabetical listing of all the research materials you cite. An effective works-cited entry helps your readers locate its source, primarily by citing traits (like author, title, and location) shared across most sources. These traits are referred to as the nine ***core elements***, and every source contains some combination (but not necessarily all) of them. Here is an overview of these elements.

1. Author.

The person or people who wrote or otherwise created the source—or whose work on the source you are choosing to emphasize. This could mean an author, an editor (for a work with no author), a director, a composer, a director, a performer, or a narrator. It might be a full name or a Twitter handle.

- **One author:** Ng, Celeste.
- **Two authors:** Miller, Brenda, and Suzanne Paola.
- **Three or more authors:** Raabe, William A., et al.

2. Title of Source.

The title of the specific source you are citing. This could be a whole book or a short poem within it, if your focus is on that poem. This could be a specific blog entry or an entire album. Shorter works or works that are part of a larger whole usually use quotation marks, while longer or stand-alone works use italics.

- **Essay:** "Once More to the Lake."
- **Television episode:** "Stolen Phone."
- **Play:** *The Tragedy of Hamlet, Prince of Denmark.*
- **Book:** *The Dirty Dust.*

3. Title of Container,

A larger source containing the source you are citing. When citing a full, stand-alone source, element 3 = element 2. However, when citing an essay within a book or an episode of a television show, the container is the book or show. Italicize most containers.

- **Book:** F*rames of Mind: A Rhetorical Reader,*
- **Television show:** *Broad City,*
- **Website:** *The Toast,*

4. Other Contributors,

Noteworthy contributors to the work not listed in element 1. These may include editors, translators, performers, etc. Introduce each name (or set of names) with a description of the role played. If listed after element 2, capitalize the description; if listed after element 3, do not.

- , adapted by Spike Lee,
- , performance by Octavia Spencer,
- , translated by Alan Titley,

5. Version,

Description of a source that appears in more than one version. This appears most frequently for books that exist in multiple editions, whether these are numbered or indicated merely as "revised," "expanded," or similar. It may also apply to the "director's cut" of a film, a version of software, or similar.

- director's cut,
- 15th ed.,

6. Number,

Number indicating source's place in a sequence. This could refer to a volume and/or issue number for journals, to volume numbers for books that appear in multiple volumes, or to season and episode numbers for shows.

- **Television episode:** season 2, episode 1,
- **Book:** vol. 6,
- **Journal Article:** vol. 119, no. 3,

7. Publisher,

Organization that delivers the source to the public. Publishers should be listed for books, films, television shows, and similar, but ***not*** for periodicals, works published directly by authors or editors, Websites for which the publisher's name is the same as the title, or Websites that do not produce the works they house (examples: *YouTube, EccoHost,* or *WordPress*).

- U of Chicago P,
- Metropolitan Museum of Art,
- Lucasfilm,

8. Publication date,

When the source was made available to the public. This could mean when a work was published or republished in print or online, or when it was released in theaters or on *iTunes*, broadcast on television, or performed live. It might be a year, a month, a specific date, or even a specific time.

- 2016,
- Spring 2016,
- 24 Mar. 2015,
- 10 Jan. 2016, 9:30 p.m.,

9. Location,

Where to find the specific source. This could be a page number or range for print sources; a direct URL or DOI for online sources; or another type of identifier for specific source types. This is also the place to record the location of a lecture, live performance, or similar.

- pp. 30-36.
- www.newyorker.com/magazine/2015/07/20/the-really-big-one/.
- doi:10.1002/cplx.21590.
- Sheraton Hotel, New Orleans.

Not all sources contain all of the nine core elements, and some of them contain additional or optional elements, which you'll learn about in the sections that follow.

Containers within Containers

Some sources are housed in containers within larger containers. For instance, if you cite an article (source) from a journal (container #1) that you accessed through a service like *ProQuest* (container #2), or if you discuss an episode (source) of a television show (container #1) that you accessed on a service like *Netflix* (container #2), then you will need to include information about that larger container, too. This will help readers retrace your steps.

To create a works-cited entry for a source found in a container within a container, do the following:

- List core elements 1 (author) and 2 (title of source).
- List core elements 3-9 that provide information about the first container.
- List core elements 3-9 that provide information about the second container.

In the following example, a writer has identified and ordered source information for a television episode using the core elements. She used this process to create the works-cited entry that follows.

SOURCE

1. Author.	Dan Nowak.
2. Title of Source.	"Unraveling."
CONTAINER 1	
3. Title of Container,	*The Killing,*
4. Other Contributors,	directed by Lodge Kerrigan,
5. Version,	
6. Number,	season 4, episode 2,
7. Publisher,	AMC,
8. Publication date,	1 Aug. 2014.
9. Location.	

CONTAINER 2

1. Title of Container, *Netflix,*
2. Other Contributors,
3. Version,
4. Number,
5. Publisher,
6. Publication date,
7. Location. www.netflix.com/watch/70306003.

Nowak, Dan. "Unraveling." *The Killing,* directed by Lodge Kerrigan, season 4, episode 2, AMC, 1 Aug. 2014. *Netflix,* www.netflix.com/watch/70306003.

WORKS-CITED ENTRY

The sections that follow will examine how to format these elements for specific source types. For every entry that is listed on your works-cited page, double-space within and between entries on the list, and indent the second and subsequent lines of each entry one-half inch. (**See 10b** for full manuscript guidelines.)

MLA Entries for Periodicals

Periodicals include scholarly journals, magazines, and newspapers. For each works-cited entry, include as many of the nine core elements (described at the beginning of this section) as possible. Figure 10.1 shows where you can find this information in a print scholarly journal. Figure 10.2 shows where you can find the information in an online scholarly journal.

Scholarly Journals

1. An Article in a Scholarly Journal

When citing a print text, include the volume number (**vol.**) and issue number (**no.**) and be sure to include "**p.**" or "**pp.**" before page numbers.

Harriss, M. Cooper. "One Blues Invisible: Civil Rights and Civil Religion in Ralph Ellison's Second Novel." *African American Review,* vol. 47, no. 2, 2014, pp. 247-66.

When citing an online text, include page numbers (if available) and be sure to include the full URL or DOI for the article, followed by a period.

Maeseele, Thomas. "From Charity to Welfare Rights? A Study of Social Care Practices." *Social Work and Society: The International Online-Only Journal,* vol. 10, no. 1, 2010, www.socwork.net/sws/article/view/35/90.

Author
(last name, first name)

Title of source

Harkin, Patricia. "The Reception of Reader-Response Theory." *College Composition and Communication,* vol. 56, no. 3, 2005, pp. 410-25.

Title of container | Publication date | Location | Number

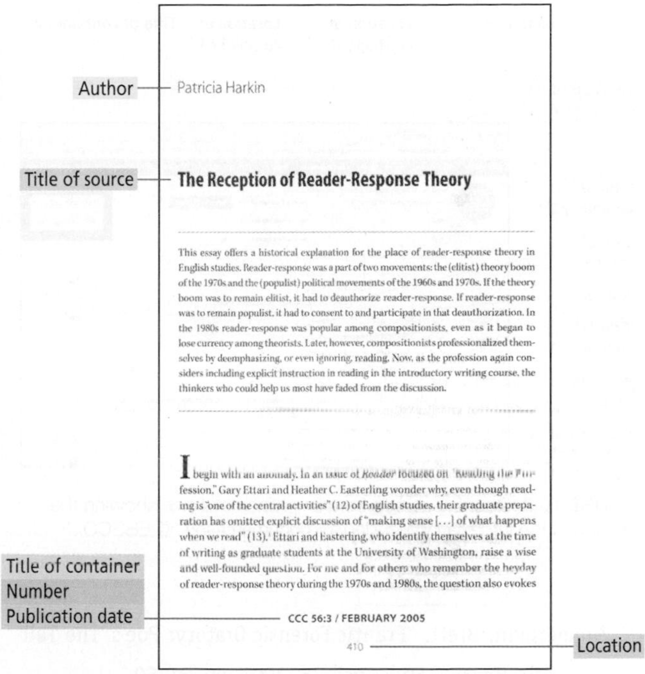

Author — Patricia Harkin

Title of source — **The Reception of Reader-Response Theory**

This essay offers a historical explanation for the place of reader-response theory in English studies. Reader-response was a part of two movements: the (elitist) theory boom of the 1970s and the (populist) political movements of the 1960s and 1970s. If the theory boom was to remain elitist, it had to deauthorize reader-response. If reader-response was to remain populist, it had to consent to and participate in that deauthorization. In the 1980s reader-response was popular among compositionists, even as it began to lose currency among theorists. Later, however, compositionists professionalized themselves by deemphasizing, or even ignoring, reading. Now, as the profession again considers including explicit instruction in reading in the introductory writing course, the thinkers who could help us most have faded from the discussion.

I begin with an anomaly. In an issue of *Reader* focused on "Reading the Profession," Gary Ettari and Heather C. Easterling wonder why, even though reading is "one of the central activities" (12) of English studies, their graduate preparation has omitted explicit discussion of "making sense [...] of what happens when we read" (13).[1] Ettari and Easterling, who identify themselves at the time of writing as graduate students at the University of Washington, raise a wise and well-founded question. For me and for others who remember the heyday of reader-response theory during the 1970s and 1980s, the question also evokes

Title of container
Number
Publication date — CCC 56:3 / FEBRUARY 2005

410 — Location

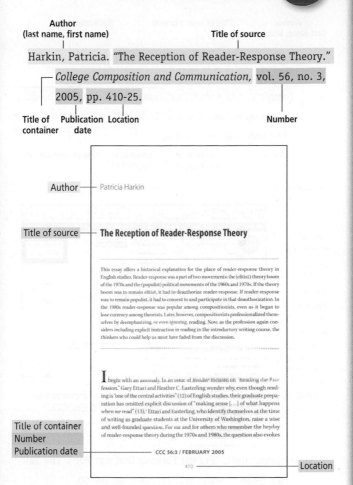

FIGURE 10.1 First page of a journal article showing the location of the information needed for documentation. © College Composition and Communication/National Council of Teachers of English.

2. An Article in a Scholarly Journal from an Online Database

Indicate the database you used to access the source and include the full URL or DOI, followed by a period.

Kerness, Bonnie, et al. "Race and the Politics of Isolation in U.S. Prisons." *Atlantic Journal of Communication,* vol. 22, no. 1, 2014, pp. 21-41. *Academic Search Complete,* doi:10.1080/15456870.2014.860146.

3. An Article with a Title within Its Title

If the article you are citing contains a title that is normally enclosed in quotation marks, use single quotation marks for the interior title.

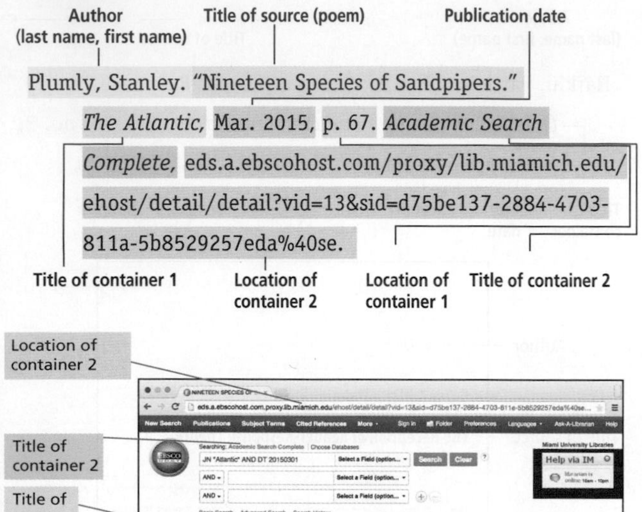

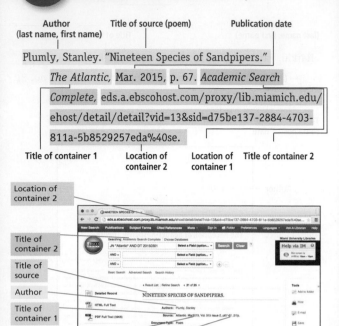

FIGURE 10.2 Opening screen from an online database showing the location of the information needed for documentation. © EBSCO.

Zimmerman, Brett. "Frantic Forensic Oratory: Poe's 'The Tell-Tale Heart.'" *Style,* vol. 35, 2001, pp. 34-50.

If the article you are citing contains a title that is normally italicized, use italics for the title in your works-cited entry.

Zhang, Mingquan. "The Technological Diegesis in *The Great Gatsby*." *English Language Teaching,* vol. 1, no. 2, Dec. 2008, pp. 86-89. *ERIC,* files.eric.ed.gov/fulltext/EJ1082800.pdf.

Magazines

4. An Article in a Magazine

"Ronald Reagan." *National Review,* 28 June 2004, pp. 14-17.

Jackowe, David J. "Poison Gas Comes to America." *American History,* Dec. 2014, www.historynet.com/poison-gas-comes-to-america.htm.

If the article begins on one page (say, page 186), but then skips to page 189, include the abbreviation "**pp.**" followed by the first page number and a plus sign.

Di Giovanni, Janine. "The Shiites of Iraq." *National Geographic,* June 2004, pp. 1+.

5. An Article in a Magazine from an Online Database

For all periodical titles, include the initial article (usually "The") prior to the periodical title, as in the following example (***The*** before ***Atlantic***).

Khazan, Olga. "The Bro Whisperer: Michael Kimmel's Quest to Turn College Boys into Gentlemen—and Improve Sex on Campus." *The Atlantic,* Jan. 2015, pp. 20-21. *Academic OneFile,* connection.ebscohost.com/c/articles/99854172/bro-whisperer.

Newspapers and News Services

6. An Article in a Newspaper

Include the version of a text if there is more than one form for it (such as "**expanded ed.**" or "**2nd ed.**").

"Suicide Finding is Disputed." *The New York Times,* late ed., 11 Feb. 2015, p. B14.

Jones, Chris. "Don't Overlook the Need for Avant-Garde, Even in Chicago." *The Chicago Tribune,* 11 Feb. 2015. www.chicagotribune.com/entertainment/theater/ct-avante-garde-theater-tuta-column.html.

7. An Article in a Newspaper from an Online Database

Spiegel, Peter. "Third Time Lucky? The Latest Plan to Rescue Greece." *The Financial Times,* 17 Sep. 2013, p. 17. *Academic OneFile,* go.galegroup.com.eduproxy.tc-library.org:8080/ps/i.do?id=GALE%7CA343076709 sid=summon&v=2.1&u=new30429&it=r&p=AONE&sw=w&asid=d9006f47ca3d73b0a937c7b23f0636da.

8. A News Service

Ryan, Desmond. "Some Background on the Battle of Gettysburg." *Knight Ridder / Tribune Media Service,*

7 Oct. 1993. *Academic OneFile,* search.proquest.com.ezproxy.cul.columbia.edu/docview/259995964.

"Russians Make Giant Snow Portrait of First Astronaut." *Reuters,* 11 Apr. 2016, www.reuters.com/article/us-russia-gagarin-idUSKCN0X81PE?feedType=RSS&feedName=lifestyleMolt.

9. An Editorial or Letter to the Editor in a Newspaper

Insert a descriptor (such as "**Editorial.**" or "**Letter.**") to stand in place of a title (if none is given) or after a title. A descriptor designates a particular section of a text.

"Lynching as Racial Terrorism." Editorial. *The New York Times,* late ed., 11 Feb. 2015, p. A26.

Rossi, Claire. Letter. *The New York Times,* 21 Mar. 2016, www.nytimes.com/2016/03/21/opinion/women-in-science.html?partner=rssnyt&emc=rss&_r=0.

Book Reviews, Newsletters, and Encyclopedias

10. A Book Review

DeSanctis, Maria. "Small Comforts." Review of *A Motor-Flight through France,* by Edith Wharton. *Tin House,* vol. 16, no. 2, 2014.

Close-Up PUBLISHERS' NAMES

MLA requires that you use abbreviated forms of publishers' names in the works-cited list. In general, omit articles; abbreviations, such as *Inc.* and *Corp.*; and words such as *Publishers, Books,* and *Press*. If the publisher's name includes a person's name, use the last name only. Finally, use standard abbreviations whenever you can—*UP* for University Press and *P* for Press, for example.

Name	Abbreviation
Basic Books	Basic
Oxford University Press	Oxford UP
Alfred A. Knopf, Inc.	Knopf
Random House, Inc.	Random
University of Chicago Press	U of Chicago P

Molzhan, Laura. Review of *The Incidents,* by Ayaka Kato. *The Chicago Tribune,* 8 June 2014, www.chicagotribune.com/entertainment/theater/dance/chi-incidents-dance-review-20140608-story.html.

11. An Article in a Newsletter

Cappucci, Karen. "The Importance of Updated CORIs." *Glenwood News,* 8 Apr. 2016, p. 1.

"The Viking in Scandinavia." *HAAS Recycling Newsletter,* May 2014, www.haas-recycling.com/tl_files/downloads/newsletter/en/HAAS-Newsletter-Issue-No.8_04 2014.pdf.

12. An Article in an Encyclopedia

"Hawthorne, Nathaniel." *Encyclopaedia Britannica Online,* 20 Apr. 2015, www.britannica.com/biography/Nathaniel-Hawthorne.

MLA Entries for Books

Books follow the same guidelines as periodicals. For each works-cited entry, include as many of the nine core elements (described at the beginning of this section) as possible. Figures 10.3 and 10.4 show where you can find this information in a print book.

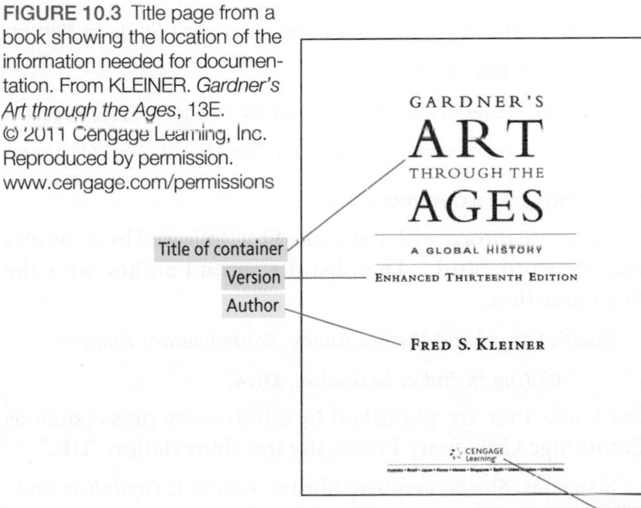

FIGURE 10.3 Title page from a book showing the location of the information needed for documentation. From KLEINER. *Gardner's Art through the Ages*, 13E. © 2011 Cengage Learning, Inc. Reproduced by permission. www.cengage.com/permissions

Author (last name, first name) | Title of container

Kleiner, Fred S. *Gardner's Art through the Ages: A Global History.* Enhanced 13th ed., Cengage, 2011.

Version | Publisher | Publication date

Publication date

CENGAGE Learning

Gardner's Art through the Ages: A Global History,
Enhanced Thirteenth Edition
Fred S. Kleiner

Publisher: Clark Baxter

Senior Development Editor: Sharon Adams Poore

Assistant Editor: Kimberly Apfelbaum

Editorial Assistant: Ashley Bargende

Senior Media Editor: Wendy Constantine

Marketing Manager: Diane Wenckebach

Marketing Coordinator: Loreen Pelletier

Marketing Communications Manager: Heather Baxley

Senior Content Project Manager: Lianne Ames

Senior Art Director: Cate Barr

Print Buyer: Julio Esperas

Production Service/Layout: Joan Keyes, Dovetail Publishing Services

Text Designer: tani hasegawa

Photo Manager: John Hill

Cover Designer: tani hasegawa

Cover Image: *Woman Holding a Balance*, c. 1664 (oil on canvas), Vermeer, Jan (1632–75)/National Gallery of Art, Washington, DC, USA/The Bridgeman Art Library

Compositor: Thompson Type

© 2011, 2009, 2005 Wadsworth, Cengage Learning

ALL RIGHTS RESERVED. No part of this work covered by the copyright herein may be reproduced, transmitted, stored, or used in any form or by any means graphic, electronic, or mechanical, including but not limited to photocopying, recording, scanning, digitizing, taping, Web distribution, information networks, or information storage and retrieval systems, except as permitted under Section 107 or 108 of the 1976 United States Copyright Act, without the prior written permission of the publisher.

For product information and technology assistance, contact us at Cengage Learning Customer & Sales Support, 1-800-354-9706
For permission to use material from this text or product, submit all requests online at **www.cengage.com/permissions.**
Further permissions questions can be emailed to **permissionrequest@cengage.com**

Library of Congress Control Number: 2009932089

ISBN-13: 978-0-495-79986-3
ISBN-10: 0-495-79986-6

Wadsworth
20 Channel Center Street
Boston, MA 02210
USA

Cengage Learning is a leading provider of customized learning solutions with office locations around the globe, including Singapore, the United Kingdom, Australia, Mexico, Brazil, and Japan. Locate your local office at **international.cengage.com/region**

Cengage Learning products are represented in Canada by Nelson Education, Ltd.

For your course and learning solutions, visit **www.cengage.com**

Purchase any of our products at your local college store or at our preferred online store **www.ichapters.com**

Printed in the United States of America
1 2 3 4 5 6 7 13 12 11 10 09

FIGURE 10.4 Copyright page from a book showing the location of the copyright information. From KLEINER. *Gardner's Art through the Ages*, 13E. © 2011 Cengage Learning, Inc. Reproduced by permission. www.cengage.com/permissions

Authors

13. A Book by One Author

Miller, Laura. *The Magician's Book: A Skeptic's Guide to Narnia.* Back Bay, 2009.

Douglass, Frederick. My Bondage and My Freedom, 1855. *Project Gutenberg,* www.gutenberg.org/files/202/202-h/202-h.htm.

14. A Book by Two Authors

List the first author with last name first, followed by a comma and the word "**and.**" Then list the second author with the first name first.

Gulati, Varun, and Mythili Anoop. *Contemporary Women's Writing in India*. Lexington, 2014.

For books that are published by a university press (such as Cambridge University Press), use the abbreviation "**UP.**"

Slaughter, Sheila, and Gary Rhodes. *Academic Capitalism and the New Economy: Markets, State, and Higher Education.*

Johns Hopkins UP, 2009, jhupbooks.press.jhu.edu/content/academic-capitalism-and-new-economy.

15. A Book by Three or More Authors

Include only the name of the first author (last name first), followed by a comma and **et al.** ("and others").

Orr, Catherine M., et al. *Rethinking Women's and Gender Studies*. Routledge, 2011.

The following text is published by National Academies Press; the word "Press" is abbreviated with the letter "**P.**"

Beatty, Alexandra S., et al. *Climate Change Education*. The National Academies P, 2014, www.nap.edu/read/18807/.

16. Two or More Books by the Same Author

List books by the same author in alphabetical order by title. After the first entry, use three unspaced hyphens followed by a period in place of the author's name.

Ede, Lisa. *Situating Composition: Composition Studies and the Politics of Location*. Southern Illinois UP, 2004.

---. *Work in Progress*. 6th ed., Bedford, 2004.

17. A Book by a Corporate Author

If a text is both authored and published by the same organization, begin with the title of the text. If the corporate author is not the same as the publisher, begin with the name of the corporate author.

Grade Expectations: How Marks and Education Policies Shape Students' Ambitions. Organisation for Economic Cooperation and Development, 2012, doi:10.1787/19963777.

The Home Depot. *Home Improvement 1-2-3*. 2nd ed., Meredith Books, 2003.

18. An Edited Book

An edited book is a work prepared for publication by a person other than the author. If your focus is on the *author's* work, begin your citation with the author's name.

Twain, Mark. *The Adventures of Huckleberry Finn*. Edited by Michael Patrick Hearn, Norton, 2001.

If your focus is on the *editor's* work, begin your citation with the editor's name, followed by a comma and the word "**editor.**" (For two editors, treat the entry as you would a book by two authors, but include the word **editors** after the second name. For three or more editors, include only the first editor's name (last name first), followed by a comma and the words "**et al., editors.**")

Hearn, Michael Patrick, editor. *The Adventures of Huckleberry Finn*. By Mark Twain, Norton, 2001.

19. A Translation

If your focus is on the *translator's* work, place that name first in your citation, followed by the word "**translator**." If your focus is on the *author's* work, follow the first entry under "An Edited Book."

Rabassa, Gregory, translator. *One Hundred Years of Solitude*. By Gabriel García Márquez, Avon, 1991.

20. A Subsequent Edition of a Book

When citing an edition other than the first, include the edition number after the title of the book. The edition number usually appears on the work's cover and title page.

Yaghijian, Lucretia B. *Writing Theology Well: A Rhetoric for Theological and Biblical Writers*. 2nd ed., Bloomsbury, 2015.

Miner, Dorothy, et al., editors. *Teaching Chemistry to Students with Disabilities: A Manual for High Schools, Colleges, and Graduate Programs*. 4th ed., American Chemical Society, 2001. *ERIC*, files.eric.ed.gov/fulltext/ED476798.pdf.

21. A Republished Book

Include the original publication date after the title of a republished book.

Wharton, Edith. *The House of Mirth*. 1905. Scribner's, 1975.

22. A Book in a Series

If the cover or title page indicates that the book is part of a series, include the series name, neither italicized nor enclosed in quotation marks, and the series number (if applicable) after the publication information.

Davis, Bertram H. *Thomas Percy*. Twayne, 1981. Twayne's English Authors 313.

23. A Multivolume Work

When all volumes of a multivolume work have the same title, include the number of the volume you are using.

Writings of Charles S. Peirce: A Chronological Edition. Vol. 4, edited by Max H. Fisch, Indiana UP, 2000.

If you use two or more volumes that have the same title, cite the entire work.

Writings of Charles S. Peirce: A Chronological Edition. Edited by Max H. Fisch, Indiana UP, 2000. 6 vols.

24. An Illustrated Book or a Graphic Narrative

An illustrated book is a work in which illustrations accompany the text. If your focus is on the *author's* work, begin your citation with the author's name. After the title, include the words "**illustrated by**" followed by the illustrator's name and the publication information.

Frost, Robert. *Stopping by Woods on a Snowy Evening*, illustrated by Susan Jeffers, Penguin, 2001.

If your focus is on the *illustrator's* work, begin your citation with the illustrator's name followed by a comma and the word "**illustator.**" After the title of the work, provide the author's name, preceded by the word "**By**."

Jeffers, Susan, illustrator. *Stopping by Woods on a Snowy Evening*. By Robert Frost, Penguin, 2001.

For a graphic novel, where the text and illustrations work together to tell a story, use the same citation you would for a book. If the author and illustrator are different people, cite them in one of the two ways described for an illustrated book.

Bechdel, Alison. *Fun Home: A Family Tragicomic*. Houghton, 2006.

25. The Foreword, Preface, or Afterword of a Book

Campbell, Richard. Preface. *Media and Culture: An Introduction to Mass Communication*, by Bettina Fabos, Bedford, 2005, pp. vi-xi.

26. A Book with a Title within Its Title

If the book you are citing contains a title that is normally italicized (a novel, play, or long poem, for example), do not italicize the interior title.

Fulton, Joe B. *Mark Twain in the Margins: The Quarry Farm Marginalia and* A Connecticut Yankee in King Arthur's Court. U of Alabama P, 2000.

If the book you are citing contains a title that is normally enclosed in quotation marks (a short story or poem), keep the quotation marks.

Hawkins, Hunt, and Brian W. Shaffer, editors. *Approaches to Teaching Conrad's "Heart of Darkness" and "The Secret Sharer."* MLA, 2002.

27. Sacred Texts

The New English Bible with the Apocrypha. Oxford Study ed., Oxford UP, 1976.

Holy Qur'an. Translated by M. H. Shakir, Tahrike Tarsile Qur'an, 1999.

28. A Book Accessed through an E-reader

Sonnenberg, Brittani. *Home Leave: A Novel.* Kindle ed., Hachette, 2014.

Parts of Books

29. A Short Story, Play, or Poem in a Collection

Bukowski, Charles. "lonely hearts." *The Flash of Lightning behind the Mountain: New Poems,* Ecco, 2004, pp. 115-16.

30. An Essay in an Anthology or Edited Collection

Crevel, René. "From *Babylon*." *Surrealist Painters and Poets: An Anthology,* edited by Mary Ann Caws. MIT P, 2001, pp. 175-77.

31. More than One Work from the Same Anthology

Provide a complete citation for the anthology, but list each work from that anthology separately (with a cross-reference to the entire anthology). Entries should appear in alphabetical order.

Agar, Eileen. "Am I a Surrealist?" Caws, *Surrealist Painters,* pp. 3-7.

Caws, Mary Ann, editor. *Surrealist Painters and Poets: An Anthology*. MIT P, 2001.

Crevel, René. "From *Babylon*." Caws, *Surrealist Painters,* pp. 175-77.

32. A Scholarly Article Reprinted in a Collection

Booth, Wayne C. "Why Ethical Criticism Can Never Be Simple." *Style*, vol. 32, no. 2, 1998, pp. 351-64. Reprinted in *Mapping the Ethical Turn: A Reader in Ethics, Culture, and Literary Theory*, edited by Todd F. Davis and Kenneth Womack. UP of Virginia, 2001, pp. 16-29.

33. An Article in a Reference Book

For a signed article, begin with the author's name.

Birch, Dinah. "Expressionism." *The Oxford Companion to English Literature*. 7th ed., Oxford UP, 2009.

For an unsigned article, begin with the title.

"Cubism." *The Encyclopedia Americana*. 2012 ed.

MLA Entries for Internet-Specific Sources

When citing Websites, podcasts, *YouTube* videos, and blogs, include as many of the nine core elements (described at the beginning of this section) as possible. Figure 10.5 shows where you can find this information on a Website.

34. An Entire Website

When citing a Website, include the full URL for that site.

Nelson, Cary, and Bartholomew Brinkman, editors. *Modern American Poetry*. Dept. of English, U of Illinois, Urbana-Champaign, 2014, www.english.illinois.edu/maps/poets.htm.

35. A Document within a Website

When citing a document or an article within a Website, include the full URL for the document or article.

Nix, Elizabeth. "6 Viking Leaders You Should Know." *History.com*, A&E Television Networks, 6 Feb. 2014, www.history.com/news/history-lists/6-viking-leaders-you-should-know.

36. A Home Page for a Course

Davis, Brian. Home page. Dept. of Physics and Physical Oceanography, U of North Carolina, Wilmington, Fall 2015, www.people.uncw.edu/davis/phy201.html.

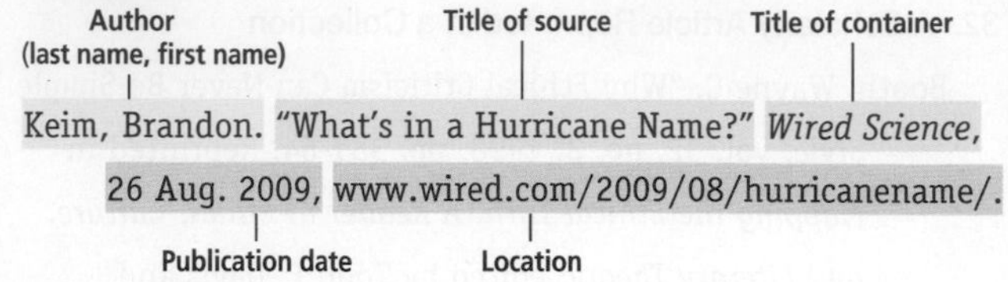

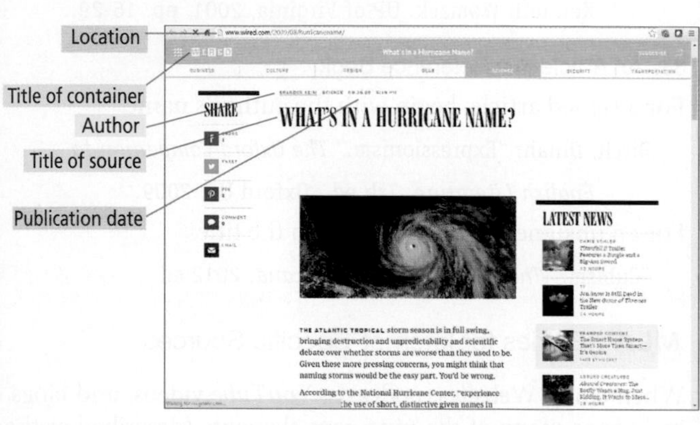

FIGURE 10.5 Part of an online article showing the location of the information needed for documentation. Wired.com © 2011 Condé Nast Digital. All rights reserved. Image from NOAA.

37. A Podcast or a Radio Program Accessed Online

When citing a podcast or radio program online, include the full URL.

"Teenage Skeptic Takes on Climate Scientists." *Morning Edition*, narrated by David Kestenbaum, National Public Radio, 15 Apr. 2008, www.npr.org/templates/story.php?storyId 89619306.

38. An Online Video (*YouTube*)

Because videos posted to online sites can be removed at any time, you should provide as much information as possible in your citation. In the following example, a date of access in included after the full URL for the video.

Mohr, Nicole. "How to Analyze a Poem." *YouTube*, 27 Oct. 2013. www.youtube.com/watch?v=5lVHsfk0vV8. Accessed 22 Mar. 2016.

39. A Television Program Streamed via *Netflix* or *Amazon*

Shows that are streamed through online services are often available for a certain period of time. For this reason, you may want to include the date you accessed a program that is streamed online.

"Episode 4." *Call the Midwife*, season 4, BBC One, 8 Feb. 2015. *Netflix*, www.netflix.com/search/call%20the%20midwife?jbv=70245163&jbp=0&jbr=0. Accessed 22 Mar. 2016.

40. A Blog, Tweet, or Social Networking Post

O'Connor, Brendan. "The Downtown Void." *The Awl*, 17 Mar. 2016, www.theawl.com/2016/03/the-downtown-void.

For a tweet, use the full tweet as the title. Include the date and time, as well as the full tweet's URL.

@tim_cook. "Andy Grove was one of the giants of the technology world. He loved our country and epitomized America at its best. Rest in peace." *Twitter*, 21 March 2016, 10:35 p.m., twitter.com/tim_cook/status/712073584194105344.

41. A Comment on a Blog, Tweet, or Other Online Forum

Often commenters use screen names or pseudonyms to identify themselves. Treat the name exactly as it appears onscreen.

foxinthe_snow. Comment on "My Other Parent," by Nicole Soojung Callahan. *The Toast*, 22 Dec. 2014, www.aka-sf.org/my-other-parent-by-nicole-soojung-callahan/.

42. An App (or any Computer Software)

Paper—Stories from Facebook, version 1.2.6. *Facebook*, 11 Mar. 2016, www.facebook.com/paper.

43. A Source Accessed through an App

Dolce, Chris. "Winter Storm Selene: 2,000-Mile-Plus Snow Swath." *The Weather Channel*, version 7.3.2, 22 Mar. 2016, 8:45 a.m.

44. Email

Mauk, Karen R. "Today." Received by Stephen R. Mandell, 28 June 2015.

MLA Entries for Other Sources

45. A Photograph or Painting

For a photograph or painting viewed at a museum or other location, provide the name of the photographer or artist (last name first), followed by the title of the work in italics. Note the year in which the work was created, as well as the name of the place where it was viewed and its city. If the name of the museum contains the city name, omit the city.

Stieglitz, Alfred. *The Steerage*. 1907, Los Angeles County Museum of Art.

A photograph or painting without a title is treated the same, but in place of the italicized title, add a brief description of the work. If the work was accessed online, include the full URL where the work was viewed.

Burns, Patrick. Panoramic print of Providence, Rhode Island. 1988, Worcester Art Museum, vps343.pairvps.com:8080/emuseum/view/objects/asitem/search@/15/title-desc?t:state:flow=d8ad95ba-419f-450a-a5dc-8214e37e7e6f.

46. A Cartoon/Comic Strip

Trudeau, Gary. "Doonesbury." *The Philadelphia Inquirer*, 15 Sept. 2003, p. E13.

Stossel, Sage. "Star Wars: The Next Generation." *The Atlantic Online*, 20 May 1999, www.theatlantic.com/past/unbound/sage/ss990519.htm.

47. An Advertisement

If the source you use is not one that readers would be able to identify, include a description in your citation.

Microsoft. Advertisement. *National Review*, 8 June 2010.

48. A Map

Like the previous example, include a description in your citation if readers might not be able to identify the source.

"Philadelphia, Pennsylvania." Map. *U.S. Gazetteer*, 2016, pennsylvania.hometownlocator.com/maps/countymap,cfips,101,c,philadelphia.cfm.

49. A Film

Include the title of the film (italicized), the distributor, and the date, along with other information that may be useful to readers, such as the name of the director, names of performers, and the screenwriter.

If you focus on the film, place it first in the citation.

Citizen Kane. Directed by Orson Welles, performances by Welles and Agnes Moorehead, RKO, 1941.

If you focus on the contribution of a particular person, begin with the person's name.

Welles, Orson, director. *Citizen Kane*. RKO, 1941.

If you cite a film on DVD or Blu-ray, include the original release date.

Cowperthwaite, Gabriela, director. *Blackfish*. Magnolia Home Entertainment, 2013.

50. A Television Program

If the program is part of a series, begin with the episode title. Include the original air date.

"War Feels Like War." *P.O.V.*, PBS, 6 Jul. 2004.

If you accessed the program online, provide the previous information and include the season and episode number, as well as the full URL for the episode.

"The Miseducation of Susan Ross." *Scandal*, season 5, episode 6, ABC, 31 Mar. 2016, abc.go.com/shows/scandal/episode-guide/season-05/16-the-miseducation-of-susan-ross.

51. An Audio Recording

Malloy, Dave. "No One Else." *Natasha, Pierre, and the Great Comet of 1812*, Sh-K-Boom, 2013.

Adele. "When We Were Young." 25, Sony, 2015. *iTunes*, itun.es/us/HIPQp.

52. An Image or Video on a Website

Einspruch, Franklin. "View Out the Window." *The Boston Globe*, 21 Feb. 2015, www.bostonglobe.com/arts/2015/02/21-the-poetry-boston-snowfall/maV2CoJKQfkbFAAdnh08tL/story.html.

53. A Dissertation

For a published dissertation, place the title in italics and be sure to include the full URL or DOI for the work.

Rodriguez, Jason Anthony. *Bureaucracy and Altruism: Managing the Contradictions of Teaching*. Dissertation. U of Texas, Arlington, 2003. *ProQuest*, search.proquest .com.ezproxy.cul.columbia.edu/docview/305227623.

For an unpublished dissertation, place the title in quotation marks.

Pfeffer, Miki. "An 'Enlarging Influence': Women of New Orleans, Julia Ward Howe, and the Women's Department at the Cotton Centennial Exposition, 1884-1885."

Dissertation. U of New Orleans, 2011.

54. A Government Publication

For a work by a government agency, begin the citation with the name of the government, followed by a comma and the name of the organizational unit (if applicable), followed by the agency. These entities are arranged from largest to smallest, as shown in the following examples. Do not abbreviate words such as "Department" or "Government Printing Office."

United States, Congress, Senate, Office of Consumer Affairs. *2014 Consumer's Resource Handbook*, Government Publishing Office, 2014.

United States, Department of Justice, Office of Justice Programs. *Violence Against Women: Estimates from the Redesigned National Crime Victimization Survey*, by Ronet Bachman and Linda E. Salzman, Aug. 1995, www.bjs.gov/content/pub/pdf/FEMVIED.PDF.

If you cite legislation of the United States Congress, include the number and session. If there is a document type (such as a report) and number, include that information, as well.

United States, Congress, Senate, Committee on Energy and Natural Resources. *Keystone XL Pipeline*. Government Publishing Office, 2015. 114th Congress, 1st session, Report 114-1.

55. A Pamphlet

Cite a pamphlet as you would a book. If no author is listed, begin with the title (italicized).

The Darker Side of Tanning. American Academy of Dermatology, 2010.

56. A Lecture

If you attend a lecture or other public address, state that at the end of your citation with the word "**Lecture**" or "**Address**."

Grimm, Mary. "An Afternoon with Mary Grimm." Visiting Writers Program, Dept. of English, Wright State U, 16 Apr. 2004. Lecture.

57. A Personal Interview or Letter

For a personal interview, begin with the interview subject and use the phrase "**Personal Interview**," followed by the date of the interview.

Tannen, Deborah. Personal Interview. 8 June 2015.

When citing a letter, begin with the letter writer's name and use the phrase "**Personal Letter**," followed by the date of the letter.

Tan, Amy. Personal Letter. 7 Apr. 2016.

58. A Published Interview

Include the phrase "**Interview by**" after the title of the interview. For an interview accessed online, include the full URL for the piece.

"Bill Gates: The *Rolling Stone* Interview." Interview by Jeff Goodell, 13 Mar. 2014, *RollingStone.com*, www.rollingstone.com/culture/news/bill-gates-the-rolling-stone-interview-20140313.

59. A Published Letter

Joyce, James. "Letter to Louis Gillet." *James Joyce*, by Richard Ellmann, Oxford UP, 1965, p. 631.

3 Content Notes

Content notes—multiple bibliographic citations or other material that does not fit smoothly into your essay—are indicated by a **superscript** (raised numeral) in the text. Notes can appear either as footnotes at the bottom of the page or as endnotes on a separate sheet entitled **Notes**, placed after the last page of the essay and before the works-cited

Close-Up HOW TO CITE SOURCES NOT LISTED IN THIS CHAPTER

The examples listed in this chapter represent the sources you will most likely encounter in your research. If you encounter a source that is not listed here, find the model that most closely matches it, and adapt the guidelines for your use.

For example, suppose you wanted to include **an obituary** from a print newspaper in your list of works cited. The models that most closely resemble this type of entry are *an editorial in a newspaper* (entry 9). If you used these models as your guide, your entry would look like this:

Boucher, Geoff, and Elaine Woo. "Michael Jackson's Life Was Infused with Fantasy and Tragedy." Obituary. *The Los Angeles Times,* 2 Jul. 2009, p. 4.

list. Content notes are double-spaced within and between entries. The first line is indented one-half inch, and subsequent lines are typed flush left.

For Multiple Citations

In the Essay

Many researchers emphasize the necessity of having dying patients share their experiences.[1]

In the Note

1. Kübler-Ross 27; Stinnette 43; Poston 70; Cohen and Cohen 31-34; Burke 1: 91-95.

For Other Material

In the Essay

The massacre during World War I is an event the survivors could not easily forget.[2]

In the Note

2. For a firsthand account of these events, see Bedoukian 178-81.

10b MLA-Style Manuscript Guidelines

Although MLA essays do not usually include abstracts or internal headings, this situation is changing. Be sure you know what your instructor expects.

The guidelines in the three checklists that follow are based on the *MLA Handbook* 8th edition.

10c Model MLA-Style Research Paper

The following student essay, "The Great Debate: *Wikipedia* and College-Level Research," uses MLA documentation style. It includes MLA-style in-text citations, three charts, a notes page, and a works-cited list.

CHECKLIST

Typing Your Essay

When typing your essay, use the student essay in **10c** as your model.

- ❑ Leave a one-inch margin at the top and bottom and on both sides of the page. Double-space your essay throughout.
- ❑ Capitalize all important words in your title, but not prepositions, articles, coordinating conjunctions, or the *to* in infinitives (unless they begin or end the title or subtitle). Do not italicize your title or enclose it in quotation marks. Never put a period after the title.
- ❑ Number all pages of your essay consecutively—including the first—in the upper right-hand corner, one-half inch from the top, flush right. Type your last name followed by a space before the page number on every page.
- ❑ Set off quotations of more than four lines of prose or more than three lines of poetry by indenting the whole quotation one-half inch. If you quote two or more paragraphs, indent the first line of each paragraph an additional quarter inch. (If the first sentence does not begin a paragraph, do not indent it. Indent the first line only in successive paragraphs.)
- ❑ Citations should follow MLA documentation style. See 10a

CHECKLIST

Using Visuals

See 39d

- ❑ Insert visuals into the text as close as possible to where they are discussed.
- ❑ For **tables**, follow these guidelines: *Above the table*, label each table with the word **Table** followed by an arabic numeral (for instance, **Table 1**). Double-space, and type a descriptive caption, with the first line flush with the left-hand margin; indent subsequent lines one-quarter inch. Capitalize the caption as if it were a title.

  Below the table, type the word **Source**, followed by a colon and all source information. Type the first line of the source information flush with the left-hand margin; indent subsequent lines one-quarter inch.
- ❑ Label other types of visual material—graphs, charts, photographs, drawings, and so on—**Fig.** (Figure) followed by an arabic numeral (for example, **Fig. 2**). Directly below the visual, type the label and a title or caption on the same line, followed by source information. Type all lines flush with the left-hand margin.
- ❑ Do not include the source of the visual in the works-cited list unless you use other material from that source elsewhere in the essay.

CHECKLIST

Preparing the MLA Works-Cited List

When typing your works-cited list, follow these guidelines:

See 10a3

- ❑ Begin the works-cited list on a new page after the last page of text or content notes, numbered as the next page of the essay.
- ❑ Center the title **Works Cited** one inch from the top of the page. Double-space between the title and the first entry.
- ❑ List entries alphabetically, with last name first. Use the author's full name as it appears on the title page. If a source has no listed author, alphabetize it by the first word of the title (not counting the article).
- ❑ Type the first line of each entry flush with the left-hand margin; indent subsequent lines one-half inch.
- ❑ Double-space within and between entries.

Title Pages

Although MLA does not require a separate title page, some instructors prefer that you include one. If so, follow this format:

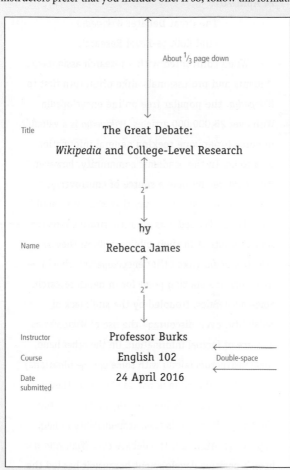

1″ ½″

James 1

Student's last name and page number on every page (including the first)

Rebecca James

Professor Burks

English 102

24 April 2016

Center title →

The Great Debate: *Wikipedia* and College-Level Research

Indent ½″ →

When confronted with a research assignment, students and professionals alike often turn first to *Wikipedia,* the popular free online encyclopedia. With over 26,000,000 articles, *Wikipedia* is a valuable resource for anyone seeking general information on a topic. In the academic community, however, *Wikipedia* has become a source of controversy. Many college instructors say that students should not rely on *Wikipedia* as an authoritative research source or cite it in their bibliographies; they say that *Wikipedia* (like other encyclopedias) should be used only as a starting point for in-depth research. Some academics, troubled by the site's lack of reliability, even discourage the use of *Wikipedia* as a source of factual information. On the other hand, some instructors (along with some college librarians) believe that the issue is not so clear-cut. They say that *Wikipedia* is here to stay and that if the site has problems, it is their responsibility to help improve it. All in all, the debate over *Wikipedia* has been a positive development because it has led the academic community to confront the challenges of open, collaborative software on the web.

Double-space

1″ 1″

Thesis statement

Wikipedia is the most popular wiki, an open-source website that allows users to edit as well

Outline point I: Definition of wiki and explanation of *Wikipedia*

1″

James 2

as contribute content. Derived from a Hawaiian word meaning "quick," the term *wiki* suggests the swiftness and ease with which users can access information on and contribute content to a site ("Wiki"). In accordance with the site's policies, users can edit existing articles and add new articles using *Wikipedia*'s editing tools, which do not require specialized programming knowledge or expertise. Since its creation in 2001 by Jimmy Wales, *Wikipedia* has grown into a huge database of articles on topics ranging from contemporary rock bands to obscure scientific and technical concepts. Because anyone can edit or add content to the site, however, many members of the academic community consider *Wikipedia* unreliable.

Parenthetical documentation refers to material accessed from a website

Student's original conclusions; no documentation necessary

Without a professional editorial board to oversee its development, *Wikipedia* has several shortcomings that limit its trustworthiness. As *Wikipedia*'s own "Researching with *Wikipedia*" page concedes, "not everything in *Wikipedia* is accurate, comprehensive, or unbiased." "Reliability of *Wikipedia*," an article on *Wikipedia*, discusses the many problems that have been identified, presenting criticisms under categories such as "areas of reliability," "susceptibility to bias," and "false biographical information." Academics have similar objections. Villanova University communication department chair Maurice L. Hall has reservations about *Wikipedia*:

Outline point II: Introduction to *Wikipedia*'s drawbacks

Quotations from Internet source, introduced by author's name, are not followed by a paragraph or page number because this information was not provided in the electronic text

> As an open source that is not subjected to traditional forms of peer review, *Wikipedia* must be considered only as reliable as the credibility of the footnotes it uses. But

Quotation of more than four lines is typed as a block, indented 1", and double-spaced, with no quotation marks

James 3

> I also tell students that the information can be skewed in directions of ideology or other forms of bias, and so that is why it cannot be taken as a final authority. (qtd. in Burnsed)

Qtd. in indicates that Hall's comments were quoted in Burnsed's article

In fact, in 2007, *Wikipedia*'s unreliability led Middlebury College's history department to prohibit students from citing Wikipedia as a research source—although it does not prohibit them from using the site for reference. Since then, however, many academics have qualified their criticisms of *Wikipedia*, arguing that although the site is not a reliable research source, it is a valuable stepping stone to more in-depth research. As retired reference librarian Joe Schallan explains, "*Wikipedia* can be useful, especially as a starting point for information on offbeat topics or niche interests that traditional encyclopedias omit." However, he believes that information from *Wikipedia* should be taken "with a very large grain of salt."

Because it is an open-source site, *Wikipedia* is not always reliable or accurate. Although many *Wikipedia* articles include citations, many others—especially those that are underdeveloped—do not. In addition, because anyone can create or edit them, *Wikipedia* articles can be inaccurate, biased, and even targets for vandalism. For example, some *Wikipedia* users tamper with the biographies of especially high-profile political or cultural figures.[1] According to the article "*Wikipedia* Vandalism Detection," seven percent of *Wikipedia*'s articles are vandalized in some way (Adler et al. 277). Although *Wikipedia* has an extensive protection policy that restricts the kinds of edits that can be

Outline point III: *Wikipedia*'s unreliability

Superscript number identifies content note

James 4

made to its articles ("*Wikipedia*: Protection Policy"), there are limitations to *Wikipedia*'s control measures.

Outline point IV: *Wikipedia*'s poor writing

Because they can be edited by anyone, *Wikipedia* articles are often poorly written. Emory University English professor Mark Bauerlein asserts that *Wikipedia* articles are written in a "flat, featureless, factual style" (153). Even though *Wikipedia* has instituted a coding system to label the shortcomings of its less-developed articles, a warning about an article's poor writing style is likely to go unnoticed by the typical user. Bauerlein argues that the poor writing of many *Wikipedia* articles reaffirms to students that sloppy writing and grammatical errors are acceptable in their own writing as well:

> Students relying on *Wikipedia* alone, year in and year out, absorb the prose as proper knowledge discourse, and knowledge itself seems blank and uninspiring. (153-54)

Parenthetical documentation is placed one space after end punctuation

Thus, according to Bauerlein, *Wikipedia* articles have actually lowered the standards for what constitutes acceptable college-level writing.

Outline point V. A: *Wikipedia*'s popularity and benefits: Wilson's findings (charts)

Despite *Wikipedia*'s drawbacks, there is no denying the popularity of the site among both college students and professionals, who turn to it first for general factual information on a variety of topics. According to Jodi L. Wilson, more than seventy percent of *Wikipedia* contributors are at least twenty-two years old, with the majority of users having higher-education degrees (885-87).[2] Figs. 1 and 2 show a breakdown of the people who most commonly consult *Wikipedia*.

Superscript number identifies content note

Figures summarize relevant data. Source information is typed directly below the figures.

James 5

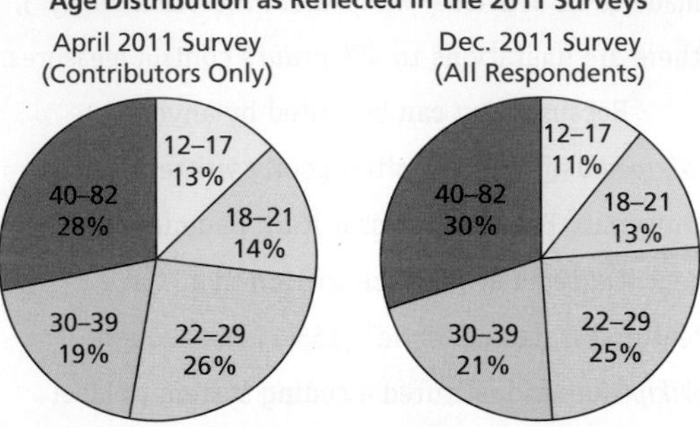

Fig. 1. Jodi L. Wilson, "Proceed with Extreme Caution: Citation to *Wikipedia* in Light of Contributor Demographics and Content Policies." *Vanderbilt Journal of Entertainment & Technology Law*, vol. 16, no. 4, 2014, p. 886. *Academic Search Complete*, web.a.ebscohost.com.ezproxy.cul.columbia.edu/ehost/detail/detail?vid=4&sid=14afe0c2-3351-4754-93dc-2371d2724d5d.

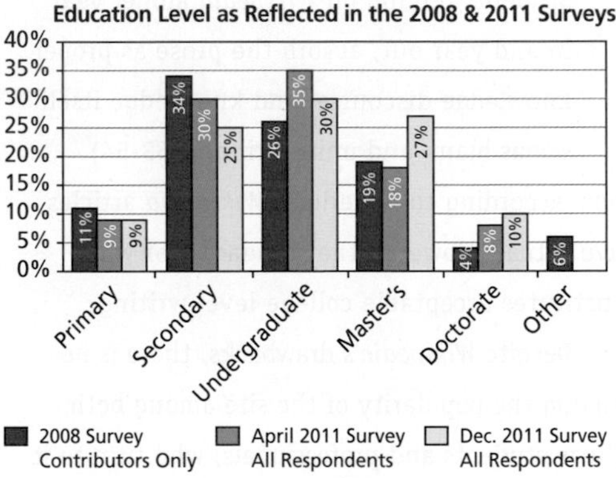

Fig. 2. Jodi L. Wilson, "Proceed with Extreme Caution: Citation to *Wikipedia* in Light of Contributor Demographics and Content Policies." *Vanderbilt Journal of Entertainment & Technology Law*, vol. 16, no. 4, 2014, p. 886. *Academic Search Complete*, web.a.ebscohost.com.ezproxy.cul.columbia.edu/ehost/detail/detail?vid=4&sid=14afe0c2-3351-4754-93dc-2371d2724d5d.

James 6

Outline point V. B: *Wikipedia*'s popularity and benefits: comprehensive abstracts, links to other sources, and current and comprehensive bibliographies

There are good reasons why so many educated adults use *Wikipedia*. Longer *Wikipedia* articles often include comprehensive abstracts that summarize their content. *Wikipedia* articles also often include links to other *Wikipedia* articles, allowing users to navigate quickly through related content. In addition, many *Wikipedia* articles link to other online and print sources, including reliable peer-reviewed sources. Another benefit, noted earlier by Villanova University's Maurice L. Hall, is the inclusion of current and comprehensive bibliographies in some *Wikipedia* articles. According to Alison J. Head and Michael B. Eisenberg, "*Wikipedia* plays an important role when students are formulating and defining a topic."[3] Assuming that *Wikipedia* users make the effort to connect an article's content with more reliable, traditional research sources, *Wikipedia* can be a valuable first step for serious researchers.

Superscript number identifies content note

Outline point VI: *Wikipedia*'s advantages over other online encyclopedias

Wikipedia has advantages over other online encyclopedias. Because users can update articles in real time from any location, *Wikipedia* offers up-to-the-minute coverage of political and cultural events as well as timely information on popular culture topics that receive little or no attention in other reference sources. In addition, because *Wikipedia* has such a broad user base, more topics are covered in *Wikipedia* than in other online resources. For example, a student researching the history of video gaming would find *Wikipedia*'s "Wii U" article, with its numerous pages of information and nearly two hundred references, to be a valuable resource.

James 7

Encyclopaedia Britannica does not contain a comparable article on this popular game console. Even when there is little information on a particular topic, *Wikipedia* allows users to create "stub" articles, which provide minimal information that users can expand over time. Thus, by offering immediate access to information on relatively obscure topics, *Wikipedia* can be a valuable first step in finding reliable research sources on such topics.

Outline point VII: *Wikipedia's* ongoing improvements

In their 2014 study, Marcus Messner et al. found that *Wikipedia* has become an even more comprehensive and reliable database of information and that it is gaining increasing acceptance in the academic community. *Wikipedia*'s "About" page claims that the continual editing of articles "generally results in an upward trend of quality and a growing consensus over a neutral representation of information." In fact, *Wikipedia* has instituted control measures to help weed out inaccurate or biased information and to make its content more reliable. For example, evaluating articles on the basis of accuracy, neutrality, completeness, and style, *Wikipedia* ranks its best articles as "featured" and its second-best articles as "good."[4] Although no professional editorial board oversees the development of content within *Wikipedia,* experienced users may become editors, and this role allows them to monitor the process by which content is added and updated. Users may also use the "Talk" page to discuss an article's content and make suggestions for improvement. With such controls in

Superscript number identifies content note

place, some *Wikipedia* articles are comparable in scope and accuracy to articles in professionally edited online resources.

Outline point VIII: *Wikipedia*'s content

Although critics argue that the collaborative nature of the wiki format does not necessarily help improve content, the study by Messner et al. seems to suggest the opposite. In examining trends of content development in *Wikipedia* nutritional health articles, Messner et al. affirm that *Wikipedia*'s reliability has improved over time. They explain, "this study's goal was to close a gap in the current research and analyze the online rankings of *Wikipedia* articles on nutritional topics and the types of references they are based on" (Messner et al.).

Messner et al. summarize their findings with a positive conclusion:

> [W]hile *Wikipedia* has grown and expanded over time with reference numbers increasing, the overall quality of articles has at a minimum stayed consistently reliable and has even increased for some of the articles in recent years. This shows that as *Wikipedia* continues to grow, there has been an overall consolidation, creating a better and more reliable source for information on health and nutrition.

Supporting this conclusion, Fig. 3 illustrates how, in recent years, *Wikipedia* articles more consistently include references to reliable sources.

James 9

In offering increasingly more consistent and well-researched coverage, *Wikipedia* is becoming a more reliable source of information than some of its critics might like to admit.

Chart summarizes relevant data. Source information is typed directly below the figure.

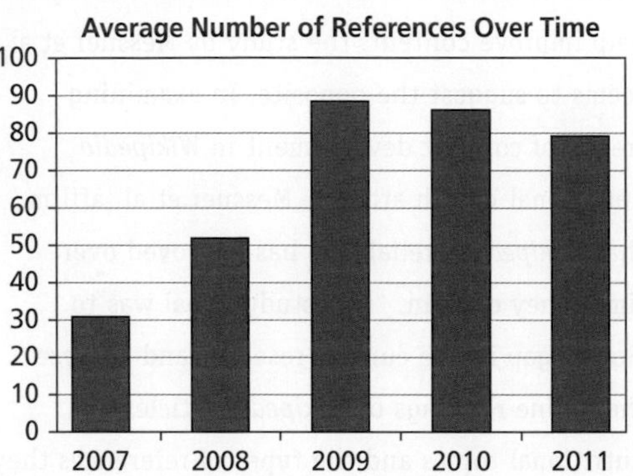

Fig. 3. Marcus Messner, et al., "Influencing Public Opinion from Corn Syrup to Obesity: A Longitudinal Analysis of the References for Nutritional Entries on *Wikipedia*." *First Monday*, vol. 19, no. 11, 2014. *Google Scholar*, www.firstmonday.dk/ojs/index.php/fm/article/view/4823.

Outline point IX: Academic community's reservations about *Wikipedia*

Some argue that the academic community's reservations about *Wikipedia* have less to do with *Wikipedia*'s shortcomings and more to do with resistance to emergent digital research technologies. Harvard Law professor Jonathan L. Zittrain suggests that academia has, in effect, fallen behind, observing that "so many projects by universities and libraries are about knowledge and information online, . . . [but academics] just couldn't get *Wikipedia* going, or anything like it" (qtd. in Foster). A recent study suggested one

Ellipsis indicates that the student has omitted words from the quotation

James 10

reason for *Wikipedia*'s bad reputation among many college instructors: "the perceived detrimental effects of the use of Web 2.0 applications not included in the university suite" (Bayliss 36). Although Jimmy Wales, cofounder of *Wikipedia,* acknowledges that *Wikipedia* should serve only as a starting point for more in-depth research, he calls for the academic community to recognize *Wikipedia* as one of several new, important digital platforms that change the way people learn and disseminate knowledge. "Instead of fearing the power, complexity, and extraordinary potential of these new platforms," Wales says, "we should be asking how we can gain from their success" (qtd. in Goldstein). As many instructors and librarians argue, members of the academic community are uniquely qualified to improve *Wikipedia* by expanding stub articles and by writing new articles about their areas of expertise.

Outline point X: Instructors' and librarians' efforts to use and improve *Wikipedia*

In recent years, librarians across the country have committed their time and resources to enhancing *Wikipedia* articles that pertain to their own special collections and areas of expertise—and, in general, have become more comfortable with *Wikipedia*. In his research, Colorado Mesa University business professor Johnny Snyder found that "faculty and librarians seem to be using *Wikipedia* more than students . . ." (161). He goes on to explain, "This result was unexpected, as students in the twenty-first century are being classified as 'digital natives' and

James 11

are embedded in technology and information seeking activities, while librarians and faculty are perceived to be more skeptical about this information source" (Snyder 161). June L. Power, an access service/reference librarian at the University of North Carolina at Pembroke, concedes, "Okay, I am ready for the criticism. What self-respecting librarian turns to *Wikipedia* for reference work? I admit it—this one does" (139). Power describes *Wikipedia*'s value to librarians and students alike: "While I won't complete deep research using only *Wikipedia*, being able to find quick information about a topic is something for which *Wikipedia* is an excellent tool" (139). Snyder, Power, and others believe that it is the responsibility of the academic community to bridge the divide between traditional research sources and the digital tools and technologies students are increasingly using to conduct college-level research.

Already, college instructors have found new uses and benefits of *Wikipedia* by incorporating it into their classrooms. In fact, *Wikipedia* has implemented an education program as part of its outreach and collaboration initiative to help instructors around the world build writing assignments based on *Wikipedia*. *Wikipedia*'s "Education Program" page offers guidelines and other resources for incorporating *Wikipedia* into the classroom, noting that this program marks "[t]he end of throwaway assignments and the

Outline poin[t] XI: *Wikiped[ia]* in the classroom

James 12

beginning of real-world impact for student editors." Jeff Byers, a chemistry professor at Middlebury College (where one of the more famous *Wikipedia* "bans" was instituted not long ago), has students in his advanced organic chemistry course write *Wikipedia* entries. Similarly, in her article "Writing for the World: *Wikipedia* as an Introduction to Academic Writing," Christine M. Tardy, an associate professor of writing, rhetoric, and discourse at DePaul University, encourages instructors to use *Wikipedia* in the classroom and outlines some sample writing assignments that can help students "gain a real sense of audience and enjoy the satisfaction of seeing their work published on a high-traffic global website" (18). Instructors like Byers and Tardy emphasize the collaborative nature of *Wikipedia* writing assignments, which offer students a unique opportunity to experience the kinds of writing they are likely to do after college. Additionally, *Wikipedia* writing assignments encourage students to use critical thinking skills, since they require students to evaluate the articles they find on the site and to use *Wikipedia* bibliographies as a starting place to find more suitable research sources.

Outline point III: Academics' changing view of *Wikipedia*

With emerging research on *Wikipedia* use and with new efforts by colleges and universities around the country to incorporate *Wikipedia* into the classroom, the debate surrounding *Wikipedia* seems to be shifting. Although instructors used to seek ways to prevent students from using *Wikipedia*

James 13

as a research source, some in the academic community are now acknowledging the importance and usefulness of this online resource—at least for general reference. Many former critics are acknowledging that *Wikipedia* offers academics an opportunity to participate in emergent digital technologies that have changed the ways students conduct research. In other words, instructors acknowledge, they need to come to terms with *Wikipedia* and develop guidelines for its use. More and more academics are realizing that improving *Wikipedia* actually benefits students, since the site is often the first place students go when starting a research project. To its credit, *Wikipedia* has taken steps to improve the site's reliability and accuracy, and *Wikipedia*'s outreach and collaboration initiative is building a comprehensive list of best practices for continuing to enhance the quality of *Wikipedia* over time.

Conclusion restates the thesis and summarizes key points

Like any encyclopedia, *Wikipedia* is not a suitable source for college-level research. Beyond this fact, however, it may also not yet be as reliable as some other reference sources. Still, it is a valuable starting point for research. As academics and others continue to examine *Wikipedia*'s strengths and weaknesses, they may become more open to its use and more willing to work to improve it. In this sense, the debate over *Wikipedia* is likely to have a positive outcome. Meanwhile, however, students should exercise caution when evaluating general information they find on *Wikipedia* and refrain from citing it as a source.

1"

James 14

Notes

Center title

Indent 1/2"

Double-space

1. In one well-known example, the reputation of journalist John Seigenthaler was tarnished when a *Wikipedia* user edited his biography to claim inaccurately that Seigenthaler was involved in the Kennedy assassination, a lie that spread to other online sources.

2. Wilson cautions that, although the majority of *Wikipedia* users are educated adults, researchers should be careful to consider the credibility of the *Wikipedia* contributors to articles they use in their research.

1" 1"

3. Head and Eisenberg also note, however, that "when students are in a deep research mode, . . . it is library databases, such as *JSTOR* and *PsycINFO*, for instance, that students use more frequently than *Wikipedia*."

4. In addition, *Wikipedia*'s policies state that the information in its articles must be verifiable and must be based on documented, preexisting research.

1"

½"

James 15

Center title

Works Cited

"About *Wikipedia*." *Wikipedia*, 8 Mar. 2016, 15:07, en.wikipedia.org/wiki/Wikipedia:About.

Adler, B. Thomas, et al. "*Wikipedia* Vandalism Detection: Combining Natural Language, Metadata, and Reputation Features." *Lecture Notes in Computer Science*, vol. 6609, 2011, pp. 277-88. *Google Scholar*, link.springer.com/chapter/10.1007/978-3-642-19437-5_23#page-1.

Bauerlein, Mark. *The Dumbest Generation: How the Digital Age Stupefies Young Americans and Jeopardizes Our Future (or, Don't Trust Anyone Under 30)*. Penguin, 2008.

Bayliss, Gemma. "Exploring the Cautionary Attitude toward *Wikipedia* in Higher Education: Implications for Higher Education Institutions." *New Review of Academic Librarianship*, vol. 19, no.1, 2013, pp. 36-57. *Academic Search Complete*, doi:10.1080/13614533.2012.740439.

Burnsed, Brian. "*Wikipedia* Gradually Accepted in College Classrooms." *USNews.com*, 20 June 2011, www.usnews.com/education/best-colleges/articles/2011/06/20/wikipedia-gradually-accepted-in-college-classrooms.

Foster, Andrea L. "Professor Predicts Bleak Future for the Internet." *Chronicle of Higher Education*, 18 Apr. 2008, p. A29, www.chronicle.com/article/Professor-Predicts-Bleak-Fu/31556.

Goldstein, Evan R. "The Dumbing of America?" *Chronicle of Higher Education*, 21 Mar. 2008,

Double-space

1"

1"

Newspaper article accessed from an online database

1"

James 16

p. B4, www.chronicle.com/article/The-Dumbing-of-America-/22127.

Head, Alison J., and Michael B. Eisenberg. "How Today's College Students Use *Wikipedia* for Course-Related Research." *First Monday,* vol. 15, no. 3, 2010. *Google Scholar,* papers.ssrn.com/sol3/papers.cfm?abstract_id=2281527.

Messner, Marcus, et al. "Influencing Public Opinion Opinion from Corn Syrup to Obesity: A Longitudinal Analysis of the References for Nutritional Entries on *Wikipedia*." *First Monday,* vol. 19, no. 11, 2014. *Google Scholar,* www.firstmonday.dk/ojs/index.php/fm/article/view/4823.

Power, June L. "Access the Web: Mobile Apps for Librarians." *Journal of Access Services,* vol. 10, no. 2, 2013, pp. 138–43. *Academic Search Complete,* doi:10.1080/15367967.2013.767690.

"Protection Policy." *Wikipedia,* 10 Mar. 2016, 16:23, en.wikipedia.org/wiki/Protection_policy.

"Reliability of *Wikipedia*." *Wikipedia,* 12 Mar. 2016, 11:02, en.wikipedia.org/wiki/Reliability_of_Wikipedia.

"Researching with *Wikipedia*." *Wikipedia,* 8 Mar. 2016, 15:25, en.wikipedia.org/wiki/Wikipedia:Researching_with_Wikipedia.

Schallan, Joe. "*Wikipedia* Woes." Letter. *American Libraries,* Apr. 2010, p. 9.

Snyder, Johnny. "*Wikipedia*: Librarians' Perspectives on Its Use as a Reference

Journal article without pagination accessed from *Google Scholar*

Signed letter to the editor in a monthly magazine

James 17

Source." *Reference & User Services Quarterly,* vol. 53, no. 2, 2013, pp. 155-63. *Academic Search Complete,* go.galegroup.com.eduproxy.tc-library.org:8080/ps/i.do?id=GALE%7CA361943129.

Tardy, Christine M. "Writing for the World: *Wikipedia* as an Introduction to Academic Writing." *English Teaching Forum,* vol. 48, no. 1, 2010, pp. 12+. *ERIC,* eric.ed.gov/?q=Writing+for+the+World%3a+Wikipedia+%09as+an+Introduction+to+Academic+Writing&id=EJ914884.

Article in an online encyclopedia

"Wiki." *Encyclopaedia Britannica,* 2014, www. britannica.com/topic/wiki.

Unsigned document within a website

"*Wikipedia* Education Program." *Wikipedia,* 10 Mar. 2016, 17:43, wikimediafoundation.org/wiki/Wikipedia_Education_Program.

Wilson, Jodi L. "Proceed with Extreme Caution: Citation to *Wikipedia* in Light of Contributor Demographics and Content Policies." *Vanderbilt Journal of Entertainment & Technology Law,* vol. 16, no. 4, 2014, pp. 857-908. *Academic Search Complete,* web.a.ebscohost.com.ezproxy.cul.columbia.edu/ehost/detail/detail?vid=4&sid=14afe0c2-3351-4754-93dc-2371d2724d5d.

Directory of APA In-Text Citations

1. A work by a single author (p. 166)
2. A work by two authors (p. 166)
3. A work by three to five authors (p. 166)
4. A work by six or more authors (p. 166)
5. Works by authors with the same last name (p. 167)
6. A work by a corporate author (p. 167)
7. A work with no listed author (p. 167)
8. A personal communication (p. 167)
9. An indirect source (p. 167)
10. A specific part of a source (p. 167)
11. An electronic source (p. 163)
12. Two or more works within the same parenthetical reference (p. 163)
13. A table (p. 163)

Directory of APA Reference List Entries

PRINT SOURCES: *Entries for Articles*

Articles in Scholarly Journals

1. An article in a scholarly journal with continuous pagination throughout an annual volume (p. 169)
2. An article in a scholarly journal with separate pagination in each issue (p. 169)
3. A book review in a scholarly journal (unsigned) (p. 170)

Articles in Magazines and Newspapers

4. A magazine article (p. 170)
5. A newspaper article (p. 171)
6. A newspaper editorial (unsigned) (p. 171)
7. A letter to the editor of a newspaper (p. 171)

PRINT SOURCES: *Entries for Books*

Authors

8. A book with one author (p. 172)
9. A book with more than one author (p. 173)
10. A book with no listed author or editor (p. 173)

11. A book with a corporate author (p. 173)
12. An edited book (p. 173)

Editions, Multivolume Works, and Forewords

13. A work in several volumes (p. 173)
14. The foreword, preface, or afterword of a book (p. 173)

Parts of Books

15. A selection from an anthology (p. 173)
16. An article in a reference book (p. 174)

Government and Technical Reports

17. A government report (p. 174)
18. A technical report (p. 174)

ENTRIES FOR MISCELLANEOUS PRINT SOURCES

Letters

19. A personal letter (p. 174)
20. A published letter (p. 174)

ENTRIES FOR OTHER SOURCES

Television Broadcasts, Films, Audio Recordings, Interviews, and Software

21. A television broadcast (p. 174)
22. A television series (p. 175)
23. A film (p. 175)
24. An audio recording (p. 175)
25. A recorded interview (p. 175)
26. A transcription of a recorded interview (p. 175)
27. Software or an app (p. 175)

ELECTRONIC SOURCES: *Entries for Sources from Internet Sites*

Internet-Specific Sources

28. An online article also published in a print source (p. 177)
29. An article in an Internet-only journal (p. 177)
30. A document from a university website (p. 177)
31. An online document (no author identified, no date) (p. 177)
32. An email (p. 177)

33. A blog article or entry (p. 178)
34. A comment on a blog or an online forum (p. 178)
35. An online video (*YouTube*) (p. 178)
36. A podcast (p. 178)
37. A social networking post (*Facebook* post, tweet, etc.) (p. 178)
38. A searchable database (p. 179)

Abstracts and Newspaper Articles

39. An abstract (p. 179)
40. An article in a daily newspaper (p. 179)

CHAPTER 11

APA Documentation Style

11a Using APA Style

APA style* is used extensively in the social sciences. APA documentation has three parts: *parenthetical references in the body of the paper*, a *reference list*, and optional *content footnotes*.

1 Parenthetical References

APA documentation uses short parenthetical references in the body of the essay keyed to an alphabetical list of references at the end of the essay. A typical parenthetical reference consists of the author's last name (followed by a comma) and the year of publication.

> Many people exhibit symptoms of depression after the death of a pet (Russo, 2016).

If the author's name appears in an introductory phrase, include the year of publication there as well.

> According to Russo (2016), many people exhibit symptoms of depression after the death of a pet.

When quoting directly, include the page number, preceded by **p.** in parentheses after the quotation.

> According to Weston (2015), children from one-parent homes read at "a significantly lower level than those from two-parent homes" (p. 58).

Note: A long quotation (forty words or more) is not set in quotation marks. It is set as a block, and the entire quotation is double-spaced and indented one-half inch from the left margin. Parenthetical documentation is placed one space after the final punctuation.

---

*APA documentation format follows the guidelines set in the *Publication Manual of the American Psychological Association*, 6th ed. Washington, DC: APA, 2010.

Sample APA In-Text Citations

1. A Work by a Single Author

Many college students suffer from sleep deprivation (Anton, 2009).

2. A Work by Two Authors

There is growing concern over the use of psychological testing in elementary schools (Albright & Glennon, 2013).

3. A Work by Three to Five Authors

If a work has more than two but fewer than six authors, mention all names in the first reference; in subsequent references in the same paragraph, cite only the first author followed by **et al.** ("and others"). When the reference appears in later paragraphs, include the year.

First Reference

(Sparks, Wilson, & Hewitt, 2015)

Subsequent References in the Same Paragraph

(Sparks et al.)

References in Later Paragraphs

(Sparks et al., 2015)

4. A Work by Six or More Authors

When a work has six or more authors, cite the name of the first author followed by **et al.** and the year in all references.

(Miller et al., 2016)

Close-Up CITING WORKS BY MULTIPLE AUTHORS

When referring to multiple authors in the text of your essay, join the last two names with **and**.

According to Rosen, Wolfe, and Ziff (2015). . . .

Parenthetical references (as well as reference list entries) require an **ampersand (&)**.

(Rosen, Wolfe, & Ziff, 2015)

5. Works by Authors with the Same Last Name

If your reference list includes works by two or more authors with the same last name, use each author's initials in all in-text citations.

> Both F. Bor (2013) and S. D. Bor (2012) concluded that no further study was needed.

6. A Work by a Corporate Author

If the name of a corporate author is long, abbreviate it after the first citation.

First Reference

> (National Institute of Mental Health [NIMH], 2015)

Subsequent Reference

> (NIMH, 2015)

7. A Work with No Listed Author

If a work has no listed author, cite the first two or three words of the title (followed by a comma) and the year. Use quotation marks around titles of periodical articles and chapters of books; use italics for titles of books, periodicals, brochures, reports, and the like.

> ("New Immigration," 2014)

8. A Personal Communication

Cite letters, memos, telephone conversations, personal interviews, emails, messages from electronic bulletin boards, and so on only in the text of your essay—*not* in the reference list

> (R. Takaki, personal communication, October 17, 2015)

9. An Indirect Source

> Cogan and Howe offer very different interpretations of the problem (cited in Swenson, 2015).

10. A Specific Part of a Source

Use abbreviations for the words *page* (**p.**), and *pages* (**pp.**), but spell out *chapter* and *section.*

> These theories have an interesting history (Lee, 2013, chapter 2).

11. An Electronic Source

For an electronic source that does not show page numbers, use the paragraph number preceded by the abbreviation **para.**

> Conversation at the dinner table is an example of a family ritual (Kulp, 2015, para. 3).

In the case of an electronic source that has neither page nor paragraph numbers, cite both the heading in the source and the number of the paragraph following the heading in which the material is located.

> Healthy eating is a never-ending series of free choices (Shapiro, 2016, Introduction section, para. 2).

If the source has no headings, you may not be able to specify an exact location.

12. Two or More Works within the Same Parenthetical Reference

List works by different authors in alphabetical order, separated by semicolons.

> This theory is supported by several studies (Barson & Roth, 2005; Rose, 2010; Tedesco, 2014).

List two or more works by the same author or authors in order of date of publication (separated by commas), with the earliest date first.

> This theory is supported by several studies (Rhodes & Dollek, 2011, 2013, 2015).

For two or more works by the same author published in the same year, designate the work whose title comes first alphabetically *a*, the one whose title comes next *b*, and so on; repeat the year in each citation.

> This theory is supported by several studies (Shapiro, 2014a, 2014b).

13. A Table

If you use a table from a source, give credit to the author in a note at the bottom of the table. Do not include this information in the reference list.

> *Note*. From "Predictors of Employment and Earnings Among JOBS Participants," by P. A. Neenan and D. K. Orthner, 1996, *Social Work Research, 20*(4), p. 233.

2 Reference List

The **reference list** gives the publication information for all the sources you cite. It should appear at the end of your essay on a new numbered page titled **References**. Entries in the reference list should be arranged alphabetically. Double-space within and between reference list entries. The first line of each entry should start at the left margin, with the second and subsequent lines indented one-half inch. (**See 12b** for full manuscript guidelines.)

APA PRINT SOURCES Entries for Articles

Article citations include the author's name (last name first); the date of publication (in parentheses); the title of the article; the title of the periodical (italicized); the volume number (italicized); the issue number, if any (in parentheses); and the inclusive page numbers (including all digits). Figure 11.1 on page 164 shows where you can find this information.

Capitalize the first word of the article's title and subtitle as well as any proper nouns. Do not underline or italicize the title of the article or enclose it in quotation marks. Give the periodical title in full, and capitalize all words except articles, prepositions, and conjunctions of fewer than four letters. Use **p.** or **pp.** when referring to page numbers in newspapers, but omit this abbreviation when referring to page numbers in journals and popular magazines.

Articles in Scholarly Journals

1. An Article in a Scholarly Journal with Continuous Pagination throughout an Annual Volume

Case, C. A., Hensley, R., & Anderson, A. (2014). Reflecting on heterosexual and male privilege: Interventions to raise awareness. *Journal of Social Issues, 70*, 722-740.

2. An Article in a Scholarly Journal with Separate Pagination in Each Issue

Zell, E., Krizan, Z., & Teeter, S. R. (2015). Evaluating gender similarities and differences using metasynthesis. *American Psychologist, 70*(1), 10-20.

Note: Do not leave a space between the volume and issue numbers.

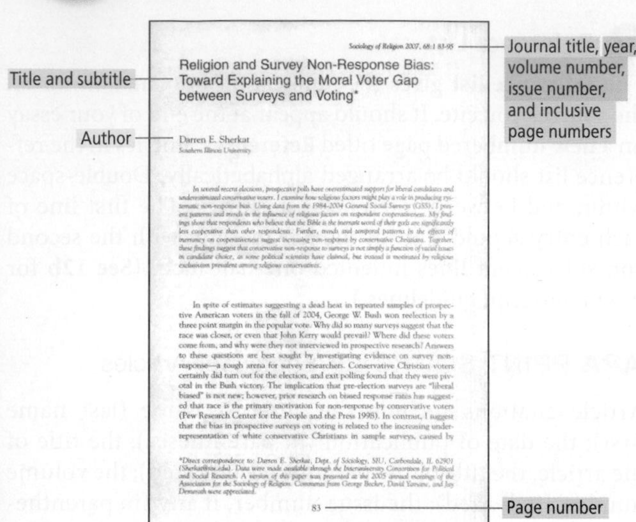

Sociology of Religion 2007, 68:1 83-95

Religion and Survey Non-Response Bias: Toward Explaining the Moral Voter Gap between Surveys and Voting*

Darren E. Sherkat
Southern Illinois University

In several recent elections, prospective polls have overestimated support for liberal candidates and underestimated conservative voters. I examine how religious factors might play a role in producing systematic non-response bias. Using data from the 1984-2004 General Social Surveys (GSS), I present patterns and trends in the influence of religious factors on respondent cooperativeness. My findings show that respondents who believe that the Bible is the inerrant word of their gods are significantly less cooperative than other respondents. Further, trends and temporal patterns in the effects of inerrancy on cooperativeness suggest increasing non-response by conservative Christians. Together, these findings suggest that conservative non-response to surveys is not simply a function of racial issues in candidate choice, as some political scientists have claimed, but instead is motivated by religious exclusivism prevalent among religious conservatives.

In spite of estimates suggesting a dead heat in repeated samples of prospective American voters in the fall of 2004, George W. Bush won reelection by a three point margin in the popular vote. Why did so many surveys suggest that the race was closer, or even that John Kerry would prevail? Where did these voters come from, and why were they not interviewed in prospective research? Answers to these questions are best sought by investigating evidence on survey non-response—a tough arena for survey researchers. Conservative Christian voters certainly did turn out for the election, and exit polling found that they were pivotal in the Bush victory. The implication that pre-election surveys are "liberal biased" is not new; however, prior research on biased response rates has suggested that race is the primary motivation for non-response by conservative voters (Pew Research Center for the People and the Press 1998). In contrast, I suggest that the bias in prospective surveys on voting is related to the increasing underrepresentation of white conservative Christians in sample surveys, caused by

Direct correspondence to: Darren E. Sherkat, Dept. of Sociology, SIU, Carbondale, IL 62901 (Sherkat@siu.edu). Data were made available through the Interuniversity Consortium for Political and Social Research. A version of this paper was presented at the 2005 annual meetings of the Association for the Sociology of Religion. Comments from George Becker, David Yamane, and Jay Demerath were appreciated.

83

FIGURE 11.1 First page of an article showing the location of the information needed for documentation. © Association for the Sociology of Religion.

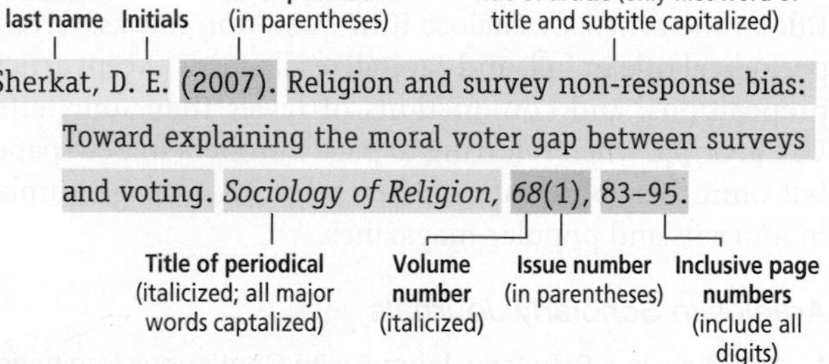

3. A Book Review in a Scholarly Journal (Unsigned)

A review with no author should be listed by title, followed by a description of the reviewed work in brackets.

> Coming of age and joining the cult of thinness [Review of the book *The cult of thinness*, by Sharlene Nagy Hesse-Biber]. (2008, June). *Psychology of Women Quarterly, 32*(2), 221–222.

Articles in Magazines and Newspapers

4. A Magazine Article

> Drevitch, G. (2014, May–June). Pop psychology. *Psychology Today, 47*, 40.

5. A Newspaper Article

If an article appears on nonconsecutive pages, give all page numbers, separated by commas (for example, **A1, A14**). If the article appears on consecutive pages, indicate the full range of pages (for example, **A7–A9**).

> Jargon, J. (2010, December 27). On McDonald's menu: Variety, caution. *Wall Street Journal,* pp. A1, A14.

6. A Newspaper Editorial (Unsigned)

An editorial with no author should be listed by title, followed by the label **Editorial** in brackets.

> The plight of the underinsured [Editorial]. (2008, June 12). *The New York Times,* p. A30.

7. A Letter to the Editor of a Newspaper

> Mania, M. (2015, February 19). Superfluous selfie sticks [Letter to the editor]. *The New York Times,* p. A24.

APA PRINT SOURCES Entries for Books

Book citations include the author's name (last name first); the year of publication (in parentheses); the book title (italicized); and publication information. Figures 11.2 and 11.3 on page 166 show where you can find this information.

Capitalize only the first word of the title and subtitle and any proper nouns. Include any additional necessary information—edition, report number, or volume number, for example—in parentheses after the title. In the publication information, write out in full the names of associations, corporations, and university presses. Include the words **Book** and **Press**, but do not include terms such as **Publishers, Co.**, or **Inc.**

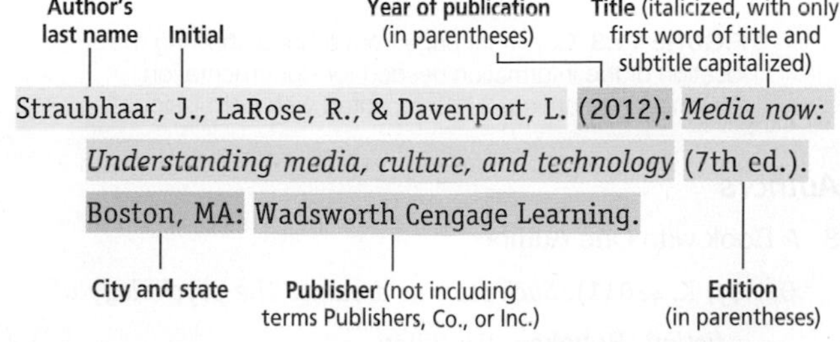

MEDIA NOW — Title

Understanding Media, Culture, and Technology — Subtitle

SEVENTH EDITION — Edition

JOSEPH STRAUBHAAR — Authors
University of Texas, Austin

ROBERT LA ROSE
Michigan State University

LUCINDA DAVENPORT
Michigan State University

WADSWORTH
CENGAGE Learning

Australia • Brazil • Japan • Korea • Mexico • Singapore • Spain • United Kingdom • United States

Publisher

FIGURE 11.2 Title page from a book showing the location of the information needed for documentation. © Cengage Learning, 2012; reprinted with permission.

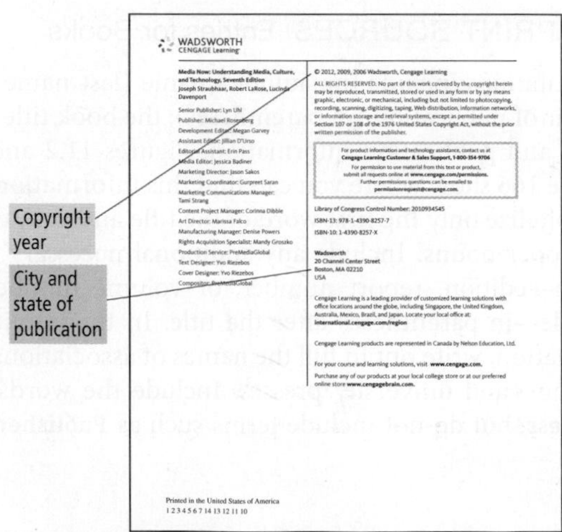

WADSWORTH
CENGAGE Learning

Media Now: Understanding Media, Culture, and Technology, Seventh Edition
Joseph Straubhaar, Robert LaRose, Lucinda Davenport

Senior Publisher: Lyn Uhl
Publisher: Michael Rosenberg
Development Editor: Megan Garvey
Assistant Editor: Jillian D'Urso
Editorial Assistant: Erin Pass
Media Editor: Jessica Badiner
Marketing Director: Jason Sakos
Marketing Coordinator: Gurpreet Saran
Marketing Communications Manager: Tami Strang
Content Project Manager: Corinna Dibble
Art Director: Marissa Falco
Manufacturing Manager: Denise Powers
Rights Acquisition Specialist: Mandy Groszko
Production Service: PreMediaGlobal
Text Designer: Yvo Riezebos
Cover Designer: Yvo Riezebos
Compositor: PreMediaGlobal

For product information and technology assistance, contact us at
Cengage Learning Customer & Sales Support, 1-800-354-9706
For permission to use material from this text or product,
submit all requests online at **www.cengage.com/permissions.**
Further permissions questions can be emailed to
permissionrequest@cengage.com.

Library of Congress Control Number: 2010934545

ISBN-13: 978-1-4390-8257-7

ISBN-10: 1-4390-8257-X

Wadsworth
20 Channel Center Street
Boston, MA 02210
USA

Cengage Learning is a leading provider of customized learning solutions with office locations around the globe, including Singapore, the United Kingdom, Australia, Mexico, Brazil, and Japan. Locate your local office at: **international.cengage.com/region**

Cengage Learning products are represented in Canada by Nelson Education, Ltd.

For your course and learning solutions, visit **www.cengage.com.**

Purchase any of our products at your local college store or at our preferred online store **www.cengagebrain.com.**

Printed in the United States of America
1 2 3 4 5 6 7 14 13 12 11 10

FIGURE 11.3 Copyright page from a book showing the location of the information needed for documentation. © Cengage Learning, 2012; reprinted with permission.

Authors

8. A Book with One Author

Oatley, K. (2011). *Such stuff as dreams: The psychology of fiction*. Hoboken, NJ: Wiley.

9. A Book with More Than One Author

List up to seven authors by last name and initials, using an ampersand (&) to connect the last two names. For more than seven authors, insert an ellipsis (three spaced periods) and add the last author's name.

Wolfinger, D., Knable, P., Richards, H. L., & Silberger, R. (2007). *The chronically unemployed.* New York, NY: Berman Press.

10. A Book with No Listed Author or Editor

Teaching in a wired classroom. (2012). Philadelphia, PA: Drexel Press.

11. A Book with a Corporate Author

When the author and the publisher are the same, include the word **Author** at the end of the citation instead of repeating the publisher's name.

League of Women Voters of the United States. (2008). *Local league handbook*. Washington, DC: Author.

12. An Edited Book

Wienroth, M., & Rodriques, E. (Eds.). (2015). *Knowing new biotechnologies: Social aspects of technological convergence*. New York, NY: Routledge.

Editions, Multivolume Works, and Forewords

13. A Work in Several Volumes

O'Connor, E. E., & Garofalo, L. (2010). *Documenting Latin America: Gender, race, and nation*. (Vols. 1–2). New York, NY: Pearson.

14. The Foreword, Preface, or Afterword of a Book

Taylor, T. (1979). Preface. In B. B. Ferencz, *Less than slaves* (pp. ii–ix). Cambridge, MA: Harvard University Press.

Parts of Books

15. A Selection from an Anthology

Give inclusive page numbers preceded by **pp.** (in parentheses) after the title of the anthology. The title of the selection is not enclosed in quotation marks.

Lorde, A. (1984). Age, race, and class. In P. S. Rothenberg (Ed.), *Racism and sexism: An integrated study* (pp. 352–360). New York, NY: St. Martin's Press.

Note: If you cite two or more selections from the same anthology, give the full citation for the anthology in each entry.

16. An Article in a Reference Book

Edwards, P. (Ed.). (2006). Determinism. In *The encyclopedia of philosophy* (Vol. 2, pp. 359–373). New York, NY: Macmillan.

Government and Technical Reports

17. A Government Report

U.S. Department of Health and Human Services, National Institutes of Health, National Institute of Mental Health. (2007). *Motion pictures and violence: A summary report of research* (DHHS Publication No. ADM 91-22187). Washington, DC: Government Printing Office.

18. A Technical Report

Attali, Y., & Powers, D. (2008). *Effect of immediate feedback and revision on psychometric properties of open-ended GRE® subject test items* (ETS GRE Board Research Report No. 04-05). Princeton, NJ: Educational Testing Service.

APA ENTRIES FOR MISCELLANEOUS PRINT SOURCES

Letters

19. A Personal Letter

References to unpublished personal letters, like references to all other personal communications, should be included only in the text of the essay, not in the reference list.

20. A Published Letter

Joyce, J. (1931). Letter to Louis Gillet. In Richard Ellmann, *James Joyce* (p. 631). New York, NY: Oxford University Press.

APA ENTRIES FOR OTHER SOURCES

Television Broadcasts, Films, Audio Recordings, Interviews, and Software

21. A Television Broadcast

Murphy, J. (Executive Producer). (2006, March 4). *The CBS evening news* [Television broadcast]. New York, NY: Columbia Broadcasting Service.

22. A Television Series Episode

Bedard, B. (Writer). (2014). Best new girl [Television series episode]. In J. Solloway (Executive Producer), *Transparent*. Los Angeles, CA: Amazon Studios.

23. A Film

Colson, C., Winfrey, O., Gardner, D., and Kleiner, J. (Producers), & DuVernay, A. (Director). (2014). *Selma* [Motion picture]. United States: Paramount Pictures.

24. An Audio Recording

Beck. (2014). Don't let it go. On *Morning phase* [MP3]. Los Angeles, CA: Capitol Records.

Knowles, B., & Asher, J. (2013). Heaven. On *Beyoncé* [CD]. New York, NY: Columbia Records.

25. A Recorded Interview

Bartel, S. S. (1978, November 5). Interview by L. Clark [Tape recording]. Billy Graham Center, Wheaton College. BGC Archives, Wheaton, IL.

26. A Transcription of a Recorded Interview

Berry, D. W. (1986, February 14). *Interview with Donald Wesley Berry—Collection 325*. Billy Graham Center, Wheaton College. BGC Archives, Wheaton, IL.

27. Software or an App

Sharp, S. (2009). Career Selection Tests (Version 7.0) [Software]. Chico, CA: Avocation Software.

Handup. (2014). *Handup vote* (Version 2.0.1) [Mobile application software]. Retrieved from http://itunes.apple.com

APA ELECTRONIC SOURCES — Entries for Sources from Internet Sites

APA guidelines for documenting electronic sources focus on web sources, which often do not include all the bibliographic information that print sources do. For example, web sources may not include page numbers or a place of publication. At a minimum, a web citation should have a title, a date (the date of publication, update, or retrieval), and a Digital Object Identifier (DOI) (when available) or an electronic address (URL). If possible, also include the author(s) of a source. Figure 11.4 shows where you can find this information.

When you need to divide a URL at the end of a line, break it after a double slash or before most other punctuation (do not add a hyphen). Do not add a period at the end of the URL.

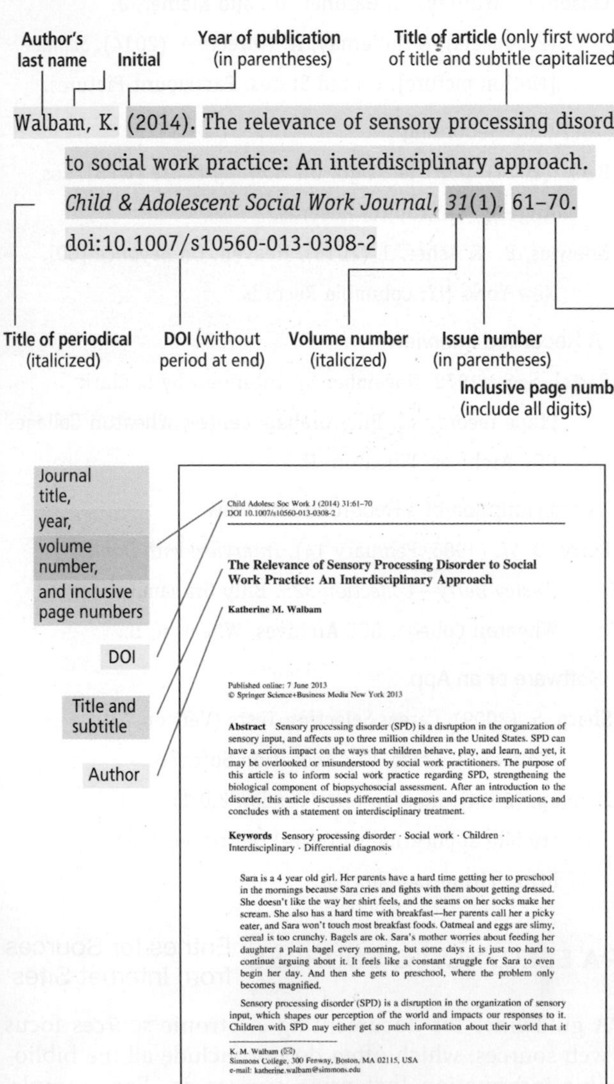

Child Adolesc Soc Work J (2014) 31:61–70
DOI 10.1007/s10560-013-0308-2

The Relevance of Sensory Processing Disorder to Social Work Practice: An Interdisciplinary Approach

Katherine M. Walbam

Published online: 7 June 2013
© Springer Science+Business Media New York 2013

Abstract Sensory processing disorder (SPD) is a disruption in the organization of sensory input, and affects up to three million children in the United States. SPD can have a serious impact on the ways that children behave, play, and learn, and yet, it may be overlooked or misunderstood by social work practitioners. The purpose of this article is to inform social work practice regarding SPD, strengthening the biological component of biopsychosocial assessment. After an introduction to the disorder, this article discusses differential diagnosis and practice implications, and concludes with a statement on interdisciplinary treatment.

Keywords Sensory processing disorder · Social work · Children · Interdisciplinary · Differential diagnosis

Sara is a 4 year old girl. Her parents have a hard time getting her to preschool in the mornings because Sara cries and fights with them about getting dressed. She doesn't like the way her shirt feels, and the seams on her socks make her scream. She also has a hard time with breakfast—her parents call her a picky eater, and Sara won't touch most breakfast foods. Oatmeal and eggs are slimy, cereal is too crunchy. Bagels are ok. Sara's mother worries about feeding her daughter a plain bagel every morning, but some days it is just too hard to continue arguing about it. It feels like a constant struggle for Sara to even begin her day. And then she gets to preschool, where the problem only becomes magnified.

Sensory processing disorder (SPD) is a disruption in the organization of sensory input, which shapes our perception of the world and impacts our responses to it. Children with SPD may either get so much information about their world that it

K. M. Walbam (✉)
Simmons College, 300 Fenway, Boston, MA 02115, USA
e-mail: katherine.walbam@simmons.edu

Springer

FIGURE 11.4 Part of an online article showing the location of the information needed for documentation. https://ebscohost.com

Internet-Specific Sources

28. An Online Article Also Published in a Print Source

If the article has a DOI, you do not need to include the retrieval date or the URL. Always include the volume number (italicized) and the issue number (in parentheses, if available).

Rutledge, P. C., Park, A., & Sher, K. J. (2008). 21st birthday drinking: Extremely extreme. *Journal of Consulting and Clinical Psychology, 76*(3), 511–516. doi:10.1037/0022-006X.76.3.511

29. An Article in an Internet-Only Journal

If the article does not have a DOI, include the URL. Always include the URL (when available) for the archived version of the article. If you accessed the article through an online database, include the URL for the home page of the journal. (If a single URL links to multiple articles, include the URL for the journal's home page.) No retrieval date is needed for content that is not likely to be changed or updated—for example, a journal article or a book.

Hill, S. A., & Laugharne, R. (2006). Patient choice survey in general adult psychiatry. *Psychiatry On-Line*. Retrieved from http://www.priory.co.uk/psych.htm

30. A Document from a University Website

Beck, S. E. (2008, April 3). *The good, the bad & the ugly: Or, why it's a good idea to evaluate web sources.* Retrieved July 7, 2014, from New Mexico State University Library website: http://lib.nmsu.edu/instruction/evalcrit.html

31. An Online Document (No Author Identified, No Date)

A document with no author or date should be listed by title, followed by the abbreviation **n.d.** (for "no date"), the retrieval date, and the URL.

The stratocaster appreciation page. (n.d.). Retrieved July 27, 2015, from http://members.tripod.com/~AFH

32. An Email

As with all other personal communications, citations for email should be included only in the text of your essay, not in the reference list.

33. A Blog Article or Entry

List the author's name—or, if that is not available, the author's screen name. In brackets after the title, provide information that will help readers access this particular post. APA style recommends the term Web log post, but ask your instructor if Blog post is an acceptable alternative.

Sullivan, A. (2015, February 15). The war [Web log post]. On *The daily dish*. Retrieved from http://dish.andrewsullivan.com/2015/02/06/the-war-4/

34. A Comment on a Blog or an Online Forum

Jamie. (2010, June 26). Re: Trying to lose 50 million pounds [Web log comment]. Retrieved from http://blogs.wsj.com/numbersguy

Silva, T. (2007, March 9). Severe stress can damage a child's brain [Online forum comment]. Retrieved from http://groups.google.com/group/sci.psychology.psychotherapy.moderated

35. An Online Video (*YouTube*)

Learning Without Borders. (2012, February 1). The purpose of education [Video file]. Retrieved from https://www.youtube.com/watch?v=DdNAUJWJN08

36. A Podcast

Koenig, S., & Snyder, J. (Producers). (2014). The alibi [Podcast episode]. In *Serial*. Chicago, IL: Chicago Public Media.

37. A Social Networking Post (*Facebook* post, tweet, etc.)

Provide up to the first forty words of a *Facebook*, *Twitter*, *Instagram*, or similar post. For a tweet, begin with the author's listed name, followed by the author's *Twitter* name in brackets (as in the first example below).

Muna, D. [DemitriMuna]. (2014, February 21). Opposed to GM foods? Stop eating grapefruit; they are genetically modified. There was no such thing as a grapefruit before the 18th century [Tweet]. Retrieved from https://twitter.com/demitrimuna/status/569349630887985152

Psychology Today. (2015, February 18). Do people just not get you? This may be why: https://www.psychologytoday.com/articles/200909/are-you-misunderstood? [Facebook status update]. Retrieved from https://www.facebook.com/psychologytoday

38. A Searchable Database

Include the database name only if the material you are citing is obscure, out of print, or otherwise difficult to locate. No retrieval date is needed.

Murphy, M. E. (1940, December 15). When war comes. *Vital Speeches of the Day, 7*(5), 139–144. Retrieved from http://www.vsotd.com

Abstracts and Newspaper Articles

39. An Abstract

Qiong, L. (2008, July). After the quake: Psychological treatment following the disaster. *China Today, 57*(7), 18–21. Abstract retrieved from http://www.chinatoday.com.cn/ctenglish/index.htm

40. An Article in a Daily Newspaper

Lowrey, A. (2014, February 20). Study finds greater income inequality in nation's thriving cities. *The New York Times*. Retrieved from http://www.nytimes.com

3 Content Footnotes

APA format permits content notes, indicated by **superscripts** in the text. The notes are listed on a separate numbered page, titled **Footnotes**, after the reference list and before any appendices. Double-space all notes, indenting the first line of each note one-half inch and beginning subsequent lines flush left. Number the notes with superscripts that correspond to the numbers in your text.

11b APA-Style Manuscript Guidelines

Social science essays label sections with headings. Sections may include an introduction (untitled), followed by headings such as **Background, Method, Results**, and **Conclusion**.

Each section of a social science essay is a complete unit with a beginning and an end so that it can be read separately and still make sense out of context. The body of the essay may include charts, graphs, maps, photographs, flowcharts, or tables.

CHECKLIST

Typing Your Essay

When you type your essay, use the student essay in **11c** as your model.

- ❑ Leave one-inch margins at the top and bottom and on both sides. Double-space your essay throughout.
- ❑ Indent the first line of every paragraph and the first line of every content footnote one-half inch from the left-hand margin.
- ❑ Set off a **long quotation** (more than forty words) in a block format by indenting the entire quotation one-half inch from the left-hand margin. Do not indent the first line further.
- ❑ Number all pages consecutively. Each page should include a **page header** (or **running head**) typed one-half inch from the top of the page. Type the page header flush left and the page number flush right.
- See 39b ❑ Center major headings, and type them with uppercase and lowercase letters. Place minor headings flush left, typed with uppercase and lowercase letters. Use boldface for both major and minor headings.
- See 39c ❑ Format items in a series as a numbered list.
- ❑ Arrange the pages of the essay in the following order:
  - ❑ **Title page** (page 1) with a running head (in all uppercase letters), page number, title, your name, and the name of your school. (Your instructor may require additional information.)
  - ❑ **Abstract and keywords** (page 2)
  - ❑ **Text of essay** (beginning on page 3)
  - ❑ **Reference list** (new page)
  - ❑ **Content footnotes** (new page)
  - ❑ **Appendices** (start each appendix on a new page)
- See 11a ❑ Citations should follow APA documentation style.

CHECKLIST

Using Visuals

APA style distinguishes between two types of visuals: **tables** and **figures** (charts, graphs, photographs, and diagrams). In manuscripts not intended for publication, tables and figures are included in the text. A short table or figure should appear on the page where it is discussed; a long table or figure should be placed on a separate page just after the page where it is discussed.

Tables

Number all **tables** consecutively. Each table should have a *label* and a *title*.

- ❑ The **label** consists of the word **Table** (not in italics), along with an arabic numeral, typed flush left above the table.
- ❑ Double-space and type a brief explanatory **title** for each table (in italics) flush left below the label. Capitalize the first letters of principal words of the title.

Table 7

Frequency of Negative Responses of Dorm Students to

Questions Concerning Alcohol Consumption

Figures

Number all **figures** consecutively. Each figure should have a *label* and a *caption*.

- ❑ The **label** consists of the word ***Figure*** (typed flush left below the figure) followed by the figure number (both in italics).
- ❑ The **caption** explains the figure and serves as a title. Double-space the caption, but do not italicize it. Capitalize only the first word and any proper nouns, and end the caption with a period. The caption follows the label (on the same line).

Figure 1. Duration of responses measured in seconds.

Note: If you use a table or figure from an outside source, include full source information in a note at the bottom of the table or figure. This information does not appear in your reference list.

CHECKLIST

Preparing the APA Reference List

When typing your reference list, follow these guidelines:

- ❑ Begin the reference list on a new page after the last page of text, numbered as the next page of the essay.
- ❑ Center the title **References** at the top of the page.
- ❑ List the items in the reference list alphabetically (with author's last name first).
- ❑ Type the first line of each entry at the left margin. Indent subsequent lines one-half inch.
- ❑ Separate the major divisions of each entry with a period and one space.
- ❑ Double-space the reference list within and between entries.

Close-Up ARRANGING ENTRIES IN THE APA REFERENCE LIST

- Single-author entries precede multiple-author entries that begin with the same name.

  Field, S. (2015).

  Field, S., & Levitt, M. P. (2012).

- Entries by the same author or authors are arranged according to date of publication, starting with the earliest date.

  Ruthenberg, H., & Rubin, R. (2013).

  Ruthenberg, H., & Rubin, R. (2015).

- Entries with the same author or authors and date of publication are arranged alphabetically according to title. Lowercase letters (*a*, *b*, *c*, and so on) that indicate the order of publication are placed within parentheses.

  Wolk, E. M. (2016a). Analysis . . .

  Wolk, E. M. (2016b). Hormonal . . .

11c Model APA-Style Research Paper

The following student essay, "Sleep Deprivation in College Students," uses APA documentation style. It includes a title page, an abstract, a reference list, a table, and a bar graph. The web citations in this student essay do not have DOIs, so URLs have been provided instead.

½"

Running head: SLEEP DEPRIVATION 1 Page header

Sleep Deprivation in College Students — Title

Andrew J. Neale — Your name

University of Texas — School

Psychology 215, Section 4 — Course title

Dr. Reiss — Instructor's name

March 12, 2015 — Date

SLEEP DEPRIVATION 1″ 2 Page header on every page

Center heading

Abstract

A survey was conducted of 50 first-year college students in an introductory biology class. The survey consisted of five questions regarding the causes and results of sleep deprivation and specifically addressed the students' study methods and the grades they received on the fall midterm. The study's hypothesis was that although students believe that forgoing sleep to study will yield better grades, sleep deprivation may actually cause a decrease in performance. The study concluded that while only 43% of the students who received either an A or a B on the fall midterm deprived themselves of sleep in order to cram for the test, 90% of those who received a C or a D were sleep deprived.

Abstract typed as a single paragraph in block format (not indented)

Keywords: sleep disorders, sleep deprivation, grade performance, grades and sleep, forgoing sleep

An optional list of keywords helps readers find your work in databases. Check with your instructor to see if this list is required.

SLEEP DEPRIVATION 3

Sleep Deprivation in College Students

Full title (centered)

Indent ½"

Introduction

For many college students, sleep is a luxury they feel they cannot afford. Bombarded with tests and assignments and limited by a 24-hour day, students often attempt to make up time by doing without sleep. Unfortunately, students may actually hurt their academic performance by failing to get enough sleep. According to several psychological and medical studies, sleep deprivation can lead to memory loss and health problems, both of which can harm a student's academic performance.

Double-space

Thesis statement

Background

Heading (centered and boldfaced)

Sleep is often overlooked as an essential part of a healthy lifestyle. Each day, millions of Americans wake up without having gotten enough sleep. This fact indicates that for many people, sleep is viewed as a luxury rather than a necessity. As National Sleep Foundation Executive Director Richard L. Gelula observes, "Some of the problems we face as a society—from road rage to obesity—may be linked to lack of sleep or poor sleep" (National Sleep Foundation, 2002, para. 3). In fact, according to the National Sleep Foundation, sleep deprivation "jolts the immune system into action, reflecting the same type of immediate response shown during exposure to stress . . ." (2012, para. 1).

1" 1"

Literature review (paras. 2–7)

Quotation requires its own documentation and a page number (or a paragraph number for Internet sources)

Sleep deprivation is particularly common among college students, many of whom have busy lives and are required to absorb a great deal of material before their exams. It is common for

1"

SLEEP DEPRIVATION 4

college students to take a quick nap between classes or fall asleep while studying in the library because they are sleep deprived. Approximately 44% of young adults experience daytime sleepiness at least a few days a month (National Sleep Foundation, 2002, para. 6). In particular, many students are sleep deprived on the day of an exam because they stayed up all night studying. These students believe that if they read and review immediately before taking a test—even though this usually means losing sleep—they will remember more information and thus get better grades. However, this is not the case.

Student uses past tense when discussing other researchers' studies

A study conducted by professors Mary Carskadon at Brown University in Providence, Rhode Island, and Amy Wolfson at the College of the Holy Cross in Worcester, Massachusetts, showed that high school students who got adequate sleep were more likely to do well in their classes (Carpenter, 2001). According to this study, students who went to bed early on both weeknights and weekends earned mainly A's and B's. The students who received D's and F's averaged about 35 minutes less sleep per day than the high achievers (cited in Carpenter, 2001). The results of this study suggest that sleep is associated with high academic achievement.

Cited in indicates an indirect source

Once students reach college, however, many believe that sleep is a luxury they can do without. For example, students believe that if they use the time they would normally sleep to study, they

SLEEP DEPRIVATION 5

will do better on exams. A survey of 144 undergraduate students in introductory psychology classes disproved this assumption. According to this study, "long sleepers," those individuals who slept 9 or more hours out of a 24-hour day, had significantly higher grade point averages (GPAs) than "short sleepers," individuals who slept less than 7 hours out of a 24-hour day. Therefore, contrary to the belief of many college students, more sleep is often associated with a high GPA (Kelly, Kelly, & Clanton, 2001).

Many students believe that sleep deprivation is not the cause of their poor performance, but rather that a host of other factors is to blame. A study in the *Journal of American College Health* tested the effect that several factors have on a student's performance in school, as measured by students' GPAs. Some of the factors considered were exercise, sleep, nutritional habits, social support, time management techniques, stress management techniques, and spiritual health (Trockel, Barnes, & Egget, 2000). The most significant correlation discovered in the study was between GPA and the sleep habits of students. Sleep deprivation had a more negative impact on GPAs than any other factor (Trockel et al., 2000).

First reference includes all three authors; *et al.* replaces second and third authors in subsequent reference in same paragraph

Despite these findings, many students continue to believe that they will be able to remember more material if they do not sleep before an exam. They fear that sleeping will interfere with their ability to retain information.

SLEEP DEPRIVATION 6

Pilcher and Walters (1997), however, showed that sleep deprivation actually impaired learning skills. In this study, one group of students was sleep deprived, while the other got 8 hours of sleep before the exam. The students in each group estimated how well they had performed on the exam. The students who were sleep deprived believed their performance on the test was better than did those who were not sleep deprived, but actually the performance of the sleep-deprived students was significantly worse than that of those who got 8 hours of sleep prior to the test (Pilcher & Walters, 1997, cited in Bubolz, Brown, & Soper, 2001). This study supports the hypothesis that sleep deprivation harms cognitive performance.

Student uses past tense when discussing his own research study

A survey of students in an introductory biology class at the University of Texas, which demonstrated the effects of sleep deprivation on academic performance, also supported the hypothesis that despite students' beliefs, forgoing sleep does not lead to better test scores.

Method

To determine the causes and results of sleep deprivation, a study of the relationship between sleep and test performance was conducted. Fifty first-year college students in an introductory biology class were surveyed, and their performance on the fall midterm was analyzed.

Each student was asked to complete a survey consisting of the following five questions about their sleep patterns and their performance on the fall midterm:

1. Do you regularly deprive yourself of sleep when studying for an exam?
2. Did you deprive yourself of sleep when studying for the fall midterm?
3. What was your grade on the exam?
4. Do you feel your performance was helped or harmed by the amount of sleep you had?
5. Will you deprive yourself of sleep when you study for the final exam?

Numbered list is indented 1/2" and set in block format

To maintain confidentiality, the students were asked not to put their names on the survey. Also, to determine whether the students answered question 3 truthfully, the group grade distribution from the surveys was compared to the number of A's, B's, C's, and D's shown in the instructor's record of the test results. The two frequency distributions were identical.

Results

Analysis of the survey data indicated a significant difference between the grades of students who were sleep deprived and the grades of those who were not. The results of the survey are presented in Table 1.

Table 1 introduced

The grades in the class were curved so that out of 50 students, 10 received A's, 20 received B's, 10 received C's, and 10 received D's. For the purposes of this survey, an A or B on the exam indicates that the student performed well.

SLEEP DEPRIVATION 8

A grade of C or D on the exam is considered a poor grade.

Table placed on page where it is discussed

Table 1

Results of Survey of Students in University of Texas Introduction to Biology Class Examining the Relationship between Sleep Deprivation and Academic Performance

Table created by student; no documentation necessary

Grade totals	Sleep deprived	Not sleep deprived	Usually sleep deprived	Improved	Harmed	Continue sleep deprivation?
A = 10	4	6	1	4	0	4
B = 20	9	11	8	8	1	8
C = 10	10	0	6	5	4	7
D = 10	8	2	2	1	3	2
Total	31	19	17	18	8	21

Statistical findings in table discussed

Of the 50 students in the class, 31 (or 62%) said they deprived themselves of sleep when studying for the fall midterm. Of these students, 17 (or 34% of the class) reported that they regularly deprive themselves of sleep before an exam.

Of the 31 students who said they deprived themselves of sleep when studying for the fall midterm, only 4 earned A's, and the majority of the A's in the class were received by those students who were not sleep deprived. Even more significant was the fact that of the 4 students who were sleep deprived and got A's, only one student claimed to usually be sleep deprived on the day of an exam. Thus, assuming the students who earn A's in a class do well in general, it is possible that sleep deprivation did not help or harm these students' grades. Not surprisingly, of the 4 students who received A's and were sleep deprived, all said they would continue this behavior pattern.

The majority of those who deprived themselves of sleep received B's and C's on the exam. A total of 20 students earned a grade of B on the exam. Of those students, only 9, or 18% of the class, said they were deprived of sleep when they took the test.

Students who said they were sleep deprived when they took the exam received the majority of the poor grades. Ten students got C's on the midterm, and of these 10 students, 100% said they were sleep deprived when they took the test. Of the 10 students (20% of the class) who got D's, 8 said they were sleep deprived. Figure 1 shows the significant relationship that was found between poor grades on the exam and sleep deprivation.

Figure 1 Introduced

Conclusion

For many students, sleep is viewed as a luxury rather than as a necessity. Particularly during exam periods, students use the hours in which they would normally sleep to study. However, this behavior does not seem to be effective. The survey discussed here reveals a definite correlation between sleep deprivation and lower exam scores. In fact, the majority of students who performed well on the exam,

SLEEP DEPRIVATION 10

Figure placed as close as possible to discussion in essay

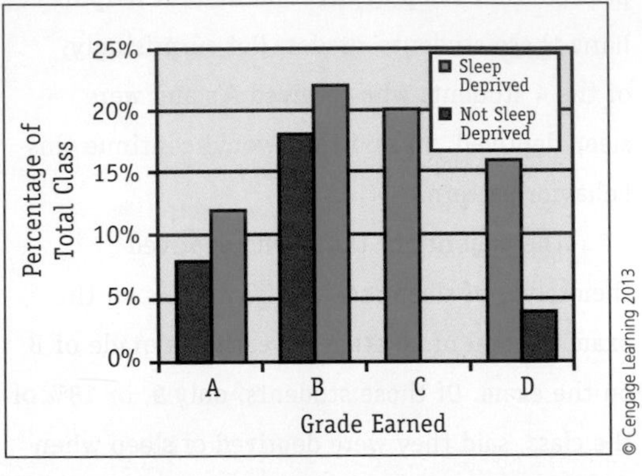

Label and caption

(No source information needed for graph based on student's original data)

Figure 1. Results of a survey of students in a University of Texas Introduction to Biology class, examining the relationship between sleep deprivation and academic performance.

earning either A's or B's, were not deprived of sleep. Therefore, students who choose studying over sleep should consider that sleep deprivation may actually lead to impaired academic performance.

SLEEP DEPRIVATION 1" 11

References ← Center heading

Bubolz, W., Brown, F., & Soper, B. (2001). Sleep habits and patterns of college students: A preliminary study. *Journal of American College Health*, *50*, 131–135.

Carpenter, S. (2001). Sleep deprivation may be undermining teen health. *Monitor on Psychology*, *32*(9). Retrieved from http://www.apa.org/monitor/oct01/sleepteen.html

Kelly, W. E., Kelly, K. E., & Clanton, R. C. (2001). The relationship between sleep length and grade-point average among college students. *College Student Journal*, *35*(1), 84–90.

National Sleep Foundation. (2002, April 2). *Epidemic of daytime sleepiness linked to increased feelings of anger, stress and pessimism*. Retrieved from http://www.sleepfoundation.org

National Sleep Foundation. (2012, July 1). *Sleep deprivation effect on the immune system mirrors physical stress*. Retrieved from http://www.sleepfoundation.org

Trockel, M., Barnes, M., & Egget, D. (2000). Health-related variables and academic performance among first-year college students: Implications for sleep and other behaviors. *Journal of American College Health*, *49*, 125–131.

Indent ½"

Double-space

Entries listed in alphabetical order

URL is provided for web citation that does not have a DOI

Directory of Chicago-Style Endnotes and Bibliography Entries

PRINT SOURCES: *Entries for Articles*

Articles in Scholarly Journals

1. An article in a scholarly journal with continuous pagination throughout an annual volume (p. 198)
2. An article in a scholarly journal with separate pagination in each issue (p. 198)

Articles in Magazines and Newspapers

3. An article in a weekly magazine (signed/unsigned) (p. 199)
4. An article in a monthly magazine (signed) (p. 199)
5. An article in a monthly magazine (unsigned) (p. 199)
6. An article in a newspaper (signed) (p. 199)
7. An article in a newspaper (unsigned) (p. 200)
8. A letter to the editor of a newspaper (p. 200)
9. A book review in a newspaper (p. 200)

PRINT SOURCES: *Entries for Books*

Authors and Editors

10. A book by one author or editor (p. 201)
11. A book by two or three authors or editors (p. 201)
12. A book by more than three authors or editors (p. 202)
13. A book with no listed author or editor (p. 202)
14. A book by a corporate author (p. 202)
15. A book with an author and an editor (p. 202)
16. A book quoted in a secondary source (p. 203)

Editions and Multivolume Works

17. A subsequent edition of a book (p. 203)
18. A multivolume work (p. 203)

Parts of Books

19. A chapter in a book (p. 203)
20. An essay in an anthology (p. 204)

Religious Works

21. Sacred texts (p. 204)

ENTRIES FOR MISCELLANEOUS PRINT AND NONPRINT SOURCES

Interviews

22. A personal interview (p. 204)
23. A published interview (p. 204)

Letters and Government Documents

24. A personal letter (p. 205)
25. A government document (p. 205)

DVDs and Recordings

26. A DVD (p. 205)
27. An audio recording (p. 205)

ELECTRONIC SOURCES: *Entries for Sources from Online Publications*

Articles, Books, and Reference Works on the Internet

28. An article in an online scholarly journal (p. 206)
29. An article in an online magazine (p. 206)
30. An article in an online newspaper (p. 207)
31. An article in an encyclopedia (p. 207)
32. A book (p. 207)
33. A government publication (p. 208)

ELECTRONIC SOURCES: *Entries for Sources from an Online Database*

Sources from an Online Database

34. A scholarly journal article (p. 208)

ELECTRONIC SOURCES: *Entries for Sources from Internet Sites*

Internet-Specific Sources

35. A website (p. 209)
36. An email (p. 209)
37. A listserv posting (p. 209)
38. A blog article or entry (p. 209)
39. A podcast (p. 210)
40. An online video (*YouTube*) (p. 210)
41. A social networking post (*Facebook* post, tweet, etc.) (p. 210)

CHAPTER 12

Chicago Documentation Style

12a Using Chicago Humanities Style

The Chicago Manual of Style includes two citation methods, a notes-bibliography style used in history, in the humanities, and in some social science disciplines, and an author-date style used in the sciences and social sciences. **Chicago humanities style*** has two parts: *notes at the end of the essay* (**endnotes**) and usually a *list of bibliographic citations* (**bibliography**). (Chicago style encourages the use of endnotes, but allows the use of footnotes at the bottom of the page.)

1 Endnotes and Footnotes

The notes format calls for a **superscript** (raised numeral) in the text after source material you have either quoted or referred to. This numeral, placed after all punctuation marks except dashes, corresponds to the numeral that precedes the endnote or footnote.

Endnote and Footnote Format: Chicago Style

In the Text

> By November of 1942, the Allies had proof that the Nazis were engaged in the systematic killing of Jews.[1]

In the Note

> 1. David S. Wyman, *The Abandonment of the Jews: America and the Holocaust 1941–1945* (New York: Pantheon Books, 1984), 65.

---

* Chicago humanities style follows the guidelines set in *The Chicago Manual of Style*, 16th ed. Chicago: University of Chicago Press, 2010. The manuscript guidelines and sample research paper at the end of this chapter follow guidelines set in Kate L. Turabian's *A Manual for Writers of Research Papers, Theses, and Dissertations*, 8th ed. Chicago: University of Chicago Press, 2013. Turabian style, which is based on Chicago style, addresses formatting concerns specific to college writers.

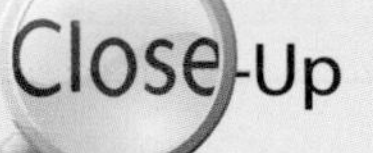

SUBSEQUENT REFERENCES TO THE SAME WORK

In an essay with no bibliography, use the full citation in the first note for a work; in subsequent references to the same work, list only the author's last name, a comma, an abbreviated title, another comma, and a page number. In an essay with a bibliography, you may use the short form for all notes.

First Note on Espinoza

1. J. M. Espinoza. *The First Expedition of Vargas in New Mexico, 1692* (Albuquerque: University of New Mexico Press, 1949), 10–12.

Subsequent Note

5. Espinoza, *First Expedition,* 29.

Note: You may use the abbreviation *ibid.* ("in the same place") for subsequent references to the same work as long as there are no intervening references. *Ibid.* takes the place of the author's name, the work's title, and the page number if they are the same as those in the previous note. If the page number is different, cite *Ibid.* and the page number.

First Note on Espinoza

1. J. M. Espinoza. *The First Expedition of Vargas in New Mexico, 1692* (Albuquerque: University of New Mexico Press, 1949), 10–12.

Next Note

2. Ibid., 23.

2 Bibliography

The **bibliography** provides complete publication information for the works consulted. Bibliography entries are arranged alphabetically by the author's last name or the first major word of the title (if there is no author). Single-space within an entry; double-space between entries.

Sample Chicago-Style Endnotes and Bibliography Entries

CHICAGO PRINT SOURCES Entries for Articles

Article citations generally include the name of the author (last name first); the title of the article (in quotation marks); the title of the periodical (in italics); the volume number, issue number, and date; and the page reference. Months are spelled out in full, not abbreviated.

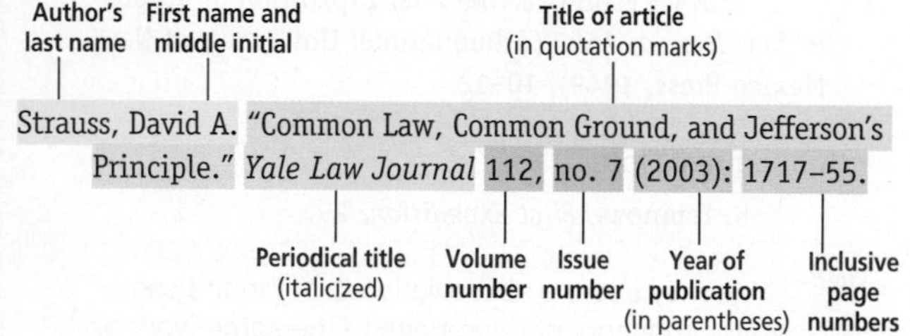

Articles in Scholarly Journals

1. An Article in a Scholarly Journal with Continuous Pagination throughout an Annual Volume

Endnote

1. John Huntington, "Science Fiction and the Future," *College English* 37 (Fall 1975): 341.

Bibliography

Huntington, John. "Science Fiction and the Future." *College English* 37 (Fall 1975): 340-58.

2. An Article in a Scholarly Journal with Separate Pagination in Each Issue

Endnote

2. R. G. Sipes, "War, Sports, and Aggression: An Empirical Test of Two Rival Theories," *American Anthropologist* 4, no. 2 (1973): 80.

Bibliography

Sipes, R. G. "War, Sports, and Aggression: An Empirical Test of Two Rival Theories." *American Anthropologist* 4, no. 2 (1973): 65-84.

Articles in Magazines and Newspapers

3. An Article in a Weekly Magazine (Signed/Unsigned)

Endnote

Signed

3. Pico Iyer, "A Mum for All Seasons," *Time,* April 8, 2002, 51.

Unsigned

3. "Burst Bubble," *New Scientist,* July 27, 2002, 24.

Although both endnotes above specify page numbers, the corresponding bibliography entries include page numbers only when the pages are consecutive (as in the second example that follows).

Bibliography

Signed

Iyer, Pico. "A Mum for All Seasons." *Time,* April 8, 2002.

Unsigned

"Burst Bubble." *New Scientist,* July 27, 2002, 24-25.

4. An Article in a Monthly Magazine (Signed)

Endnote

4. Tad Suzuki, "Reflecting Light on Photo Realism," *American Artist,* March 2002, 47.

Bibliography

Suzuki, Tad. "Reflecting Light on Photo Realism." *American Artist,* March 2002, 46-51.

5. An Article in a Monthly Magazine (Unsigned)

Endnote

5. "Repowering the U.S. with Clean Energy Development," *BioCycle,* July 2002, 14.

Bibliography

"Repowering the U.S. with Clean Energy Development." *BioCycle,* July 2002, 14.

6. An Article in a Newspaper (Signed)

Endnote

Because the pagination of newspapers can change from edition to edition, Chicago style recommends not giving page numbers for newspaper articles.

6. Francis X. Clines, "Civil War Relics Draw Visitors, and Con Artists," *New York Times,* August 4, 2002, national edition.

Bibliography

Clines, Francis X. "Civil War Relics Draw Visitors, and Con Artists." *New York Times,* August 4, 2002, national edition.

7. An Article in a Newspaper (Unsigned)

Endnote

7. "Feds Lead Way in Long-Term Care," *Atlanta Journal-Constitution,* July 21, 2002, sec. E.

Note: Omit the initial article the from the newspaper's title, but include a city name in the title, even if it is not part of the actual title.

If you provide a note or mention the name of the newspaper and publication date in your text, you do not need to list unsigned articles or other newspaper items in your bibliography.

8. A Letter to the Editor of a Newspaper

Endnote

8. Arnold Stieber, letter to the editor, *Seattle Times,* July 4, 2009.

Bibliography

Stieber, Arnold. Letter to the editor. *Seattle Times,* July 4, 2009.

9. A Book Review in a Newspaper

Endnote

9. Janet Maslin, "The Real Lincoln Bedroom: Love in a Time of Strife," review of *The Lincolns: Portrait of a Marriage,* by Daniel Mark Epstein, *New York Times,* July 3, 2008.

Bibliography

Maslin, Janet. "The Real Lincoln Bedroom: Love in a Time of Strife." Review of *The Lincolns: Portrait of a Marriage,* by Daniel Mark Epstein. *New York Times,* July 3, 2008.

CHICAGO PRINT SOURCES Entries for Books

Capitalize the first, last, and all major words of titles and subtitles. Chicago style italicizes book titles.

Author's last name | **First name and middle initial** | **Title** (italicized, all major words capitalized) | **City and state** (to clarify unfamiliar or ambiguous city)

Wartenberg, Thomas E. *The Nature of Art.* Belmont, CA: Wadsworth, 2002.

Publisher's name | **Year of publication**

Authors and Editors

10. A Book by One Author or Editor

Endnote

10. Robert Dallek, *An Unfinished Life: John F. Kennedy, 1917–1963* (New York: Little, Brown, 2003), 213.

Bibliography

Dallek, Robert. *An Unfinished Life: John F. Kennedy, 1917–1963.* New York: Little, Brown, 2003.

If the book has an editor rather than an author, add a comma and **ed.** after the name: **John Fields, ed.** Follow with a comma in a note.

11. A Book by Two or Three Authors or Editors

Endnote

Two Authors

11. Jack Watson and Grant McKerney, *A Cultural History of the Theater* (New York: Longman, 1993), 137.

Three Authors

11. Nathan Caplan, John K. Whitmore, and Marcella H. Choy, *The Boat People and Achievement in America: A Study of Economic and Educational Success* (Ann Arbor: University of Michigan Press, 1990), 51.

Bibliography

Two Authors

Watson, Jack, and Grant McKerney. *A Cultural History of the Theater*. New York: Longman, 1993.

Three Authors

Caplan, Nathan, John K. Whitmore, and Marcella H. Choy. *The Boat People and Achievement in America: A Study of Economic and Educational Success.* Ann Arbor: University of Michigan Press, 1990.

12. A Book by More Than Three Authors or Editors

Endnote

Chicago style favors **et al.** rather than **and others** after the first name in endnotes. Add a comma and **eds.** after the names of the editors in both the endnotes and the bibliography.

12. Robert E. Spiller et al., eds., *Literary History of the United States* (New York: Macmillan, 1953), 24.

Bibliography

List all authors' or editors' names in the bibliography.

Spiller, Robert E., Willard Thorp, Thomas H. Johnson, and Henry Seidel Canby, eds. *Literary History of the United States*. New York: Macmillan, 1953.

13. A Book with No Listed Author or Editor

Endnote

13. *Merriam-Webster's Guide to Punctuation and Style*, 4th ed. (Springfield, MA: Merriam-Webster, 2008), 22.

Bibliography

Merriam-Webster's Guide to Punctuation and Style. 4th ed. Springfield, MA: Merriam-Webster, 2008.

14. A Book by a Corporate Author

If a publication issued by an organization does not identify a person as the author, the organization is listed as the author even if its name is repeated in the title, in the series title, or as the publisher.

Endnote

14. National Geographic Society, *National Parks of the United States*, 6th ed. (Washington, DC: National Geographic Society, 2009), 77.

Bibliography

National Geographic Society. *National Parks of the United States*. 6th ed. Washington, DC: National Geographic Society, 2009.

15. A Book with an Author and an Editor

Endnote

15. William Bartram, *The Travels of William Bartram*, ed. Mark Van Doren (New York: Dover Press, 1955), 85.

Bibliography

Bartram, William. *The Travels of William Bartram*. Edited by Mark Van Doren. New York: Dover Press, 1955.

16. A Book Quoted in a Secondary Source

Endnote

16. Henry Adams, *Mont Saint-Michel and Chartres* (New York: Penguin Books, 1986), 296, quoted in Karen Armstrong, *A History of God: The 4000-Year Quest of Judaism, Christianity and Islam* (New York: Ballantine Books, 1993), 203-4.

Bibliography

Adams, Henry. *Mont Saint-Michel and Chartres,* 296. New York: Penguin Books, 1986. Quoted in Armstrong, *A History of God,* 203-4.

Armstrong, Karen. *A History of God: The 4000-Year Quest of Judaism, Christianity, and Islam.* New York: Ballantine Books, 1993.

Editions and Multivolume Works

17. A Subsequent Edition of a Book

Endnote

17. Laurie G. Kirszner and Stephen R. Mandell, *The Concise Cengage Handbook,* 5th ed. (Boston: Wadsworth, 2017), 52.

Bibliography

Kirszner, Laurie G., and Stephen R. Mandell. *The Concise Cengage Handbook.* 5th ed. Boston: Wadsworth, 2017.

18. A Multivolume Work

Endnote

18. Kathleen Raine, *Blake and Tradition* (Princeton, NJ: Princeton University Press, 1968), 1:143.

Bibliography

Raine, Kathleen. *Blake and Tradition.* Vol. 1. Princeton, NJ: Princeton University Press, 1968.

Parts of Books

19. A Chapter in a Book

Endnote

19. Roy Porter, "Health, Disease, and Cure," in *Quacks: Fakers and Charlatans in Medicine* (Stroud, UK: Tempus Publishing, 2003), 188.

Bibliography

Porter, Roy. "Health, Disease, and Cure." In *Quacks: Fakers and Charlatans in Medicine,* 182-205. Stroud, UK: Tempus Publishing, 2003.

20. An Essay in an Anthology

Endnote

20. G. E. R. Lloyd, "Science and Mathematics," in *The Legacy of Greece,* ed. Moses Finley (New York: Oxford University Press, 1981), 270.

Bibliography

Lloyd, G. E. R. "Science and Mathematics." In *The Legacy of Greece,* edited by Moses Finley, 256-300. New York: Oxford University Press, 1981.

Religious Works

21. Sacred Texts

References to religious works (such as the Bible or Qur'an) are usually limited to the text or notes and not listed in the bibliography. In citing the Bible, include the book (abbreviated), the chapter (followed by a colon), and the verse numbers. Identify the version, but do not include a page number.

Endnote

21. Phil. 1:9-11 (King James Version).

CHICAGO ENTRIES FOR MISCELLANEOUS PRINT AND NONPRINT SOURCES

Interviews

22. A Personal Interview

Endnote

22. Cornel West, interview by author, tape recording, June 8, 2013.

Personal interviews are cited in the notes or text but are usually not listed in the bibliography.

23. A Published Interview

Endnote

23. Gwendolyn Brooks, interview by George Stavros, *Contemporary Literature* 11, no. 1 (Winter 1970): 12.

Bibliography

Brooks, Gwendolyn. Interview by George Stavros. *Contemporary Literature* 11, no. 1 (Winter 1970): 1-20.

Letters and Government Documents

24. A Personal Letter

Endnote

24. Julia Alvarez, letter to the author, April 10, 2013.

Personal letters are mentioned in the text or a note but are not listed in the bibliography.

25. A Government Document

Endnote

25. US Department of Transportation, *The Future of High-Speed Trains in the United States: Special Study, 2007* (Washington, DC: Government Printing Office, 2008), 203.

Bibliography

US Department of Transportation. *The Future of High-Speed Trains in the United States: Special Study, 2007.* Washington, DC: Government Printing Office, 2008.

DVDs and Recordings

26. A DVD

Endnote

26. *Steve Jobs: The Lost Interview*, directed by Paul Sen (New York: Magnolia Home Entertainment, 2012), DVD, 72 min.

Bibliography

Steve Jobs: The Lost Interview. Directed by Paul Sen. New York: Magnolia Home Entertainment, 2012. DVD, 72 min.

27. An Audio Recording

Endnote

27. Bob Marley and the Wailers, "Crisis," *Kaya,* Kava Island Records 423 095-3, 1978, compact disc.

Bibliography

Marley, Bob, and the Wailers. "Crisis." *Kaya*. Kava Island Records 423 095-3, 1978, compact disc.

CHICAGO ELECTRONIC SOURCES Entries for Sources from Online Publications

Citations of sources from online publications usually include the author's name; the title of the article; the title of the publication; the publication information and date; the page numbers (if applicable); and the DOI (digital object identifier), a permanent identifying number, or URL (followed by a period). If no publication date is available or if your instructor or discipline requires one, include an access date before the DOI or URL.

You may break a DOI or URL that continues to a second line after a colon or double slash; before a comma, a period, a hyphen, a question mark, a percent symbol, a number sign, a tilde, or an underscore; or before or after an ampersand or equals sign.

Author's last name | First name | Title of article (in quotation marks)

Dekoven, Marianne. "Utopias Limited: Post-Sixties and Postmodern American Fiction." *Modern Fiction Studies* 41, no. 1 (1995). doi:10.1353/mfs.1995.0002.

Volume number | Issue number | Year of publication (in parentheses) | DOI | Title of periodical (italicized)

Articles, Books, and Reference Works on the Internet

28. An Article in an Online Scholarly Journal

Endnote

28. Richard J. Schaefer, "Editing Strategies in Television Documentaries," *Journal of Communication* 47, no. 4 (1997): 80, doi:10.1111/j1460-2446.1997.tb02726.x.

Bibliography

Schaefer, Richard J. "Editing Strategies in Television Documentaries." *Journal of Communication* 47, no. 4 (1997): 69–89. doi:10.1111/j1460-2446.1997.tb02726.x.

29. An Article in an Online Magazine

Endnote

29. Steven Levy, "I Was a Wi-Fi Freeloader," *Newsweek*, October 9, 2002, http://www.msnbc.com/news/816606.asp.

If there is no DOI for a source, cite the URL.

Bibliography

Levy, Steven. "I Was a Wi-Fi Freeloader." *Newsweek,* October 9, 2002. http://www.msnbc.com/news/816606.asp.

30. An Article in an Online Newspaper

Endnote

30. William J. Broad, "Piece by Piece, the Civil War *Monitor* Is Pulled from the Atlantic's Depths," *New York Times*, July 18, 2002, http://query.nytimes.com.

Bibliography

Broad, William J. "Piece by Piece, the Civil War *Monitor* Is Pulled from the Atlantic's Depths." *New York Times*, July 18, 2002. http://query.nytimes.com.

31. An Article in an Encyclopedia

If the reference book lists entries alphabetically, put the abbreviation **s.v.** (Latin for *sub verbo*, "under the word") before the entry name. If there is no publication or revision date for the entry, give the date of access before the DOI or URL.

Endnote

31. *Encyclopaedia Britannica Online*, s.v. "Adams, John," accessed July 5, 2015, http://www.britannica.com/EBchecked/topic/5132/John-Adams.

Dictionary and encyclopedia entries are not listed in the bibliography.

32. A Book

Endnote

32. Frederick Douglass, *My Bondage and My Freedom* (Boston, 1855), http://etext.virginia.edu/toc/modeng/public/DouMybo.html.

Bibliography

Douglass, Frederick. *My Bondage and My Freedom*. Boston, 1855. http://etext.virginia.edu/toc/modeng/public/DouMybo.html.

Older works available online may not include all publication information. Give the DOI or URL as the last part of the citation.

33. A Government Publication

Endnote

33. US Department of Transportation, Federal Motor Carrier Safety Administration, *Safety Belt Usage by Commercial Motor Vehicle Drivers (SBUCMVD) 2007 Survey, Final Report* (Washington, DC: Government Printing Office, 2008), http://www.fmcsa.dot.gov/safety-security/safety-belt/exec-summary-2007.htm.

Bibliography

US Department of Transportation. Federal Motor Carrier Safety Administration. *Safety Belt Usage by Commercial Motor Vehicle Drivers (SBUCMVD) 2007 Survey, Final Report*. Washington, DC: Government Printing Office, 2008. http://www.fmcsa.dot.gov/safety-security/safety-belt/exec-summary-2007.htm.

CHICAGO ELECTRONIC SOURCES — Entries for Sources from an Online Database

Sources from an Online Database

Many articles and other materials published in print and electronically are also archived and available online through free or subscription databases.

34. A Scholarly Journal Article

Endnote

34. Monroe Billington, "Freedom to Serve: The President's Committee on Equality of Treatment and Opportunity in the Armed Forces, 1949–1950," *Journal of Negro History* 51, no. 4 (1966): 264, http://www.jstor.org/stable/2716101.

Use a DOI, a number that applies to an article in all of the media in which it may be published, rather than a URL if one is available. If you use a URL, cite the shorter, more stable form that will take you to the article's location in a database.

Bibliography

Billington, Monroe. "Freedom to Serve: The President's Committee on Equality of Treatment and Opportunity in the Armed Forces, 1949–1950," *Journal of Negro*

History 51, no. 4 (1966): 262–74. http://www.jstor.org/stable/2716101.

If there is no stable URL, include the name of the database and put any identifying database number in parentheses: (**ERIC**). If the article or document does not have a date of publication or revision, include an access date.

CHICAGO ELECTRONIC SOURCES Entries for Sources from Internet Sites

Internet-Specific Sources

35. A Website

Endnote

35. David Perdue, "Dickens's Journalistic Career," David Perdue's Charles Dickens Page, accessed October 25, 2015, http://www.fidnet.com/~dap1955/dickens.

Titles of websites are in regular type (roman). Titles of pages or sections on a site are in quotation marks. If there is no date of publication, give an access date. Website content is not usually listed in a bibliography.

36. An Email

Endnote

36. Meg Halverson, "Scuba Report," email message to author, April 2, 2015.

Email messages can also be mentioned in the text; they are not listed in the bibliography.

37. A Listserv Posting

Include the name of the list, the date of the individual posting, and the URL for the archive.

Endnote

37. Dave Shirlaw to Underwater Archeology discussion list, September 6, 2014, http://lists.asu.edu/archives/sub-arch.html.

Listserv postings are not listed in the bibliography.

38. A Blog Article or Entry

Note the genre (blog) after the blog's title.

Endnote

38. Anne Curzane, "Electronic Innovation >>>," *Lingua Franca*, blog, February 16, 2015, http://chronicle.com/blogs/linguafranca/2015/02/16/electronic-innovation/.

Blog posts are not included in the bibliography.

39. A Podcast

Endnote

39. HowStuffWorks, "The Father of Plastics," podcast audio, *Stuff You Missed in History Class*, 2015, MP3, 28:18, accessed September 18, 2015, http://www.missedinhistory.com/podcasts/the-father-of-plastics/.

Bibliography

HowStuffWorks. "The Father of Plastics." Podcast audio. *Stuff You Missed in History Class*. 2015, MP3, 28:18. Accessed September 18, 2015. http://www.missedinhistory.com/podcasts/the-father-of-plastics/.

40. An Online Video (*YouTube*)

Endnote

40. John Green and CrashCourse, *Conflict in Israel and Palestine: Crash Course World History 223*, online video, 12:52, January 28, 2015, https://www.youtube.com/watch?v=1wo2TLlMhiw.

Bibliography

Green, John, and CrashCourse. *Conflict in Israel and Palestine: Crash Course World History 223*. Online video, 12:52. January 28, 2015. https://www.youtube.com/watch?v=1wo2TLlMhiw.

41. A Social Networking Post (*Facebook* post, tweet, etc.)

No bibliography entry is needed. Include information about the post (such as the writer's *Twitter* name) within the text of your essay or include a note such as the following.

Endnote

41. Celeste Ng, Twitter post, February 18, 2015, 8:55 a.m., https://twitter.com/pronounced_ing/.

12b Chicago Humanities Manuscript Guidelines

CHECKLIST

Typing Your Essay

When you type your essay, use the student essay in **12c** as your model.

- ❑ On the title page, type the full title of your essay. Also include your name, the course title, and the date.
- ❑ Double-space all text in your essay. Single-space block quotations, table titles, figure captions, footnotes, endnotes, and bibliography entries. Double-space between footnotes, endnotes, and bibliography entries.
- ❑ Leave a one-inch margin at the top, at the bottom, and on both sides of the page.
- ❑ Indent the first line of each paragraph one-half inch. Set off a long prose block quotation (five or more lines) from the text by indenting the quotation one-half inch from the left-hand margin. Do not use quotation marks. Double-space before and after the block quotation.
- ❑ Number all pages consecutively at the top of the page (centered or flush right) or centered at the bottom. Page numbers should appear at a consistent distance (at least three-fourths of an inch) from the top margin. Do not number the title page; the first full page of the essay is page 1.
- ❑ Use superscript numbers to indicate in-text citations. Type superscript numbers at the end of cited material (quotations, paraphrases, or summaries). Place the note number at the end of a sentence or clause (with no intervening space). The number follows any punctuation mark except a dash, which it precedes.
- ❑ Citations should follow **Chicago humanities documentation style**. See 12a

CHECKLIST

Using Visuals

According to *The Chicago Manual of Style,* there are two types of visuals: **tables** and **figures** (or **illustrations**), including charts, graphs, photographs, maps, and diagrams.

Tables

- ❑ Give each **table** a label and a consecutive arabic number (**Table 1, Table 2**) followed by a period.

continued

Using Visuals *(continued)*

- ❑ Give each table a concise descriptive title in noun form without a period. Place the title after the table number.
- ❑ Place both the label and the title flush left above the table.
- ❑ Place source information flush left below the table, introduced by the word **Source** or **Sources**. Otherwise style the source as a complete footnote.

  Source: David E. Fisher and Marshall Jon Fisher, *Tube: The Invention of Television* (Washington, DC: Counterpoint Press, 1996), 185.

  If you do not cite this source elsewhere in your essay, do not list it in your bibliography.

Figures

- ❑ Give each **figure** a label, a consecutive arabic number, and a caption.
- ❑ Place the label, the number, and a period flush left below the figure. Then, leave a space and add the caption.
- ❑ Place source information (credit line) at the end of the caption after a period.

  Figure 1. Television and its influence on young children. Photograph from ABC Photos.

CHECKLIST

Preparing the Chicago-Style Endnotes Page

When typing your endnotes page, follow these guidelines:

- ❑ Begin the endnotes on a new page after the last page of the text of the essay and preceding the bibliography.
- ❑ Type the title **Notes** and center it one inch from the top of the page. Then double-space and type the first note.
- ❑ Number the page on which the endnotes appear as the next page of the essay.
- ❑ Type and number notes in the order in which they appear in the essay, beginning with number 1. Type the note number on (not above) the line, followed by a period and one space.
- ❑ Indent the first line of each note one-half inch; type subsequent lines flush with the left-hand margin.
- ❑ Single-space lines within a note. Double-space between notes.
- ❑ Break DOIs and URLs after a colon or double slashes, before punctuation marks (period, single slash, comma, hyphen, and so on), or before or after the symbols = and &.

CHECKLIST

Preparing the Chicago-Style Bibliography

When typing your bibliography, follow these guidelines:

- ❑ Begin entries on a separate page after the endnotes.
- ❑ Type the title **Bibliography** and center it one inch from the top of the page. Then double-space and type the first entry.
- ❑ List entries alphabetically according to the author's last name.
- ❑ Type the first line of each entry flush with the left-hand margin. Indent subsequent lines one-half inch.
- ❑ Single-space within an entry; double-space between entries.

12c Model Chicago Humanities Research Paper (Excerpts)

The following pages are from a student essay, "The Flu of 1918 and the Potential for Future Pandemics," written for a history course. It uses Chicago humanities documentation and has a title page, notes page, and bibliography. The web citations in this student essay do not have DOIs, so URLs have been provided instead.

Title page is not numbered

Title boldfaced and centered

The Flu of 1918 and the Potential for Future Pandemics

Name

Course title

Date

Rita Lin

American History 301

May 3, 2015

1" ¾" 1

The Flu of 1918 and the Potential for Future Pandemics

Title if required by instructor (centered and boldfaced)

Indent ½" → In November 2002, a mysterious new illness surfaced in China. By May 2003, what became known as SARS (Severe Acute Respiratory Syndrome) had been transported by air travelers to Europe, South America, South Africa, Australia, and North America, and the worldwide death toll had grown to 250.[1] By June 2003, there were more than 8,200 suspected cases of SARS in 30 countries and 750 deaths related to the outbreak, including 30 in Toronto. Just when SARS appeared to be waning in Asia, a second outbreak in Toronto, the hardest hit of all cities outside of Asia, reminded everyone that SARS remained a deadly threat.[2] As SARS continued to claim more victims and expand its reach, fears of a new pandemic spread throughout the world.

Double-space the text of the essay

Introduction

Superscript numbers refer to endnotes

1" 1"

The belief that a pandemic could occur in the future is not a far-fetched idea. During the twentieth century, there were three, and the most deadly one, in 1918, had several significant similarities to the SARS outbreak. As David Brown points out, the 1918 influenza pandemic is in many ways a mirror reflecting the causes and symptoms, as well as the future potential, of SARS. Both are caused by a virus, lead to respiratory illness, and spread through casual contact and coughing. Outbreaks of both are often traced to one individual, quarantine is the major weapon against the spread of both, and both probably arose from mutated animal viruses. Moreover, as Brown observes, the greatest fear regarding SARS was that it would become so

1"

2

widespread that transmission chains would be undetectable, and health officials would be helpless to restrain outbreaks. Such was the case with the 1918 influenza, which also began mysteriously in China and was transported around the globe (at that time by World War I military ships). By the time the flu lost its power in the spring of 1919, just one year later, it had killed more than 50 million people worldwide,[3] more than twice as many as those who died during the four and a half years of World War I. Thus, if SARS is a reflection of the potential for a future flu pandemic—and experts believe it is—the international community needs to acknowledge the danger, accelerate its research, and develop an extensive virus surveillance system.

Thesis statement

History of 1918 pandemic

Clearly, the 1918 flu was different from anything previously known to Americans. Among the peculiarities of the pandemic were its origin and cause. In the spring of 1918, the virus, in relatively mild form, mysteriously appeared on a Kansas military base. After apparently dying out, the flu returned to the United States in late August. At that point, the influenza was no ordinary flu; it "struck with incredible speed, often killing a victim within hours of contact[,] . . . so fast that such infections rarely had time to set in."[4] Unlike previous strains, the 1918 flu struck healthy young people.

Brackets indicate that comma was added by student writer

Center title (boldfaced) and double-space before first note

1"

10

Notes

1. Nancy Shute, "SARS Hits Home," *U.S. News & World Report*, May 5, 2003, 42.

Indent ½"

2. "Canada Waits for SARS News as Asia Under Control," *Sydney Morning Herald*, June 2, 2003, http://www.smh.com.au.

Single-space within a note; double-space between notes

3. David Brown, "A Grim Reminder in SARS Fight: In 1918, Spanish Flu Swept the Globe, Killing Millions," MSNBC News Online, June 4, 2003, http://www.msnbc.com/news/921901.asp.

A long URL for an online newspaper article can be shortened after the first single slash

4. Doug Rekenthaler, "The Flu Pandemic of 1918: Is a Repeat Performance Likely?—Part 1 of 2," Disaster Relief: New Stories, February 22, 1999, http://www.disasterrelief.org /Disasters/990219Flu.

Endnotes listed in order in which they appear in the essay

5. Lynette Iezzoni, *Influenza 1918: The Worst Epidemic in American History* (New York: TV Books, 1999), 40.

6. "1918 Influenza Timeline," *Influenza 1918*, 1999, http://www.pbs.org/wgbh/amex/influenza /timeline/index.html.

Subsequent references to the same source include author's last name, shortened title, and page number(s)

Ibid. is used for a subsequent reference to the same source when there are no intervening references

7. Iezonni, *Influenza 1918,* 131–32.

8. Brown, "Grim Reminder."

9. Iezonni, *Influenza 1918,* 88–89.

10. Ibid., 204.

1"

13

Bibliography

Center title (boldfaced) and double-space before first entry

"1918 Influenza Timeline." *Influenza 1918,* 1999. http://www.pbs.org/wgbh/amex/influenza /timeline/index.html.

Billings, Molly. "The Influenza Pandemic of 1918." Human Virology at Stanford: Interesting Viral Web Pages, June 1997. http://www.stanford .edu/group/virus/uda/index.html.

Brown, David. "A Grim Reminder in SARS Fight: In 1918, Spanish Flu Swept the Globe, Killing Millions." MSNBC News Online, June 4, 2003. http://www.msnbc.com/news/921901.asp.

"Canada Waits for SARS News as Asia Under Control." *Sydney Morning Herald,* June 2, 2003. http://www.smh.com.au/text.

Cooke, Robert. "Drugs vs. the Bug of 1918: Virus' Deadly Code Is Unlocked to Test Strategies to Fight It." *Newsday,* October 1, 2002.

Crosby, Alfred W., Jr. *America's Forgotten Pandemic: The Influenza of 1918.* New York: Cambridge University Press, 1989.

Dandurant, Daren. "Virus Changes Can Make Flu a Slippery Foe to Combat." MSNBC News Online, January 17, 2003. http://www.msnbc.com /local/sco/m8052.asp.

First line of each entry is flush with the left-hand margin; subsequent lines are indented 1/2"

Single-space within entries; double-space between them

URLs are provided for web citations that do not have DOIs

Entries are listed alphabetically according to the author's last name

Directory of CSE Reference List Entries

PRINT SOURCES: *Entries for Articles*

Articles in Scholarly Journals

1. An article in a journal paginated by issue (p. 222)
2. An article in a journal with continuous pagination (p. 222)

Articles in Magazines and Newspapers

3. A magazine article (signed) (p. 222)
4. A magazine article (unsigned) (p. 222)
5. A newspaper article (signed) (p. 222)
6. A newspaper article (unsigned) (p. 223)

PRINT SOURCES: *Entries for Books*

Authors

7. A book with one author (p. 223)
8. A book with more than one author (p. 223)
9. An edited book (p. 223)
10. An organization as author (p. 224)

Parts of Books

11. A chapter or other part of a book with a separate title but with the same author (p. 224)
12. A chapter or other part of a book with a different author (p. 224)

Professional and Technical Publications

13. Published proceedings of a conference (p. 224)
14. A technical report (p. 224)

ENTRIES FOR MISCELLANEOUS PRINT AND NONPRINT SOURCES

Films, Recordings, and Maps

15. An audio recording (p. 225)
16. A film, DVD, or Blu-ray (p. 225)
17. A map (p. 225)

ELECTRONIC SOURCES: *Entries for Sources from Internet Sites*

Internet-Specific Sources

18. An article in an online scholarly journal (p. 226)
19. An online book (p. 226)
20. An online image (p. 226)
21. A podcast (p. 226)

CHAPTER 13

CSE and Other Documentation Styles

13a Using CSE Style

CSE style,* recommended by the Council of Science Editors (CSE), is used in biology, zoology, physiology, anatomy, and genetics. CSE style has two parts—*documentation in the text* and a *reference list.*

1 Documentation in the Text

CSE style permits either of two documentation formats: *citation-sequence format* or *name-year format.*

Citation-Sequence Format The **citation-sequence format** calls for either superscripts (raised numbers) in the text of the essay (the preferred form) or numbers inserted parenthetically in the text of the essay.

> One study[1] has demonstrated the effect of low dissolved oxygen.

These numbers refer to a list of references at the end of the essay. Entries are numbered in the order in which they appear in the text of the essay. For example, if **James** is mentioned first in the text, **James** will be number 1 in the reference list. When you refer to more than one source in a single note, the numbers are separated by a hyphen if they are in sequence and by a comma if they are not.

> Some studies[2-3] dispute this claim.
>
> Other studies[3,6] support these findings.

---

*CSE style follows the guidelines set in the style manual of the Council of Science Editors: *Scientific Style and Format: The CSE Manual for Authors, Editors, and Publishers,* 8th ed. Chicago: University of Chicago Press, 2014.

Name-Year Format The **name-year format** calls for the author's name and the year of publication to be inserted parenthetically in the text. If the author's name is used to introduce the source material, only the date of publication is needed in the parenthetical citation.

A great deal of heat is often generated during this process (McGinness 2010).

According to McGinness (2010), a great deal of heat is often generated during this process.

When two or more works are cited in the same parentheses, the sources are arranged chronologically (from earliest to latest) and separated by semicolons.

Epidemics can be avoided by taking tissue cultures (Domb 2010) and by intervention with antibiotics (Baldwin and Rigby 2005; Martin and others 2006; Cording 2010).

Note: The citation **Baldwin and Rigby 2005** refers to a work by two authors; the citation **Martin and others 2006** refers to a work by three or more authors.

2 Reference List

The format of the reference list depends on the documentation format you use. If you use the **name-year** documentation format, your reference list will resemble the reference list for an **APA** essay (**see Chapter 11**). If you use the **citation-sequence** documentation style (as in the essay in **13c**), your sources will be listed by number, in the order in which they appear in your essay, on a **References** page. In either case, double-space within and between entries; type each number flush left, followed by a period and one space; and align the second and subsequent lines with the first letter of the author's last name. (The following examples illustrate citation-sequence documentation style.)

CSE PRINT SOURCES Entries for Articles

List the author or authors by last name; after one space, list the initial or initials (unspaced) of the first and middle names (followed by a period); the title of the article (not in quotation marks, and with only the first word capitalized); the abbreviated name of the journal (with all major words capitalized, but not italicized or underlined); the year (followed by a semicolon); the volume number, the issue number (in parentheses), followed by a colon; and inclusive page numbers. No spaces separate the year, the volume number, and the page numbers.

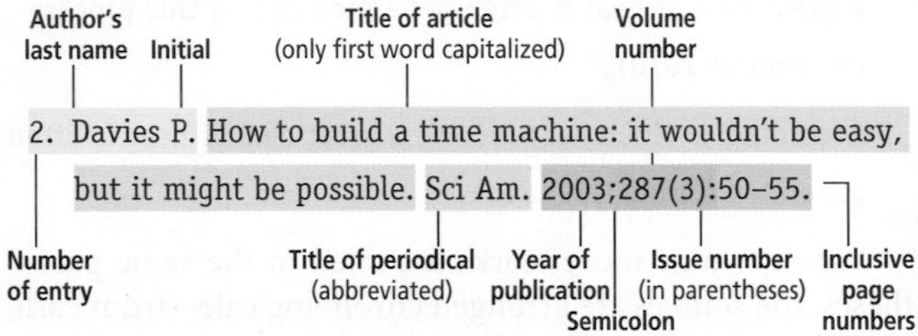

Articles in Scholarly Journals

1. An Article in a Journal Paginated by Issue

1. Sarmiento JL, Gruber N. Sinks for anthropogenic carbon. Phy Today. 2002;55(8):30-36.

2. An Article in a Journal with Continuous Pagination

2. Brazil K, Krueger P. Patterns of family adaptation to childhood asthma. J Pediatr Nurs. 2002;17:167-173.

Note: Omit the month (and the day for weeklies) and issue number for journals with continuous pagination through an annual volume.

Articles in Magazines and Newspapers

3. A Magazine Article (Signed)

3. Nadis S. Using lasers to detect E.T. Astronomy. 2002 Sep:44-49.

Note: Month names longer than three letters are abbreviated by their first three letters.

4. A Magazine Article (Unsigned)

4. Brown dwarf glows with radio waves. Astronomy. 2001 Jun:28.

5. A Newspaper Article (Signed)

5. Husted B. Don't wiggle out of untangling computer wires. Atlanta Journal-Constitution. 2002 Jul 21;Sect Q:1 (col 1).

6. A Newspaper Article (Unsigned)

6. Scientists find gene tied to cancer risk. New York Times (Late Ed.). 2002 Apr 22;Sect A:18 (col 6).

CSE PRINT SOURCES Entries for Books

List the author or authors (last name first); the title (not underlined, and with only the first word capitalized); the place of publication; the full name of the publisher (followed by a semicolon); the year (followed by a period); and the total number of pages (including back matter, such as the index).

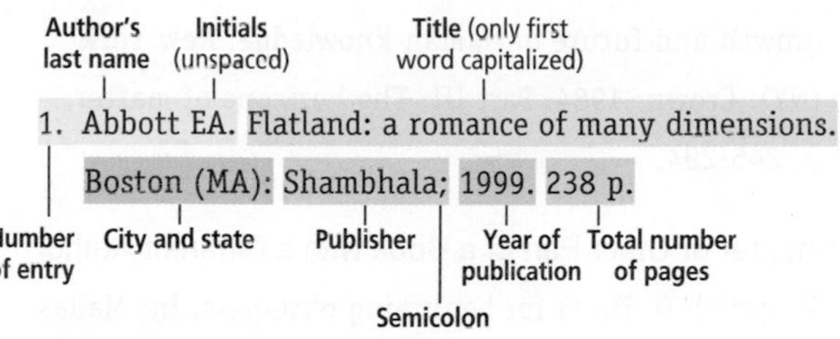

Authors

7. A Book with One Author

7. Hawking SW. A brief history of time: from the big bang to black holes. New York (NY): Bantam; 1995. 198 p.

Note: No comma follows the author's last name, and no period separates the unspaced initials of the first and middle names.

8. A Book with More Than One Author

8. Horner JR, Gorman J. Digging dinosaurs. New York (NY): Workman; 1988. 210 p.

9. An Edited Book

9. Goldfarb TD, editor. Taking sides: clashing views on controversial environmental issues. 2nd ed. Guilford (CT): Dushkin; 1987. 323 p.

Note: The publisher's state, province, or country can be added within parentheses to clarify the location. The two-letter postal service abbreviation can be used for the state or province.

10. An Organization as Author

10. National Institutes of Health (US). Human embryonic stem-cell derived neurons treat stroke in rats. Bethesda (MD): US Dept. of Health and Human Services; 2008. 92 p.

Parts of Books

11. A Chapter or Other Part of a Book with a Separate Title but with the Same Author

11. Asimov I. Exploring the earth and cosmos: the growth and future of human knowledge. New York (NY): Crown; 1984. Part III, The horizons of matter; p. 245-294.

12. A Chapter or Other Part of a Book with a Different Author

12. Gingerich O. Hints for beginning observers. In: Mallas JH, Kreimer E, editors. The Messier album: an observer's handbook. Cambridge (GB): Cambridge Univ Pr; 1978. p. 194-195.

Professional and Technical Publications

13. Published Proceedings of a Conference

13. Al-Sherbini A. New applications of lasers in photobiology and photochemistry. Modern Trends of Physics Research, 1st International Conference; 2004 May 12-14; Cairo, Egypt. Melville (NY): American Institute of Physics; 2005. 14 p.

14. A Technical Report

14. Forman GL. Feature selection for text classification. 2007 Feb 12. Hewlett-Packard technical reports HPL-2007-16R1. 24 p. http://www.hpl.hp.com/techreports/2007/HPL-2007-16R1.html.

Note: See pages 225–26 for information on citing online sources.

CSE ENTRIES FOR MISCELLANEOUS PRINT AND NONPRINT SOURCES

Films, Recordings, and Maps

15. An Audio Recording

15. Nye B. Undeniable: evolution and the science of creation [CD]. New York: Macmillan Audio; 2014. 4 discs: 569 min.

16. A Film, DVD, or Blu-ray

16. Tyson ND, narrator. Cosmos: a spacetime odyssey [DVD]. Fox TV, producer. Los Angeles: 20th Century Fox; 2014. 4 discs: 572 min.

17. A Map

A Sheet Map

17. Amazonia: a world resource at risk [ecological map]. Washington (DC): National Geographic Society; 2008. 1 sheet.

A Map in an Atlas

17. Central Africa [political map]. In: Hammond citation world atlas. Maplewood (NJ): Hammond; 2008. p. 114-115. Color, scale 1:13,800,000.

CSE ELECTRONIC SOURCES

Entries for Sources from Internet Sites

With Internet sources, include a description of the medium, the date of access, and the URL.

Author's last name | Initials (unspaced) | Title of article (only first word capitalized) | Title of periodical (abbreviated)

3. Sarra SA. The method of characteristics with applications to conservation laws. J Online Math and Its Apps. 2003 [accessed 2015 Aug 26]; 3. http://www.joma.org/vol3/articles/sarra/sarra.html.

Number of entry | Year of publication | Date of access (abbreviated: in brackets) | Semicolon | Volume number | URL

Internet-Specific Sources

18. An Article in an Online Scholarly Journal

18. Lasko P. The *Drosophila melanogaster* genome: translation factors and RNA binding proteins. J Cell Biol. 2000 [accessed 2015 Feb 15]; 150(2):F51-56. http://www.jcb.org/search.dtl.

19. An Online Book

19. Bohm D. Causality and chance in modern physics. Philadelphia: Univ of Pennsylvania Pr; c1999 [accessed 2014 Aug 17]. http://www.netlibrary.com/ebook_info .asp?product_id517169.

20. An Online Image

20. Muroe R. Atoms [cartoon]. xkcd.com. [accessed 2014 Feb 23]. http://xkcd.com/1490/.

21. A Podcast

21. Adams R. Energy and empire by George Gonzales [podcast, episode 235]. The Atomic Show. Atomic Insights. 2015 Feb 26, 21 min. [accessed 2015 Mar 1]. http://atomicinsights.com/atomic-show-235-energy-and-empire-by-george-gonzales/.

13b CSE-Style Manuscript Guidelines

CHECKLIST

Typing Your Essay

When you type your essay, use the student essay in **13c** as your model.

- ❑ Do not include a title page. Type your name, the course, and the date flush left one inch from the top of the first page.
- ❑ If required, include an **abstract** (a 250-word summary of the essay) on a separate numbered page.
- ❑ Double-space throughout.

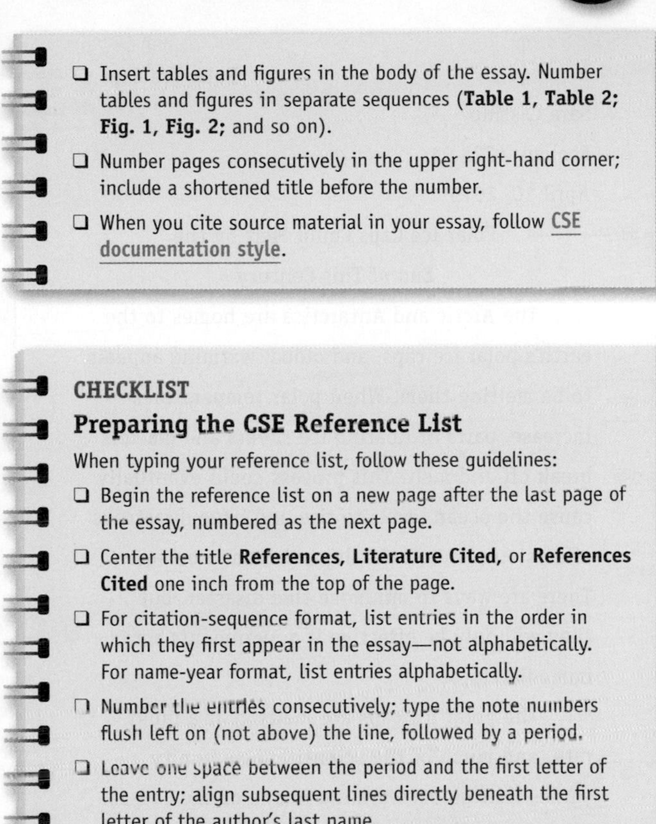

❑ Insert tables and figures in the body of the essay. Number tables and figures in separate sequences (**Table 1, Table 2; Fig. 1, Fig. 2;** and so on).

❑ Number pages consecutively in the upper right-hand corner; include a shortened title before the number.

❑ When you cite source material in your essay, follow **CSE documentation style**.

See 13a

CHECKLIST

Preparing the CSE Reference List

When typing your reference list, follow these guidelines:

❑ Begin the reference list on a new page after the last page of the essay, numbered as the next page.

❑ Center the title **References, Literature Cited,** or **References Cited** one inch from the top of the page.

❑ For citation-sequence format, list entries in the order in which they first appear in the essay—not alphabetically. For name-year format, list entries alphabetically.

❑ Number the entries consecutively; type the note numbers flush left on (not above) the line, followed by a period.

❑ Leave one space between the period and the first letter of the entry; align subsequent lines directly beneath the first letter of the author's last name.

❑ Double-space within and between entries.

13c Model CSE-Style Research Paper (Excerpts)

The following pages are from a student essay that explores the dangers of global warming for humans and wildlife. The essay, which cites seven sources and includes a line graph, illustrates CSE citation-sequence format.

1″ ½″

Polar Ice Caps 1

Abbreviated title and page number

Sara Castillo

Ecology 4223.01

April 10, 2015

Center title →

Polar Ice Caps Could Melt by the End of This Century

Indent ½″ →

The Arctic and Antarctica are homes to the earth's polar ice caps, and global warming appears to be melting them. When polar temperatures increase, parts of floating ice sheets and glaciers break off and melt. This process could eventually cause the ocean levels to rise and have disastrous effects on plants, animals, and human beings. There are ways to minimize this disaster, but they will only be effective if governments act immediately.

Double-space

Introduction

Thesis statement

The polar ice caps are melting at a rapid rate, and much of the scientific community agrees that global warming is one of the causes. The greenhouse effect, the mechanism that causes global warming, occurs when molecules of greenhouse gases in the atmosphere reflect the rays of the sun back to the earth. This mechanism enables our planet to maintain a temperature adequate for life. However, as the concentration of greenhouse gases in the atmosphere increases, more heat from the sun is retained, and the temperature of the earth rises.[1]

1″ 1″

Superscript numbers correspond to sources in the reference list

Greenhouse gases include carbon dioxide (CO_2), methane, and nitrous oxide.[2] Since the beginning of the industrial revolution in the late 1800s, people have been burning fossil fuels

1″

Polar Ice Caps 2

that create CO_2.[3] This CO_2 has led to an increase in the greenhouse effect and has contributed to the global warming that is melting the polar ice caps. As Figure 1 shows, the surface temperature of the earth has increased by about 1 degree Celsius (1.8 degrees Fahrenheit) since the 1850s. Some scientists have predicted that temperatures will increase even further.

Figure 1 Introduced

Figure placed close to where it is discussed

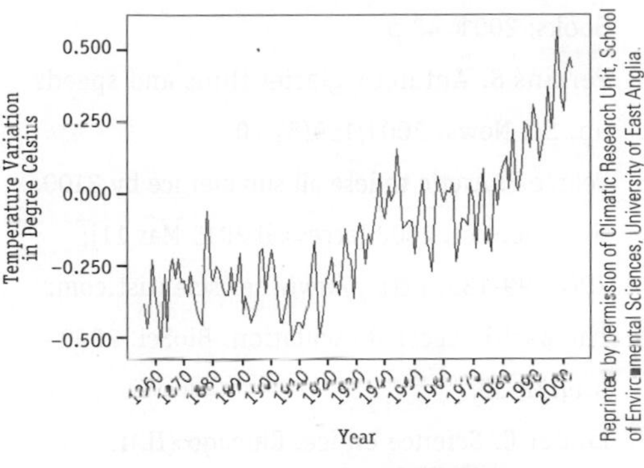

Fig. 1. Global temperature variation from the average during the base period 1860-2000 (adapted from Climatic research unit: data: temperature 2003). [accessed 2015 Mar 11]. http://www.cru.uea.ac.uk/cru/data/temperature.

Label, caption, and full source information

It is easy to see the effects of global warming. For example, the Pine Island Glacier in Antarctica was depleted at a rate of 1.6 meters per year between 1992 and 1999. This type of melting is very likely to increase the fresh water that

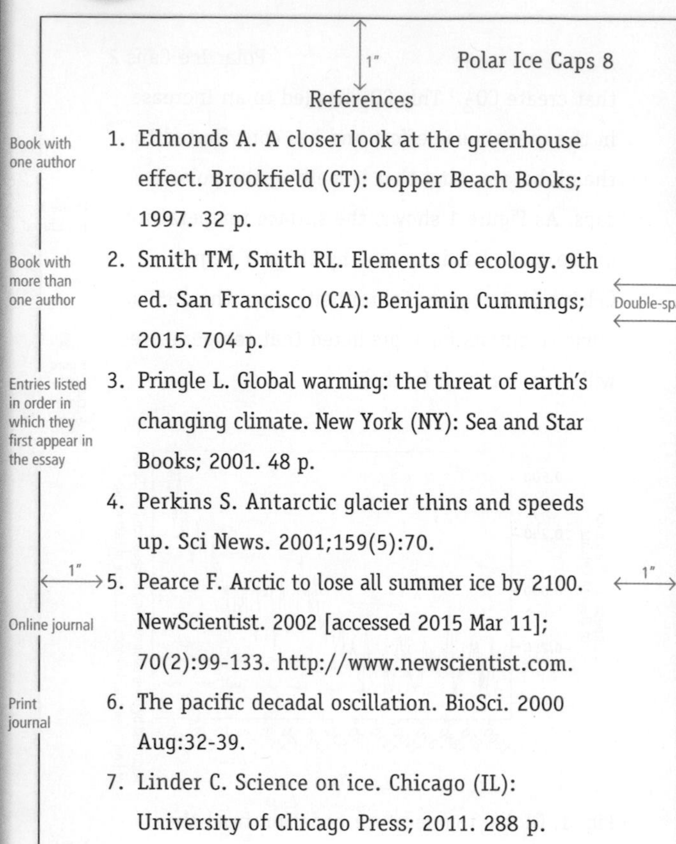

1"
Polar Ice Caps 8
References
Book with one author
1. Edmonds A. A closer look at the greenhouse effect. Brookfield (CT): Copper Beach Books; 1997. 32 p.
Book with more than one author
2. Smith TM, Smith RL. Elements of ecology. 9th ed. San Francisco (CA): Benjamin Cummings; 2015. 704 p.
Double-space
Entries listed in order in which they first appear in the essay
3. Pringle L. Global warming: the threat of earth's changing climate. New York (NY): Sea and Star Books; 2001. 48 p.
4. Perkins S. Antarctic glacier thins and speeds up. Sci News. 2001;159(5):70.
1"
5. Pearce F. Arctic to lose all summer ice by 2100. NewScientist. 2002 [accessed 2015 Mar 11]; 70(2):99-133. http://www.newscientist.com.
1"
Online journal
Print journal
6. The pacific decadal oscillation. BioSci. 2000 Aug:32-39.
7. Linder C. Science on ice. Chicago (IL): University of Chicago Press; 2011. 288 p.

13d Using Other Documentation Styles

The following style manuals describe documentation formats and manuscript guidelines used in various fields.

CHEMISTRY

Coghill, Anne M., and Lorrin R. Garson, eds. *The ACS Style Guide: Effective Communication of Scientific Information*. 3rd ed. Washington: American Chemical Society, 2006. Print.

GEOLOGY

Hansen, Wallace R., ed. *Suggestions to Authors of the Reports of the United States Geological Survey*. 7th ed. Washington: GPO, 1991. Print.

GOVERNMENT DOCUMENTS

Cheney, Debora. *The Complete Guide to Citing Government Information Resources: A Manual for Social Science & Business Research*. 3rd ed. Bethesda: Congressional Information Service, 2002. Print.

United States Government Printing Office. *Style Manual*. Washington: GPO, 2009. Print.

JOURNALISM

Associated Press. *The Associated Press Stylebook and Briefing on Media Law 2015*. 46th ed. New York: Basic, 2015. Print.

LAW

The Bluebook: A Uniform System of Citation. Comp. Editors of Columbia Law Review et al. 19th ed. Cambridge: Harvard Law Review Association, 2010. Print.

MATHEMATICS

American Mathematical Society. *AMS Author Handbook*. Providence: American Mathematical Society, 2014. Web.

MEDICINE

Iverson, Cheryl. *AMA Manual of Style: A Guide for Authors and Editors*. 10th ed. Oxford: Oxford UP, 2007. Print.

MUSIC

Holoman, D. Kern. *Writing about Music: A Style Sheet*. 2nd ed. Berkeley: U of California P, 2008. Print.

PHYSICS

American Institute of Physics. *AIP Style Manual*. 5th ed. Melville: American Institute of Physics, 2000. Print.

SCIENTIFIC AND TECHNICAL WRITING

Rubens, Philip, ed. *Science and Technical Writing: A Manual of Style*. 2nd ed. New York: Routledge, 2001. Print.

PART 4

Writing Grammatical Sentences

14 Revising Run-Ons 234

14a Recognizing Comma Splices and Fused Sentences 234
14b Correcting Comma Splices and Fused Sentences 234

15 Revising Fragments 236

15a Recognizing Fragments 236
15b Correcting Fragments 237
15c Using Fragments Intentionally 239

16 Understanding Agreement 240

16a Making Subjects and Verbs Agree 240
16b Making Pronouns and Antecedents Agree 243

17 Using Verbs 245

17a Using Irregular Verbs 245
17b Understanding Tense 248
17c Understanding Mood 251
17d Understanding Voice 252

18 Using Pronouns 253

18a Understanding Pronoun Case 253
18b Determining Pronoun Case in Special Situations 254
18c Revising Pronoun Reference Errors 256

19 Using Adjectives and Adverbs 258

19a Using Adjectives 258
19b Using Adverbs 259
19c Using Comparative and Superlative Forms 259

CHAPTER 14

Revising Run-Ons

14a Recognizing Comma Splices and Fused Sentences

See A2.3

A **run-on** is an error that occurs when two independent clauses are joined incorrectly. There are two kinds of run-ons: *comma splices* and *fused sentences.*

A **comma splice** is a run-on that occurs when two independent clauses are joined with just a comma. **A fused sentence** is a run-on that occurs when two independent clauses are joined with no punctuation.

Comma Splice: Charles Dickens created the character of Mr. Micawber, he also created Uriah Heep.

Fused Sentence: Charles Dickens created the character of Mr. Micawber he also created Uriah Heep.

14b Correcting Comma Splices and Fused Sentences

To correct a comma splice or fused sentence, use one of the following four strategies:

1. Add a period between the clauses, creating two separate sentences.
2. Add a semicolon between the clauses, creating a compound sentence.
3. Add a coordinating conjunction between the clauses, creating a compound sentence.
4. Subordinate one clause to the other, creating a complex sentence.

1 Add a Period

You can add a period between the independent clauses, creating two separate sentences. This is a good strategy to use when the clauses are long or when they are not closely related.

> In 1894, Frenchman Alfred Dreyfus was falsely convicted of treason~~,~~ *. His* ~~his~~ struggle for justice pitted the army against the civil libertarians.

2 Add a Semicolon

You can add a semicolon between two closely related clauses that convey parallel or contrasting information. The result will be a compound sentence. See 29a See 21a1

> Chippendale chairs have straight legs*;* however, Queen Anne chairs have curved legs.

Note: When you use a **transitional word or phrase** (such as *however, therefore*, or *for example*) to connect two independent clauses, the transitional element must be preceded by a semicolon and followed by a comma. If you use a comma alone, you create a comma splice. If you omit punctuation entirely, you create a fused sentence. See 20b

3 Add a Coordinating Conjunction

You can use a coordinating conjunction (*and, or, but, nor, for, so, yet*) to join two closely related clauses of equal importance into one **compound sentence**. The coordinating conjunction you choose indicates the relationship between the clauses: addition (*and*), contrast (*but, yet*), causality (*for, so*), or a choice of alternatives (*or, nor*). Be sure to add a comma before the coordinating conjunction. See 21a1

> Elias Howe invented the sewing machine, *and* Julia Ward Howe was a poet and social reformer.

4 Create a Complex Sentence

When the ideas in two independent clauses are not of equal importance, you can use an appropriate subordinating conjunction or a relative pronoun to join the clauses into one **complex sentence**, placing the less important idea in the dependent clause. See 21a2

Stravinsky's 1913 ballet *The Rite of Spring* shocked Parisians~~.~~ *because* the dancing seemed erotic.

Lady Mary Wortley Montagu*, who* had suffered from smallpox herself, ~~she~~ helped spread the practice of inoculation in the eighteenth century.

CHAPTER 15

Revising Fragments

15a Recognizing Fragments

A **fragment** is an incomplete sentence—a clause or a phrase—that is punctuated as if it were a sentence. A sentence may be incomplete for any of the following reasons:

- **It has no subject.**

  Many astrophysicists now believe that galaxies are distributed in clusters. And even form supercluster complexes.

- **It has no verb.**

  Every generation has its defining moments. Usually the events with the most news coverage.

- **It has neither a subject nor a verb.**

  Researchers are engaged in a variety of studies. Suggesting a link between alcoholism and heredity. (*Suggesting* is a **verbal**, which cannot serve as a sentence's main verb.)

See A1.3

See A2.3

- **It is a dependent clause.**

  Bishop Desmond Tutu was awarded the Nobel Peace Prize. Because he struggled to end apartheid.

  The pH meter and the spectrophotometer are two scientific instruments. That changed the chemistry laboratory dramatically.

Note: A sentence cannot consist of a single clause that begins with a subordinating conjunction (such as *because*) or a relative pronoun (such as *that*); moreover, unless it is a question, a sentence cannot consist of a single clause beginning with *when, where, who, which, what, why*, or *how*.

15b Correcting Fragments

If you identify a fragment in your writing, use one of the following three strategies to correct it.

1 Attach the Fragment to an Independent Clause

In most cases, the simplest way to correct a fragment is by attaching it to an adjacent independent clause that contains the missing words.

> President Lyndon Johnson did not seek a second term~~.~~ *for* ~~For~~ a number of reasons. (**prepositional phrase** fragment) See A2.3

> Students sometimes take a leave of absence~~.~~ *to* ~~To~~ decide on definite career goals. (**verbal phrase** fragment) See A2.3

> The pilot changed course~~.~~ *, realizing* ~~Realizing~~ that the weather was worsening. (verbal phrase fragment)

> Brian was the star forward of the Blue Devils~~.~~ *, the* ~~The~~ team with the best record. (**appositive** fragment) See 18b3

> Fairy tales are full of damsels in distress~~.~~ *, such* ~~Such~~ as Rapunzel. (appositive fragment)

> People with dyslexia have trouble reading~~.~~ *and* ~~And~~ may also find it difficult to write. (part of compound predicate)

> They took only a compass and a canteen~~.~~ *and* ~~And~~ some trail mix. (part of compound object)

> Property taxes rose sharply~~.~~ *although* ~~Although~~ city services declined. (**dependent clause** fragment) See A2.3

> The battery is dead~~.~~ *, which* ~~Which~~ means the car won't start. (dependent clause fragment)

Close-Up LISTS

When a fragment takes the form of a list, add a colon to connect the list to the independent clause that introduces it.

See 32a1

Tourists often outnumber residents in at least four European cities~~.~~ : Venice, Florence, Canterbury, and Bath.

2 Delete the Subordinating Conjunction or Relative Pronoun

When a fragment consists of a dependent clause that is punctuated as though it were a complete sentence, you can correct it by attaching it to an adjacent independent clause, as illustrated in **15b1**. Alternatively, you can simply delete the subordinating conjunction or relative pronoun.

Property taxes rose sharply. ~~Although city~~ *City* services declined. (subordinating conjunction *although* deleted)

The battery is dead. ~~Which~~ *This* means the car won't start. (relative pronoun *which* replaced by *this*, a word that can serve as the sentence's subject)

Note: Simply deleting the subordinating conjunction or relative pronoun, as in the two examples above, is usually the least desirable way to revise a sentence fragment because it is likely to create two choppy sentences and obscure the connection between them.

3 Supply the Missing Subject or Verb

Another way to correct a fragment is to add the missing words (a subject or a verb or both) that are needed to make the fragment a sentence.

In 1948, India became independent. ~~Divided~~ *It was divided* into the nations of India and Pakistan. (verbal phrase fragment)

A familiar trademark can increase a product's sales. ~~Reminding~~ *It reminds* shoppers that the product has a longstanding reputation. (verbal phrase fragment)

FRAGMENTS INTRODUCED BY TRANSITIONS

Some fragments are word groups that are introduced by transitional words and phrases, such as *also*, *finally*, *in addition*, and *now*, but are missing subjects and verbs. To correct such a fragment, you need to add the missing subject and verb.

See 20b

Finally, *he found* a new home for the family.

In addition, *we need* three new keyboards for the computer lab.

15c Using Fragments Intentionally

Fragments are often used in speech as well as in personal email, text messages, and other informal writing—as well as in journalism, creative writing, and advertising. In professional and academic writing, however, sentence fragments are generally not acceptable.

CHECKLIST

Using Fragments Intentionally

In college writing, it is permissible to use fragments in the following special situations:

- ❑ In lists
- ❑ In captions that accompany visuals
- ❑ In topic outlines
- ❑ In quoted dialogue
- ❑ In bulleted or numbered lists in *PowerPoint* presentations
- ❑ In titles and subtitles of essays and reports

CHAPTER 16

Understanding Agreement

See 23a4

Agreement is the correspondence between words in number, gender, or person. Subjects and verbs agree in **number** (singular or plural) and **person** (first, second, or third); pronouns and their antecedents agree in number, person, and **gender** (masculine, feminine, or neuter).

16a Making Subjects and Verbs Agree

Singular subjects take singular verbs, and plural subjects take plural verbs.

See 17b1

Present tense verbs, except *be* and *have*, add *-s* or *-es* when the subject is third-person singular. (Third-person singular subjects include nouns; the personal pronouns *he*, *she*, *it*, and *one*; and many **indefinite pronouns**.)

See 16a4

The President has the power to veto congressional legislation.

She frequently cites statistics to support her points.

In every group, somebody emerges as a natural leader.

Present tense verbs do not add *-s* or *-es* when the subject is a plural noun, a first-person or second-person pronoun (*I*, *we*, *you*), or a third-person plural pronoun (*they*).

Experts recommend that dieters avoid processed meat.

At this stratum, we see rocks dating back ten million years.

They say that even some wealthy people have defaulted on their student loans.

In the following situations, making subjects and verbs agree can be challenging for writers.

1 When Words Come between Subject and Verb

If a modifying phrase comes between the subject and the verb, the verb should agree with the subject, not with the last word in the modifying phrase.

The sound of the drumbeats builds in intensity in Eugene O'Neill's play *The Emperor Jones*.

The games won by the intramural team are few and far between.

This rule also applies to phrases introduced by *along with, as well as, in addition to, including*, and *together with.*

Heavy rain, along with high winds, causes hazardous driving conditions.

2 When Compound Subjects Are Joined by *And*

Compound subjects joined by *and* usually take plural verbs.

Air bags and antilock brakes are standard on all new models.

There are, however, two exceptions to this rule:

- Compound subjects joined by *and* that stand for a single idea or person are treated as a unit and take singular verbs.

  Rhythm and blues is a forerunner of rock and roll.

- When *each* or *every* precedes a compound subject joined by *and*, the subject takes a singular verb.

  Every desk and file cabinet was searched before the letter was found.

3 When Compound Subjects Are Joined by *Or*

Compound subjects joined by *or* (or by *either . . . or*, or *neither . . . nor*) may take either a singular or a plural verb.

If both subjects are singular, use a singular verb; if both are plural, use a plural verb. If one subject is singular and the other is plural, the verb agrees with the subject that is nearer to it.

Either radiation treatments or chemotherapy is combined with surgery for effective results.

Either chemotherapy or radiation treatments are combined with surgery for effective results.

4 With Indefinite Pronoun Subjects

Most indefinite pronouns—*another, anyone, everyone, one, each, either, neither, anything, everything, something, nothing, nobody*, and *somebody*—are singular and take singular verbs. ml 44c3

Anyone is welcome to apply for this grant.

Some indefinite pronouns—*both, many, few, several, others*—are plural and take plural verbs.

Several of the articles are useful.

A few indefinite pronouns—*some, all, any, more, most,* and *none*—can be singular or plural, depending on the noun they refer to.

Some of this trouble is to be expected. (*Some* refers to *trouble.*)

Some of the spectators are getting restless. (*Some* refers to *spectators.*)

5 With Collective Noun Subjects

A **collective noun** names a group of persons or things—for instance, *navy, union, association, band.* When a collective noun refers to the group as a unit (as it usually does), it takes a singular verb; when it refers to the individuals or items that make up the group, it takes a plural verb.

To many people, the royal family symbolizes Great Britain. (The family, as a unit, is the symbol.)

The family all eat at different times. (Each family member eats separately.)

Phrases that name fixed amounts—*three-quarters, twenty dollars, the majority*—are treated like collective nouns. When the amount denotes a unit, it takes a singular verb; when it denotes part of the whole, it takes a plural verb.

Three-quarters of his usual salary is not enough to live on.

Three-quarters of the patients improve dramatically after treatment.

Note: *The number* is always singular, and *a number* is always plural: *The number of voters has declined; A number of students have missed the opportunity to preregister.*

6 When Singular Subjects Have Plural Forms

A singular subject takes a singular verb even if the form of the subject is plural.

Statistics deals with the collection and analysis of data.

When such a word has a plural meaning, however, use a plural verb.

The statistics prove him wrong.

7 When Subject-Verb Order Is Inverted

Even when word order is inverted so that the verb comes before the subject (as it does in questions and in sentences beginning with *there is* or *there are*), the subject and verb must agree.

ml 44f

Is either answer correct?

There are currently thirteen US courts of appeals.

8 With Linking Verbs

A linking verb should agree with its subject, not with the subject complement.

See 19a

The problem was termites.

Termites were the problem.

9 With Relative Pronouns

When you use a relative pronoun (*who, which, that,* and so on) to introduce a dependent clause, the verb in the dependent clause agrees in number with the pronoun's **antecedent**, the word to which the pronoun refers.

See A1.2

The farmer is among the ones who suffer during a grain embargo.

The farmer is the only one who suffers during a grain embargo.

16b Making Pronouns and Antecedents Agree

A pronoun must agree with its **antecedent**—the word or word group to which the pronoun refers.

Singular pronouns—such as *he, him, she, her, it, me, myself,* and *oneself*—should refer to singular antecedents. Plural pronouns—such as *we, us, they, them,* and *their*—should refer to plural antecedents.

1 With Compound Antecedents

In most cases, use a plural pronoun to refer to a **compound antecedent** (two or more words connected by *and*).

> Mormonism and Christian Science were similar in their beginnings.
>
> However, there are several exceptions to this general rule:

- Use a singular pronoun when a compound antecedent is preceded by *each* or *every*.

  > Every programming language and software package has its limitations.

- Use a singular pronoun to refer to two or more singular antecedents linked by *or* or *nor*.

  > Neither Thoreau nor Whitman lived to see his work read widely.

- When one part of a compound antecedent is singular and one part is plural, the pronoun agrees in person and number with the antecedent that is nearer to it.

  > Neither the boy nor his parents had fastened their seat belts.

2 With Collective Noun Antecedents

If the meaning of a collective noun antecedent is singular (as it will be in most cases), use a singular pronoun. If the meaning is plural, use a plural pronoun.

> The teachers' union announced its plan to strike. (The members acted as a unit.)

> The team moved to their positions. (Each member acted individually.)

3 With Indefinite Pronoun Antecedents

See 16a4 Most **indefinite pronouns**—*each, either, neither, one, anyone*, and the like—are singular and take singular pronouns.

> Neither of the men had his proposal ready by the deadline.

Each of these neighborhoods has its own traditions and values.

A few indefinite pronouns are plural; some others can be singular or plural.

Close-Up PRONOUN-ANTECEDENT AGREEMENT

In speech and in informal writing, many people use the plural pronouns *they* or *their* with singular indefinite pronouns that refer to people, such as *someone, everyone,* and *nobody*.

Everyone can present their own viewpoint.

In college writing, however, you should avoid using a plural pronoun with a singular indefinite pronoun subject. Instead, you can use both the masculine and the feminine pronoun.

Everyone can present his or her own viewpoint.

Or, you can make the sentence's subject plural.

All participants can present their own viewpoints.

The use of *his* to refer to a singular indefinite pronoun (*Everyone can present* his *own viewpoint*) is considered sexist language.

See 26c2

CHAPTER 17

Using Verbs

17a Using Irregular Verbs

A **regular verb** forms both its past tense and its past participle by adding *-d* or *-ed* to the **base form** of the verb (the present tense form of the verb that is used with *I*).

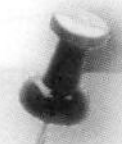

Principal Parts of Regular Verbs

Base Form	Past Tense Form	Past Participle
smile	smiled	smiled
talk	talked	talked

Irregular verbs do not follow this pattern. The chart that follows lists the principal parts of the most frequently used irregular verbs.

Frequently Used Irregular Verbs

Base Form	Past Tense Form	Past Participle
arise	arose	arisen
awake	awoke, awaked	awoke, awaked
be	was/were	been
beat	beat	beaten
begin	began	begun
bend	bent	bent
bet	bet, betted	bet
bite	bit	bitten
blow	blew	blown
break	broke	broken
bring	brought	brought
build	built	built
burst	burst	burst
buy	bought	bought
catch	caught	caught
choose	chose	chosen
cling	clung	clung
come	came	come
cost	cost	cost
deal	dealt	dealt
dig	dug	dug
dive	dived, dove	dived
do	did	done
drag	dragged	dragged
draw	drew	drawn
drink	drank	drunk
drive	drove	driven
eat	ate	eaten

Base Form	Past Tense Form	Past Participle
fall	fell	fallen
fight	fought	fought
find	found	found
fly	flew	flown
forget	forgot	forgotten, forgot
freeze	froze	frozen
get	got	gotten
give	gave	given
go	went	gone
grow	grew	grown
hang (suspend)	hung	hung
have	had	had
hear	heard	heard
keep	kept	kept
know	knew	known
lay (place/put)	laid	laid
lead	led	led
lend	lent	lent
let	let	let
lie (recline)	lay	lain
make	made	made
prove	proved	proved, proven
read	read	read
ride	rode	ridden
ring	rang	rung
rise	rose	risen
run	ran	run
say	said	said
see	saw	seen
set (place)	set	set
shake	shook	shaken
shrink	shrank, shrunk	shrunk, shrunken
sing	sang	sung
sink	sank	sunk
sit	sat	sat
speak	spoke	spoken
speed	sped, speeded	sped, speeded
spin	spun	spun
spring	sprang	sprung
stand	stood	stood
steal	stole	stolen
strike	struck	struck, stricken
swear	swore	sworn
swim	swam	swum
swing	swung	swung
take	took	taken
teach	taught	taught

continued

Frequently Used Irregular Verbs *(continued)*

Base Form	Past Tense Form	Past Participle
throw	threw	thrown
wake	woke, waked	waked, woken
wear	wore	worn
wring	wrung	wrung
write	wrote	written

Close-Up *LIE/LAY AND SIT/SET*

Lie means "to recline" and does not take an object ("He likes to *lie* on the floor"); *lay* means "to place" or "to put" and does take an object ("He wants to *lay* a rug on the floor").

Base Form	Past Tense Form	Past Participle
lie	lay	lain
lay	laid	laid

Sit means "to assume a seated position" and does not take an object ("She wants to *sit* on the table"); *set* means "to place" or "to put" and usually takes an object ("She wants to *set* a vase on the table").

Base Form	Past Tense Form	Past Participle
sit	sat	sat
set	set	set

17b Understanding Tense

ml 44a2 Tense is the form a verb takes to indicate when an action occurred or when a condition existed.

1 Using the Simple Tenses

The **simple tenses** include *present, past*, and *future*:

- The **present tense** usually indicates an action that is taking place at the time it is expressed or an action that occurs regularly.

  I see your point. (an action taking place when it is expressed)

We wear wool in the winter. (an action that occurs regularly)

Close-Up SPECIAL USES OF THE PRESENT TENSE

The present tense has four special uses:

1. **To indicate future time:** The grades arrive next Thursday.
2. **To state a generally held belief:** Studying pays off.
3. **To state a scientific truth:** An object at rest tends to stay at rest.
4. **To discuss a literary work:** *Family Installments* tells the story of a Puerto Rican family.

- The **past tense** indicates that an action has already taken place.

  John Glenn orbited the earth three times on February 20, 1962. (an action completed in the past)

  As a young man, Mark Twain traveled through the Southwest. (an action that occurred once or many times in the past but did not extend into the present)

- The **future tense** indicates that an action will or is likely to take place.

  Halley's Comet will reappear in 2061. (a future action that will definitely occur)

  The growth of community colleges will probably continue. (a future action that is likely to occur)

2 Using the Perfect Tenses

The **perfect tenses** indicate actions that were or will be completed before other actions or conditions. The perfect tenses are formed with the appropriate tense form of the auxiliary verb *have* plus the past participle:

- The **present perfect** tense can indicate either of two kinds of continuing action beginning in the past.

Dr. Kim has finished studying the effects of BHA on rats. (an action that began in the past and is finished at the present time)

My mother has invested her money wisely. (an action that began in the past and extends into the present)

- The **past perfect** tense indicates an action occurring before a certain time in the past.

  By 1946, engineers had built the first electronic digital computer.

- The **future perfect** tense indicates that an action will be finished by a certain future time.

  By Tuesday, the transit authority will have run out of money.

3 Using the Progressive Tenses

The **progressive tenses** indicate continuing action. They are formed with the appropriate tense of the verb *be* plus the present participle:

- The **present progressive** tense indicates that something is happening at the time it is expressed in speech or writing.

  The volcano is erupting, and lava is flowing toward the town.

- The **past progressive** tense can indicate either of two kinds of past action.

  Roderick Usher's actions were becoming increasingly bizarre. (a continuing action in the past)

  The French revolutionary Marat was stabbed to death while he was bathing. (an action occurring at the same time in the past as another action)

- The **future progressive** tense indicates a continuing action in the future.

  The treasury secretary will be monitoring the money supply very carefully.

- The **present perfect progressive** tense indicates action continuing from the past into the present and possibly into the future.

  Rescuers have been working around the clock.

- The **past perfect progressive** tense indicates that a past action went on until another one occurred.

    President Kennedy had been working on civil rights legislation before he was assassinated.

- The **future perfect progressive** tense indicates that an action will continue until a certain future time.

    By eleven o'clock, we will have been driving for seven hours.

17c Understanding Mood

Mood is the form a verb takes to indicate whether a writer is making a statement, asking a question, giving a command, or expressing a wish or a contrary-to-fact statement. There are three moods in English:

- The **indicative** mood states a fact, expresses an opinion, or asks a question: *Jackie Robinson had a great impact on professional baseball.*
- The **imperative** mood is used in commands and direct requests: *Use a dictionary.*
- The **subjunctive** mood is used to express wishes, contrary-to-fact conditions, and requests or recommendations.

The **present subjunctive** is used in *that* clauses after words such as *ask, demand, suggest, require,* and *recommend.* The present subjunctive uses the base form of the verb, regardless of the subject.

Captain Ahab demanded that his crew hunt the white whale.

The report recommended that doctors be more flexible.

The **past subjunctive** is used in **conditional statements** (statements beginning with *if, as if,* or *as though* that are contrary to fact and statements that express a wish). The past subjunctive has the same form as the past tense of the verb, except for the verb *be,* which uses *were,* even with singular subjects.

If John went home, he could see Marsha. (John is not home.)

The father acted as if he were having the baby. (The father couldn't be having the baby.)

I wish I were more organized. (expresses a wish)

Note: In many situations, the subjunctive mood can sound stiff or formal. To eliminate the need for a subjunctive construction, rephrase the sentence.

> The group asked ~~that~~ the city council ^to ban smoking in public places.

17d Understanding Voice

Voice is the form a verb takes to indicate whether the subject of the verb acts or is acted upon. When the subject of a verb does something—that is, acts—the verb is in the **active voice**. When something is done to the subject of a verb—that is, the subject is acted upon—the verb is in the **passive voice**.

> **Active Voice:** Hart Crane wrote *The Bridge*.
>
> **Passive Voice:** *The Bridge* was written by Hart Crane.

Because the active voice emphasizes the person or thing performing an action, it is usually clearer and stronger than the passive voice. For this reason, you should usually use the active voice in your college writing.

> *The students chose investigative*
> ^~~Investigative~~ reporter Bob Woodward ~~was chosen by the students~~ as the graduation speaker.

Some scientific disciplines, however, encourage the use of the passive voice. The purpose is to convey objectivity—to shift the focus away from the scientists and to emphasize the experimental results.

> Grits are eaten throughout the South. (Passive voice emphasizes the fact that grits are eaten; who eats them is not important.)
>
> DDT was found in soil samples. (Passive voice emphasizes the discovery of DDT; who found it is not important.)

CHAPTER 18

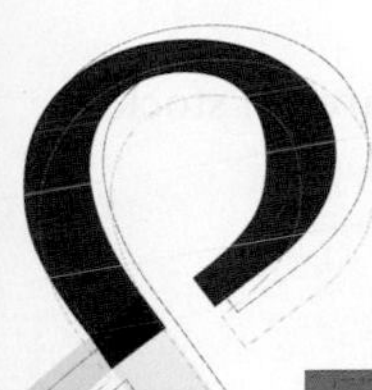

Using Pronouns

18a Understanding Pronoun Case

Pronouns change **case** to indicate their function in a sentence. English has three cases: *subjective, objective,* and *possessive.*

Pronoun Case Forms

Subjective							
I	he, she	it	we	you	they	who	whoever
Objective							
me	him, her	it	us	you	them	whom	whomever
Possessive							
my mine	his, her hers	its	our ours	your yours	their theirs	whose	

1 Subjective Case

A pronoun takes the **subjective case** in these situations.

Subject of a Verb: I bought a new mountain bike.

Subject Complement: It was he for whom the men were looking.

2 Objective Case

A pronoun takes the **objective case** in these situations.

Direct Object: Our sociology teacher asked Adam and me to work on the project.

Indirect Object: The plumber's bill gave them quite a shock.

Object of a Preposition: We own ten shares of stock between us.

Close-Up *I* AND *ME*

I is not necessarily more appropriate than *me*. In the following situation, *me* is correct.

> Just between you and me [not *I*], I think the data are inconclusive. (*Me* is the object of the preposition *between*.)

3 Possessive Case

A pronoun takes the **possessive case** when it indicates ownership. The possessive case is also used before a gerund. See A1.3

> Napoleon approved of their [not *them*] ruling Naples. (*Ruling* is a gerund.)

18b Determining Pronoun Case in Special Situations

1 In Comparisons with *Than* or *As*

When a comparison ends with a pronoun, the pronoun's function in the sentence determines your choice of pronoun case. If the pronoun functions as a subject, use the subjective case; if it functions as an object, use the objective case. You can determine the function of the pronoun by completing the comparison.

> Darcy likes John more than I. (. . . more than *I* like John; *I* is the subject.)
>
> Darcy likes John more than me. (. . . more than she likes *me*; *me* is the object.)

2 With *Who* and *Whom*

The case of the pronouns *who* and *whom* depends on their function *within their own clause*. When a pronoun serves as the subject of its clause, use *who* or *whoever*; when it functions as an object, use *whom* or *whomever*.

> The Salvation Army gives food and shelter to whoever is in need. (*Whoever* is the subject of the dependent clause.)
>
> I wonder whom jazz musician Miles Davis influenced. (*Whom* is the object of *influenced* in the dependent clause.)

Close-Up PRONOUN CASE IN QUESTIONS

To determine the case of *who* at the beginning of a question, use a personal pronoun to answer the question. The case of *who* should be the same as the case of the personal pronoun.

> Who wrote *The Age of Innocence*? She wrote it. (subject)
>
> Whom do you support for mayor? I support him. (object)

3 With Appositives

An **appositive** is a noun or noun phrase that identifies or renames an adjacent noun or pronoun. The case of a pronoun in an appositive depends on the function of the word the appositive identifies or renames. ml 44c4

> Two artists, he and Smokey Robinson, recorded for Motown Records. (*Artists* is the subject of the sentence, so the pronoun in the appositive *he and Smokey Robinson* takes the subjective case.)
>
> We heard two Motown recording artists, Smokey Robinson and him. (*Artists* is the object of the verb *heard*, so the pronoun in the appositive *Smokey Robinson and him* takes the objective case.)

4 With *We* and *Us* before a Noun

When a first-person plural pronoun directly precedes a noun, the case of the pronoun depends on the function of the noun in the sentence.

> We women must stick together. (*Women* is the subject of the sentence, so the pronoun *we* takes the subjective case.)

Good teachers make learning easy for us students. (*Students* is the object of the preposition *for*, so the pronoun *us* takes the objective case.)

18c Revising Pronoun Reference Errors

ml 44c1 An **antecedent** is the word or word group to which a pronoun refers. The connection between a pronoun and its antecedent should be clear.

Alicia forgot her cell phone.

The students missed their train.

1 Ambiguous Antecedents

Sometimes it is not clear to which antecedent a pronoun—for example, *this*, *that*, *which*, or *it*—refers. In such cases, eliminate the ambiguity by substituting a noun for the pronoun.

The accountant took out his calculator and added up the list of numbers. Then, he put ~~it~~ *the calculator* back in his briefcase. (The pronoun *it* can refer either to *calculator* or to *list of numbers*.)

Sometimes a pronoun—for example, *this*—does not seem to refer to any specific antecedent. In such cases, supply a noun to clarify the reference.

Some one-celled organisms contain chlorophyll yet are considered animals. This *paradox* illustrates the difficulty of classifying single-celled organisms. (What does *this* refer to?)

2 Remote Antecedents

The farther a pronoun is from its antecedent, the more difficult it is for readers to make a connection between them. If a pronoun and its antecedent are far apart, replace the pronoun with a noun.

During the mid-1800s, many Czechs began to immigrate to America. By 1860, about 23,000 Czechs had left their country. By 1900, 13,000 Czech immigrants were coming to ~~its~~ *America's* shores each year.

3 Nonexistent Antecedents

Sometimes a pronoun refers to an antecedent that does not appear in the sentence. In such cases, replace the pronoun with a noun.

Our township has decided to build a computer lab in the elementary school. ~~They~~ *Teachers* feel that fourth-graders should begin using computers. (What does *they* refer to?)

Close-Up *WHO, WHICH, AND THAT*

In general, *who* refers to people or to animals that have names. *Which* and *that* refer to objects, events, or unnamed animals. When referring to an antecedent, be sure to choose the appropriate pronoun (*who, which*, or *that*).

David Henry Hwang, who wrote the Tony Award–winning play *M. Butterfly*, also wrote *Yellow Face* and *Chinglish*.

The spotted owl, which lives in old-growth forests, is in danger of extinction.

Houses that are built today are usually more energy efficient than those built twenty years ago.

Never use *that* to refer to a person:

The man ~~that~~ *who* won the trophy is my neighbor.

Note: Use *which* to introduce nonrestrictive clauses, which are set off by commas. Use *that* to introduce restrictive clauses, which are not set off by commas. (*Who* can introduce either restrictive or nonrestrictive clauses.) See 28d1

CHAPTER 19

Using Adjectives and Adverbs

Adjectives modify nouns and pronouns. **Adverbs** modify verbs, adjectives, or other adverbs—or entire phrases, clauses, or sentences.

MULTILINGUAL TIP
For information on correct placement of adjectives and adverbs in a sentence, **see 44d1.**
For information on correct order of adjectives in a series, **see 44d2.**

The function of a word in a sentence, not its form, determines whether it is an adjective or an adverb. Although many adverbs (such as *immediately* and *hopelessly*) end in *-ly*, others (such as *almost* and *very*) do not. Moreover, some words that end in *-ly* (such as *lively*) are adjectives.

19a Using Adjectives

Use an **adjective**, not an adverb, to modify a noun or a pronoun. Also use an adjective as a subject complement. See A1.3 A subject complement is a word that follows a linking verb and modifies the sentence's subject, not its verb. A **linking verb** does not show physical or emotional action. *Seem, appear, believe, become, grow, turn, remain, prove, look, sound, smell, taste, feel,* and the forms of the verb *be* are (or can be used as) linking verbs.

> Michelle seemed brave. (*Seemed* shows no action, so it is a linking verb. Because *brave* is a subject complement that modifies the noun *Michelle*, it takes the adjective form.)

> Michelle smiled bravely. (*Smiled* shows action, so it is not a linking verb. Because *bravely* modifies *smiled*, it takes the adverb form.)

Note: Sometimes the same verb can function as either a linking verb or an action verb.

> He looked hungry. (Here, *looked* is a linking verb; *hungry* modifies the subject.)

He looked <u>hungrily</u> at the sandwich. (Here, *looked* is an action verb; *hungrily* modifies the verb.)

19b Using Adverbs

Use an **adverb**, not an adjective, to modify a verb, an adjective, or another adverb—or an entire phrase, clause, or sentence.

> Most students did ~~great~~ very well on the midterm. (*Very* modifies *well*; *well* modifies *did*.)

> My parents dress a lot more ~~conservative~~ conservatively than my friends do. (*More* modifies *conservatively*; *conservatively* modifies *dress*.)

Close-Up USING ADJECTIVES AND ADVERBS

In informal speech, adjective forms such as *good, bad, sure, real, slow, quick*, and *loud* are often used to modify verbs, adjectives, and adverbs. Avoid these informal modifiers in college writing.

> The program ran ~~real good~~ really well the first time we tried it, but the new system performed ~~bad~~ badly.

19c Using Comparative and Superlative Forms

Most adjectives and adverbs have **comparative** and **superlative** forms.

Comparative and Superlative Forms

Form	Function	Example
Positive	Describes a quality; indicates no comparison	big, easily

continued

Comparative and Superlative Forms *(continued)*

Form	Function	Example
Comparative	Indicates comparison between two qualities (greater or lesser)	bigger, more easily
Superlative	Indicates comparison among more than two qualities (greatest or least)	biggest, most easily

1 Regular Comparative and Superlative Forms

To form the comparative and superlative, all one-syllable adjectives and many two-syllable adjectives (particularly those that end in *-y, -ly, -le, -er*, and *-ow*) add *-er* or *-est*: slower, funnier; slowest, funniest. (Note that a final *y* becomes *i* before the *-er* or *-est* is added.)

Other two-syllable adjectives and all long adjectives form the comparative with *more* and the superlative with *most*: more famous, more incredible; most famous, most incredible.

Adverbs ending in *-ly* also form the comparative with *more* and the superlative with *most*: more slowly; most slowly. Other adverbs use the *-er* and *-est* endings: sooner; soonest.

All adjectives and adverbs form the comparative with *less* (less lovely; less slowly) and the superlative with *least* (least lovely; least slowly).

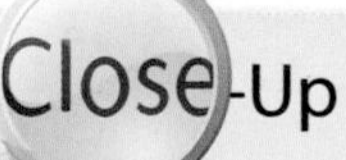

USING COMPARATIVES AND SUPERLATIVES

- Never use both *more* and *-er* to form the comparative, and never use both *most* and *-est* to form the superlative.

  Nothing could have been ~~more~~ easier.

  Jack is the ~~most~~ meanest person I know.

- Never use the superlative when comparing only two things.

  Stacy is the *older* ~~oldest~~ of the two sisters.

- Never use the comparative when comparing more than two things.

  We chose the *earliest* ~~earlier~~ of the four appointments.

2 Irregular Comparative and Superlative Forms

Some adjectives and adverbs have irregular comparative and superlative forms.

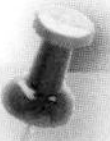

Irregular Comparative and Superlative Forms

	Positive	Comparative	Superlative
Adjectives:	good	better	best
	bad	worse	worst
	a little	less	least
	many, much, some	more	most
Adverbs:	well	better	best
	badly	worse	worst

Close-Up ILLOGICAL COMPARATIVE AND SUPERLATIVE FORMS

Many adjectives—for example, *perfect, unique, excellent, impossible, parallel, empty*, and *dead*—are **absolutes**; therefore, they have no comparative or superlative forms.

I saw ~~the most~~ ^a^ unique vase in the museum.

These adjectives can, however, be modified by words that suggest approaching the absolute state—*nearly* or *almost*, for example.

He revised until his draft was almost perfect.

Note: Some adverbs, particularly those indicating time, place, and degree (*almost, very, here, immediately*), do not have comparative or superlative forms.

PART 5

Writing Effective Paragraphs and Sentences

20 Writing Effective Paragraphs 264

20a Writing Unified Paragraphs 264
20b Writing Coherent Paragraphs 265
20c Writing Well-Developed Paragraphs 266
20d Writing Introductory and Concluding Paragraphs 267

21 Writing Varied Sentences 269

21a Varying Sentence Structure 269
21b Varying Sentence Length 271
21c Varying Sentence Openings 272

22 Writing Concise Sentences 273

22a Eliminating Wordiness 274
22b Eliminating Unnecessary Repetition 275
22c Tightening Rambling Sentences 276

23 Revising Awkward or Confusing Sentences 277

23a Revising Unnecessary Shifts 278
23b Revising Mixed Constructions 279
23c Revising Faulty Predication 279

24 Using Parallelism 280

24a Using Parallelism Effectively 280
24b Revising Faulty Parallelism 281

25 Placing Modifiers Carefully 282

25a Revising Misplaced Modifiers 282
25b Revising Intrusive Modifiers 284
25c Revising Dangling Modifiers 284

26 Choosing Words 285

26a Choosing the Right Word 285
26b Avoiding Inappropriate Language 287
26c Avoiding Offensive Language 288

CHAPTER 20

Writing Effective Paragraphs

A **paragraph** is a group of related sentences. A paragraph may be complete in itself or part of a longer piece of writing.

CHECKLIST

When to Begin a New Paragraph

- ❑ Begin a new paragraph whenever you move from one major point to another.
- ❑ Begin a new paragraph whenever you move your readers from one time period or location to another.
- ❑ Begin a new paragraph whenever you introduce a major new step in a process.
- ❑ Begin a new paragraph when you want to emphasize an important idea.
- ❑ Begin a new paragraph every time a new person speaks.
- ❑ Begin a new paragraph to signal the end of your introduction and also the beginning of your conclusion.

20a Writing Unified Paragraphs

A paragraph is **unified** when it develops a single main idea. The **topic sentence** states the main idea of the paragraph, and the other sentences in the paragraph support that idea.

Topic sentence

Support

I was a listening child, careful to hear the very different sounds of Spanish and English. Wide-eyed with hearing, I'd listen to sounds more than words. First, there were English (*gringo*) sounds. So many words were still unknown that when the butcher or the lady at the drugstore said something to me, exotic polysyllabic sounds would bloom in the midst of their sentences. Often the speech of people in public seemed to me very loud, booming with confidence. The man behind the counter would literally ask, "What can I do for you?" But by being so firm and so clear, the sound of his voice said that he was a *gringo;* he belonged in public society. (Richard Rodriguez, *Aria: Memoir of a Bilingual Childhood*)

Note: A topic sentence usually comes at the beginning of a paragraph, but it may appear in the middle or at the end—or even be implied.

20b Writing Coherent Paragraphs

A paragraph is **coherent** when all its sentences clearly relate to one another. **Transitional words and phrases** establish coherence by reinforcing the spatial, chronological, and logical connections among the sentences in a paragraph.

> Napoleon certainly made a change for the worse by leaving his small kingdom of Elba. After Waterloo, he went back to Paris, and he abdicated for a second time. A hundred days after his return from Elba, he fled to Rochefort in hope of escaping to America. Finally, he gave himself up to the English captain of the ship *Bellerophon*. Once again, he suggested that the Prince Regent grant him asylum, and once again, he was refused. In the end, all he saw of England was the Devon coast and Plymouth Sound as he passed on to the remote island of St. Helena. After six years of exile, he died on May 5, 1821, at the age of fifty-two. (Norman Mackenzie, *The Escape from Elba*)

Topic sentence

Transitional words and phrases establish chronology of events

Using Transitional Words and Phrases

To Signal Sequence or Addition

again, also, besides, first . . . second . . . third, furthermore, in addition, moreover, one . . . another, too

To Signal Time

after, afterward, as soon as, at first, at the same time, before, earlier, finally, in the meantime, later, meanwhile, next, now, since, soon, subsequently, then, until

To Signal Comparison

also, in comparison, likewise, similarly

To Signal Contrast

although, but, despite, even though, however, in contrast, instead, meanwhile, nevertheless, nonetheless, on the contrary, on the one hand . . . on the other hand, still, whereas, yet

continued

Using Transitional Words and Phrases *(continued)*

To Introduce Examples

for example, for instance, namely

To Signal Narrowing of Focus

after all, indeed, in fact, in other words, in particular, specifically, that is

To Introduce Conclusions or Summaries

as a result, consequently, in conclusion, in other words, in summary, therefore, thus, to conclude

To Signal Concession

admittedly, certainly, granted, naturally, of course

To Introduce Causes or Effects

accordingly, as a result, because, consequently, hence, since, so, then, therefore

See 24a

Note: **Parallel** words, phrases, and clauses ("He was a patriot. . . . He was a reformer. . . . He was an innovator. . . .") and repeated key words and phrases ("He invented a new type of printing press. . . . This printing press . . .") can also help writers achieve coherence.

20c Writing Well-Developed Paragraphs

A paragraph is **well developed** when it includes the support—examples, statistics, expert opinion, and so on—that readers need to understand and accept its main idea.

Topic sentence

Specific examples

Specific examples

From Thanksgiving until Christmas, children are bombarded with ads for violent toys and games. Toy manufacturers persist in thinking that only toys that appeal to children's aggressiveness will sell. One television commercial praises the merits of a commando team that attacks and captures a miniature enemy base. Toy soldiers wear realistic uniforms and carry automatic rifles, pistols, knives, grenades, and ammunition. Another commercial shows laughing children shooting one another with plastic rocket fighters and tank-like vehicles. Despite claims that they (unlike action toys) have educational value, video games have increased the level of violence. The most popular video games—such as *Grand Theft Auto V* and *Resident Evil 6*—depict graphic violence, criminal behavior, and other objectionable material. One game allows players to hack up and destroy zombies with a variety of weapons, such as swords, picks, and chainsaws as well as guns and grenades. Other best-selling games graphically simulate hand-to-hand combat on city streets. The real question is why parents buy these violent toys and games for their children. (student writer)

Note: Length alone does not determine whether a paragraph is well developed. The amount and kind of support you need depend on your audience, your purpose, and the scope of your paragraph's main idea.

20d Writing Introductory and Concluding Paragraphs

1 Introductory Paragraphs

An **introductory paragraph** prepares readers for the essay to follow and makes them want to read further. Typically, it introduces the subject, narrows it, and then states the essay's thesis.

> Although it has now faded from view, the telegraph lives on within the communications technologies that have subsequently built upon its foundations: the telephone, the fax machine, and, more recently, the Internet. And, ironically, it is the Internet—despite being regarded as a quintessentially modern means of communication—that has the most in common with its telegraphic ancestor. (Tom Standage, *The Victorian Internet*)

Thesis statement

An introductory paragraph may also arouse readers' interest with a relevant quotation, a compelling question, a definition, or a controversial statement.

Note: Avoid introductions that simply announce your subject ("In my essay, I will talk about Lady Macbeth") or that undercut your credibility ("I don't know much about alternative energy sources, but I would like to present my opinion").

CHECKLIST

Revising Introductions

- ❑ Does your introductory paragraph include a thesis statement?
- ❑ Does it lead naturally into the body of your essay?
- ❑ Does it arouse your readers' interest?
- ❑ Does it avoid statements that simply announce your subject or that undercut your credibility?

2 Concluding Paragraphs

A **concluding paragraph** reminds readers what they have read. Typically, it begins by reinforcing the essay's thesis and then moves to more general comments. If possible, it should end with a statement that readers will remember.

> As an Arab-American, I feel I have the best of two worlds. I'm proud to be part of the melting pot, proud to contribute to the tremendous diversity of cultures, customs and traditions that make this country unique. But Arab-bashing—public acceptance of hatred and bigotry—is something no American can be proud of. (Ellen Mansoor Collier, "I Am Not a Terrorist")

A concluding paragraph may also include a prediction, a warning, a recommendation, or a relevant quotation.

Note: Avoid conclusions that just repeat your introduction in different words, offer apologies, or undercut your credibility ("Of course, I am not an expert" or "At least this is my opinion").

CHECKLIST

Revising Conclusions

- ❑ Does your concluding paragraph sum up your essay, perhaps by reviewing the essay's main points?
- ❑ Does it do more than just repeat the introduction?
- ❑ Does it avoid apologies?
- ❑ Does it end memorably?

CHAPTER 21

Writing Varied Sentences

21a Varying Sentence Structure

Paragraphs that mix simple sentences with compound and complex sentences are more varied—and therefore more interesting—than those that do not. See A2.2

1 Using Compound Sentences

A **compound sentence** consists of two or more independent clauses joined with *coordinating conjunctions, transitional words and phrases, correlative conjunctions, semicolons*, or *colons*.

Coordinating Conjunctions

The pianist was nervous, but the concert was a success.

Note: Remember to use a comma before the coordinating conjunction—*and, or, nor, but, for, so*, and *yet*—that joins the two independent clauses. See A2.3

Transitional Words and Phrases Frequently used transitional words and phrases include conjunctive adverbs such as *consequently, finally, still*, and *thus*, as well as expressions such as *for example, in fact*, and *for instance*. See 20b

The saxophone does not belong to the brass family; in fact, it is a member of the woodwind family.

Note: Use a semicolon—not a comma—before the transitional word or phrase that joins the two independent clauses.

Correlative Conjunctions

Either he left his coat in his locker, or he left it on the bus.

Semicolons

Alaska is the largest state; Rhode Island is the smallest.

Colons

He got his orders: he was to leave on Sunday.

Close-Up USING COMPOUND SENTENCES

When you join independent clauses to create a compound sentence, you help readers to see the relationships between your ideas. Compound sentences can indicate the following relationships:

- Addition (*and, in addition, not only . . . but also*)
- Contrast (*but, however*)
- Causal relationships (*so, therefore, consequently*)
- Alternatives (*or, either . . . or*)

2 Using Complex Sentences

See A2.3

A **complex sentence** consists of one independent clause and at least one dependent clause. In a complex sentence, a **subordinating conjunction** or **relative pronoun** links the independent and dependent clauses and indicates the relationship between them.

(dependent clause) (independent clause)
[After the town was evacuated], [the hurricane began].

(independent clause) (dependent clause)
[Officials watched the storm] [that threatened to destroy the town].

(dependent clause)
Town officials, [who were very concerned], watched the storm.

Frequently Used Subordinating Conjunctions

after	before	until
although	if	when
as	once	whenever
as if	since	where
as though	that	wherever
because	unless	while

Relative Pronouns

that	whatever	who (whose, whom)
what	which	whoever (whomever)

Close-Up USING COMPLEX SENTENCES

When you join clauses to create complex sentences, you help readers to see the relationships between your ideas. Complex sentences can indicate the following relationships:

- Time relationships (*before, after, until, when, since*)
- Contrast (*however, although*)
- Causal relationships (*therefore, because, so that*)
- Conditional relationships (*if, unless*)
- Location (*where, wherever*)
- Identity (*who, which, that*)

21b Varying Sentence Length

Strings of short simple sentences can be tedious—and sometimes hard to follow, as the following paragraph illustrates.

> John Peter Zenger was a newspaper editor. He waged and won an important battle for freedom of the press in America. He criticized the policies of the British governor. He was charged with criminal libel as a result. Zenger's lawyers were disbarred by the governor. Andrew Hamilton defended him. Hamilton convinced the jury that Zenger's criticisms were true. Therefore, the statements were not libelous.

You can revise a series of choppy sentences like the ones in the paragraph above by using *coordination*, *subordination*, or *embedding* to combine sentences.

Coordination pairs similar elements—words, phrases, or clauses—giving equal weight to each.

> John Peter Zenger was a newspaper editor. He waged and won an important battle for freedom of the press in America.

Two sentences linked with *and,* creating compound sentence

He criticized the policies of the British governor and he was charged with criminal libel as a result. Zenger's lawyers were disbarred by the governor. Andrew Hamilton defended him. Hamilton convinced the jury that Zenger's criticisms were true. Therefore, the statements were not libelous.

MULTILINGUAL TIP

Some multilingual students rely on simple sentences and coordination in their writing because they are afraid of making sentence structure errors. The result is a monotonous style. To add variety, try using **subordination** and **embedding** (as illustrated below) in your sentences.

Subordination places the more important idea in an independent clause and the less important idea in a dependent clause.

Simple sentences become dependent clauses, creating two complex sentences

John Peter Zenger was a newspaper editor who waged and won an important battle for freedom of the press in America. He criticized the policies of the British governor, and he was charged with criminal libel as a result. When Zenger's lawyers were disbarred by the governor, Andrew Hamilton defended him. Hamilton convinced the jury that Zenger's criticisms were true. Therefore, the statements were not libelous.

Embedding is the working of additional words and phrases into a sentence.

The sentence *Hamilton convinced the jury . . .* becomes the phrase *convincing the jury*

John Peter Zenger was a newspaper editor who waged and won an important battle for freedom of the press in America. He criticized the policies of the British governor, and he was charged with criminal libel as a result. When Zenger's lawyers were disbarred by the governor, Andrew Hamilton defended him, convincing the jury that Zenger's criticisms were true. Therefore, the statements were not libelous.

This final revision of the original string of choppy sentences is interesting and readable because it is now composed of varied and logically linked sentences. (The short simple sentence at the end has been retained for emphasis.)

21c Varying Sentence Openings

Rather than beginning every sentence with the subject (*I, He*, or *It*, for example), begin some sentences with modifying words, phrases, or clauses.

Words

Proud and relieved, they watched their daughter receive her diploma.

Hungrily, he devoured his lunch.

Phrases

For better or for worse, credit cards are now widely available to college students.

Located on the west coast of Great Britain, Wales is part of the United Kingdom.

His artistic interests expanding, Picasso designed ballet sets and illustrated books.

Clauses

After President Woodrow Wilson was incapacitated by a stroke, his wife unofficially performed many of his duties.

CHAPTER 22

Writing Concise Sentences

A sentence is not concise simply because it is short; a **concise** sentence contains only the words necessary to make its point.

Close-Up TEXT MESSAGES

If you send texts, you already use certain strategies to make your writing concise: you omit articles and other nonessential words, and you use nonstandard spellings (*nite*), abbreviations, and shorthand (*RU home?*). However, this kind of language is not acceptable in college writing, where you need to use other strategies (such as those discussed in this chapter) to make your writing concise.

22a Eliminating Wordiness

Whenever possible, delete nonessential words—*deadwood, utility words*, and *circumlocution*—from your writing.

1 Eliminate Deadwood

The term **deadwood** refers to unnecessary phrases that take up space and add nothing to meaning.

> *Many*
> ^~~There were many~~ factors ~~that~~ influenced his decision to become a priest.
>
> The two plots are ~~both~~ similar in ~~the way~~ that they trace the characters' increasing rage.
>
> *is*
> The only truly tragic character in *Hamlet*^ ~~would have to be~~ Ophelia.
>
> *This*
> ^~~In this~~ article ~~it~~ discusses lead poisoning.

Deadwood also includes unnecessary statements of opinion, such as *I feel, it seems to me, I believe*, and *in my opinion*.

> *The*
> ~~In my opinion, I believe the~~^ characters seem undeveloped.
>
> *This*
> ~~As far as I'm concerned, this~~^ course should not be required.

2 Eliminate Utility Words

Utility words function as filler and have no real meaning in a sentence. Utility words include nouns with imprecise meanings (*factor, situation, type, aspect*, and so on); adjectives so general that they are almost meaningless (*good, bad, important*); and common adverbs denoting degree (*basically, actually, quite, very, definitely*).

Often, you can just delete a utility word; if you cannot, replace it with a more precise word.

> *Registration*
> ^~~The registration situation~~ was disorganized.
>
> It was ~~basically~~ a worthwhile book, but I didn't ~~actually~~ finish it.

3 Avoid Circumlocution

Circumlocution is taking a roundabout way to say something (using ten words when five will do). Instead of complicated constructions, use specific words and concise phrases that come right to the point.

> ~~It is not unlikely that the~~ *The* trend toward lower consumer spending will *probably* continue.

> Joe was in the army *while* ~~during the same time that~~ I was in college.

Close-Up REVISING WORDY PHRASES

If you cannot edit a wordy construction, substitute a more concise, more direct term.

Wordy	Concise
at the present time	now
due to the fact that	because
in the vicinity of	near
have the ability to	be able to

22b Eliminating Unnecessary Repetition

Although intentional repetition can add emphasis to your writing, **redundant** word groups (repeated words or phrases that say the same thing, such as *true facts* or *armed gunman*) and other kinds of unnecessary repetition can annoy readers and obscure your meaning. Correct unnecessary repetition by using one of the following strategies.

1 Delete Redundancy

> People's clothing ~~attire~~ can reveal a good deal about their personalities.

> The two candidates share several positions ~~in common~~.

2 Substitute a Pronoun

> Agatha Christie's fictional detective Miss Marple has solved many crimes. *The Murder at the Vicarage* was one of *her* ~~Miss Marple's~~ most challenging cases.

3 Create an Appositive

Red Barber, ~~was~~ a sportscaster, ~~He~~ he was known for his colorful expressions.

4 Create a Compound

John F. Kennedy was the youngest man ever elected president and ~~He was~~ the first Catholic to hold this office.

5 Create a Complex Sentence

Americans value freedom of speech, which ~~Freedom of speech~~ is guaranteed by the First Amendment.

22c Tightening Rambling Sentences

The combination of nonessential words, unnecessary repetition, and complicated syntax creates **rambling sentences**. Revising such sentences frequently requires extensive editing.

1 Eliminate Excessive Coordination

See 21a1

When you string a series of clauses together with coordinating conjunctions, you create a rambling, unfocused **compound sentence**. To revise such sentences, first identify the main idea, and state it in an independent clause; then, add the supporting details.

Wordy: Puerto Rico is a large island, and it is very mountainous, and it has steep slopes, and they fall to gentle plains along the coast.

Concise: A large island, Puerto Rico is very mountainous, with steep slopes falling to gentle plains along the coast. (Puerto Rico's mountainous terrain is the sentence's main idea.)

2 Eliminate Adjective Clauses

See A2.3

A series of **adjective clauses** is also likely to produce a rambling sentence. To revise, substitute concise modifying words or phrases for the adjective clauses.

Wordy: *Moby-Dick*, which is a novel about a white whale, was written by Herman Melville, who was friendly with Nathaniel Hawthorne, who urged him to revise the first draft.

Concise: *Moby-Dick*, a novel about a white whale, was written by Herman Melville, who revised the first draft at the urging of his friend Nathaniel Hawthorne.

3 Eliminate Passive Constructions

Unnecessary use of the passive voice can also create a rambling sentence. Correct this problem by changing passive voice to active voice. See 17d

~~Water rights are being fought for in court by~~ Indian tribes such as the Papago in Arizona and the Pyramid Lake Paiute in Nevada~~.~~ *are fighting in court for water rights.*

4 Eliminate Wordy Prepositional Phrases

When you revise, substitute adjectives or adverbs for wordy **prepositional phrases**. See A2.3

The trip was *dangerous* ~~one of danger~~ but also *exciting.* ~~one of excitement.~~

He spoke *confidently* ~~in a confident manner~~ and *authoritatively.* ~~with a lot of authority.~~

5 Eliminate Wordy Noun Constructions

Substitute strong verbs for wordy **noun phrases**. See A2.3

We have *decided* ~~made the decision~~ to postpone the meeting until ~~the appearance of~~ all the board members *appear*.

CHAPTER 23

Revising Awkward or Confusing Sentences

The most common causes of awkward or confusing sentences are *unnecessary shifts, mixed constructions,* and *faulty predication.*

23a Revising Unnecessary Shifts

1 Shifts in Tense

See 17b ml 44a2

Verb tense in a sentence or in a related group of sentences should shift only for a good reason—to indicate a change of time, for example. Unnecessary shifts in tense can be confusing.

> I registered for the advanced philosophy seminar because I wanted a challenge. However, by the first week I ^started ~~start~~ having trouble understanding the reading. (unnecessary shift from past to present)

2 Shifts in Voice

See 17d ml 44a6

Unnecessary shifts from active to passive voice (or from passive to active) can be confusing.

> F. Scott Fitzgerald wrote *This Side of Paradise*, and ^he later ^wrote *The Great Gatsby*^. ~~was written.~~ (unnecessary shift from active to passive)

3 Shifts in Mood

See 17c

Unnecessary shifts in mood can also create awkward sentences.

> Next, heat the mixture in a test tube, and ^be ~~you should make~~ sure it does not boil. (unnecessary shift from imperative to indicative)

4 Shifts in Person and Number

ml 44a1

Person indicates who is speaking (first person—*I, we*), who is spoken to (second person—*you*), and who is spoken about (third person—*he, she, it,* and *they*). Most often, unnecessary shifts between the second and the third person are responsible for awkward sentences.

> When ^you ~~one~~ look~~s~~ for a car loan, you compare the interest rates of several banks. (unnecessary shift from third to second person)

See 18c ml 44c1

Number indicates one (singular—*novel, it*) or more than one (plural—*novels, they, them*). Singular pronouns should refer to singular **antecedents** and plural pronouns to plural antecedents.

he or she
If a person does not study regularly, ~~they~~ will have a difficult time learning a foreign language. (unnecessary shift from singular to plural)

23b Revising Mixed Constructions

A **mixed construction** occurs when an introductory dependent clause, prepositional phrase, or independent clause is incorrectly used as the subject of a sentence.

,
Because she studies every day ~~explains why~~ she gets good grades. (dependent clause incorrectly used as subject)

, you can
By calling for information ~~is the way to~~ learn more about the benefits of ROTC. (prepositional phrase incorrectly used as subject)

Being
~~He was~~ late ~~was what~~ made him miss the first act. (independent clause incorrectly used as subject)

23c Revising Faulty Predication

Faulty predication occurs when a sentence's subject and predicate do not logically go together. Faulty predication often occurs in sentences that contain a linking verb—a form of the verb *be*, for example—and a subject complement.

caused
Mounting costs and decreasing revenues ~~were~~ the downfall of the hospital.

Faulty predication also occurs when a one-sentence definition contains the construction *is where* or *is when*. (In a definition, *is* must be preceded and followed by a noun or noun phrase.)

the construction of
Taxidermy is ~~where you construct~~ a lifelike representation of an animal from its preserved skin.

Finally, faulty predication occurs when the phrase *the reason is* precedes *because*. In this situation, *because* (which means "for the reason that") is redundant and should be deleted.

that
The reason we drive is ~~because~~ we are afraid to fly.

CHAPTER 24

Using Parallelism

Parallelism—the use of matching words, phrases, or clauses to express equivalent ideas—adds unity, balance, and coherence to your writing. Effective parallelism makes sentences easier to follow and emphasizes relationships between equivalent ideas, but faulty parallelism can create awkward sentences that obscure your meaning and confuse readers.

See 24b

24a Using Parallelism Effectively

1 With Items in a Series

Items in a series should be presented in parallel terms.

Eat, drink, and be merry.

Baby food consumption, toy production, and school construction are likely to decline as the US population ages.

2 With Paired Items

Paired words, phrases, or clauses should be presented in parallel terms.

The thank-you note was short but sweet.

Ask not what your country can do for you; ask what you can do for your country. (John F. Kennedy)

Paired items linked by **correlative conjunctions** (such as *not only . . . but also* and *either . . . or*) should always be parallel.

The design team paid attention not only to color but also to texture.

Either repeat physics or take calculus.

Parallelism is also used with paired elements linked by *than* or *as*.

Richard Wright and James Baldwin chose to live in Paris rather than to remain in the United States.

Success is as much <u>a matter of hard work</u> as <u>a matter of luck</u>.

Elements in <u>outlines</u> and <u>lists</u> should also be parallel.

See 5i1, 39c

24b Revising Faulty Parallelism

Faulty parallelism occurs when elements in a sentence that express equivalent ideas are not presented in parallel terms.

> Many residents of developing countries lack adequate housing, adequate food, and ^*adequate* ~~their~~ health-care facilities^ ~~are also inadequate.~~

To correct faulty parallelism, match nouns with nouns, verbs with verbs, and phrases or clauses with similarly constructed phrases or clauses.

> Popular exercises for men and women include spinning, ^*weight training* ~~weights~~, and running.

> I look forward to hearing from you and to ^*having* ~~have~~ an opportunity to tell you more about myself.

Close-Up REPEATING KEY WORDS

Although the use of similar grammatical structures may be enough to convey parallelism, sometimes sentences are even clearer if certain key words (for example, articles, prepositions, and the *to* in infinitives) are also repeated in each element of a pair or series. In the following sentence, repeating the preposition *by* makes it clear that *not* applies only to the first phrase.

> Computerization has helped industry by not allowing labor costs to skyrocket, ^*by* increasing the speed of production, and ^*by* improving efficiency.

CHAPTER 25

Placing Modifiers Carefully

A **modifier** is a word, phrase, or clause that describes, limits, or qualifies another word in a sentence. A modifier should be placed close to the word it modifies.

Wendy watched the storm, fierce and threatening. (*fierce and threatening* modifies *storm*)

Faulty modification is the awkward or confusing placement of modifiers or the modification of nonexistent words.

25a Revising Misplaced Modifiers

A **misplaced modifier** is a word or word group whose placement suggests that it modifies one thing when it is intended to modify another.

Confusing: With an IQ of just 52, the lawyer argued that his client should not get the death penalty. (Does the lawyer have an IQ of 52?)

Revised: The lawyer argued that his client, with an IQ of just 52, should not get the death penalty.

1 Placing Limiting Modifiers

Limiting modifiers—such as *almost, only, even, hardly, just, merely, nearly, exactly, scarcely,* and *simply*—should immediately precede the words they modify. Different placements change the meaning of the sentence.

Nick *just* set up camp at the edge of town. (He did it just now.)

Just Nick set up camp at the edge of town. (He did it alone.)

Nick set up camp *just* at the edge of town. (His camp was precisely at the edge.)

When a limiting modifier is placed so that it is not clear whether it modifies a word before it or a word after it, it is called a **squinting modifier**.

The life that everyone thought would fulfill her totally bored her.

To correct a squinting modifier, place the modifier so that it is clear which word it modifies.

The life that everyone thought would totally fulfill her bored her. (She was expected to be totally fulfilled.)

The life that everyone thought would fulfill her bored her totally. (She was totally bored.)

2 Relocating Misplaced Phrases

To avoid ambiguity, place phrases as close as possible to the words they modify:

- Place verbal phrases directly before or directly after the words they modify.

Roller-skating along the shore,
^Jane watched the boats.^ ~~roller skating along the shore.~~

- Place prepositional phrases immediately after the words they modify.

with no arms
Venus de Milo is a statue^ created by a famous artist^ ~~with no arms.~~

3 Relocating Misplaced Dependent Clauses

A dependent clause that serves as a modifier must be clearly related to the word it modifies.

- An **adjective clause** appears immediately *after* the word it modifies.

, which will benefit everyone,
This diet program^ will limit the consumption of possible carcinogens^ ~~, which will benefit everyone.~~

- An **adverb clause** may appear in various positions, as long as its relationship to the word it modifies is clear.

When Lincoln was president, the Civil War raged.

The Civil War raged when Lincoln was president.

25b Revising Intrusive Modifiers

An **intrusive modifier** awkwardly interrupts a sentence, making the sentence difficult to understand.

- Revise when a long modifying phrase comes between an auxiliary verb and the main verb.

Without
~~She had, without~~ giving it a second thought or considering the consequences, *she had* planned to reenlist.

- Revise when a modifier creates an awkward **split infinitive**—that is, when the modifier comes between ("splits") the word *to* and the base form of the verb.

He hoped to *defeat his opponent* quickly and easily ~~defeat his opponent.~~

Note: A split infinitive is acceptable when the intervening modifier is short, especially if the alternative would be awkward or ambiguous: *She expected to almost beat her previous record.*

25c Revising Dangling Modifiers

A **dangling modifier** is a word or phrase that cannot logically modify any word in the sentence.

Using this drug, many undesirable side effects are experienced. (Who is using this drug?)

- One way to correct this dangling modifier is to **create a new subject** by adding a word that the modifier (*using this drug*) can logically modify.

Using this drug, patients experience many undesirable side effects.

- Another way to correct the dangling modifier is to **create a dependent clause.**

When they use this drug, patients experience many undesirable side effects.

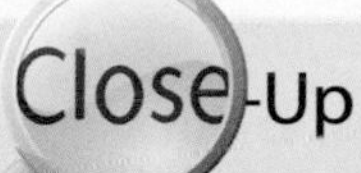

DANGLING MODIFIERS AND THE PASSIVE VOICE

Many sentences that include dangling modifiers are in the passive voice. Changing the passive voice to active voice often corrects the dangling modifier.

See 17d

ml 44a6

CHAPTER 26

Choosing Words

26a Choosing the Right Word

1 Denotation and Connotation

A word's **denotation** is its basic dictionary meaning—what it stands for without any emotional associations. A word's **connotations** are the emotional, social, and political associations it has in addition to its denotative meaning.

Word	Denotation	Connotation
politician	someone who holds a political office	opportunist; wheeler-dealer

If you use terms without considering their connotations, you risk confusing and possibly alienating readers.

Close-Up USING A THESAURUS

A **thesaurus** lists **synonyms** (words that have the same meaning—for example, *well* and *healthy*) and **antonyms** (words that have opposite meanings—for example, *courage*

(continued)

USING A THESAURUS *(continued)*

and *cowardice*). Most online dictionaries, as well as *Microsoft Word*, enable you to access a thesaurus. When you consult a thesaurus, remember that no two words have exactly the same meaning.

2 Euphemisms

A **euphemism** is a mild or polite term used in place of a blunt term to describe something that is unpleasant or embarrassing. College writing is no place for euphemisms. Say what you mean—*pregnant*, not *expecting*; *died*, not *passed away*; and *strike*, not *work stoppage*.

3 Specific and General Words

Specific words refer to particular persons, items, or events; **general** words denote entire classes or groups. *Queen Elizabeth II*, for example, is more specific than *ruler*; *jeans* is more specific than *clothing*; and *hybrid car* is more specific than *vehicle*. Although you can use general words to describe entire classes of items, you should use specific words to clarify such generalizations.

Close-Up USING SPECIFIC WORDS

Avoid general words such as *nice*, *great*, and *terrific* that say nothing and could be used in almost any sentence. These utility words convey only enthusiasm, not precise meanings. Replace them with more specific words.

See 22a2

4 Abstract and Concrete Words

Abstract words—*beauty*, *truth*, *justice*, and so on—refer to ideas, qualities, or conditions that cannot be perceived by the senses. **Concrete** words name things that readers can see, hear, taste, smell, or touch. The more concrete your words and phrases, the more vivid the images you evoke in your readers' minds.

5 Commonly Confused Words (Homophones)

Some words, such as *accept* and *except*, are pronounced alike but spelled differently. Because they are often confused, you should be careful when you use them.

accept	to receive
except	other than
affect	to have an influence on (*verb*)
effect	result (*noun*); to cause (*verb*)
its	possessive of *it*
it's	contraction of *it is*

For a full list of these and other homophones, along with their meanings and sentences illustrating their use, **see Appendix B**.

26b Avoiding Inappropriate Language

When you write, avoid language that is inappropriate for your audience and purpose.

1 Jargon

Jargon is the specialized or technical vocabulary of a trade, profession, or academic discipline. Although it is useful for communicating in the field for which it was developed, outside that field it is often confusing.

> The patient had ~~an acute myocardial infarction.~~ *a heart attack.*

2 Pretentious Diction

Good writing is clear writing, and pompous or flowery language is no substitute for clarity. Revise to eliminate **pretentious diction**, inappropriately elevated and wordy language.

> As I fell ~~into slumber~~ *asleep*, I ~~cogitated~~ *thought* about my day ~~ambling~~ *hiking* through ~~the splendor of~~ the Appalachian Mountains.

3 Clichés

Clichés are tired expressions that have lost their impact because they have been used so often. Familiar sayings such as "The bottom line," "it is what it is," and "what goes around comes around," for example, do little to enhance your writing. Avoid the temptation to use clichés in your college writing.

26c Avoiding Offensive Language

1 Stereotypes

When referring to a racial, ethnic, or religious group, use words with neutral connotations or words that the group itself uses in *formal* speech or writing. Also avoid potentially offensive labels related to age, social class, occupation, physical or mental ability, or sexual orientation.

2 Sexist Language

Avoid **sexist language**, language that reinforces and promotes gender stereotypes. Sexist language entails much more than the use of derogatory words. For example, assuming that some professions are exclusive to one gender—for instance, that *nurse* denotes only women or that *engineer* denotes only men—is sexist. So is the use of job titles such as *mailman* for *letter carrier* and *stewardess* for *flight attendant*.

Sexist language also occurs when a writer fails to apply the same terminology to both men and women. For example, you should refer to two scientists with PhDs not as Dr. Sagan and Mrs. Yallow, but as Dr. Sagan and Dr. Yallow.

In your writing, always use *women* when referring to adult females. Also avoid using the generic *he* or *him* when your subject could be either male or female. Instead, use the third-person plural or the phrase *he or she* (not *he/she*).

Sexist: Before boarding, each passenger should make certain that he has his ticket.

Revised: Before boarding, passengers should make certain that they have their tickets.

Revised: Before boarding, each passenger should make certain that he or she has a ticket.

Note: Be careful not to use *they* or *their* to refer to a singular antecedent.

Drivers
~~Any driver~~ caught speeding should have their driving privileges suspended.

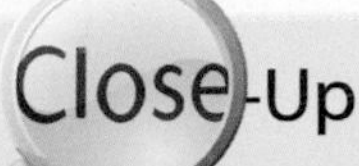

Close-Up ELIMINATING SEXIST LANGUAGE

For most sexist usages, there are nonsexist alternatives.

Sexist Usage	Possible Revisions
1. Mankind	People, human beings
Man's accomplishments	Human accomplishments
Man-made	Synthetic
2. Female engineer (lawyer, accountant, etc.), male model	Engineer (lawyer, accountant, etc.), model
3. Policeman/woman	Police officer
Salesman/woman/girl	Salesperson/sales representative
Businessman/woman	Businessperson, executive
4. Everyone should complete his application by Tuesday.	Everyone should complete his or her application by Tuesday. All students should complete their applications by Tuesday.

PART 6

Understanding Punctuation

Quick Guide to Sentence Punctuation: Commas, Semicolons, Colons, Dashes, Parentheses (Chart) 292

27 Using End Punctuation 293

27a Using Periods 293
27b Using Question Marks 294
27c Using Exclamation Points 295

28 Using Commas 295

28a Setting Off Independent Clauses 295
28b Setting Off Items in a Series 296
28c Setting Off Introductory Elements 297
28d Setting Off Nonessential Material 297
28e Using Commas in Other Conventional Contexts 300
28f Using Commas to Prevent Misreading 301
28g Editing Misused Commas 301

29 Using Semicolons 302

29a Separating Independent Clauses 302
29b Separating Items in a Series 303
29c Editing Misused Semicolons 303

30 Using Apostrophes 304

30a Forming the Possessive Case 304
30b Indicating Omissions in Contractions 305
30c Forming Plurals 306
30d Editing Misused Apostrophes 307

31 Using Quotation Marks 307

31a Setting Off Quoted Speech or Writing 307
31b Setting Off Titles 311
31c Setting Off Words Used in Special Ways 311
31d Using Quotation Marks with Other Punctuation 311
31e Editing Misused Quotation Marks 313

32 Using Other Punctuation Marks 313

32a Using Colons 313
32b Using Dashes 315
32c Using Parentheses 316
32d Using Brackets 317
32e Using Slashes 317
32f Using Ellipses 318

(Further explanations and examples are located in the sections listed in parentheses after each example.)

SEPARATING INDEPENDENT CLAUSES

With a Comma and a Coordinating Conjunction

The House approved the bill, but the Senate rejected it. (**28a**)

With a Semicolon

Paul Revere's *The Boston Massacre* is traditional American protest art; Edward Hicks's paintings are socially conscious art with a religious strain. (**29a**)

With a Semicolon and a Transitional Word or Phrase

Thomas Jefferson brought two hundred vanilla beans and a recipe for vanilla ice cream back from France; thus, he gave America its all-time favorite ice-cream flavor. (**29a**)

With a Colon

The survey presents an interesting finding: Americans do not trust the news media. (**32a2**)

SEPARATING ITEMS IN A SERIES

With Commas

Chipmunk, *raccoon*, and *Mugwump* are Native American words. (**28b**)

With Semicolons

Laramie, Wyoming; Wyoming, Delaware; and Delaware, Ohio were three of the places they visited. (**29b**)

SETTING OFF EXAMPLES, EXPLANATIONS, OR SUMMARIES

With a Colon

She had one dream: to play professional basketball. (**32a2**)

With a Dash

"Study hard," "Respect your elders," "Don't talk with your mouth full"—Sharon had often heard her parents say these things. (**32b2**)

SETTING OFF NONESSENTIAL MATERIAL

With a Single Comma

In fact, Outward Bound has an excellent reputation. (**28d2**)

With a Pair of Commas

Jonas Salk, not Albert Sabin, developed the first polio vaccine. (**28d3**)

With Dashes

Neither of the boys—both nine-year-olds—had any history of violence. (**32b1**)

With Parentheses

In some European countries (notably Sweden and Denmark), high-quality day care is offered at little or no cost to parents. (**32c1**)

CHAPTER 27

Using End Punctuation

27a Using Periods

Use a period to signal the end of most sentences, including indirect questions.

Something is rotten in Denmark.

They wondered whether the water was safe to drink.

Also use periods in most abbreviations.

Mr. Spock	Aug.	Dr. Livingstone
9 p.m.	etc.	1600 Pennsylvania Ave.

If an abbreviation ends the sentence, do not add another period.

He promised to be there at 6 a.m./

However, do add a question mark if the sentence is a question.

Did he arrive at 6 p.m.?

If the abbreviation falls *within* a sentence, use normal punctuation after the period.

He promised to be there at 6 p.m., but he forgot.

Close-Up ABBREVIATIONS WITHOUT PERIODS

Abbreviations composed of all capital letters do not usually require periods unless they stand for initials of people's names (E. B. White).

(continued)

ABBREVIATIONS WITHOUT PERIODS *(continued)*

Familiar abbreviations of names of corporations or government agencies and abbreviations of scientific and technical terms do not require periods.

TMZ NYPD DNA CIA WCAU-FM NFL

Acronyms—new words formed from the initial letters or first few letters of a series of words—do not include periods.

hazmat Nascar NATO modem

Clipped forms (commonly accepted shortened forms of words, such as *gym, dorm, math*, and *fax*) do not use periods.

Postal abbreviations do not include periods.

TX CA MS PA FL NY

Use periods to mark divisions in dramatic, poetic, and biblical references.

Hamlet 2.2.1–5 (act, scene, lines)

Paradise Lost 7.163–167 (book, lines)

Judges 4.14 (chapter, verse)

See 10a1

Note: In MLA parenthetical references, titles of classic literary works and books of the Bible are often abbreviated: **(*Ham.* 2.2.1-5)**; **(Judg. 4.14)**.

Note: When you type an electronic address (URL), do not end it with a period, and do not add spaces after periods within the address.

27b Using Question Marks

Use a question mark to signal the end of a direct question.

Who was at the door?

Use a question mark in parentheses to indicate uncertainty about a date or number.

Aristophanes, the Greek playwright, was born in 448 (?) BC and died in 380 (?) BC.

Close-Up **EDITING MISUSED QUESTION MARKS**

- Use a period, not a question mark, with an indirect question.

  The personnel officer asked whether he knew how to type?.

- Do not use a question mark to convey sarcasm. Instead, suggest your attitude through your choice of words.

  I refused his ^not very^ generous (?) offer.

27c Using Exclamation Points

An exclamation point is used to signal the end of an emotional or emphatic statement, an emphatic interjection, or a forceful command.

Remember the Maine!

"No! Don't leave!" he cried.

Note: Except for recording dialogue, do not use exclamation points in college writing. Even in informal writing, use exclamation points sparingly—and never use two or more in a row.

CHAPTER 28 Using Commas

28a Setting Off Independent Clauses

Use a comma when you form a compound sentence by linking two independent clauses with a **coordinating conjunction** (*and, but, or, nor, for, yet, so*) or with a pair of **correlative conjunctions**. See A1.7

The House approved the bill, but the Senate rejected it.

Either the hard drive is full, or the modem is too slow.

Note: You may omit the comma if two clauses connected by a coordinating conjunction are very short: *Love it* or *leave it.*

28b Setting Off Items in a Series

Use commas between items in a series of three or more **coordinate elements** (words, phrases, or clauses joined by a coordinating conjunction).

Chipmunk, *raccoon*, and *Mugwump* are Native American words.

You may pay by check, with a credit or debit card, or in cash.

Brazilians speak Portuguese, Colombians speak Spanish, and Haitians speak French and Creole.

Note: To avoid ambiguity, use a comma before the *and* (or other coordinating conjunction) that separates the last two items in a series: *He was inspired by his parents, the Dalai Lama, and Mother Teresa.*

Use a comma between items in a series of two or more **coordinate adjectives**—adjectives that modify the same word or word group—unless they are joined by a conjunction.

She brushed her long, shining hair.

The baby was tired and cranky and wet. (no commas required)

CHECKLIST

Punctuating Adjectives in a Series

- ❑ If you can reverse the order of the adjectives or insert *and* between the adjectives without changing the meaning, the adjectives are coordinate, and you should use a comma.

  She brushed her long, shining hair.
  She brushed her shining, long hair.
  She brushed her long [and] shining hair.

- ❑ If you cannot reverse the order, the adjectives are not coordinate, and you should not use a comma.

  Ten red balloons fell from the ceiling.
  Red ten balloons fell from the ceiling.
  Ten [and] red balloons fell from the ceiling.

Note: Numbers—such as *ten*—are not coordinate with other adjectives.

MULTILINGUAL TIP

For information on the order of adjectives in a series, see 44d2.

28c Setting Off Introductory Elements

An introductory dependent clause, verbal phrase, or prepositional phrase is generally set off from the rest of the sentence by a comma.

When war came to Baghdad, many victims were children. (dependent clause)

If an introductory *dependent clause* is short and designates time, you may omit the comma—provided the sentence will be clear without it: *When I exercise I drink plenty of water.*

Pushing onward, Scott struggled toward the South Pole. (verbal phrase)

During the Depression, movie attendance rose. (prepositional phrase)

If an introductory *prepositional phrase* is short and no ambiguity is possible, you may omit the comma: *After lunch I took a four-hour nap.*

Close-Up TRANSITIONAL WORDS AND PHRASES

When a transitional word or phrase begins a sentence, it is usually set off with a comma.

See 20b

However, any plan that is enacted must be fair.

In other words, we cannot act hastily.

28d Setting Off Nonessential Material

Use commas to set off nonessential material whether it appears at the beginning, in the middle, or at the end of a sentence.

1 Nonrestrictive Modifiers

Use commas to set off **nonrestrictive modifiers**, which supply information that is not essential to the meaning of the words they modify. (*Do not* use commas to set off **restrictive modifiers**, which supply information that is essential to the meaning of the words they modify.)

Nonrestrictive (commas required): Actors, who have inflated egos, are often insecure. (*All* actors—not just those with inflated egos—are insecure.)

Restrictive (no commas): Actors who have inflated egos are often insecure. (Only those actors with inflated egos—not all actors—are insecure.)

In the following examples, commas set off only nonrestrictive modifiers—those that supply nonessential information. Commas do not set off restrictive modifiers, which supply essential information.

Adjective Clauses

Nonrestrictive: He ran for the bus, which was late as usual.

Restrictive: Speaking in public is something that most people fear.

Prepositional Phrases

Nonrestrictive: The clerk, with a nod, dismissed me.

Restrictive: The man with the gun demanded their money.

Verbal Phrases

Nonrestrictive: The marathoner, running his fastest, beat his previous record.

Restrictive: The candidates running for mayor have agreed to a debate.

Appositives

Nonrestrictive: *Citizen Kane*, Orson Welles's first film, made him famous.

Restrictive: The film *Citizen Kane* made Orson Welles famous.

CHECKLIST

Restrictive and Nonrestrictive Modifiers

To determine whether a modifier is restrictive or nonrestrictive, answer these questions:

- ❑ Is the modifier essential to the meaning of the word it modifies (*The man* with the gun, not just any man)? If so, it is restrictive and does not take commas.
- ❑ Is the modifier introduced by *that* (*something that most people fear*)? If so, it is restrictive. *That* cannot introduce a nonrestrictive clause.
- ❑ Can you delete the relative pronoun without causing ambiguity or confusion (*something [that] most people fear*)? If so, the clause is restrictive.
- ❑ Is the appositive more specific than the noun that precedes it (*the film* Citizen Kane)? If so, it is restrictive.

Close-Up USING COMMAS WITH *THAT* AND *WHICH*

- *That* introduces only restrictive clauses, which are not set off by commas.

  I bought a used car that cost $2,000.

- *Which* introduces only nonrestrictive clauses, which are set off by commas.

  The used car I bought, which cost $2,000, broke down after a week.

2 Transitional Words and Phrases

Transitional words and phrases qualify, clarify, and make connections. Because they are not essential to the sentence's meaning, however, they are always set off by commas when they interrupt a clause or when they begin or end a sentence. See 20b

The Outward Bound program, for example, is considered safe.

In fact, Outward Bound has an excellent reputation.

Other programs are not so safe, however.

Note: When a transitional word or phrase joins two independent clauses, it must be preceded by a semicolon and followed by a comma; *Laughter is the best medicine; of course, penicillin also comes in handy sometimes.*

3 Contradictory Phrases

A phrase that expresses a contradiction is usually set off from the rest of the sentence by one or more commas.

> This medicine is taken after meals, never on an empty stomach.
>
> Jonas Salk, not Albert Sabin, developed the first polio vaccine.

4 Miscellaneous Nonessential Elements

Other nonessential elements usually set off by commas include tag questions, names in direct address, mild interjections, and *yes* and *no*.

> This is your first day on the job, isn't it?
>
> I wonder, Mr. Honeywell, whether Mr. Albright deserves a raise.
>
> Well, it's about time.
>
> Yes, that's what I thought.

28e Using Commas in Other Conventional Contexts

1 With Direct Quotations

In most cases, use commas to set off a direct quotation from the **identifying tag**, the phrase that identifies the speaker (*he said, she answered*, and so on).

> Emerson said, "I greet you at the beginning of a great career."
>
> "I greet you at the beginning of a great career," Emerson said.
>
> "I greet you," Emerson said, "at the beginning of a great career."

When the identifying tag comes between two complete sentences, however, the tag is introduced by a comma but followed by a period.

> "Winning isn't everything," Coach Vince Lombardi once said. "It's the only thing."

2 With Titles or Degrees Following a Name

Michael Crichton, MD, wrote *Jurassic Park*.

Hamlet, Prince of Denmark, is Shakespeare's most famous character.

3 In Dates and Addresses

On August 30, 1983, the space shuttle *Challenger* exploded.

Her address is 600 West End Avenue, New York, NY 10024.

When only the month and year are given, do not use a comma to separate the month from the year: *August 1983*. Do not use a comma to separate the street number from the street or the state name from the zip code.

28f Using Commas to Prevent Misreading

In some cases, a comma is used to avoid ambiguity. For example, consider the following sentence.

Those who can, sprint the final lap.

Without the comma, *can* appears to be an auxiliary verb ("Those who can sprint . . ."), and the sentence seems incomplete. The comma tells readers to pause and thus prevents confusion.

Also use a comma to acknowledge the omission of a repeated word, usually a verb, and to separate words repeated consecutively.

Pam carried the box; Tim, the suitcase.

Everything bad that could have happened, happened.

28g Editing Misused Commas

Do not use commas in the following situations.

1 To Set Off Restrictive Modifiers

The film*,* *Avatar*, was directed by James Cameron.

They planned a picnic, in the park.

2 Between a Subject and Its Predicate

A woman with dark red hair, opened the door.

3 Before or After a Series

Three important criteria are, fat content, salt content, and taste.

The provinces Quebec, Ontario, and Alberta, are in Canada.

4 Between a Verb and an Indirect Quotation or Indirect Question

General Douglas MacArthur vowed, that he would return.

The landlord asked, if we would sign a two-year lease.

5 In Compounds That Are Not Composed of Independent Clauses

During the 1400s plagues, and pestilence were common. (compound subject)

Many nontraditional students are returning to college, and tend to do well there. (compound predicate)

6 Before a Dependent Clause at the End of a Sentence

Jane Addams founded Hull House in 1889, because she wanted to help Chicago's poor.

CHAPTER 29

Using Semicolons

The **semicolon** is used only between items of equal grammatical rank: two independent clauses, two phrases, and so on.

29a Separating Independent Clauses

Use a semicolon between closely related independent clauses that convey parallel or contrasting information but are not joined by a coordinating conjunction.

Paul Revere's *The Boston Massacre* is an early example of American protest art; Edward Hicks's later "primitive" paintings are socially conscious art with a religious strain.

Note: Using only a comma or no punctuation at all between independent clauses creates a **run-on**. See Ch. 14

Also use a semicolon between two independent clauses when the second clause is introduced by a transitional word or phrase (the transitional element is followed by a comma).

Thomas Jefferson brought two hundred vanilla beans and a recipe for vanilla ice cream back from France; thus, he gave America its all-time favorite ice cream flavor.

29b Separating Items in a Series

Use semicolons between items in a series when one or more of the items already include commas.

I have visited Laramie, Wyoming; Wyoming, Delaware; and Delaware, Ohio.

29c Editing Misused Semicolons

Do not use semicolons in the following situations.

1 Between a Dependent and an Independent Clause

Because drugs can now suppress the body's immune reaction;, fewer organ transplants are rejected.

2 To Introduce a List

Millions of people spend time every day on four of the most popular social networking sites;: *Facebook*, *Twitter*, *LinkedIn* and *Pinterest*.

CHAPTER 30

Using Apostrophes

Use an apostrophe to form the possessive case, to indicate omissions in contractions, and to form certain plurals.

30a Forming the Possessive Case

The possessive case indicates ownership. In English, the possessive case of nouns and indefinite pronouns is indicated either with a phrase that includes the word *of* (the hands *of* the clock) or with an apostrophe and, in most cases, an *s* (the clock's hands).

1 Singular Nouns and Indefinite Pronouns

To form the possessive case of **singular nouns** and **indefinite pronouns**, add -'*s*.

"The Monk's Tale" is one of Chaucer's *Canterbury Tales.*

When we would arrive was anyone's guess.

2 Singular Nouns Ending in -*s*

To form the possessive case of **singular nouns that end in -*s***, add -'*s* in most cases.

Chris's goal was to become a surgeon.

Reading Henry James's *The Ambassadors* was not Maris's idea of fun.

The class's time was changed to 8 a.m.

Note: With some singular nouns that end in -*s*, pronouncing the possessive ending as a separate syllable can sound awkward. In such cases, it is acceptable to use just an apostrophe: *Crispus Attucks' death, Achilles' left heel, Aristophanes'* play.

3 Regular Plural Nouns

To form the possessive case of **regular plural nouns** (those that end in -*s* or -*es*), add only an apostrophe.

Laid-off employees received two weeks' severance pay and three months' medical benefits.

The Lopezes' three children are triplets.

4 Irregular Plural Nouns

To form the possessive case of **nouns that have irregular plurals**, add *-'s*.

The Children's Hour is a play by Lillian Hellman.

5 Compound Nouns or Groups of Words

To form the possessive case of **compound words or groups of words**, add *-'s* to the last word.

The President accepted the Secretary of Defense's resignation.

This is someone else's responsibility.

6 Two or More Items

To indicate **individual ownership** of two or more items, add *-'s* to each item.

Ernest Hemingway's and Gertrude Stein's writing styles have some similarities.

To indicate **joint ownership**, add *-'s* only to the last item.

Lewis and Clark's expedition has been the subject of many books.

30b Indicating Omissions in Contractions

Apostrophes replace omitted letters in contractions that combine a pronoun and a verb (*he* + *will* = *he'll*) or the elements of a verb phrase (*do* + *not* = *don't*).

Frequently Used Contractions

it's (it is, it has)	let's (let us)
he's (he is, he has)	we've (we have)
she's (she is, she has)	they're (they are)

continued

Frequently Used Contractions *(continued)*

who's (who is, who has)	we'll (we will)
isn't (is not)	I'm (I am)
wouldn't (would not)	we're (we are)
couldn't (could not)	you'd (you would)
don't (do not)	we'd (we would)
won't (will not)	they'd (they had)

Note: Contractions are very informal. Do not use contractions in college writing unless you are quoting a source that uses them.

Close-Up USING APOSTROPHES

Be careful not to confuse contractions (which always include apostrophes) with the possessive forms of personal pronouns (which never include apostrophes).

Contractions	Possessive Forms
Who's on first?	Whose book is this?
They're playing our song.	Their team is winning.
It's raining.	Its paws were muddy.
You're a real pal.	Your résumé is very impressive.

Note: In informal writing, an apostrophe may also be used to replace the century in a year: *class of '12, the '60s*. In college writing, however, write out the year in full: *class of 2012, the sixties*.

30c Forming Plurals

In a few special situations, add -*'s* to form plurals.

- **Plurals of Letters**

  The Italian language has no *j*'s, *k*'s, or *w*'s.

- **Plurals of Words Referred to as Words**

  The supervisor would accept no *if*'s, *and*'s, or *but*'s.

See 35c

Note: Elements spoken of as themselves (letters, numerals, or words) are set in italic type; the plural ending, however, is not.

30d Editing Misused Apostrophes

Do not use apostrophes in the following situations.

1 With Plural Nouns That Are Not Possessive

The Thompson's are not at home.

Down vest's are very warm.

The Philadelphia 76er's have had good years and bad.

2 To Form the Possessive Case of Personal Pronouns

This ticket must be your's or her's.

The next turn is their's.

Her doll had lost it's right eye.

The next great moment in history is our's.

CHAPTER 31

Using Quotation Marks

Use quotation marks to set off brief passages of quoted speech or writing, to set off titles, and to set off words used in special ways. Do not use quotation marks when quoting long passages of prose or poetry.

31a Setting Off Quoted Speech or Writing

When you quote a word, phrase, or brief passage of someone's speech or writing, enclose the quoted material in a pair of quotation marks.

> Gloria Steinem said, "We are becoming the men we once hoped to marry."

Galsworthy writes that Aunt Juley is "prostrated by the blow" (329). (Note that in this example from a student essay, the end punctuation follows the parenthetical documentation.)

Close-Up USING QUOTATION MARKS WITH DIALOGUE

When you record **dialogue** (conversation between two or more people), enclose the quoted words in quotation marks. Begin a new paragraph each time a new speaker is introduced.

When you are quoting several paragraphs of dialogue by one speaker, begin each new paragraph with quotation marks. However, use closing quotation marks only at the end of the *entire quoted passage* (not at the end of each paragraph).

Special rules govern the punctuation of a quotation when it is used with an **identifying tag**—a phrase (such as *he said*) that identifies the speaker or writer.

1 Identifying Tag in the Middle of a Quoted Passage

Use a pair of commas to set off an identifying tag that interrupts a quoted passage.

> "In the future," pop artist Andy Warhol once said, "everyone will be world famous for fifteen minutes."

If the identifying tag follows a complete sentence but the quoted passage continues, use a period after the tag. Begin the new sentence with a capital letter, and enclose it in quotation marks.

> "Be careful," Erin warned. "Reptiles can be tricky."

2 Identifying Tag at the Beginning of a Quoted Passage

Use a comma after an identifying tag that introduces quoted speech or writing.

> The Raven repeated, "Nevermore."

Use a colon instead of a comma before a quotation if the identifying tag is a complete sentence. See 32a

She gave her final answer: "No."

3 Identifying Tag at the End of a Quoted Passage

Use a comma to set off a quotation from an identifying tag that follows it.

"Be careful out there," the sergeant warned.

If the quotation ends with a question mark or an exclamation point, use that punctuation mark instead of the comma. In this situation, the identifying tag begins with a lowercase letter even though it follows end punctuation.

"Is Ankara the capital of Turkey?" she asked.

"Oh boy!" he cried.

Note: For information on using quotation marks with other punctuation, **see 31d**.

Close-Up QUOTING LONG PROSE PASSAGES

Do *not* enclose a **long prose passage** (more than four lines) in quotation marks. Instead, set it off by indenting the entire passage one-half inch from the left-hand margin. Double-space above and below the quoted passage, and double-space between lines within it. Introduce the passage with a colon, and place parenthetical documentation one space after the end punctuation.

The following portrait of Aunt Juley illustrates several of the devices Galsworthy uses throughout *The Forsyte Saga*, such as a journalistic detachment, a sense of the grotesque, and an ironic stance:

> Aunt Juley stayed in her room, prostrated by the blow. Her face, discoloured by tears, was divided into compartments by the little ridges of pouting flesh which had swollen

(continued)

QUOTING LONG PROSE PASSAGES *(continued)*

with emotion. . . . Her warm heart could not bear the thought that Ann was lying there so cold. (329)

Many similar portraits of characters appear throughout the novel.

When you quote a long prose passage that is a single paragraph, do not indent the first line. When quoting two or more paragraphs, however, indent the first line of each paragraph (including the first) an additional one-quarter inch. If the first sentence of the quoted passage does not begin a paragraph in the source, do not indent it—but do indent the first line of each subsequent paragraph. If the passage you are quoting includes material set in quotation marks, keep those quotation marks.

Close-Up QUOTING POETRY

Treat one line of poetry like a short prose passage: enclose it in quotation marks and run it into the text. If you quote two or three lines of poetry, separate the lines with **slashes**, and run the quotation into the text. (Leave one space before and one space after the slash.)

See 32e

If you quote more than three lines of poetry, set them off like a long prose passage. (For special emphasis, you may set off fewer lines in this way.) Do not use quotation marks, and be sure to reproduce *exactly* the spelling, capitalization, and indentation of the quoted lines.

Wilfred Owen, a poet who was killed in action in World War I, expressed the horrors of war with vivid imagery:

Bent double, like old beggars under sacks.
Knock-kneed, coughing like hags, we cursed
    through sludge.
Till on the haunting flares we turned our backs
And towards our distant rest began to trudge.
    (lines 1-4)

31b Setting Off Titles

Titles of short works and titles of parts of long works are enclosed in quotation marks. Other titles are italicized.

Titles Requiring Quotation Marks

Articles in Magazines, Newspapers, and Professional Journals

"Why Johnny Can't Write"

Essays, Short Stories, Short Poems, and Songs

"Fenimore Cooper's Literary Offenses"
"Flying Home"
"The Road Not Taken"
"The Star-Spangled Banner"

Chapters or Sections of Books

"Miss Sharp Begins to Make Friends" (Chapter 10 of *Vanity Fair*)

Episodes of Radio or Television Series

"Lucy Goes to the Hospital" (*I Love Lucy*)

See **35a** for a list of titles that require italics.

31c Setting Off Words Used in Special Ways

Enclose a word used in a special or unusual way in quotation marks. (If you use *so-called* before the word, do not use quotation marks as well.)

> It was clear that adults approved of children who were "readers," but it was not at all clear why this was so. (Annie Dillard)

31d Using Quotation Marks with Other Punctuation

At the end of a quotation, punctuation is sometimes placed before the quotation marks and sometimes placed after the quotation marks:

- Place the comma or period *before* the closing quotation marks.

> Many, like poet Robert Frost, think about "the road not taken," but not many have taken "the one less traveled by."

- Place a semicolon or colon *after* the closing quotation marks.

  Students who do not pass the test receive “certificates of completion”; those who pass are awarded diplomas.

  Taxpayers were pleased with the first of the candidate’s promised “sweeping new reforms”: a balanced budget.

- If a question mark, exclamation point, or dash is part of the quotation, place the punctuation mark *before* the closing quotation marks.

  “Who’s there?” she demanded.

  “Stop!” he cried.

  “Should we leave now, or—” Vicki paused, unable to continue.

- If a question mark, exclamation point, or dash is not part of the quotation, place the punctuation mark *after* the closing quotation marks.

  Did you finish reading “The Black Cat”?

  Whatever you do, don’t yell “Uncle”!

  The first story—Updike’s “*A&P*”—provoked discussion.

Close-Up QUOTATIONS WITHIN QUOTATIONS

Use *single* quotation marks to enclose a quotation within a quotation.

Claire noted, “Liberace always said, ‘I cried all the way to the bank.’ ”

Also use single quotation marks within a quotation to set off a title that would normally be enclosed in double quotation marks.

I think what she said was, “Play it, Sam. Play ‘As Time Goes By.’ ”

Use *double* quotation marks around quotations or titles within a long prose passage.

See 31a

31e Editing Misused Quotation Marks

Do not use quotation marks in the following situations.

1 To Set Off Indirect Quotations

Do not use quotation marks to set off **indirect quotations** (someone else's written or spoken words that are not quoted exactly).

> Freud wondered "what women wanted."

2 To Set Off Slang or Technical Terms

> Dawn is "into" running.
>
> "Biofeedback" is sometimes used to treat migraines.

Note: Do not use quotation marks (or italics) to set off titles of your own essays.

CHAPTER 32

Using Other Punctuation Marks

32a Using Colons

The **colon** is a strong punctuation mark that points readers ahead to the material that follows it. When a colon introduces a list or series, explanatory material, or a quotation, it must be preceded by a complete sentence.

1 Introducing Lists or Series

Use colons to set off lists or series, including those introduced by phrases such as *the following* or *as follows*.

> Waiting tables requires three skills: memory, speed, and balance.

2 Introducing Explanatory Material

Use colons to introduce material that explains, exemplifies, or summarizes.

She had one dream: to play professional basketball.

Sometimes a colon separates two independent clauses with the second illustrating or clarifying the first.

The survey presents an interesting finding: Americans do not trust the news media.

Note: When a complete sentence follows a colon, the sentence may begin with either a capital or a lowercase letter. However, if the sentence is a quotation, the first word is always capitalized (unless it is not capitalized in the source).

3 Introducing Quotations

See 31a When you quote a **long prose passage**, always introduce it with a colon. Also use a colon before a short quotation when it is introduced by a complete sentence.

With dignity, Bartleby repeated the words again: "I prefer not to."

Other Conventional Uses of Colons

To Separate a Title from a Subtitle

Family Installments: Memories of Growing Up Hispanic

To Separate Minutes from Hours

6:15 a.m.

See 41a **After the Salutation in a Business Letter**

Dear Dr. Evans:

4 Editing Misused Colons

Do not use colons in the following situations.

- After *namely, for example, such as,* or *that is.*

The Eye Institute treats patients with a wide variety of conditions, such as, myopia, glaucoma, and cataracts.

- Between verbs and their objects or complements or between prepositions and their objects.

James Michener wrote, *Hawaii, Centennial, Space*, and *Poland*.

Hitler's armies marched through, the Netherlands, Belgium, and France.

32b Using Dashes

1 Setting Off Nonessential Material

Like commas, dashes can set off nonessential material, but unlike commas, dashes call attention to the material they set off. Indicate a dash with two unspaced hyphens (which your word-processing program will automatically convert to a dash). See 28d

For emphasis, you may use dashes to set off explanations, qualifications, examples, definitions, and appositives.

Neither of the boys—both nine-year-olds—had any history of violence.

Too many parents learn the dangers of swimming pools the hard way—after their toddlers have drowned.

2 Introducing a Summary

Use a dash to introduce a statement that summarizes a list or series that appears before it.

"Study hard," "Respect your elders," "Don't talk with your mouth full"—Sharon had often heard her parents say these things.

3 Indicating an Interruption

In dialogue, a dash may indicate a hesitation or an unfinished thought.

"I think—no, I know—that this is the worst day of my life," Julie sighed.

Note: Because a series of dashes can make a passage seem disorganized and out of control, you should be careful not to overuse them.

32c Using Parentheses

1 Setting Off Nonessential Material

Use **parentheses** to enclose material that expands, clarifies, illustrates, or supplements. (Note that unlike dashes, parentheses tend to de-emphasize the words they enclose.)

> In some European countries (notably Sweden and France), superb day care is offered at little or no cost to parents.

When a complete sentence set off by parentheses falls within another sentence, it should not begin with a capital letter or end with a period.

> Because the area is so cold (temperatures average in the low twenties), it is virtually uninhabitable.

When the parenthetical sentence does *not* fall within another sentence, however, it must begin with a capital letter and end with appropriate punctuation.

> The region is very cold. (Temperatures average in the low twenties.)

Close-Up USING PARENTHESES WITH COMMAS

Never use a comma before an opening parenthesis. (A comma may follow the closing parenthesis, however.)

> George Orwell's *1984*, (1949), which focuses on the dangers of a totalitarian society, should be required reading.

2 Using Parentheses in Other Situations

Use parentheses around letters and numbers that identify points on a list, dates, cross-references, and documentation.

> All reports must include the following components: (1) an opening summary, (2) a background statement, and (3) a list of conclusions.

Russia defeated Sweden in the Great Northern War (1700–1721).

Other scholars also make this point (see p. 54).

One critic has called the novel "puerile" (Arvin 72).

32d Using Brackets

When one set of parentheses falls within another, use **brackets** in place of the inner set.

In her classic study of American education between 1945 and 1960 (*The Troubled Crusade* [New York: Books, 1963]), Diane Ravitch addresses issues such as progressive education, race, educational reforms, and campus unrest.

Also use brackets within quotations to indicate to readers that the bracketed words are yours and not those of your source. You can bracket an explanation, a clarification, a correction, or an opinion.

"Even at Princeton he [F. Scott Fitzgerald] felt like an outsider."

If a quotation contains an error, indicate that the error is not yours by following it with the Latin word *sic* ("thus") in brackets.

As the website notes, "The octopuss [sic] is a cephalopod mollusk with eight arms."

Note: Use brackets to indicate changes you make in order to fit a quotation smoothly into your sentence. See 8a

32e Using Slashes

1 Separating One Option from Another

The either/or fallacy is a common error in logic.

Writer/director M. Night Shyamalan spoke at the film festival.

In this situation, do not leave a space before or after the slash.

2 Separating Lines of Poetry Run into the Text

The poet James Schevill writes, "I study my defects / And learn how to perfect them."

In this situation, leave one space before and one space after the slash.

32f Using Ellipses

Use ellipses in the following situations.

1 Indicating an Omission in Quoted Prose

Use an **ellipsis**—three *spaced* periods—to indicate that you have omitted words from a prose quotation. (Note that an ellipsis in the middle of a quoted passage can indicate the omission of a word, a sentence or two, or even a whole paragraph or more.) When deleting material from a quotation, be very careful not to change the meaning of the original passage.

Original: "When I was a young man, being anxious to distinguish myself, I was perpetually starting new propositions." (Samuel Johnson)

With Omission: "When I was a young man, . . . I was perpetually starting new propositions."

Note that when you delete words immediately after a punctuation mark (such as the comma in the above example), you retain the punctuation mark before the ellipsis.

When you delete material at the end of a sentence, place the ellipsis *after* the sentence's period or other end punctuation.

According to humorist Dave Barry, "from outer space Europe appears to be shaped like a large ketchup stain. . . ." (period followed by ellipsis)

Never begin a quoted passage with an ellipsis.

When you delete material between sentences, place the ellipsis *after* any punctuation that appears in the original passage.

Deletion from Middle of One Sentence to End of Another: According to Donald Hall, "Everywhere one meets the idea that reading is an activity desirable in itself. . . . People surround the idea of reading with piety and do not take into account the purpose of reading." (period followed by ellipsis)

Deletion from Middle of One Sentence to Middle of Another: "When I was a young man, . . . I found that generally what was new was false." (Samuel Johnson) (comma followed by ellipsis)

Note: If a quoted passage already contains an ellipsis, MLA recommends that you enclose your own ellipses in brackets to distinguish them from those that appear in the original quotation.

Close-Up USING ELLIPSES

If a quotation ending with an ellipsis is followed by parenthetical documentation, the final punctuation comes *after* the documentation.

> As Jarman argues, "Compromise was impossible . . ." (161).

2 Indicating an Omission in Quoted Poetry

Use an ellipsis when you omit a word or phrase from a line of poetry. When you omit one or more lines of poetry, use a line of spaced periods. (The length may be equal either to the line above it or to the missing line—but it should not be longer than the longest line of the poem.)

Original:

Stitch! Stitch! Stitch!
In poverty, hunger, and dirt,
And still with a voice of dolorous pitch,
Would that its tone could reach the Rich,
She sang this "Song of the Shirt"!
(Thomas Hood)

With Omission:

Stitch! Stitch! Stitch!
In poverty, hunger, and dirt,
. . . .
She sang this "Song of the Shirt"!

PART 7

Understanding Spelling and Mechanics

33 Becoming a Better Speller 322

33a The *ie/ei* Combinations 322
33b Doubling Final Consonants 322
33c Silent e before a Suffix 323
33d *y* before a Suffix 323
33e *seed* Endings 323
33f *-able, -ible* 323
33g Plurals 323

34 Knowing When to Capitalize 324

34a Capitalizing Proper Nouns 325
34b Capitalizing Important Words in Titles 327
34c Editing Misused Capitals 328

35 Using Italics 328

35a Setting Off Titles and Names 328
35b Setting Off Foreign Words and Phrases 329
35c Setting Off Elements Spoken of as Themselves and Terms Being Defined 329
35d Using Italics for Emphasis 330

36 Using Hyphens 330

36a Breaking a Word at the End of a Line 330
36b Dividing Compound Words 331

37 Using Abbreviations 333

37a Abbreviating Titles 333
37b Abbreviating Organization Names and Technical Terms 333
37c Abbreviating Dates, Times of Day, Temperatures, and Numbers 334
37d Editing Misused Abbreviations 335

38 Using Numbers 336

38a Spelled-Out Numbers versus Numerals 336
38b Conventional Uses of Numerals 337

CHAPTER 33

Becoming a Better Speller

Like most students, you probably use a spell checker when you write. A spell checker, however, does not eliminate your need to know how to spell. For one thing, a spell checker will only check words that are listed in its dictionary. In addition, a spell checker will not tell you that you have confused two homophones, such as *principle* and *principal.* Finally, a spell checker will not catch typos that create new words, such as *form* for *from.* For this reason, you still need to proofread your essays.

Memorizing just a few simple rules (and their exceptions) can help you identify and correct words that you have misspelled.

33a The *ie/ei* Combinations

Use *i* before *e* (*belief, chief*) except after *c* (*ceiling, receive*) or when pronounced *ay*, as in *neighbor* or *weigh.* **Exceptions:** *either, neither, foreign, leisure, weird*, and *seize.* In addition, if the *ie* combination is not pronounced as a unit, the rule does not apply: *atheist, science.*

33b Doubling Final Consonants

The only words that double their consonants before a suffix that begins with a vowel (*-ed* or *-ing*) are those that pass the following three tests:

1. They have one syllable or are stressed on the last syllable.
2. They have only one vowel in the last syllable.
3. They end in a single consonant.

The word *tap* satisfies all three conditions: it has only one syllable, it has only one vowel (*a*), and it ends in a single consonant (*p*). Therefore, the final consonant doubles before a suffix beginning with a vowel (*tapped, tapping*).

33c Silent e before a Suffix

When a suffix that begins with a consonant is added to a word ending in a silent *e*, the *e* is usually kept: *hope/hopeful*. **Exceptions:** *argument, truly, ninth, judgment*, and *abridgment*.

When a suffix that begins with a vowel is added to a word ending in a silent *e*, the *e* is usually dropped: *hope/hoping*. **Exceptions:** *changeable, noticeable*, and *courageous*.

33d y before a Suffix

When a word ends in a consonant plus *y*, the *y* usually changes to an *i* when a suffix is added (*beauty* + *ful* = *beautiful*). The *y* is kept, however, when the suffix *-ing* is added (*tally* + *ing* = *tallying*) and in some one-syllable words (*dry* + *ness* = *dryness*).

When a word ends in a vowel plus *y*, the *y* is kept (*joy* + *ful* = *joyful*). **Exception:** *day* + *ly* = *daily*.

33e *seed* Endings

Endings with the sound *seed* are nearly always spelled *cede*, as in *precede*. **Exceptions:** *supersede, exceed, proceed*, and *succeed*.

33f -able, -ible

If the root of a word is itself a word, the suffix *-able* is most commonly used (*comfortable, agreeable*). If the root of a word is not a word, the suffix *-ible* is most often used (*compatible, incredible*).

33g Plurals

Most nouns form plurals by adding *-s*: *tortilla/tortillas, boat/boats*. There are, however, a number of exceptions:

- **Words Ending in *-f* or *-fe*** Some words ending in *-f* or *-fe* form plurals by changing the *f* to *v* and adding *-es* or *-s*: *life/lives, self/selves*. Others add just *-s*: *belief/beliefs, safe/safes*.
- **Words Ending in *-y*** Most words that end in a consonant followed by *y* form plurals by changing the *y* to *i* and

adding *-es*: *baby/babies.* **Exceptions:** proper nouns such as *Kennedy* (plural *Kennedys*).

- **Words Ending in *-o*** Most words that end in a consonant followed by *o* add *-es* to form the plural: *tomato/tomatoes, hero/heroes.* **Exceptions:** *silo/silos, piano/pianos, memo/memos, soprano/sopranos.*
- **Words Ending in *-s, -ss, -sh, -ch, -x,* and *-z*** Words ending in *-s, -ss, -sh, -ch, -x,* and *-z* form plurals by adding *-es*: *Jones/Joneses, kiss/kisses, rash/rashes, lunch/lunches, box/boxes, buzz/buzzes.* **Exceptions:** Some one-syllable words that end in *-s* or *-z* double their final consonants when forming plurals: *quiz/quizzes.*
- **Compound Nouns** Hyphenated compound nouns whose first element is more important than the others form the plural with the first element: *sister-in-law/sisters-in-law, editor-in-chief/editors-in-chief.*
- **Foreign Plurals** Some words, especially those borrowed from Latin or Greek, keep their foreign plurals.

Singular	Plural
basis	bases
criterion	criteria
datum	data
memorandum	memoranda
stimulus	stimuli

Note: Some linguists find Latin and Greek plural endings pretentious and encourage the use of English plural forms—for example, *condominiums* rather than *condominia, stadiums* rather than *stadia*, and *octopuses* rather than *octopi.*

CHAPTER 34

Knowing When to Capitalize

In addition to capitalizing the first word of a sentence (including a quoted sentence) and the pronoun *I*, always capitalize *proper nouns* and *important words in titles.*

Close-Up **REVISING CAPITALIZATION ERRORS**

In *Microsoft Word*, the AutoCorrect tool will automatically capitalize certain words—such as the first word of a sentence or the days of the week. Be sure to proofread your work, though, since AutoCorrect will sometimes introduce capitalization errors into your writing.

34a Capitalizing Proper Nouns

Proper nouns—the names of specific persons, places, or things—are capitalized, and so are adjectives formed from proper nouns.

1 Specific People's Names

Always capitalize people's names: Kirsten Gillibrand, Barack Obama.

Capitalize a title when it precedes a person's name (Senator Kirsten Gillibrand) or is used instead of the name (Dad). Do not capitalize titles that *follow* names (Kirsten Gillibrand, the senator from New York) or those that refer to the general position, not the particular person who holds it (a stay-at-home dad).

You may, however, capitalize titles that indicate very high-ranking positions even when they are used alone or when they follow a name: the Pope; Barack Obama, President of the United States. Never capitalize a title denoting a family relationship when it follows an article or a possessive pronoun (an uncle, his mom).

Capitalize titles that represent academic degrees or abbreviations of those degrees even when they follow a name: Dr. Sanjay Gupta; Sanjay Gupta, MD.

2 Names of Particular Structures, Special Events, Monuments, and So On

the Brooklyn Bridge	the Taj Mahal
the Great Wall	Mount Rushmore
the World Series	the *Titanic*

Note: Capitalize a common noun, such as *bridge, river, lake,* or *county*, when it is part of a proper noun (Lake Erie, Kings County).

3 Places and Geographical Regions

Saturn the Straits of Magellan
Budapest the Western Hemisphere

Capitalize *north, south, east,* and *west* when they denote particular geographical regions but not when they designate directions.

There are more tornadoes in Kansas than in the East. (*East* refers to a specific region.)

Turn west at Broad Street and continue north to Market. (*West* and *north* refer to directions, not specific regions.)

4 Days of the Week, Months, and Holidays

Saturday Cinco de Mayo
January Diwali

5 Historical Periods, Events, Documents, and Names of Legal Cases

the Industrial Revolution the Treaty of Versailles
the Battle of Gettysburg *Brown v. Board of Education*

Note: Names of court cases are italicized in the text of essays but not in works-cited entries.

6 Philosophic, Literary, and Artistic Movements

Naturalism Dadaism
Neoclassicism Expressionism

7 Races, Ethnic Groups, Nationalities, and Languages

African American Korean
Latino/Latina Farsi

Note: When the words *black* and *white* denote races, they have traditionally not been capitalized. Current usage is divided on whether or not to capitalize *black*.

8 Religions and Their Followers; Sacred Books and Figures

Islam the Qur'an Buddha
the Talmud Jews God

Note: It is not necessary to capitalize pronouns referring to God (although some people do so).

9 Specific Groups and Organizations

the Democratic Party
the International Brotherhood of Electrical Workers
the New York Yankees
the American Civil Liberties Union
the National Rifle Association
the Rolling Stones

Note: When the name of a group or organization is abbreviated, the **abbreviation** uses capital letters in place of the capitalized words. See 37b

IBEW ACLU NRA

10 Businesses, Government Agencies, and Other Institutions

General Electric
the Environmental Protection Agency
Lincoln High School
the University of Maryland

11 Brand Names and Words Formed from Them

Velcro Coke Post-it Rollerblades AstroTurf

Note: Brand names that over long use have become synonymous with the product—for example, *nylon* and *aspirin*—are no longer capitalized. (Consult a dictionary to determine whether or not to capitalize a familiar brand name.) In general, however, use generic references, not brand names, in college writing—for example, *photocopy*, not *Xerox*.

34b Capitalizing Important Words in Titles

In general, capitalize all words in titles with the exception of articles (*a*, *an*, and *the*), prepositions, coordinating conjunctions, and the *to* in infinitives. If an article, preposition, or coordinating conjunction is the *first* or *last* word in the title, however, do capitalize it.

The Declaration of Independence
Across the River and into the Trees
Madame Curie: A Biography
"What Friends Are For"

34c Editing Misused Capitals

Do not capitalize the following:

- Seasons (summer, fall, winter, spring)
- Names of centuries (the twenty-first century)
- Names of general historical periods (the automobile age)
- Diseases and other medical terms (unless a proper noun is part of the name) or unless the disease is an **acronym**: smallpox, polio, Reyes syndrome, AIDS, Ebola

See 27a

MULTILINGUAL TIP

Do not capitalize a word simply because you want to emphasize its importance. If you are not sure whether a word should be capitalized, look it up in a dictionary.

CHAPTER 35

Using Italics

35a Setting Off Titles and Names

Use italics for the titles and names in the box that follows. All other titles are set off with **quotation marks**.

See 31b

Titles and Names Set in Italics

Books: *Twilight, Harry Potter and the Deathly Hallows*

Newspapers: *The Washington Post, The Philadelphia Inquirer*

Magazines and Journals: *Rolling Stone, Scientific American*

Online Magazines and Journals: *salon.com, theonion.com*

Websites or Home Pages: *urbanlegends.com, movie-mistakes.com*
Pamphlets: *Common Sense*
Films: *Citizen Kane, The Hunger Games*
Television Programs: *60 Minutes, The Bachelorette, American Idol*
Radio Programs: *All Things Considered, A Prairie Home Companion*
Long Poems: *John Brown's Body, The Faerie Queen*
Plays: *Macbeth, A Raisin in the Sun*
Long Musical Works: *Rigoletto, Eroica*
Software Programs: *Microsoft Word, PowerPoint*
Search Engines and Web Browsers: *Google Chrome, Safari, Internet Explorer*
Databases: *Academic Search Premier, Expanded Academic ASAP Plus*
Paintings and Sculpture: *Guernica, Pietà*
Video Games: *Halo: Combat Evolved, Grand Theft Auto V*
Ships: *Lusitania*, U.S.S. *Saratoga* (S.S. and U.S.S. are not italicized.)
Trains: *City of New Orleans, The Orient Express*
Aircraft: *The Hindenburg, Enola Gay* (Only particular aircraft, not makes or types such as Piper Cub or Airbus, are italicized.)
Spacecraft: *Challenger, Enterprise*

Names of sacred books, such as the Bible and the Qur'an, and well-known documents, such as the Constitution and the Declaration of Independence, are neither italicized nor placed within quotation marks.

35b Setting Off Foreign Words and Phrases

Use italics to set off foreign words and phrases that have not become part of the English language.

> "*C'est la vie*," Madeleine said when she saw the long line for basketball tickets.
>
> *Spirochaeta plicatilis* is a corkscrew-like bacterium.

If you are not sure whether a foreign word has been assimilated into English, consult a dictionary.

35c Setting Off Elements Spoken of as Themselves and Terms Being Defined

Use italics to set off letters, numerals, and words that refer to the letters, numerals, and words themselves.

Is that a *p* or a *g*?

I forget the exact address, but I know it has a *3* in it.

Why doesn't *though* rhyme with *cough*?

Also use italics to set off words and phrases that you go on to define.

A closet *drama* is a play meant to be read, not performed.

Note: When you quote a dictionary definition, put the word you are defining in italics and the definition itself in quotation marks.

Infer means "to draw a conclusion"; *imply* means "to suggest."

35d Using Italics for Emphasis

Italics may occasionally be used for emphasis.

Initially, poetry might be defined as a kind of language that says *more* and says it *more intensely* than does ordinary language. (Lawrence Perrine, *Sound and Sense*)

However, overuse of italics is distracting. Instead of italicizing, indicate emphasis with word choice and sentence structure.

CHAPTER 36

Using Hyphens

Hyphens have two conventional uses: to break a word at the end of a line and to link words in certain compounds.

36a Breaking a Word at the End of a Line

Sometimes you will want to intentionally break a word with a hyphen—for example, to fill in excessive space at the end of a line when you want to enhance a document's visual appeal.

When you break a word at the end of a line, divide it only between syllables, consulting a dictionary if necessary. Never divide a word at the end of a page, and never hyphenate a one-syllable word. In addition, never leave a single letter at the end of a line or carry only one or two letters to the next line.

If you divide a **compound word** at the end of a line, put the hyphen between the elements of the compound (*snow-mobile*, not *snowmo-bile*).

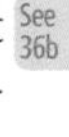

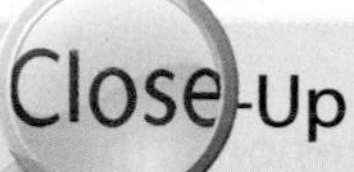

DIVIDING ELECTRONIC ADDRESSES (URLS)

MLA style recommends that you break the URL after a mark of punctuation (such as a slash, period, or hyphen). In addition, omit *http://* or *https://* when noting the URL.

36b Dividing Compound Words

A **compound word** is composed of two or more words. Some familiar compound words are always hyphenated: *no-hitter, helter-skelter*. Other compounds are always written as one word (*fireplace*) and others as two separate words (*bunk bed*). Your dictionary can tell you whether or not a particular compound requires a hyphen.

1 Hyphenating with Compound Adjectives

A **compound adjective** is made up of two or more words that function together as an adjective. When a compound adjective *precedes* the noun it modifies, use hyphens to join its elements.

> The research team tried to use nineteenth-century technology to design a space-age project.

When a compound adjective *follows* the noun it modifies, do not use hyphens to join its elements.

> The three government-operated programs were run smoothly, but the one that was not government operated was short of funds.

Note: A compound adjective formed with an adverb ending in *-ly* is not hyphenated even when it precedes the noun: *Many upwardly mobile families are on tight budgets.*

Use **suspended hyphens**—hyphens followed by a space or by appropriate punctuation and a space—in a pair or series of compounds that have the same principal elements.

Graduates of two- and four-year colleges were eligible for the grants.

The exam called for sentence-, paragraph-, and essay-length answers.

2 Hyphenating with Certain Prefixes or Suffixes

Use a hyphen between a prefix and a proper noun or adjective.

mid-July pre-Columbian

Use a hyphen to connect the prefixes *all-*, *ex-*, *half-*, *quarter-*, *quasi-*, and *self-* and the suffix *-elect* to a noun.

ex-senator	self-centered	president-elect
quarter-moon	quasi-legal	all-inclusive

Also hyphenate to avoid certain hard-to-read combinations, such as two *i*'s (*semi-illiterate*) or more than two of the same consonant (*shell-less*).

3 Hyphenating in Compound Numerals and Fractions

Hyphenate compounds that represent numbers below one hundred (even if they are part of a larger number).

the twenty-first century three hundred sixty-five days

Also hyphenate the written form of a fraction when it modifies a noun.

a two-thirds share of the business

CHAPTER 37

Using Abbreviations

Generally speaking, **abbreviations** are not appropriate in college writing except in tables, charts, and works-cited lists. Some abbreviations are acceptable only in scientific, technical, or business writing or only in a particular discipline. If you have questions about the appropriateness of a particular abbreviation, consult a style manual for the appropriate field.

> **Close-Up** ABBREVIATIONS IN ELECTRONIC COMMUNICATIONS
>
> Like emoticons and acronyms, which are popular in personal email and instant messages, shorthand abbreviations and symbols—such as GR8 and 2NITE—are common in text messages. Although they are acceptable in informal electronic communication, such abbreviations are not appropriate in college writing or in business communication.

37a Abbreviating Titles

Titles before and after proper names are usually abbreviated.

Mr. Homer Simpson	Rep. John Lewis
Henry Kissinger, PhD	Dr. Martin Luther King, Jr.

Do not, however, use an abbreviated title without a name.

The ~~Dr.~~ *doctor* diagnosed hepatitis.

37b Abbreviating Organization Names and Technical Terms

Well-known businesses and government, social, and civic organizations are frequently referred to by capitalized initials.

See 27a These **abbreviations** fall into two categories: those in which the initials are pronounced as separate units (EPA, MTV) and **acronyms**, in which the initials are pronounced as a word (NATO, FEMA).

To save space, you may use accepted abbreviations for complex technical terms that are not well known, but be sure to spell out the full term the first time you mention it, followed by the abbreviation in parentheses.

> Citrus farmers have been using ethylene dibromide (EDB), a chemical pesticide, for more than twenty years. Now, however, EDB has contaminated water supplies.

Close-Up ABBREVIATIONS IN MLA DOCUMENTATION

MLA documentation style requires abbreviations of publishers' company names—for example, **Columbia UP** for *Columbia University Press*—in the works-cited list. Do not, however, use such abbreviations in the text of an essay. See 10a2

MLA style permits the use of abbreviations that designate parts of written works (**ch. 3, sec. 7**)—but only in the works-cited list and parenthetical documentation.

Finally, MLA recommends abbreviating citations for classic literary works and for books of the Bible in parenthetical citations: **(*Oth.*)** for *Othello*, **(Exod.)** for Exodus. These words should not be abbreviated in the text of an essay or in the works-cited list.

37c Abbreviating Dates, Times of Day, Temperatures, and Numbers

50 BC (*BC* follows the date)
3:03 p.m. (lowercase)
AD 432 (*AD* precedes the date)
180°F (Fahrenheit)

Always capitalize *BC* and *AD*. (The alternatives *BCE*, for "before the Common Era," and *CE*, for "Common Era," are also capitalized.) The abbreviations *a.m.* and *p.m.* are used only when they are accompanied by numbers: *I'll see you in the morning* (not *in the a.m.*).

Avoid the abbreviation *no.* except in technical writing, and then use it only before a specific number: *The unidentified substance was labeled no. 52.*

37d Editing Misused Abbreviations

In college writing, the following are not abbreviated.

1 Latin Expressions

and so on.
Poe wrote "The Gold Bug," "The Tell-Tale Heart,"^ ~~etc.~~

for example,
Many musicians (~~e.g.,~~^ Bruce Springsteen) have been influenced by Bob Dylan.

2 Names of Days, Months, or Holidays

Saturday, December *Christmas*
On^ ~~Sat., Dec.~~ 23, I started my^ ~~Xmas~~ shopping.

3 Names of Streets and Places

Drive *New York City.*
He lives on Riverside^ ~~Dr.~~ in^ ~~NYC.~~

Exceptions: The abbreviations *US* (*US Coast Guard*), *St.* (*St. Albans*), and *Mt.* (*Mt. Etna*) are acceptable, as is *DC* in *Washington, DC.*

4 Names of Academic Subjects

Psychology *literature*
^~~Psych.~~ and English^ ~~lit.~~ are required courses.

5 Units of Measurement

MLA style does not permit abbreviations for units of measurement and requires that you spell out words such as *inches, feet, years, miles, pints, quarts,* and *gallons.*

In technical and business writing, however, some units of measurement are abbreviated when they are preceded by a numeral.

The hurricane had winds of 35 mph.

One new hybrid gets over 50 mpg.

6 Symbols

The symbols =, +, and # are acceptable in technical and scientific writing but not in nontechnical college writing. The symbols % and $ are acceptable only when used with See 38b numerals (15%, $15,000), not with spelled-out numbers.

CHAPTER 38

Using Numbers

Convention determines when to use a **numeral** (22) and when to spell out a number (twenty-two). Numerals are commonly used in scientific and technical writing and in journalism, but they are used less often in academic or literary writing.

See Ch. 11 Note: The guidelines in this chapter are based on the *MLA Handbook*, 8th ed. (2016). APA style, however, requires that all numbers below ten be spelled out if they do not represent specific measurements and that the numbers ten and above be expressed in numerals.

38a Spelled-Out Numbers versus Numerals

Unless a number falls into one of the categories listed in **38b**, spell it out *if you can do so in one or two words.*

The Hawaiian alphabet has only twelve letters.

Class size stabilized at twenty-eight students.

The subsidies are expected to total about two million dollars.

Numbers *more than two words* long are expressed in figures.

The dietitian prepared 125 sample menus.

The developer of the community purchased 300,000 doorknobs and 153,000 faucets.

Never begin a sentence with a numeral. If necessary, reword the sentence.

Faulty: 250 students are currently enrolled.

Revised: Current enrollment is 250 students.

Note: When one number immediately precedes another in a sentence, spell out the first, and use a numeral for the second: *five 3-quart containers.*

38b Conventional Uses of Numerals

Use numerals in the following situations:

- **Addresses:** 1920 Walnut Street, Philadelphia, PA 19103
- **Dates:** January 15, 1929 1914–1919
- **Exact Times:** 9:16 10 a.m. or 10:00 a.m. (but spell out times of day when they are used with *o'clock:* ten o'clock)
- **Exact Sums of Money:** $25.11 $6,752.00
- **Divisions of Works:** Act 5 lines 17–28 page 42
- **Percentages and Decimals:** 80% 3.14

Note: You may spell out a percentage (*eighty percent*) if you use percentages infrequently in an essay, provided it can be expressed in two or three words. Always use a numeral (not a spelled-out number) with a % symbol.

- **Measurements with Symbols or Abbreviations:** 32° 15 cc
- **Ratios and Statistics:** 20 to 1 a mean of 40
- **Scores:** a lead of 6 to 0
- **Identification Numbers:** Route 66 Track 8 Channel 12

PART 8

Composing in Various Genres

39 Designing Effective Documents 340

39a Creating an Effective Visual Format 340
39b Using Headings 341
39c Constructing Lists 342
39d Using Visuals 344

40 Composing in Digital Environments 347

40a Considering Audience and Purpose 347
40b Writing in a Wired Classroom 347

41 Writing in the Workplace 350

41a Writing Letters of Application 350
41b Designing Résumés 352
41c Writing Memos 352
41d Writing Emails 352

42 Developing and Delivering Presentations 355

42a Getting Started 356
42b Planning Your Speech 356
42c Preparing Your Presentation Notes 357
42d Preparing Visual Aids 358
42e Rehearsing Your Speech 361
42f Delivering Your Speech 362

43 Composing in the Disciplines 362

Composing in the Disciplines: An Overview (Chart) 364

CHAPTER 39

Designing Effective Documents

Document design is a set of guidelines that help you determine how to design a piece of written work—print or digital—so that it communicates your ideas clearly and effectively. All well-designed documents share the same general characteristics: an effective format, clear headings, useful lists, and helpful visuals.

39a Creating an Effective Visual Format

An effective document contains visual cues that help readers identify, read, and interpret information on a page.

1 Margins

Margins frame a page and keep it from looking overcrowded. Because a page with narrow (or no) margins can make a document difficult to read, margins should be at least one inch all around. If the material you are writing about is highly technical or unusually difficult, use wider margins (one and a half inches).

In general, you should **justify** (uniformly align, except for paragraph indentations) the left-hand margin.

2 White Space

White space is the area of a page that is intentionally left blank. Used effectively, white space can isolate material and focus a reader's attention on it. You can use white space around a block of text—a paragraph or a section, for example—or around visuals such as charts, graphs, and photographs.

3 Color

Color (when used in moderation) can emphasize and classify information—such as the headings in a résumé or the bars on a graph—while also making it visually appealing. Remember, however, that too many colors can distract or confuse readers.

4 Typeface and Type Size

Typefaces are distinctively designed sets of letters, numbers, and punctuation marks. The typeface you choose should be suitable for your purpose and audience. In your academic writing, avoid fancy or elaborate typefaces—script or old English, for example—that call attention to themselves and are difficult to read. Instead, select a typeface that is simple and direct—Cambria, Times New Roman, or Arial, for example. For most of your academic essays, use 10- or 12-point type (headings will sometimes be larger).

5 Line Spacing

Line spacing refers to the amount of space between the lines of a document. If the lines are too far apart, the text will seem to lack cohesion; if the lines are too close together, the text will appear crowded and be difficult to read. The type of writing you do can determine line spacing: the paragraphs of business letters, memos, and some reports are usually single-spaced and separated by a double space, but the paragraphs of academic essays are usually double-spaced.

39b Using Headings

Headings serve some useful purposes in a text:

- Headings tell readers that a new idea is being introduced.
- Headings emphasize key ideas.
- Headings indicate how information is organized in a text.

1 Number of Headings

The number of headings you use depends on the document. A long, complicated document will need more headings than a shorter, less complicated one. Keep in mind that too few headings will not be of much use, but too many headings will make your document look like an outline.

2 Phrasing

Headings should be brief, informative, and to the point. They can be single words—**Summary** or **Introduction**, for example—or they can be phrases (always stated in **parallel terms**): **Traditional Family Patterns, Alternate Family Patterns, Modern Family Patterns**. Finally, headings can be questions (**How Do You Choose a Major?**) or statements (**Choose Your Major Carefully**). See 24a

3 Indentation

Different style guides provide different guidelines concerning the placement of headings. For example, the APA style guide makes the following recommendations: first-level headings should be centered, second-level headings should be justified left, and third-level headings should be indented one-half inch. Consult the appropriate style guide for the guidelines on this issue.

4 Typographical Emphasis

You can emphasize important words in headings by using **boldface,** *italics*, or ALL CAPITAL LETTERS. Used in moderation, these distinctive type styles make a text easier to read. Used excessively, however, they slow readers down.

5 Consistency

Headings at the same level should have the same typeface, type size, spacing, and color. Thus, if one first-level heading is boldfaced and centered, all other first-level headings must be boldfaced and centered. Using consistent patterns reinforces the connection between content and ideas and makes a document easier to understand.

Note: Never separate a heading from the text that goes with it. If a heading is at the bottom of one page and the text that goes with it is on the next page, move the heading onto the next page so that readers can see the heading and the text together.

39c Constructing Lists

By breaking a long discussion into a series of key ideas, a list makes information easier to understand. By isolating individual pieces of information in this way, a list directs readers to important information on a page.

CHECKLIST

Constructing Effective Lists

When constructing a list, follow these guidelines:

- ❑ **Indent each item.** Each item in a list should be indented so that it stands out from the text around it.

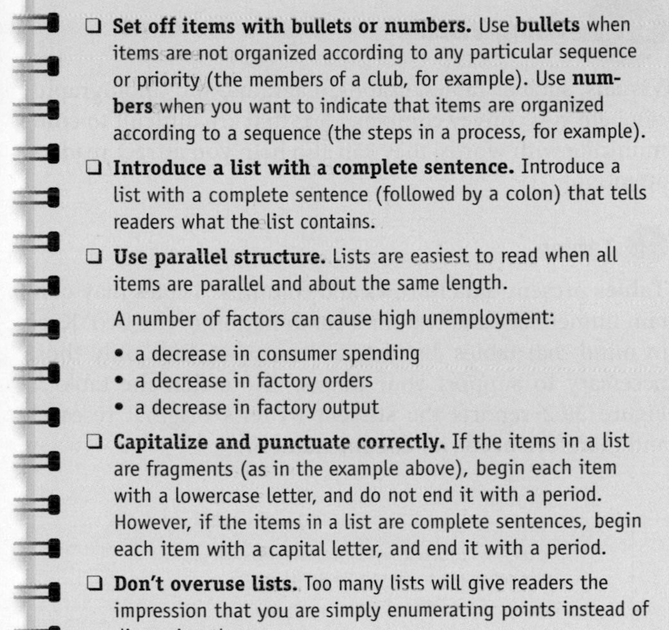

- ❑ **Set off items with bullets or numbers.** Use **bullets** when items are not organized according to any particular sequence or priority (the members of a club, for example). Use **numbers** when you want to indicate that items are organized according to a sequence (the steps in a process, for example).
- ❑ **Introduce a list with a complete sentence.** Introduce a list with a complete sentence (followed by a colon) that tells readers what the list contains.
- ❑ **Use parallel structure.** Lists are easiest to read when all items are parallel and about the same length.

  A number of factors can cause high unemployment:

  - a decrease in consumer spending
  - a decrease in factory orders
  - a decrease in factory output
- ❑ **Capitalize and punctuate correctly.** If the items in a list are fragments (as in the example above), begin each item with a lowercase letter, and do not end it with a period. However, if the items in a list are complete sentences, begin each item with a capital letter, and end it with a period.
- ❑ **Don't overuse lists.** Too many lists will give readers the impression that you are simply enumerating points instead of discussing them.

Figure 39.1 shows a page from a student's report that incorporates some of the effective design elements discussed in **39a–c.** Notice that the use of different typefaces and type sizes contributes to the document's overall readability.

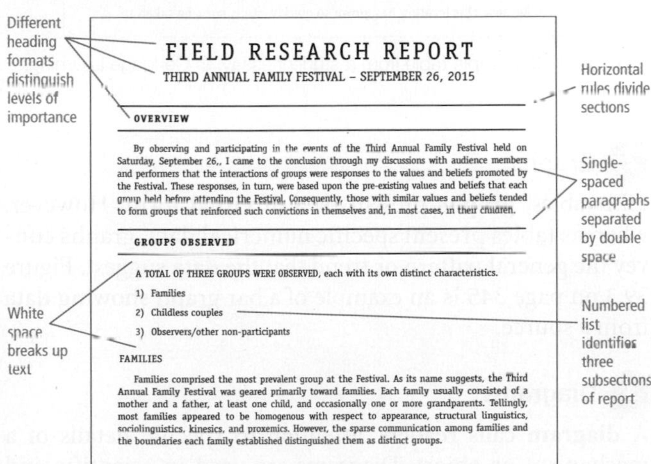

FIELD RESEARCH REPORT

THIRD ANNUAL FAMILY FESTIVAL – SEPTEMBER 26, 2015

OVERVIEW

By observing and participating in the events of the Third Annual Family Festival held on Saturday, September 26,, I came to the conclusion through my discussions with audience members and performers that the interactions of groups were responses to the values and beliefs promoted by the Festival. These responses, in turn, were based upon the pre-existing values and beliefs that each group held before attending the Festival. Consequently, those with similar values and beliefs tended to form groups that reinforced such convictions in themselves and, in most cases, in their children.

GROUPS OBSERVED

A TOTAL OF THREE GROUPS WERE OBSERVED, each with its own distinct characteristics.

1) Families
2) Childless couples
3) Observers/other non-participants

FAMILIES

Families comprised the most prevalent group at the Festival. As its name suggests, the Third Annual Family Festival was geared primarily toward families. Each family usually consisted of a mother and a father, at least one child, and occasionally one or more grandparents. Tellingly, most families appeared to be homogenous with respect to appearance, structural linguistics, sociolinguistics, kinesics, and proxemics. However, the sparse communication among families and the boundaries each family established distinguished them as distinct groups.

FIGURE 39.1 A well-designed page from a student's report. © Cengage Learning.

39d Using Visuals

Visuals, such as tables, graphs, diagrams, and photographs, can help you convey complex ideas that are difficult to communicate with words; they can also help you attract readers' attention.

1 Tables

Tables present data in rows and columns. Tables may contain numerical data, text, or a combination of the two. Keep in mind that tables distract readers, so include only those necessary to support your points. (Note that the table in Figure 39.2 reports the student writer's original research and therefore needs no documentation.)

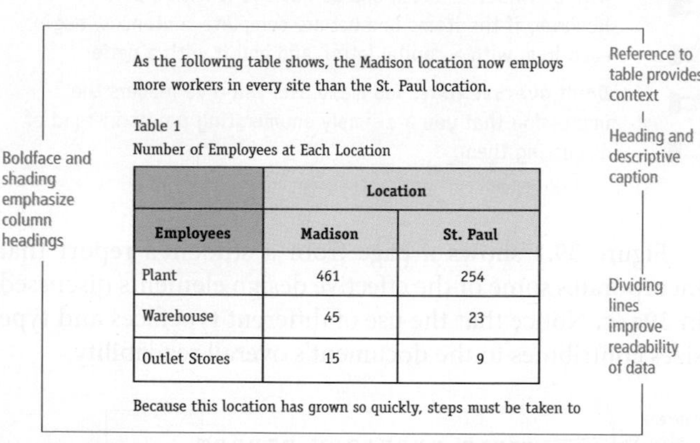
As the following table shows, the Madison location now employs more workers in every site than the St. Paul location.

Table 1
Number of Employees at Each Location

	Location	
Employees	**Madison**	**St. Paul**
Plant	461	254
Warehouse	45	23
Outlet Stores	15	9

Because this location has grown so quickly, steps must be taken to

FIGURE 39.2 Sample table from a student essay. © Cengage Learning.

2 Graphs

Like tables, **graphs** present data in visual form. However, whereas tables present specific numerical data, graphs convey the general pattern or trend that the data suggest. Figure 39.3 on page 345 is an example of a bar graph showing data from a source.

3 Diagrams

A **diagram** calls readers' attention to specific details of a mechanism or object. Diagrams are used in scientific and technical writing to clarify concepts that are difficult to explain in words. Figure 39.4 below, which illustrates the sections of an orchestra, serves a similar purpose in a music education essay.

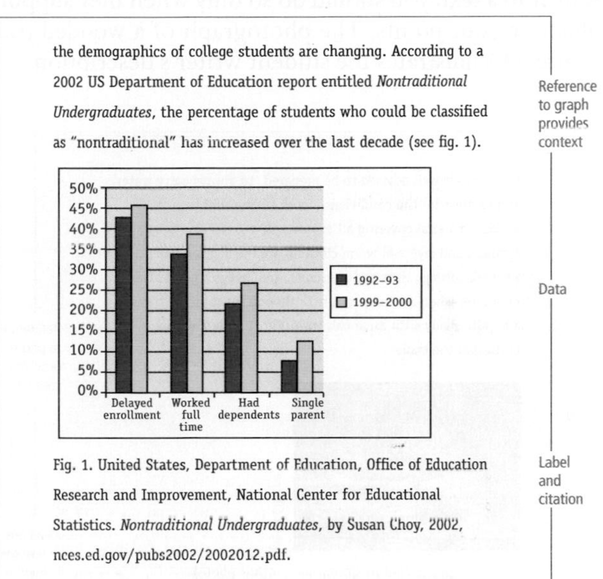
the demographics of college students are changing. According to a 2002 US Department of Education report entitled *Nontraditional Undergraduates*, the percentage of students who could be classified as "nontraditional" has increased over the last decade (see fig. 1).

Fig. 1. United States, Department of Education, Office of Education Research and Improvement, National Center for Educational Statistics. *Nontraditional Undergraduates*, by Susan Choy, 2002, nces.ed.gov/pubs2002/2002012.pdf.

FIGURE 39.3 Sample graph from a student essay. Data © US Department of Education. © Cengage Learning.

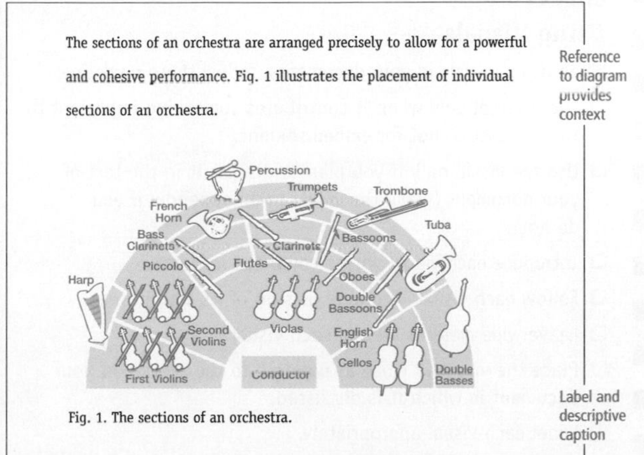
The sections of an orchestra are arranged precisely to allow for a powerful and cohesive performance. Fig. 1 illustrates the placement of individual sections of an orchestra.

Fig. 1. The sections of an orchestra.

FIGURE 39.4 Sample diagram from a student essay. © Cengage Learning.

4 Photographs

Photographs enable you to show exactly what something or someone looks like. Although it is easy to paste photographs directly into a text, you should do so only when they support or illustrate your points. The photograph of a wooded trail in Figure 39.5 illustrates the student writer's description.

travelers are well advised to be prepared, to always carry water, and to dress for the conditions. Loose fitting, lightweight wicking material covering all exposed skin is necessary in summer, and layers of warm clothing are needed for cold-weather outings. Hats and sunscreen are always a good idea no matter what the temperature, although most of the trails are quite shady with huge oak trees. Fig. 1 shows a shady portion of the trail.

Reference to photo provides context

Photo sized and placed appropriately within text with consistent white space above and below

Laurie Kirszner

Fig. 1. Greenbelt Trail in springtime (author photo).

Label and descriptive caption

FIGURE 39.5 Sample photograph from a student essay.

CHECKLIST
Using Visuals

When using visuals in your documents, follow these guidelines:

- ❑ Use a visual only when it contributes something important to the discussion, not for embellishment.
- ❑ Use the visual only if you plan to discuss it in the text of your document (place the visual in an appendix if you do not).
- ❑ Introduce each visual with a complete sentence.
- ❑ Follow each visual with a discussion of its significance.
- ❑ Leave wide margins around each visual.
- ❑ Place the visual as close as possible to the section of your document in which it is discussed.
- ❑ Label each visual appropriately.
- ❑ Document each visual borrowed from a source.

CHAPTER 40

Composing in Digital Environments

Online communication is different from print communication, specifically in the ways readers interact with the text. In order to write effectively for this type of audience, you should be aware of the demands of writing in digital environments.

40a Considering Audience and Purpose

The most obvious difference between digital communication and print communication is the nature of the **audience.** Audiences for print documents simply read a discussion. Audiences for electronic documents, however, can post responses and sometimes communicate directly with the writer.

The **purpose** of electronic communication is sometimes different from that of print communication. Unlike print documents, which appear as finished products, electronic documents are often open-ended. In fact, with wikis (**see 40b3**), readers are encouraged to add or edit content and, in this way, to participate in the creation of a document.

Internet documents also tend to be shorter and more to the point than articles written for print magazines and newspapers. Because most people read Internet articles on the screen, they may be reluctant to read articles that are more than a page or two in length.

Today the line between print and electronic documents is blurring. For example, scholarly articles may be published in online-only journals, and news stories may appear both in print and online. When a print article is published online, it usually includes web-specific elements such as links or streaming video. As online writing becomes the norm, writers need to understand its advantages and its unique features.

40b Writing in a Digital Classroom

Increasingly, instructors are using the Internet as well as specific web-based technology to teach writing. Some of the most popular tools that students can use to create web-based content in digital writing environments are discussed here.

Close-Up SYNCHRONOUS AND ASYNCHRONOUS COMMUNICATION

With **synchronous communication,** all parties involved in the communication process are present at the same time and can be involved in a real-time conversation. Chat rooms, discussion boards, and instant messaging are examples of synchronous communication. Synchronous communication tools are often used in online environments.

With **asynchronous communication,** there is a delay between the time a message is sent and the time it is received. Asynchronous exchanges occur in emails, texts, blogs, wikis, web forums, and discussion groups. With asynchronous communication, students can post comments or send email messages and read comments posted by their instructors or other students.

1 Using Email

Email enables you to exchange ideas with classmates, ask questions of your instructors, and communicate with the writing center or other campus services. You can insert email links in web documents, and you can transfer files as email attachments from one computer to another. In many classes, you submit writing assignments to instructors as email attachments.

Close-Up EMAILS TO INSTRUCTORS

When you write email messages to your instructors, keep in mind that your communication should be fairly formal. Use the type of language that you would use to address a supervisor in a work environment. Include clear subject lines, and use appropriate salutations ("Dear Professor Jewett," never "Hi Prof") and complimentary closes.

2 Using Blogs

A **blog** is like an online journal. Some writing instructors encourage students to create and maintain blogs that function as online writing journals. Blogs are not limited to text; they can contain photographs, videos, music, audio, and personal artwork as well as links to other blogs or websites. Most course management systems, such as *Blackboard* and *Canvas, make* it easy to create a blog. In addition, Web 2.0 technologies, such as *Blogger* and *WordPress*, are open-source platforms that students can use to create their own blogs.

3 Using Wikis

A **wiki** (Hawaiian for *fast* or *quick*) is a website that allows users to add, remove, or change content. With wikis, individuals can work together on a project, adding, deleting, and modifying content as the need arises. Some writing instructors create wikis to encourage students to collaborate on reports, encyclopedia entries, or brochures. The result is a project that is the collective work of all the students who contributed to it.

4 Using Listservs

Listservs (sometimes called **discussion lists**) are electronic mailing lists. They enable individuals to communicate with groups of people interested in particular topics. Subscribers to a listserv send emails to a main email address, and these messages are automatically routed to all members of the group. Listservs can be especially useful in composition classes, permitting students to post comments on reading assignments as well as to discuss other subjects with the entire class.

5 Using Podcasts

A **podcast** is any broadcast—audio or visual—that has been converted to an MP3 or similar format for playback on the Internet or with an MP3 playback device. Podcasting is becoming increasingly common in college classrooms. Instructors podcast class lectures that students can access at their leisure. Instructors also use podcasts to give feedback on students' projects, to distribute supplementary material such as audio recordings or speeches, or to communicate class information or news.

6 Using *Twitter* and *Facebook*

Some instructors use *Twitter* as a tool to teach writing. For example, because tweets force students to be concise, some writing instructors ask students to tweet their thesis statements to the class. In addition, instructors can use *Twitter* as an easy way to get in touch with students (*Don't forget. Class cancelled tomorrow.*) and to reinforce important course concepts (*Your arguments must be supported by evidence. Look out for logical fallacies.*).

Some instructors form *Facebook* groups and post links to websites, documents, and other links on the group pages. Students can post questions about class assignments and discuss topics that interest them.

CHAPTER 41

Writing in the Workplace

Whether you are writing letters of application, résumés, memos, or email, you should always be concise, avoid digressions, and try to sound as natural as possible.

41a Writing Letters of Application

A **letter of application** (electronic or print) summarizes your qualifications for a particular job.

Begin your letter of application by identifying the job you are applying for and telling where you heard about it. In the body of your letter, provide the specific information that will convince readers you are qualified for the position. Conclude by stating that you have enclosed your résumé and that you will be available for an interview. (A sample letter of application appears on page 351.)

Sample Letter of Application

246 Hillside Drive
Urbana, IL 61801
kr237@metropolis.105.com
March 19, 2015

Heading

Mr. Maurice Snyder, Personnel Director
Guilford, Fox, and Morris
22 Hamilton Street
Urbana, IL 61822

Inside address

Dear Mr. Snyder:

Salutation (followed by a colon)

My college advisor, Dr. Raymond Walsh, has told me that you are interested in hiring a part-time intern. I believe that my academic background and my work experience qualify me for this position.

I am presently a junior accounting major at the University of Illinois. During the past year, I have taken courses in taxation, trusts, and business law. I am also proficient in *QuickBooks* and *Sage 50*. Last spring, I gained practical accounting experience by working in our department's tax clinic.

← Double-space

After I graduate, I hope to earn a master's degree in taxation and then return to the Urbana area. I believe that my experience in taxation as well as my familiarity with the local business community will enable me to make a contribution to your firm.

← Single-space

I have enclosed a résumé for your review. I will be available for an interview any time after March 23.

Sincerely yours,

Complimentary close

Sandra Kraft

Written signature

Sandra Kraft
Enc.: Résumé

Typed signature
Additional data

Note: After you have been interviewed, be sure to send a **follow-up email** to the person (or persons) who interviewed you. Because many applicants do not write follow-up emails, they can make a very positive impression.

41b Designing Résumés

A **résumé** lists relevant information about your education, job experience, goals, and personal interests.

The majority of résumés are submitted electronically as email attachments, although some hiring managers still prefer paper résumés. Either way, the guidelines are the same.

The most common way to arrange the information in your résumé is in **chronological order,** listing your education and work experience in sequence, moving from latest to earliest job. Your résumé should be brief (one page, if possible), clear, and logically organized. Emphasize important information with italics, bullets, boldface, or different fonts. (A sample résumé appears on page 353.)

41c Writing Memos

Memos communicate information within an organization. Begin your memo with a purpose statement, followed by a background section. In the body of your memo, support your main point. If your memo is short, use bulleted or numbered lists to emphasize information. If it is more than two or three paragraphs, use headings to designate individual sections. End your memo by stating your conclusions and recommendations. (A sample memo appears on page 354.)

41d Writing Emails

In many workplaces, virtually all internal (and many external) communications are transmitted as email. Although personal email tends to be informal, business email observes the conventions of standard written communication.

Sample Résumé: Chronological Order

KAREN L. OLSON

SCHOOL
3812 Hamilton St. Apt. 18
Philadelphia, PA 19104
215-382-0831
olsont@dunm.ocs.drexel.edu

HOME
110 Ascot Ct.
Harmony, PA 16037
412-452-2944

EDUCATION

DREXEL UNIVERSITY, Philadelphia, PA 19104
Bachelor of Science in Graphic Design
Anticipated Graduation: May 2016
Cumulative Grade Point Average: 3.2 on a 4.0 scale

COMPUTER SKILLS AND COURSEWORK

HARDWARE

Familiar with both Macintosh and PC systems

SOFTWARE

Adobe Creative Cloud, QuarkXPress 2015, CorelDRAW Graphics Suite X7

COURSES

Corporate Identity, Environmental Graphics, Typography, Photography, Painting and Printmaking, Sculpture, Computer Imaging, Art History

EMPLOYMENT EXPERIENCE

THE TRIANGLE, Drexel University, Philadelphia, PA 19104
January 2013–present
Graphics Editor. Design all display advertisements submitted to Drexel's student newspaper.

UNISYS CORPORATION, Blue Bell, PA 19124
June–September 2013, Cooperative Education
Graphic Designer. Designed interior pages as well as covers for target marketing brochures. Created various logos and spot art designed for use on interoffice memos and departmental publications.

CHARMING SHOPPES, INC., Bensalem, PA 19020
June–December 2012, Cooperative Education
Graphic Designer/Fashion Illustrator. Created graphics for future placement on garments. Did some textile designing. Drew flat illustrations of garments to scale in computer. Prepared presentation boards.

DESIGN AND IMAGING STUDIO, Drexel University, Philadelphia, PA 19104
October 2011–June 2012
Monitor. Supervised computer activity in studio. Answered telephone. Assisted other graphic design students in using computer programs.

ACTIVITIES AND AWARDS

The Triangle, Graphics Editor: 2012–present
Kappa Omicron Nu Honor Society, vice president: 2012–present
Graphics Group, vice president: 2011–present
Dean's List: spring 2011, fall and winter 2012

REFERENCES AND PORTFOLIO

Available upon request.

Sample Memo

Opening component

TO: Ina Ellen, Senior Counselor
FROM: Kim Williams, Student Tutor Supervisor
SUBJECT: Construction of a Tutoring Center
DATE: November 10, 2015

Purpose statement

This memo proposes the establishment of a tutoring center in the Office of Student Affairs.

Body

BACKGROUND

Under the present system, tutors must work with students at a number of facilities scattered across the university campus. As a result, tutors waste a lot of time running from one facility to another and are often late for appointments.

NEW FACILITY

I propose that we establish a tutoring facility adjacent to the Office of Student Affairs. The two empty classrooms next to the office, presently used for storage of office furniture, would be ideal for this use. We could furnish these offices with the desks and file cabinets already stored in these rooms.

BENEFITS

The benefits of this facility would be the centralizing of the tutoring services and the proximity of the facility to the Office of Student Affairs. The tutoring facility could also use the secretarial services of the Office of Student Affairs.

Conclusion

RECOMMENDATIONS

To implement this project, we would need to do the following:

1. Clean up and paint rooms 331 and 333
2. Use folding partitions to divide each room into five single-desk offices
3. Use stored office equipment to furnish the center

These changes would do much to improve the tutoring service. I look forward to discussing this matter with you in more detail.

Close-Up WRITING EMAILS

The following rules can help you communicate effectively in an electronic business environment:

- Write in complete sentences. Avoid slang, imprecise diction, and abbreviations.
- Use an appropriate tone. Address readers with respect, just as you would in a standard business letter.
- Include a subject line that clearly identifies your content.
- Make your message as short as possible. Because most emails are read on the screen, long discussions are difficult to follow.
- Use short paragraphs, leaving an extra space between paragraphs.
- Use lists and internal headings to focus your discussion and to break it into manageable parts.
- Reread and edit your email after you have written it.
- Proofread carefully before sending your email.
- Make sure that your list of recipients is accurate and that you do not send your email to unintended recipients.
- Do not send your email until you are absolutely certain that your message says exactly what you want it to say.
- Do not forward an email you receive unless you have the permission of the sender.
- Watch what you write. Keep in mind that email written at work is the property of the employer, who has the legal right to access it—even without your permission.

CHAPTER 42

Developing and Delivering Presentations

At school and on the job, you may sometimes be called upon to make **presentations.** The following guidelines can make the experience much less stressful.

42a Getting Started

Just as with writing an essay, the preparation phase of a presentation is extremely important.

Identify Your Topic The first step in planning a presentation is to identify your topic. Once you have a topic, you should decide how much information you will need.

Consider Your Audience Consider the nature of your audience. Is your audience made up of experts or of people who know very little about your topic? How much background information will you have to provide? Can you use technical terms, or should you avoid them? Do you think your audience will be interested in your topic, or will you have to create interest?

See 2c

Consider Your Purpose Your speech should have a specific purpose that you can sum up concisely. To help you zero in on your purpose, ask yourself what you are trying to accomplish with your presentation.

See 2b

Consider Your Constraints How much time do you have for your presentation? (Obviously a ten-minute presentation requires more information than a three-minute presentation.) Do you know a lot about your topic, or will you have to do research?

42b Planning Your Speech

In the planning phase, you develop a thesis; then, you decide what points you will discuss and divide your speech into a few manageable sections.

PLANNING GUIDE

PRESENTATION

Your **assignment** will ask you to deliver a presentation on a particular topic.
Your **purpose** will be to inform, persuade, or entertain listeners.
Your **audience** could be people who know a lot about your topic or people who know very little about it.

INTRODUCTION

- If you think your listeners know little about your topic, begin by creating interest—possibly by identifying common ground.
- If you think your listeners know a lot about your topic, begin with some general opening remarks.
- State your thesis.

Thesis statement templates:
- As my speech will show,…
- Many people think…, but…
- Instead of…, we should…

BODY

- Establish your credibility, demonstrating why your audience should listen to you.
- Present your points one at a time.
- Support your points with specific examples and facts.
- Be sure to acknowledge and identify information from outside sources.
- Use visuals to reinforce your points and to add interest.
- Maintain eye contact with your listeners.
- Speak slowly and distinctly, and pay attention to your body language.

Topic sentence templates:
- My first (second, third) point is…
- First (second, third), I will discuss…
- One (another) reason is…

Templates for introducing support:
- According to…
- In his/her article,…
- As the following chart shows,…

CONCLUSION

- Restate your thesis, possibly listing your points.
- End with a strong closing statement.
- Remember to ask listeners if they have questions.

Closing statement templates:
- Remember, the next time you…
- For these reasons,…
- In summary,…

42c Preparing Your Presentation Notes

Most people use some form of presentation notes when they give a speech.

Full Text Some people write out the full text of their speech and refer to it during their presentation. If the type is large enough, this strategy can be useful. One disadvantage of using the full text of your speech is that it is easy to lose your place; another is that you may end up simply reading.

Notecards Some people write parts of their speech—for example, a list of key points or definitions—on notecards. With some practice, you can use notecards effectively. You have to be careful, however, not to become so dependent on the cards that you lose eye contact with your audience or begin fidgeting with the cards as you speak. Also, be sure to number the cards so that you can easily put them in order in case they get mixed up.

Outlines Some people refer to an outline when they give a speech. As they speak, they can glance down at the outline to remind themselves of a point they may have forgotten. Because an outline does not contain the full text of a speech, the temptation to read is eliminated. However, if you draw a blank, an outline gives you very little help.

iPads Some people use an iPad as a teleprompter. In order to do this, you need a stand for your iPad and an app, such as *Teleprompt+*, that turns an iPad into a teleprompter. *Teleprompt+* allows you to scroll your speech at various speeds, to pause it with a double-tap on the screen, and to time yourself as you speak. (*Teleprompt+* will even make video recordings of your presentation and of your practice sessions.)

42d Preparing Visual Aids

Visual aids can reinforce important information and make your speech easier to understand. For a simple speech, a visual aid may be no more than a definition or a few key terms, names, or dates written on the board. For a more complicated presentation, you might need charts, graphs, diagrams, photographs, or presentation software.

Microsoft PowerPoint, the most commonly used **presentation software** package, enables you to prepare attractive, professional slides (see Figure 42.1). This program contains many options for backgrounds, color schemes, and special effects, and also lets you supplement your slides with sound and video.

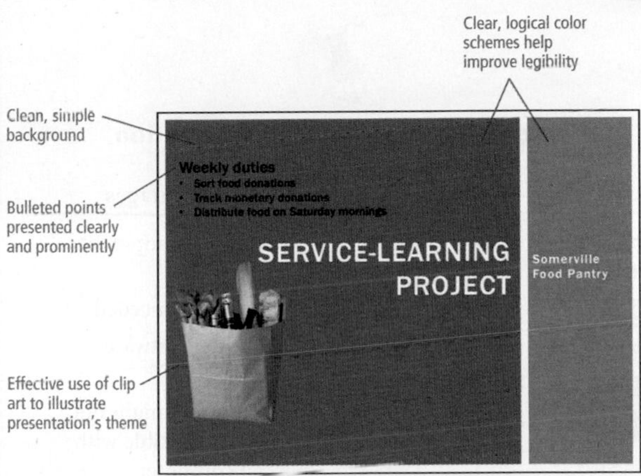

FIGURE 42.1 Effective *PowerPoint* slide. © Cengage Learning.

Prezi, available free on the Internet at <prezi.com>, is a presentation tool that is gaining in popularity. Many people think that *Prezi* presentations are more interesting and engaging than *PowerPoint* presentations. With *Prezi*, images and text are pasted on a large screen or "stage" instead of on individual slides (see Figure 42.2). Users can move around the stage (much the way a Skycam at a football game does) and zoom in and out, depending on what they want to emphasize. In addition, videos, such as those available on *YouTube*, can easily be pasted into *Prezi*.

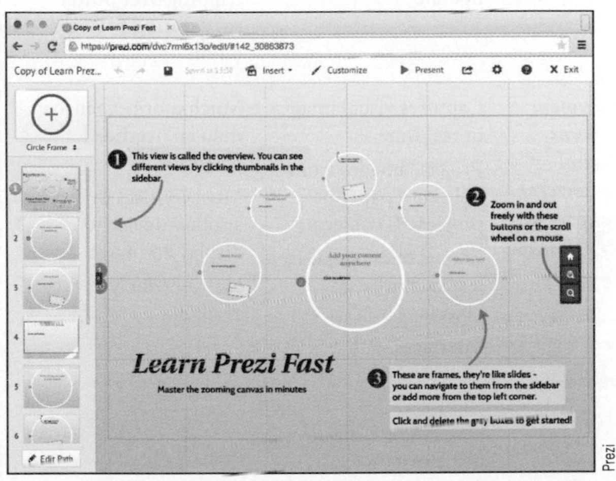

Prezi

FIGURE 42.2 *Prezi* presentation stage.

Using Visual Aids in Your Presentation

Visual Aid	Advantages	Disadvantages
Computer presentations  Bob Daemmrich/ PhotoEdit	Clear Easy to read Professional Graphics, video, sound, and animated effects Portable (USB flash drive)	Special equipment needed Expertise needed Special software needed Software might not be compatible with all computer systems
Overhead projectors  iStockphoto.com /Clickstock	Transparencies are inexpensive Transparencies are easily prepared with computer or copier Transparencies are portable Transparencies can be written on during presentation Projector is easy to operate	Transparencies can stick together Transparencies can be accidentally placed upside down Transparencies must be placed on projector by hand Some projectors are noisy Speaker must avoid tripping over power cord during presentation
Document cameras (digital visualizers) 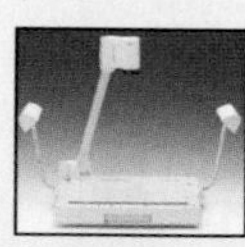 Business Wire/Handout/ Getty Images Publicity/ Getty Images	Captures visual images in real time Projects images from a sheet of paper or projects 3D objects Zooms in on small text, pictures, or objects Interfaces with a whiteboard or a computer Has a high-definition display	Much more expensive than an overhead projector Must connect to another device to display an image Not yet widely available

Visual Aid	Advantages	Disadvantages
Slide projectors Andy Crawford/ Dorling Kindersley/ Getty Images	Slides are colorful Slides look professional Projector is easy to use Order of slides can be rearranged during presentation Portable (slide carousel)	Slides are expensive to produce Special equipment needed for lettering and graphics Dark room needed for presentation Slides can jam in projector
Posters or flip charts iStockphoto.com /Mbbirdy	Low-tech and personal Good for small-group presentations Portable	May not be large enough to be seen in some rooms Artistic ability needed May be expensive if prepared professionally Must be secured to an easel
Chalkboards or whiteboards Jeffrey Coolidge/ Stone/Getty Images	Available in most rooms Easy to use Easy to erase or change information during presentation	Difficult to draw complicated graphics Handwriting must be legible Must catch errors while writing Cannot face audience when writing or drawing Very informal

42e Rehearsing Your Speech

Practice your speech often—at least five times. Do not try to memorize your entire speech, but be sure you know it well enough so that you can move from point to point without constantly looking at your notes. Finally, time yourself.

Make certain that your three-minute speech actually takes three minutes to deliver.

42f Delivering Your Speech

Keep in mind that a certain amount of nervousness is normal, so try not to focus on it too much. Once you get to the front of the room, take the time to make sure that everything you will need is there and that all your equipment is positioned properly.

When you begin speaking, pace yourself. Speak slowly and clearly, and look at the entire audience. Even though your speech is planned, it should sound natural and conversational. Use pauses to emphasize important points, and try to sound enthusiastic about your subject.

How you look will be the first thing that listeners notice about you, so dress appropriately for the occasion. (Although shorts and a T-shirt may be appropriate in some situations, they are not suitable for a classroom presentation.)

CHAPTER 43

Composing in the Disciplines

All instructors, regardless of academic discipline, have certain expectations when they read an essay. They expect to see standard English, correct grammar and spelling, logical thinking, and clear documentation of sources. In addition, they expect to see sensible organization, convincing support, and careful editing. Despite these similarities, however, instructors in various disciplines have different expectations about written work.

One way of putting these differences into perspective is to think of the various disciplines as communities of individuals who exchange ideas about issues that concern them. Just as in any community, scholars who write within a discipline have agreed to follow certain practices—conventions of style and vocabulary, for example. Without these conventions, it would be difficult or even impossible for them to communicate effectively with one another. If, for example, everyone writing about literature used a different documentation format or a different specialized vocabulary, the result would be chaos. To a large extent, then, learning to compose in a particular discipline involves learning the conventions that govern a discourse community.

The chart on pages 364–65 sums up some of the differences among disciplines in genres, style and format, documentation, and research methods and sources.

Composing in the Disciplines: An Overview

HUMANITIES

Disciplines	Genres	Style and Format
Languages Literature Philosophy History Religion Art history Music	Response Rhetorical analysis Literary analysis Annotated bibliography Bibliographic essay Book or film review	***Style*** Specialized vocabulary Direct quotations from sources ***Format*** Moderate use of internal headings or visuals

SOCIAL SCIENCES

Disciplines	Genres	Style and Format
Anthropology Psychology Economics Business Education Sociology Political science Social work Criminal justice Linguistics	Personal experience essay Book review Case study Annotated bibliography Literature review Proposal	***Style*** Specialized vocabulary, including statistical terminology ***Format*** Internal headings Visuals (graphs, maps, flowcharts, photographs) Numerical data (in tables)

NATURAL AND APPLIED SCIENCES

Disciplines	Genres	Style and Format
Natural Sciences Biology Chemistry Physics Astronomy Geology Mathematics ***Applied Sciences*** Engineering Computer science Nursing Pharmacy	Laboratory report Observation essay Literature survey Abstract Biographical essay	***Style*** Frequent use of passive voice Few direct quotations ***Format*** Internal headings Tables, graphs, and illustrations (exact formats vary)

Documentation	Research Methods and Sources
English, languages, philosophy: MLA History, art history: Chicago	Online sources Library sources (print and electronic) Interviews Observations (museums, concerts) Oral history

See Ch. 10

See Ch. 12

Documentation	Research Methods and Sources
APA	Online sources Library sources (print and electronic) Surveys Observations (behavior of groups and individuals)

See Ch. 11

Documentation	Research Methods and Sources
Biological sciences: CSE Other scientific disciplines use a variety of different documentation styles; **see 13d**	Online sources Library sources (print and electronic) Observations Experiments Surveys

See Ch. 13

Note: For information on using sources ethically across the disciplines, **see 9f.**

PART 9

Composing for Multilingual Writers

44 Grammar and Style for Multilingual Writers 368

44a Using Verbs 368
44b Using Nouns 374
44c Using Pronouns 376
44d Using Adjectives and Adverbs 378
44e Using Prepositions 380
44f Understanding Word Order 382

CHAPTER 44

Grammar and Style for Multilingual Writers

For multilingual writers (as for many native English writers), grammar can be a persistent problem. Grammatical knowledge in a second language usually develops slowly, with time and practice, and much about English is idiomatic (not subject to easy-to-learn rules). This chapter is designed to provide you with the tools you will need to address some of the most common grammatical problems faced by multilingual writers.

44a Using Verbs

1 Subject-Verb Agreement

See A1.3 English verbs change their form according to person, number, and tense. The verb in a sentence must **agree** with the subject in person and number. Person refers to *who* See 23a4 or *what* is performing the action of the verb (for example, *I*, *you*, or someone else), and number refers to *how many* people or things are performing the action (one or more than one).

See 16a In English, the rules for subject-verb agreement are very important. Unless you use the correct person and number in the verbs in your sentences, you will confuse your English-speaking audience by communicating meanings you do not intend.

2 Verb Tense

See 17b In English, the form of the verb changes to indicate tense—when the action of the verb takes place (in the past, present, or future). One problem that many nonnative speakers of English have with English verb tenses results from the large See 17a number of irregular verbs in English. For example, the first-person singular present tense of *be* is not "I be" but "I am," and the past tense is not "I beed" but "I was."

Close-Up CHOOSING THE SIMPLEST VERB FORMS

Some nonnative English speakers use verb forms that are more complicated than they need to be. They may do this because their native language uses more complicated verb forms than English does or because they "overcorrect" their verbs into complicated forms. Specifically, nonnative speakers tend to use progressive and perfect verb forms instead of simple verb forms. To communicate your ideas clearly to an English-speaking audience, choose the simplest possible verb form.

3 Auxiliary Verbs

The **auxiliary verbs** (also known as **helping verbs**) *be, have,* and *do* are used to create some present, past, and future forms of verbs in English: "Julio *is taking* a vacation"; "I *have been* tired lately"; "He *does* not *need* a license." The auxiliary verbs *be, have,* and *do* change form to reflect the time frame of the action or situation and to agree with the subject; however, the main verb remains in simple present or simple past form.

Close-Up AUXILIARY VERBS

Only auxiliary verbs, not the verbs they "help," change form to indicate person, number, and tense.

Present: We have to eat.

Past: We had to eat. (*not* "We had to ate.")

Modal auxiliaries (such as *can* and *should*) do not change form to indicate tense, person, or number. See A1.3

4 Negative Verbs

The meaning of a verb may be made negative in English in a variety of ways, chiefly by adding the words *not* or *does not* to the verb (is, is *not*; can ski, *cannot* ski; drives a car, *does not* drive a car).

Close-Up CORRECTING DOUBLE NEGATIVES

A **double negative** is an error that occurs when the meaning of a verb is made negative not just once but twice in a single sentence.

> Henry doesn't have ~~no~~ any friends. (*or* Henry ~~doesn't have~~ has no friends.)

> I looked for relevant articles, but there ~~weren't~~ were none. (*or* I looked for relevant articles, but there weren't ~~none~~ any.)

5 Phrasal Verbs

Many verbs in English are composed of two or more words that are combined to create a new idiomatic expression—for example, *check up on, run for, turn into*, and *wait on*. These verbs are called **phrasal verbs**. It is important to become familiar with phrasal verbs and their definitions so you will recognize these verbs as phrasal verbs instead of as verbs that are followed by prepositions.

Separable Phrasal Verbs Often, the words that make up a phrasal verb can be separated by a direct object. In these **separable phrasal verbs**, the object can come either before or after the preposition. For example, "Ellen turned down the job offer" and "Ellen turned the job offer down" are both correct. However, when the object is a pronoun, the pronoun must come before the preposition. Therefore, "Ellen turned it down" is correct; "Ellen turned down it" is incorrect.

Close-Up SEPARABLE PHRASAL VERBS

Verb	Definition
call off	cancel
carry on	continue
cheer up	make happy
clean out	clean the inside of

cut down	reduce
figure out	solve
fill in	substitute
find out	discover
give back	return something
give up	stop doing something or stop trying
leave out	omit
pass on	transmit
put away	place something in its proper place
put back	place something in its original place
put off	postpone
start over	start again
talk over	discuss
throw away/out	discard
touch up	repair

Inseparable Phrasal Verbs Some phrasal verbs—such as *look into* and *break into*—consist of words that can never be separated. With these **inseparable phrasal verbs**, you do not have a choice about where to place the object; the object must always follow the preposition. For example, "Anna cared for her niece" is correct, but "Anna cared her niece for" is incorrect.

Close-Up INSEPARABLE PHRASAL VERBS

Verb	Definition
come down with	develop an illness
come up with	produce
do away with	abolish
fall behind in	lag
get along with	be congenial with
get away with	avoid punishment
keep up with	maintain the same achievement or speed
look up to	admire
make up for	compensate
put up with	tolerate
run into	meet by chance
see to	arrange
show up	arrive
stand by	wait or remain loyal to
stand up for	support
watch out for	beware of or protect

6 Voice

See 17d

Verbs may be in either active or passive voice. When the subject of a sentence performs the action of the verb, the verb is in **active voice**. When the action of the verb is performed on the subject, the verb is in **passive voice**.

Karla and Miguel purchased the plane tickets. (active voice)

The plane tickets were purchased by Karla and Miguel. (passive voice)

Because your writing will usually be clearer and more concise if you use the active voice, you should use the passive voice only when you have a good reason to do so. For example, in scientific writing, it is common for writers to use the passive voice in order to convey scientific objectivity (lack of bias).

7 Transitive and Intransitive Verbs

Many nonnative English speakers find it difficult to decide whether or not a verb needs an object and in what order direct and indirect objects should appear in a sentence. Learning the difference between transitive verbs and intransitive verbs can help you with such problems.

A **transitive verb** is a verb that takes a direct object: "My father asked a question" (subject + verb + direct object). In this example, *asked* is a transitive verb; it needs an object to complete its meaning.

An **intransitive verb** is a verb that does not take an object: "The doctor smiled" (subject + verb). In this example, *smiled* is an intransitive verb; it does not need an object to complete its meaning.

A transitive verb may be followed by a direct object or by both an indirect object and a direct object. (An indirect object answers the question "To whom?" or "For whom?") The indirect object may come before or after the direct object. If the indirect object follows the direct object, the preposition *to* or *for* must precede the indirect object.

s v do
Keith wrote a letter. (subject + verb + direct object)

s v io do
Keith wrote his friend a letter. (subject + verb + indirect object + direct object)

s v do io
Keith wrote a letter *to* his friend. (subject + verb + direct object + *to/for* + indirect object)

Some verbs in English look similar and have similar meanings, except that one verb is transitive and the other is intransitive. For example, *lie* is intransitive, *lay* is transitive; *sit* is intransitive, *set* is transitive; *rise* is intransitive, *raise* is transitive. Knowing whether a verb is transitive or intransitive can help you with troublesome verb pairs such as these and also help you place the words in the correct order.

Note: It is also important to know whether a verb is transitive or intransitive because only transitive verbs can be used in the passive voice. To determine whether a verb is transitive or intransitive—that is, to determine whether or not it needs an object—consult the example phrases in a dictionary.

See 17d

8 Infinitives and Gerunds

In English, two verb forms may be used as nouns: **infinitives**, which always begin with *to* (as in *to work, to sleep, to eat*), and **gerunds**, which always end in *-ing* (as in *working, sleeping, eating*).

> To bite into this steak requires better teeth than mine. (infinitive used as a noun)
>
> Cooking is one of my favorite hobbies. (gerund used as a noun)

Sometimes the gerund and the infinitive form of the same verb can be used interchangeably. For example, "He continued *to sleep*" and "He continued *sleeping*" convey the same meaning. However, this is not always the case. Saying, "Marco and Lisa stopped *to eat* at Julio's Café" is not the same as saying, "Marco and Lisa stopped *eating* at Julio's Café." In this example, the meaning of the sentence changes depending on whether a gerund or infinitive is used.

9 Participles

In English, verb forms called **present participles** and **past participles** are frequently used as adjectives. Present participles usually end in *-ing*, as in *working, sleeping*, and *eating*, and past participles usually end in *-ed, -t*, or *-en*, as in *worked, slept*, and *eaten*.

> According to the Bible, God spoke to Moses from a burning bush. (present participle used as an adjective)
>
> Some people think raw fish is healthier than cooked fish. (past participle used as an adjective)

A **participial phrase** is a group of words consisting of the participle plus the noun phrase that functions as the object or complement of the action being expressed by the participle. To avoid confusion, the participial phrase must be placed as close as possible to the noun it modifies.

Having visited San Francisco last week, Jim and Lynn showed us pictures from their vacation. (The participial phrase is used as an adjective that modifies *Jim and Lynn*.)

10 Verbs Formed from Nouns

In English, nouns can sometimes be used as verbs, with no change in form (other than the addition of an *-s* for agreement with third-person singular subjects or the addition of past tense endings). For example, the nouns *chair, book, frame*, and *father* can all be used as verbs.

She chairs a committee on neighborhood safety.

We booked a flight to New York for next week.

I will frame my daughter's diploma after she graduates.

He fathered several children before he was thirty.

44b Using Nouns

See 33g Nouns name things: people, animals, objects, places, feelings, ideas. If a noun names one thing, it is **singular**; if a noun names more than one thing, it is **plural**.

1 Recognizing Noncount Nouns

Some English nouns do not have a plural form. These are called **noncount nouns** because what they name cannot be counted. (**Count nouns** name items that *can* be counted, such as *cat* or *desk*.)

Close-Up NONCOUNT NOUNS

The following commonly used nouns are noncount nouns. These words have no plural forms. Therefore, you should never add *-s* or *-es* to them.

advice
clothing
education
equipment
evidence
furniture
homework
information
knowledge
luggage
merchandise
revenge

2 Using Articles with Nouns

English has two kinds of **articles**, *indefinite* and *definite*.

Use an **indefinite article** (*a* or *an*) with a noun when readers are not familiar with the noun you are naming—for example, when you are introducing the noun for the first time. To say "James entered *a* building" signals to the audience that you are introducing the idea of the building for the first time. The building is indefinite, or not specific, until it has been identified.

The indefinite article *a* is used when the word following it (which may be a noun or an adjective) begins with a consonant or with a consonant sound: *a tree, a onetime offer*. The indefinite article *an* is used if the word following it begins with a vowel (*a, e, i, o,* or *u*) or with a vowel sound: *an apple, an honor.*

Use the **definite article** (*the*) when the noun you are naming has already been introduced, when the noun is already familiar to readers, or when the noun to which you refer is specific. To say "James entered *the* building" signals to readers that you are referring to the same building you mentioned earlier. The building has now become specific and may be referred to by the definite article.

Close-Up USING ARTICLES WITH NOUNS

There are two exceptions to the rules governing the use of articles with nouns:

1. **Plural nouns** do not require indefinite articles: "I love horses," not "I love a horses." (Plural nouns do, however, require definite articles: "I love the horses on the carousel in the park near my house.")
2. **Noncount nouns** may not require articles: "Love conquers all," not "A love conquers all" or "The love conquers all."

3 Using Other Determiners with Nouns

Determiners are words that function as adjectives to limit or qualify the meaning of nouns. In addition to articles, **demonstrative pronouns, possessive nouns and pronouns, numbers** (both **cardinal** and **ordinal**), and other words indicating amount or order can function in this way.

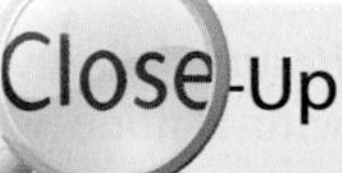

Close-Up USING OTHER DETERMINERS WITH NOUNS

- **Demonstrative pronouns** (*this, that, these, those*) communicate the following:
  1. the relative distance of the noun from the speaker's position (*this* and *these* for things that are *near, that* and *those* for things that are *far*): *this* book on my desk, *that* book on your desk; *these* shoes on my feet, *those* shoes in my closet.
  2. the number of things indicated (*this* and *that* for *singular* nouns, *these* and *those* for *plural* nouns): *this* (or *that*) flower in the vase, *these* (or *those*) flowers in the garden.
- **Possessive nouns** and **possessive pronouns** (*Ashraf's, his, their*) show who or what the noun belongs to: *Maria's* courage, *everybody's* fears, the *country's* natural resources, *my* personality, *our* groceries.
- **Cardinal** numbers (*three, fifty, a thousand*) indicate how many of the noun you mean: *seven* continents. **Ordinal** numbers (*first, tenth, thirtieth*) indicate in what order the noun appears among other items: *third* planet.
- Words other than numbers may indicate **amount** (*many, few*) and **order** (*next, last*) and function in the same ways as cardinal and ordinal numbers: *few* opportunities, *last* chance.

44c Using Pronouns

See A1.2

Any English noun may be replaced by a pronoun. For example, *doctor* may be replaced by *he* or *she, books* by *them*, and *computer* by *it*.

1 Pronoun Reference

Pronoun reference is very important in English sentences, See 18c where the noun the pronoun replaces (the **antecedent**) must be easily identified. In general, you should place the pronoun as close as possible to the noun it replaces so the noun to which the pronoun refers is clear. If this is impossible, use the noun itself instead of replacing it with a pronoun.

> **Unclear:** When Tara met Emily, she was nervous. (Does *she* refer to Tara or to Emily?)
>
> **Clear:** When Tara met Emily, Tara was nervous.
>
> **Unclear:** Stefano and Victor love his sneaker collection. (Whose sneaker collection—Stefano's, Victor's, or someone else's?)
>
> **Clear:** Stefano and Victor love Emilio's sneaker collection.

2 Pronoun Placement

Never use a pronoun immediately after the noun it replaces. For example, do not say, "Most of my classmates *they* are smart"; instead, say, "Most of my classmates are smart."

The only exception to this rule occurs with an **intensive pronoun**, which ends in *-self* and emphasizes the preceding noun or pronoun: "Marta *herself* was eager to hear the results."

3 Indefinite Pronouns

Unlike **personal pronouns** (*I, you, he, she, it, we, they, me, him, her, us*, and *them*), **indefinite pronouns** do not refer to a particular person, place, or thing. Therefore, an indefinite pronoun does not require an antecedent. **Indefinite pronoun subjects** (*anybody, nobody, each, either, someone, something, all, some*), like personal pronouns, must agree in number See 16b with the sentence's verb.

> Nobody ~~have~~ *has* failed the exam. (*Nobody* is a singular subject and requires a singular verb.)

4 Appositives

Appositives are nouns or noun phrases that identify or rename an adjacent noun or pronoun. An appositive usually follows the word it identifies or renames, but can sometimes precede it.

My parents, Mary and John, live in Louisiana. (*Mary and John* identifies *parents*.)

Note: The case of a pronoun in an appositive depends on the case of the word it identifies.

See 18a

If an appositive is *not* necessary to the meaning of the sentence, use commas to set off the appositive from the rest of the sentence. If an appositive *is* necessary to the meaning of the sentence, do not use commas.

His aunt Trang is in the hospital. (*Trang* is necessary to the meaning of the sentence because it identifies which aunt is in the hospital.)

Akta's car, a 1994 Jeep Cherokee, broke down last night. (*a 1994 Jeep Cherokee* is not necessary to the meaning of the sentence.)

5 Pronouns and Gender

A pronoun must agree in **gender** with the noun to which it refers.

My *sister* sold *her* old car.

Your *uncle* is walking *his* dog.

Note: In English, most nonhuman nouns are referred to as *it* because they do not have grammatical gender. However, exceptions are sometimes made for pets, ships, and countries. Pets are often referred to as *he* or *she*, depending on their gender, and ships and countries are sometimes referred to as *she*.

44d Using Adjectives and Adverbs

See A1. 4–5; Ch. 19

Adjectives and adverbs are words that **modify** (describe, limit, or qualify) other words.

1 Position of Adjectives and Adverbs

Adjectives in English usually appear *before* the nouns they **modify**. A native speaker of English would not say, "*Cars red and black* are involved in more accidents than *cars blue or green*" but would say instead, "*Red and black cars* are involved in more accidents than *blue or green cars*."

However, adjectives may appear *after* linking verbs ("The name seemed *familiar*."), *after* direct objects ("The coach found them *tired* but *happy*."), and *after* indefinite pronouns ("Anything *sad* makes me cry.").

Adverbs may appear before or after the verbs they describe, but they should be placed as close to the verb as possible: not "I *told* John that I couldn't meet him for lunch *politely*," but "I *politely told* John that I couldn't meet him for lunch" or "I *told* John *politely* that I couldn't meet him for lunch." When an adverb describes an adjective or another adverb, it usually comes *before* that adjective or adverb: "The essay has *basically sound* logic"; "You must express yourself *absolutely clearly*."

Never place an adverb between the verb and the direct object.

Incorrect: Rolf drank *quickly* the water.

Correct: Rolf drank the water *quickly* (or, Rolf *quickly* drank the water).

2 Order of Adjectives

A single noun may be modified by more than one adjective, perhaps even by a whole list of adjectives. Given a list of three or four adjectives, most native speakers would arrange them in a sentence in the same order. If, for example, shoes are to be described as *green* and *big*, numbering *two*, and of the type worn for playing *tennis*, a native speaker would say "two big green tennis shoes." Generally, the adjectives that are most important in completing the meaning of the noun are placed closest to the noun.

Close-Up ORDER OF ADJECTIVES

1. Articles (*a, the*), demonstratives (*this, those*), and possessives (*his, our, Maria's, everybody's*)
2. Amounts (*one, five, many, few*), order (*first, next, last*)
3. Personal opinions (*nice, ugly, crowded, pitiful*)
4. Sizes and shapes (*small, tall, straight, crooked*)
5. Age (*young, old, modern, ancient*)
6. Colors (*black, white, red, blue, dark, light*)
7. Nouns functioning as adjectives to form a unit with the noun (*soccer* ball, *cardboard* box, *history* class)

44e Using Prepositions

See A1.6 In English, prepositions (such as *to, from, at, with, among, between*) give meaning to nouns by linking them with other words and other parts of the sentence. Prepositions convey several different kinds of information:

- Relations to **time** (*at* nine o'clock, *in* five minutes, *for* a year)
- Relations of **place** (*in* the classroom, *at* the library, *beside* the chair) and **direction** (*to* the market, *onto* the stage, *toward* the freeway)
- Relations of **association** (go *with* someone, the tip *of* the iceberg)
- Relations of **purpose** (working *for* money, dieting *to* lose weight)

1 Commonly Used Prepositional Phrases

In English, the use of prepositions is often **idiomatic** rather than governed by grammatical rules. In many cases, therefore, learners of English as a second language need to memorize which prepositions are used in which phrases.

In English, some prepositions that relate to time have specific uses with certain nouns, such as days, months, and seasons:

- *On* is used with days and specific dates: *on* Tuesday, *on* September 11, 2001.
- *In* is used with months, seasons, and years: *in* November, *in* the spring, *in* 1999.
- *In* is also used when referring to some parts of the day: *in* the morning, *in* the afternoon, *in* the evening.
- *At* is used to refer to other parts of the day: *at* noon, *at* night, *at* seven o'clock.

Close-Up DIFFICULT PREPOSITIONAL PHRASES

The following phrases (accompanied by their correct prepositions) sometimes cause difficulties for multilingual writers:

according *to*	*at* least	relevant *to*
apologize *to*	*at* most	similar *to*
appeal *to*	refer *to*	subscribe *to*
different *from*		

2 Commonly Confused Prepositions

The prepositions *to, in, on, into,* and *onto* are very similar to one another and are therefore easily confused:

- ***To*** is the basic preposition of direction. It indicates movement toward a physical place: "She went *to* the restaurant"; "He went *to* the meeting." *To* is also used to form the infinitive of a verb: "He wanted *to deposit* his paycheck before noon"; "Irene offered *to drive* Maria to the baseball game."
- ***In*** indicates that something is within the boundaries of a particular space or period of time: "My son is *in* the garden"; "I like to ski *in* the winter"; "The map is *in* the car."
- ***On*** indicates position above or the state of being supported by something: "The toys are *on* the porch"; "The baby sat *on* my lap"; "The book is *on* top of the magazine."
- ***Into*** indicates movement to the inside or interior of something: "She walked *into* the room"; "I threw the stone *into* the lake"; "He put the photos *into* the box." Although *into* and *in* are sometimes interchangeable, note that usage depends on whether the subject is stationary or moving. *Into* usually indicates movement, as in "I jumped *into* the water." *In* usually indicates a stationary position relative to the object of the preposition, as in "Mary is swimming *in* the water."
- ***Onto*** indicates movement to a position on top of something: "The cat jumped *onto* the chair"; "Crumbs are falling *onto* the floor." Both *on* and *onto* can be used to indicate a position on top of something (and therefore they can sometimes be used interchangeably), but *onto* specifies that the subject is moving to a place from a different place or from an outside position.

Close-Up **PREPOSITIONS IN IDIOMATIC EXPRESSIONS**

Many nonnative speakers use incorrect prepositions in idiomatic expressions. Compare the incorrect expressions in the left-hand column below with the correct expressions in the right-hand column.

(continued)

PREPOSITIONS IN IDIOMATIC EXPRESSIONS
(continued)

Common Nonnative Speaker Usage	Native Speaker Usage
according *with*	according *to*
apologize *at*	apologize *to*
appeal *at*	appeal *to*
believe *at*	believe *in*
different *to*	different *from*
for least, *for* most	*at* least, *at* most
refer *at*	refer *to*
relevant *with*	relevant *to*
similar *with*	similar *to*
subscribe *with*	subscribe *to*

44f Understanding Word Order

Word order is extremely important in English sentences. For example, word order may indicate which word is the subject of a sentence and which is the object, or it may indicate whether a sentence is a question or a statement.

1 Standard Word Order

Like Chinese, English is an "SVO" language, or one in which the most typical sentence pattern is "subject-verb-object." (Arabic, by contrast, is an example of a "VSO" language.)

2 Word Order in Questions

Word order in questions can be particularly troublesome for speakers of languages other than English because there are so many different ways to form questions in English.

Close-Up WORD ORDER IN QUESTIONS

1. To create a **yes/no question** from a statement whose verb is a form of *be* (*am, is, are, was, were*), move the verb so it precedes the subject.

Rasheem is in his laboratory.

Is Rasheem in his laboratory?

When the statement is *not* a form of *be*, change the verb to include a form of *do* as a helping verb, and then move that helping verb so it precedes the subject.

Rasheem researched the depletion of the ozone level.

Did Rasheem research the depletion of the ozone level?

2. To create a **yes/no question** from a statement that includes one or more helping verbs, move the first helping verb so it precedes the subject.

   Rasheem is researching the depletion of the ozone layer.

   Is Rasheem researching the depletion of the ozone layer?

   Rasheem has been researching the depletion of the ozone layer.

   Has Rasheem been researching the depletion of the ozone layer?

3. To create a **question asking for information**, replace the information being asked for with an **interrogative** word (*who, what, where, why, when, how*) at the beginning of the question, and invert the order of the subject and verb as with a yes/no question.

   Rasheem is in his laboratory.

   Where is Rasheem?

   Rasheem is researching the depletion of the ozone layer.

   What is Rasheem researching?

   Rasheem researched the depletion of the ozone level.

   What did Rasheem research?

   If the interrogative word is the subject of the question, however, do *not* invert the subject and verb.

   Who is researching the depletion of the ozone level?

4. You can also form a question by adding a **tag question** (such as *won't he?* or *didn't I?*) to the end of a statement. If the verb of the main statement is *positive*, then the verb of the tag question is *negative*; if the verb of the main statement is *negative*, then the verb of the tag question is *positive*.

WORD ORDER IN QUESTIONS *(continued)*

Rasheem is researching the depletion of the ozone layer, isn't he?

Rasheem doesn't intend to write his dissertation about the depletion of the ozone layer, does he?

Grammar Review

Parts of Speech

The **part of speech** to which a word belongs depends on its function in a sentence.

Nouns

Nouns name people, animals, places, things, ideas, actions, or qualities.

A **common noun** names any of a class of people, places, or things: *artist, judge, building, event, city.*

A **proper noun,** always capitalized, refers to a particular person, place, or thing: *Mary Cassatt, World Trade Center, Crimean War.* See 34a

A **collective noun** designates a group thought of as a unit: *committee, class, family.*

An **abstract noun** refers to an intangible idea or quality: *love, hate, justice, anger, fear, prejudice.*

2 Pronouns

Pronouns are words used in place of nouns. The noun for which a pronoun stands is called its **antecedent.**

If you use a quotation in your essay, you must document it. (Pronoun *it* refers to antecedent *quotation.*)

Although different types of pronouns may have the same form, they are distinguished from one another by their function in a sentence.

A **personal pronoun** stands for a person or thing: *I, me, we, us, my, mine, our, ours, you, your, yours, he, she, it, its, him, his, her, hers, they, them, their, theirs.*

The firm made Debbie an offer, and she couldn't refuse it.

See 16a4, 16b3

An indefinite pronoun does not refer to any particular person or thing, so it does not require an antecedent. Indefinite pronouns include *another, any, each, few, many, some, nothing, one, anyone, everyone, everybody, everything, someone, something, either*, and *neither*.

Many are called, but few are chosen.

A **reflexive pronoun** ends with *-self* and refers to a recipient of the action that is the same as the actor: *myself, yourself, himself, herself, itself, oneself, themselves, ourselves, yourselves.*

They found themselves in downtown Pittsburgh.

Intensive pronouns have the same form as reflexive pronouns. An intensive pronoun emphasizes a preceding noun or pronoun.

Darrow himself was sure his client was innocent.

A **relative pronoun** introduces an adjective or noun clause in a sentence. Relative pronouns include *which, who, whom, that, what, whose, whatever, whoever, whomever*, and *whichever.*

Gandhi was the man who led India to independence. (introduces adjective clause)

Whatever happens will be a surprise. (introduces noun clause)

An **interrogative pronoun** introduces a question. Interrogative pronouns include *who, which, what, whom, whose, whoever, whatever*, and *whichever.*

Who is at the door?

A **demonstrative pronoun** points to a particular thing or group of things. *This, that, these*, and *those* are demonstrative pronouns.

This is one of Shakespeare's early plays.

A **reciprocal pronoun** denotes a mutual relationship. The reciprocal pronouns are *each other* and *one another. Each other* indicates a relationship between two individuals; *one another* denotes a relationship among more than two.

Cathy and I respect each other despite our differences.

Many of our friends do not respect one another.

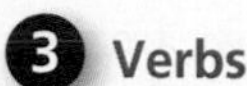 Verbs

Verbs can be classified into two groups: *main verbs* and *auxiliary verbs*.

Main Verbs **Main verbs** carry most of the meaning in a sentence or clause. Some main verbs are action verbs.

He ran for the train. (physical action)

He thought about taking the bus. (emotional action)

Other main verbs are linking verbs. A **linking verb** does not show any physical or emotional action. Its function is to link the subject to a **subject complement**, a word or phrase that renames or describes the subject.

Carbon disulfide smells bad.

Frequently Used Linking Verbs

appear	believe	look	seem	taste
be	feel	prove	smell	turn
become	grow	remain	sound	

Auxiliary Verbs **Auxiliary verbs** (also called **helping verbs**), such as *be* and *have*, combine with main verbs to form **verb phrases**. Auxiliary verbs indicate tense, voice, or mood.

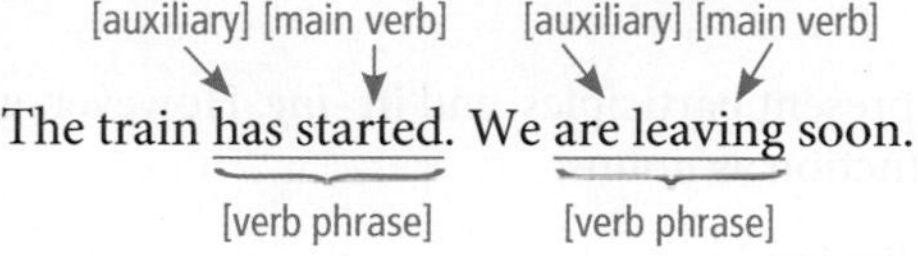

Certain auxiliary verbs, known as **modal auxiliaries**, indicate necessity, possibility, willingness, obligation, or ability.

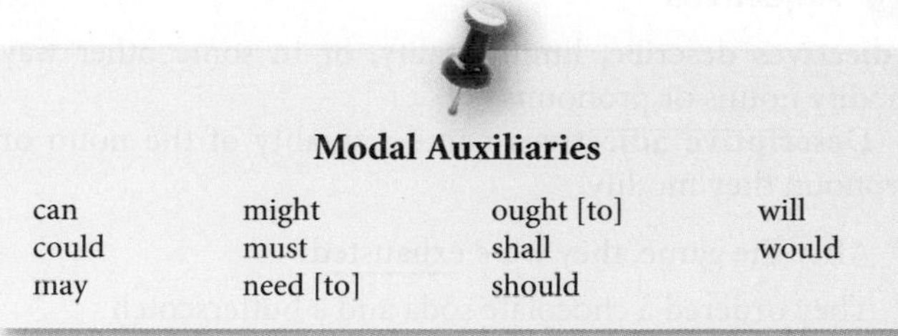

Modal Auxiliaries

can	might	ought [to]	will
could	must	shall	would
may	need [to]	should	

Verbals **Verbals**, such as *known* or *running* or *to go*, are verb forms that act as adjectives, adverbs, or nouns. A verbal can never serve as a sentence's main verb unless it is used with one or more auxiliary verbs (*He is running*). Verbals include *participles, infinitives,* and *gerunds.*

PARTICIPLES

See 17a

Virtually every verb has a **present participle**, which ends in *-ing* (*loving, learning*) and a **past participle**, which usually ends in *-d* or *-ed* (*agreed, learned*). Some verbs have irregular past participles (*gone, begun, written*). Participles may function in a sentence as adjectives or as nouns.

Twenty brands of running shoes were on display. (participle serves as adjective)

The wounded were given emergency first aid. (participle serves as noun)

INFINITIVES

An **infinitive** is made up of *to* and the base form of the verb (*to defeat*). An infinitive may function as an adjective, an adverb, or a noun.

Ann Arbor was clearly the place to be. (infinitive serves as adjective)

Carla went outside to think. (infinitive serves as adverb)

To win was everything. (infinitive serves as noun)

GERUNDS

Gerunds, like present participles, end in *-ing*. However, gerunds always function as nouns.

Seeing is believing.
Andrew loves skiing.

4 Adjectives

Adjectives describe, limit, qualify, or in some other way modify nouns or pronouns.

Descriptive adjectives name a quality of the noun or pronoun they modify.

After the game, they were exhausted.

They ordered a chocolate soda and a butterscotch sundae.

When articles, pronouns, numbers, and the like function as adjectives, limiting or qualifying nouns or pronouns, they are referred to as determiners. ml 44b3

5 Adverbs

Adverbs describe the action of verbs or modify adjectives or other adverbs (or complete phrases, clauses, or sentences). They answer the questions "How?" "Why?" "When?" "Under what conditions?" and "To what extent?"

He walked rather hesitantly toward the front of the room.

Let's meet tomorrow for coffee.

Adverbs that modify other adverbs or adjectives limit or qualify the words they modify.

He pitched an almost perfect game yesterday.

Interrogative Adverbs The **interrogative adverbs** (*how, when, why,* and *where*) introduce questions.

How are you doing?

Why did he miss class?

Conjunctive Adverbs **Conjunctive adverbs** act as transitional words, joining and relating independent clauses. See 20b

Frequently Used Conjunctive Adverbs

accordingly	furthermore	meanwhile	similarly
also	hence	moreover	still
anyway	however	nevertheless	then
besides	incidentally	next	thereafter
certainly	indeed	nonetheless	therefore
consequently	instead	now	thus
finally	likewise	otherwise	undoubtedly

6 Prepositions

A **preposition** introduces a noun or pronoun (or a phrase or clause) that functions in the sentence as a noun, linking it to other words in the sentence. The word or word group that the preposition introduces is its **object**.

They received a postcard from [prep] Bobby [obj] telling about [prep] his trip [obj].

Frequently Used Prepositions

about	beneath	inside	since
above	beside	into	through
across	between	like	throughout
after	beyond	near	to
against	by	of	toward
along	concerning	off	under
among	despite	on	underneath
around	down	onto	until
as	during	out	up
at	except	outside	upon
before	for	over	with
behind	from	past	within
below	in	regarding	without

7 Conjunctions

Conjunctions connect words, phrases, clauses, or sentences.

Coordinating Conjunctions **Coordinating conjunctions** (*and, or, but, nor, for, so, yet*) connect words, phrases, or clauses of equal weight.

Should I order chicken or fish?

Thoreau wrote *Walden* in 1854, and he died in 1862.

Correlative Conjunctions Always used in pairs, **correlative conjunctions** also link items of equal weight.

Both Hancock and Jefferson signed the Declaration of Independence.

Either I will renew my lease, or I will move.

Frequently Used Correlative Conjunctions

both . . . and	neither . . . nor
either . . . or	not only . . . but also
just as . . . so	whether . . . or

Subordinating Conjunctions Words such as *since, because*, and *although* are **subordinating conjunctions**. A subordinating conjunction introduces a dependent (subordinate) clause, connecting it to an independent (main) clause to form a complex sentence.

See 21a2

Although people may feel healthy, they can still have medical problems.

It is best to diagram your garden before you start to plant.

8 Interjections

Interjections are words used as exclamations to express emotion: *Oh! Ouch! Wow! Alas! Hey!*

A2 Sentences

1 Basic Sentence Elements

A **sentence** is an independent grammatical unit that contains a subject (a noun or noun phrase) and a predicate (a verb or verb phrase) and expresses a complete thought.

The quick brown fox jumped over the lazy dog.

It came from outer space.

2 Basic Sentence Patterns

A **simple sentence** consists of at least one subject and one predicate. Simple sentences conform to one of five patterns.

Subject + Intransitive Verb (s + v)

s v
Stock prices may fall.

Subject + Transitive Verb + Direct Object (s + v + do)

s v do
Van Gogh created *The Starry Night.*

s v do
Caroline saved Jake.

Subject + Transitive Verb + Direct Object + Object Complement (s + v + do + oc)

s v do oc
I found the exam easy.

s v do oc
The class elected Bridget treasurer.

Subject + Linking Verb + Subject Complement (s + v + sc)

s v sc
The injection was painless.

s v sc
David Cameron became Prime Minister.

Subject + Transitive Verb + Indirect Object + Direct Object (s + v + io + do)

s v io do
Cyrano wrote Roxanne a poem. (Cyrano wrote a poem *for* Roxanne.)

s v io do
Hester gave Pearl a kiss. (Hester gave a kiss *to* Pearl.)

3 Phrases and Clauses

Phrases A **phrase** is a group of related words that lacks a subject or predicate or both and functions as a single part of speech. It cannot stand alone as a sentence.

- A **verb phrase** consists of a **main verb** and all its auxiliary verbs. (Time *is flying*.)
- A **noun phrase** includes a noun or pronoun plus all related modifiers. (I'll climb *the highest mountain*.)
- See A1.6 A **prepositional phrase** consists of a preposition, its object, and any modifiers of that object. (They considered the ethical implications *of the animal experiment*.)
- See A1.3 A **verbal phrase** consists of a verbal and its related objects, modifiers, or complements. A verbal phrase may be a **participial phrase** (*encouraged by the voter turnout*), a **gerund phrase** (*taking it easy*), or an **infinitive phrase** (*to evaluate the evidence*).
- An **absolute phrase** usually consists of a noun and a participle, accompanied by modifiers. It modifies an entire independent clause rather than a particular word or phrase. (*Their toes tapping*, they watched the auditions.)

Clauses A **clause** is a group of related words that includes a subject and a predicate. An **independent** (main) **clause** can stand alone as a sentence, but a **dependent** (subordinate) **clause** cannot. It must always be combined with an independent clause to form a complex sentence.

See 21a2

[Lucretia Mott was an abolitionist.] [She was also a pioneer for women's rights.] (two independent clauses)

[Lucretia Mott was an abolitionist] [who was also a pioneer for women's rights.] (independent clause, dependent clause)

Dependent clauses may be *adjective, adverb,* or *noun* clauses:

- **Adjective clauses,** sometimes called **relative clauses,** modify nouns or pronouns and always follow the nouns or pronouns they modify. They are introduced by relative pronouns—*that, what, which, who,* and so on—or by the adverbs *where* and *when.*

  Celeste's grandparents, who were born in Romania, speak little English.

- **Adverb clauses** modify verbs, adjectives, adverbs, entire phrases, or independent clauses. They are always introduced by subordinating conjunctions.

  Mark will go wherever there's a party.

- **Noun clauses** function as subjects, objects, or complements. A noun clause may be introduced by a relative pronoun or by *whether, when, where, why,* or *how.*

  What you see is what you get.

4 Types of Sentences

A **simple sentence** is a single independent clause. A simple sentence can consist of just a subject and a predicate.

Jessica fell.

Or, a simple sentence can be expanded with modifying words and phrases.

On Halloween, Jessica fell in love with the mysterious Henry Goodyear.

A **compound sentence** consists of two or more simple sentences linked by a coordinating conjunction (preceded by a comma), by a semicolon (alone or followed by a transitional word or phrase), by correlative conjunctions, or by a colon. See 21a1

[The moon rose in the sky], and [the stars shone brightly].

[José wanted to spend a quiet afternoon]; however, [his aunt dropped by unexpectedly.]

See 21a2

A complex sentence consists of one independent clause and at least one dependent clause.

independent clause / dependent clause

[It was hard for us to believe] [that anyone could be so cruel].

A **compound-complex sentence** is a compound sentence—made up of at least two independent clauses—that also includes at least one dependent clause.

[My mother always worried] [when my father had to work late], and [she could rarely sleep more than a few minutes at a time].

Close-Up CLASSIFYING SENTENCES

Sentences can also be classified according to their function:

- **Declarative sentences** make statements; they are the most common.
- **Interrogative sentences** ask questions, usually by inverting standard subject-verb order (often with an interrogative word) or by adding a form of *do* (*Is Maggie at home? Where is Maggie? Does Maggie live here?*).
- **Imperative sentences** express commands or requests, using the second-person singular of the verb and generally omitting the pronoun subject *you* (*Go to your room. Please believe me.*).
- **Exclamatory sentences** express strong emotion and end with an exclamation point (*The killing must stop now!*).

B

Usage Review

This usage review lists words and phrases that writers often find troublesome and explains how they are used.

a, an Use *a* before words that begin with consonants and words with initial vowels that sound like consonants: *a* person, *a* historical document, *a* one-horse carriage, *a* uniform. Use *an* before words that begin with vowels and words that begin with a silent *h*: *an* artist, *an* honest person.

accept, except *Accept* is a verb that means "to receive"; *except* as a preposition or conjunction means "other than" and as a verb means "to leave out": The auditors will *accept* all your claims *except* the last two. Some businesses are *excepted* from the regulation.

advice, advise *Advice* is a noun meaning "opinion or information offered"; *advise* is a verb that means "to offer advice to": The broker *advised* her client to take his attorney's *advice*.

affect, effect *Affect* is a verb meaning "to influence"; *effect* can be a verb or a noun—as a verb it means "to bring about," and as a noun it means "result": We know how the drug *affects* patients immediately, but little is known of its long-term *effects*. The arbitrator tried to *effect* a settlement between the parties.

all ready, already *All ready* means "completely prepared"; *already* means "by or before this or that time": I was *all ready* to help, but it was *already* too late.

all right, alright Although the use of *alright* is increasing, current usage calls for *all right*.

allusion, illusion An *allusion* is a reference or hint; an *illusion* is something that is not what it seems: The poem makes an *allusion* to the Pandora myth. The shadow created an optical *illusion*.

a lot *A lot* is always two words.

among, between *Among* refers to groups of more than two things; *between* refers to just two things: The three parties agreed *among* themselves to settle the case. There will be a brief intermission *between* the two acts. (Note that *amongst* is British, not American, usage.)

amount, number *Amount* refers to a quantity that cannot be counted; *number* refers to things that can be counted: Even a small *amount* of caffeine can be harmful. Seeing their commander fall, a large *number* of troops ran to his aid.

an, a See **a, an**.

and/or In business or technical writing, use *and/or* when either or both of the items it connects can apply. In college writing, however, avoid the use of *and/or*.

as, like *As* can be used as a conjunction (to introduce a complete clause) or as a preposition; *like* should be used as a preposition only: In *The Scarlet Letter*, Hawthorne uses imagery *as* (not *like*) he does in his other works. After classes, Fred works *as* a manager of a fast food restaurant. Writers *like* Carl Sandburg appear once in a generation.

at, to Many people use the prepositions *at* and *to* after *where* in conversation: *Where* are you working *at*? Where are you going *to*? This usage is redundant and should not appear in college writing.

awhile, a while *Awhile* is an adverb; *a while*, which consists of an article and a noun, is used as the object of a preposition: Before we continue, we will rest *awhile* (modifies the verb *rest*). Before we continue, we will rest for *a while* (object of the preposition *for*).

bad, badly *Bad* is an adjective, and *badly* is an adverb: The school board decided that *Adventures of Huckleberry Finn* was a *bad* book. American automobile makers did not do *badly* this year. After verbs that refer to any of the senses or after any other linking verb, use the adjective form: He looked *bad*. He felt *bad*. It seemed *bad*.

being as, being that These awkward phrases add unnecessary words, thereby weakening your writing. Use *because* instead.

beside, besides *Beside* is a preposition meaning "next to"; *besides* can be either a preposition meaning "except" or "other than" or an adverb meaning "as well": *Beside* the tower was a wall that ran the length of the city. *Besides* its industrial uses, laser technology has many other applications. Edison invented not only the lightbulb but the phonograph *besides*.

between, among See **among, between**.

bring, take *Bring* means "to transport from a farther place to a nearer place"; *take* means "to carry or convey from a nearer place to a farther place": *Bring* me a souvenir from your trip. *Take* this message to the general, and wait for a reply.

can, may *Can* denotes ability; *may* indicates permission: If you *can* play, you *may* use my piano.

cite, site *Cite* is a verb meaning "to quote as an authority or example"; *site* is a noun meaning "a place or setting"; it is also a shortened form of *website*: Jeff *cited* five sources in his research paper. The builder cleared the *site* for the new bank. Marisa uploaded her *site* to the web.

climactic, climatic *Climactic* means "of or related to a climax"; *climatic* means "of or related to climate": The *climactic* moment of the movie occurred unexpectedly. If scientists are correct, the *climatic* conditions of Earth are changing.

complement, compliment *Complement* means "to complete or add to"; *compliment* means "to give praise": A double-blind study would *complement* their preliminary research. My instructor *complimented* me on my improvement.

conscious, conscience *Conscious* is an adjective meaning "having one's mental faculties awake"; *conscience* is a noun that means the moral sense of right and wrong: The patient will remain *conscious* during the procedure. His *conscience* would not allow him to lie.

continual, continuous *Continual* means "recurring at intervals"; *continuous* refers to an action that occurs without interruption: A pulsar is a star that emits a *continual* stream of electromagnetic radiation. (It emits radiation at regular intervals.) A small battery allows the watch to run *continuously* for five years. (It runs without stopping.)

could of, should of, would of The contractions *could've, should've*, and *would've* are often misspelled as the nonstandard constructions *could of, should of*, and *would of*. Use *could have, should have*, and *would have* in college writing.

couple, couple of *Couple* means "a pair," but *couple of* is often used colloquially to mean "several" or "a few." In your college writing, specify "four points" or "two examples" rather than using "a couple of."

criterion, criteria *Criteria*, from the Greek, is the plural of *criterion*, meaning "standard for judgment": Of all the *criteria* for hiring graduating seniors, class rank is the most important *criterion*.

data *Data* is the plural of the Latin *datum*, meaning "fact." In colloquial speech and writing, *data* is often used as the singular as well as the plural form. In college writing, use *data* only for the plural: The *data* discussed in this section *are* summarized in Appendix A.

different from, different than *Different than* is widely used in American speech. In college writing, use *different from*.

disinterested, uninterested *Disinterested* means "objective" or "capable of making an impartial judgment"; *uninterested* means "indifferent or unconcerned": The American judicial system depends on *disinterested* jurors. Finding no treasure, Hernando de Soto was *uninterested* in going farther.

don't, doesn't *Don't* is the contraction of *do not*; *doesn't* is the contraction of *does not*. Do not confuse the two: My dog *doesn't* (not *don't*) like to walk in the rain. (Note that contractions are generally not acceptable in college writing.)

economic, economical *Economic* refers to the economy—to the production, distribution, and consumption of goods. *Economical* means "avoiding waste" or "careful use of resources": There was strong *economic* growth this quarter. It is *economical* to have roommates in this city.

effect, affect See **affect, effect**.

e.g. *E.g.* is an abbreviation for the Latin *exempli gratia*, meaning "for example" or "for instance." In college writing, do not use *e.g.* Instead, use for *example* or *for instance*.

emigrate from, immigrate to To *emigrate* is "to leave one's country and settle in another"; to *immigrate* is "to come to another country and reside there." The noun forms of these words are *emigrant* and *immigrant*: My great-grandfather *emigrated from* Warsaw along with many other *emigrants* from Poland. Many people *immigrate to* the United States for economic reasons, but *immigrants* still face great challenges.

eminent, imminent *Eminent* is an adjective meaning "standing above others" or "prominent"; *imminent* means "about to occur": Oliver Wendell Holmes Jr. was an *eminent* jurist. In ancient times, a comet signaled *imminent* disaster.

enthused *Enthused*, a colloquial form of *enthusiastic*, should not be used in college writing.

etc. *Etc.*, the abbreviation of *et cetera*, means "and the rest." Do not use it in your college writing. Instead, use *and so on*—or, better yet, specify what *etc.* stands for.

everyday, every day *Everyday* is an adjective that means "ordinary" or "commonplace"; *every day* means "occurring daily": In the Gettysburg Address, Lincoln used *everyday* language. She exercises almost *every day.*

everyone, every one *Everyone* is an indefinite pronoun meaning "every person"; *every one* means "every individual or thing in a particular group": *Everyone* seems happier in the spring. *Every one* of the packages had been opened.

except, accept See **accept, except**.

explicit, implicit *Explicit* means "expressed or stated directly"; *implicit* means "implied" or "expressed or stated indirectly": The director *explicitly* warned the actors to be on time for rehearsals. Her *implicit* message was that lateness would not be tolerated.

farther, further *Farther* designates distance; *further* designates degree: I have traveled *farther* from home than any of my relatives. Critics charge that welfare subsidies encourage *further* dependence.

fewer, less Use *fewer* with nouns that can be counted: *fewer* books, *fewer* people, *fewer* dollars. Use *less* with quantities that cannot be counted: *less* pain, *less* power, *less* enthusiasm.

firstly (secondly, thirdly, . . .) Archaic forms meaning "in the first . . . second . . . third place." Use *first, second, third* instead.

further, farther See **farther, further**.

good, well *Good* is an adjective, never an adverb: She is a *good* swimmer. *Well* can function as an adverb or as an adjective. As an adverb, it means "in a good manner": She swam *well* (not *good*) in the meet. *Well* is used as an adjective meaning "in good health" with verbs that denote a state of being or feeling: I feel *well.*

got to *Got to* is not acceptable in college writing. To indicate obligation, use *have to, has to,* or *must.*

hanged, hung Both *hanged* and *hung* are past participles of *hang. Hanged* is used to refer to executions; *hung* is used to mean "suspended": Billy Budd was *hanged* for killing the master-at-arms. The stockings were *hung* by the chimney with care.

he, she Traditionally, *he* has been used in the generic sense to refer to both males and females. To acknowledge the equality of the sexes, however, avoid the generic *he*. Use plural pronouns whenever possible. **See 26c2.**

historic, historical *Historic* means "important" or "momentous"; *historical* means "relating to the past" or "based on or inspired by history": The end of World War II was a *historic* occasion. *Historical* records show that Quakers played an important part in the abolition of slavery.

hopefully The adverb *hopefully*, meaning "in a hopeful manner," should modify a verb, an adjective, or another adverb. Do not use *hopefully* as a sentence modifier meaning "it is hoped." Rather than "*Hopefully*, scientists will soon discover a cure for AIDS," write "*People hope* scientists will soon discover a cure for AIDS."

i.e. *I.e.* is an abbreviation for the Latin *id est*, meaning "that is." In college writing, do not use *i.e.* Instead, use its English equivalent.

if, whether When asking indirect questions or expressing doubt, use *whether*: He asked *whether* (not *if*) the flight would be delayed. The flight attendant was not sure *whether* (not *if*) it would be delayed.

illusion, allusion See **allusion, illusion**.

immigrate to, emigrate from See **emigrate from, immigrate to**.

implicit, explicit See **explicit, implicit**.

imply, infer *Imply* means "to hint" or "to suggest"; *infer* means "to conclude from": Mark Antony *implied* that the conspirators had murdered Caesar. The crowd *inferred* his meaning and called for justice.

infer, imply See **imply, infer**.

irregardless, regardless *Irregardless* is a nonstandard version of *regardless*. Use *regardless* or *irrespective* instead.

is when, is where These constructions are faulty when they appear in definitions: A playoff is (not *is when* or *is where*) an additional game played to establish the winner of a tie.

its, it's *Its* is a possessive pronoun; *it's* is a contraction of *it is*: *It's* no secret that the bank is out to protect *its* assets.

kind of, sort of The use of *kind of* and *sort of* to mean "rather" or "somewhat" is colloquial. These expressions should not appear in college writing: It is well known that Napoleon was rather (not *kind of*) short.

lay, lie See **lie, lay**.

leave, let *Leave* means "to go away from" or "to let remain"; *let* means "to allow" or "to permit": *Let* (not *leave*) me give you a hand.

less, fewer See **fewer, less**.

let, leave See **leave, let**.

lie, lay *Lie* is an intransitive verb (one that does not take an object) meaning "to recline." Its principal forms are *lie, lay, lain, lying*: Each afternoon she would *lie* in the sun and listen to the surf. *As I Lay Dying* is a novel by William Faulkner. By 1871, Troy had *lain* undisturbed for two thousand years. The painting shows a nude *lying* on a couch.

Lay is a transitive verb (one that takes an object) meaning "to put" or "to place." Its principal forms are *lay, laid, laid, laying*: The Federalist Papers *lay* the foundation for American conservatism. In October 1781, the British *laid* down their arms and surrendered. He had *laid* his money on the counter before leaving. We watched the stonemasons *laying* a wall.

life, lifestyle *Life* is the span of time that a living thing exists; *lifestyle* is a way of living that reflects a person's values or attitudes: Before he was hanged, Nathan Hale said, "I only regret that I have but one *life* to lose for my country." The writer Virginia Woolf was known for her unconventional *lifestyle*.

like, as See **as, like**.

loose, lose *Loose* is an adjective meaning "not rigidly fastened or securely attached"; *lose* is a verb meaning "to misplace": The marble facing of the building became *loose* and fell to the sidewalk. After only two drinks, most people *lose* their ability to judge distance.

lots, lots of, a lot of These words are colloquial substitutes for *many, much*, or *a great deal of*. Avoid their use in college writing: The students had *many* (not *lots of* or *a lot of*) options for essay topics.

man Like the generic pronoun *he, man* has been used in English to denote members of both sexes. This usage is being replaced by *human beings, people*, or similar terms that do not specify gender. **See 26c2**.

may, can See **can, may**.

may be, maybe *May be* is a verb phrase: *maybe* is an adverb meaning "perhaps": She *may be* the smartest student in the class. *Maybe* her experience has given her an advantage.

media, medium *Medium*, meaning "a means of conveying or broadcasting something," is singular; *media* is the plural form and requires a plural verb: The *media have* distorted the issue.

might have, might of *Might of* is a nonstandard spelling of the contraction of *might have* (*might've*). Use *might have* in college writing.

number, amount See **amount, number.**

OK, O.K., okay All three spellings are acceptable, but this term should be avoided in college writing. Replace it with a more specific word or words: The lecture was *adequate* (not *okay*), if uninspiring.

passed, past *Passed* is the past tense of the verb *pass*; *past* means "belonging to a former time" or "no longer current": The car must have been going eighty miles per hour when it *passed* us. In the envelope was a bill marked *past* due.

percent, percentage *Percent* indicates a part of a hundred when a specific number is referred to: "*10 percent* of his salary." *Percentage* is used when no specific number is referred to: "a *percentage* of next year's receipts." In technical and business writing, it is permissible to use the % sign after percentages you are comparing. Write out the word *percent* in college writing.

plus As a preposition, *plus* means "in addition to." Avoid using *plus* as a substitute for *and*: Include the principal, *plus* the interest, in your calculations. Your quote was too high; *moreover* (not *plus*), it was inaccurate.

precede, proceed *Precede* means "to go or come before"; *proceed* means "to go forward in an orderly way": Robert Frost's *North of Boston* was *preceded* by an earlier volume. In 1532, Francisco Pizarro landed at Tumbes and *proceeded* south.

principal, principle As a noun, *principal* means "a sum of money (minus interest) invested or lent" or "a person in the leading position"; as an adjective, it means "most important"; a *principle* is a noun meaning a rule of conduct or a basic truth: He wanted to reduce the *principal* of the loan. The *principal* of the high school is a talented administrator. Women are the *principal* wage earners in many American households. The Constitution embodies certain fundamental *principles.*

quote, quotation *Quote* is a verb. *Quotation* is a noun. In college writing, do not use *quote* as a shortened form of *quotation*: Scholars attribute these *quotations* (not *quotes*) to Shakespeare.

raise, rise *Raise* is a transitive verb, and *rise* is an intransitive verb—that is, *raise* takes an object, and *rise* does not: My grandparents *raised* a large family. The sun will *rise* at 6:12 tomorrow morning.

real, really *Real* means "genuine" or "authentic"; *really* means "actually." In college writing, do not use *real* as an adjective meaning "very."

reason is that, reason is because *Reason* should be used with *that* and not with *because*, which is redundant: The *reason* he left is *that* (not *because*) you insulted him.

regardless, irregardless See **irregardless, regardless**.

rise, raise See **raise, rise**.

set, sit *Set* means "to put down" or "to lay." Its principal forms are *set* and *setting*: After rocking the baby to sleep, he *set* her down carefully in her crib. After *setting* her down, he took a nap.

Sit means "to assume a sitting position." Its principal forms are *sit, sat*, and *sitting*: Many children *sit* in front of the television five to six hours a day. The dog *sat* by the fire. We were *sitting* in the airport when the flight was canceled.

shall, will *Will* has all but replaced *shall* to express all future action.

should of See **could of, should of, would of**.

simple, simplistic *Simple* means "plain, ordinary, or uncomplicated"; *simplistic* means "overly or misleadingly simplified": Because she had studied, Tanya thought the test was *simple*. His explanation of how the Internet works is *simplistic*.

since Do not use *since* for *because* if there is any chance of confusion. In the sentence "*Since* President Nixon traveled to China, trade between China and the United States has increased," *since* could mean either "from the time that" or "because." To be clear, use *because*.

sit, set See **set, sit**.

so Avoid using *so* as a vague intensifier meaning "very" or "extremely." Follow *so* with *that* and a clause that describes the result: She was *so* pleased with their work *that* she took them out to lunch.

sometime, sometimes, some time *Sometime* means "at some time in the future"; *sometimes* means "now and then"; *some time* means "a period of time": The president will address Congress *sometime* next week. All automobiles, no matter how reliable, *sometimes* need repairs. It has been *some time* since I read that book.

sort of, kind of See **kind of, sort of**.

supposed to, used to *Supposed to* and *used to* are often misspelled. Both verbs require the final *d* to indicate past tense.

take, bring See **bring, take.**

than, then *Than* is a conjunction used to indicate a comparison; *then* is an adverb indicating time: The new shopping center is bigger *than* the old one. He did his research; *then*, he wrote a report.

that, which, who Use *that* or *which* when referring to a thing; use *who* when referring to a person: It was a speech *that* inspired many. The movie, *which* was a huge success, failed to impress her. Anyone *who* (not *that*) takes the course will benefit.

their, there, they're *Their* is a possessive pronoun; *there* indicates place and is also used in the expressions *there is* and *there are*; *they're* is a contraction of *they are*: Watson and Crick did *their* DNA work at Cambridge University. I love Los Angeles, but I wouldn't want to live *there*. *There* is nothing we can do to resurrect an extinct species. When *they're* well treated, rabbits make excellent pets.

themselves, theirselves, theirself *Theirselves* and *theirself* are nonstandard variants of *themselves*.

then, than See **than, then.**

till, until, 'til *Till* and *until* have the same meaning, and both are acceptable. *Until* is preferred in college writing. *'Til*, a contraction of *until*, should be avoided.

to, at See **at, to.**

to, too, two *To* is a preposition that indicates direction; *too* is an adverb that means "also" or "more than is needed"; *two* expresses the number 2: Last year we flew from New York *to* California. "Tippecanoe and Tyler, *too*" was William Henry Harrison's campaign slogan. The plot was *too* complicated for the average reader. Just north of *Two* Rivers, Wisconsin, is a petrified forest.

try to, try and *Try and* is the colloquial equivalent of the more formal *try to*: He decided to *try to* (not *try and*) do better. In college writing, use *try to*.

-type Deleting this empty suffix eliminates clutter and clarifies meaning: Found in the wreckage was an incendiary (not *incendiary-type*) device.

uninterested, disinterested See **disinterested, uninterested.**

unique Because *unique* means "the only one," not "remarkable" or "unusual," never use constructions such as *the most unique* or *very unique*.

until See **till, until, 'til**.

used to See **supposed to, used to**.

utilize In most cases, replace *utilize* with *use* (*utilize* often sounds pretentious).

wait for, wait on To *wait for* means "to defer action until something occurs." To *wait on* means "to act as a waiter": I am *waiting for* (not *on*) dinner.

weather, whether *Weather* is a noun meaning "the state of the atmosphere"; *whether* is a conjunction used to introduce an alternative: The *weather* will improve this weekend. It is doubtful *whether* we will be able to ski tomorrow.

well, good See **good, well**.

were, we're *Were* is a verb; *we're* is the contraction of *we are:* The Trojans *were* asleep when the Greeks attacked. We must act now if *we're* going to succeed.

whether, if See **if, whether**.

which, who, that See **that, which, who**.

who, whom When a pronoun serves as the subject of its clause, use *who* or *whoever*; when it functions in a clause as an object, use *whom* or *whomever*: Sarah, *who* is studying ancient civilizations, would like to visit Greece. Sarah, *whom* I met in France, wants me to travel to Greece with her. **See 18b2**.

who's, whose *Who's* means "who is" or "who has"; *whose* indicates possession: *Who's* going to take calculus? *Who's* already left for the concert? The writer *whose* book was in the window was autographing copies.

will, shall See **shall, will**.

would of See **could of, should of, would of**.

your, you're *Your* indicates possession; *you're* is the contraction of *you are*: You can improve *your* stamina by jogging two miles a day. *You're* certain to be the winner.

Index

Note: Page numbers in blue type indicate definitions.

A

A, an, use as articles, 327, 375, 395
A lot, 395, 401
A number, the number, 242
Abbreviation(s), 333–36
  acronyms, 294, 327, 328, 333, 334
  in addresses, 223, 294, 335
  APA-style paper, 165, 167, 171
  capitalizing, 327, 333, 334
  CSE-style paper, 222, 223, 225
  dates, 222, 334, 335
  in digital documents, 333
  editing misused, 335–36
  measurements before, numerals in, 337
  MLA-style paper, 116, 117–18, 125, 126, 128, 294, 334, 335
  organization names, 294, 333–34
  with periods, 293–94, 333–36
  without periods, 293–94, 327, 333, 334
  plurals of, 306
  postal service, 223, 294
  of technical terms, 334, 335
  temperatures, 334
  text message, 273, 333
  times of day, 334–35
  titles of people, 333
  units of measurement, 335
-able, -ible endings, 323
Absolute(s), 261
Absolute phrase(s), 392
Abstract(s), 2
  APA reference list, 179
  APA-style paper, 184
  CSE-style paper, 226
Abstract noun(s), 385
Abstract word(s)
  concrete words *versus,* 286
  defined, 286, 385
Academic courses, abbreviating, 335
Academic degrees
  capitalizing, 325
  commas with, 301
Academic OneFile, 76
Academic writing. *See* College writing
Accept, except, 287, 395
Acronym(s), 294, 327, 328, 334
  in email, 333
  in instant messaging, 273, 333
  using, 294, 333
Act number, MLA parenthetical references, 116
Action verbs, 258–59
Active reading, 2
Active voice, 252, 372
  shift from or to passive voice, 278, 285
AD, 334
Addition
  compound sentences to indicate, 270
  to quotations, 97–98, 216
  words and phrases to signal, 265
Address(es). *See also* Electronic address(es)
  abbreviations in, 223, 294, 335
  commas in, 301
  numerals in, 337
Adjective(s), 258–61, 378–79, 388–89
  comparative form, 259–61
  without comparative forms, 261
  compound, 331–32
  coordinate, 296
  descriptive, 388
  determiners functioning as, 376
  multilingual writers and, 258, 297, 378–79
  order of, 379
  position of, 378–79
  in series, 296–97, 379
  superlative form, 259–61
  without superlative forms, 261
  using, 258–59, 378–79, 388–89
Adjective (relative) clause(s), 276, 393
  commas with, 257, 298, 299
  eliminating, 276–77
  misplaced, relocating, 283
Adverb(s), 258–61, 378–79, 389
  comparative form, 259–61
  without comparative forms, 261
  lists of, 389
  multilingual writers and, 258, 378–79
  position of, 379
  superlative form, 259–61
  without superlative forms, 261
  types, 389
  using, 259–61, 378–79, 389
Adverb clause(s), 393
  misplaced, relocating, 283–84
Adverbial conjunction(s). *See* Conjunctive adverb(s)

Advertisement(s), MLA works-cited list, 136
Advice, advise, 395
Affect, effect, 287, 395
African American, 326
Afterword
APA reference list, 173
MLA works-cited list, 131
Agreement, 240–45, 368
pronoun-antecedent, 243–45, 256–57, 278–79, 377
subject-verb, 240–43, 368
Aircraft, italicizing names of, 329
Alexa.com, 93–94
All ready, already, 395
All right, alright, 395
Allusion, illusion, 395
Alternatives, compound sentences to indicate, 270
Ambiguous antecedent(s), 256
Among, between, 395–96
Amount, 376
Amount, number, 396
Ampersand (&)
APA in-text citations, 166
APA reference list, 169, 173
An, a, use as articles, 327, 375, 395
Analysis
of assignments, 16, 43
in critical response, 8
Anatomy, documentation style. *See* CSE documentation style
And
and/or, 396
with compound antecedents, 244
compound subjects joined by, 241
with multiple authors in APA text, 166
as search operator, 73
in series, comma with, 296
And/or, 396
Annotated bibliography (student), 45
Annotation, 4–5
of electronic texts, 7
example, 4–5
of model essays, 25–30, 35–40
of text, 7
thinking critically in, 4–5
Anonymous/unsigned work(s), 133
APA in-text citations, 167
APA reference list, 170, 171, 173, 177
Chicago documentation style, 199–200, 202
CSE reference list, 223
determining legitimacy of, 93–94
MLA parenthetical references, 115
MLA works-cited list, 126, 133
Antecedent(s), 243, 256, 377, 385
agreement with pronouns, 243–45, 256–57, 278–79, 377
ambiguous, 256
collective noun, 244
compound, 244
indefinite pronoun, 244–45
nonexistent, 257
relative pronoun, 243
remote, 256–57
Anthology(ies)
APA reference list, 173–74
Chicago documentation style, 204
MLA works-cited list, 132
Anthropology, composition overview, 364–65
Antonym(s)
defined, 285
in thesaurus entry, 285–86
APA documentation style, 161–93
abbreviations, 165, 167, 171
APA style, defined, 165
checklists, 180–82
citation software, 67–69
content footnotes, 179
directory, 161–63
headings, 180, 184, 185, 342
in-text citations, 161, 165–68
manuscript guidelines, 179–82
model APA-style research paper, 182–93
reference list, 67–69, 108, 161–63, 169–79, 181, 182, 193
in the social sciences, 165
spelled-out numbers *versus* numerals, 336
Apostrophe(s), 304–07
editing misused, 307
in forming plurals, 306, 307
to indicate omissions, 305–06
in possessive case, 304–05, 306
using, 306
Applied science(s). *See* Natural and applied science(s)
Appositive(s), 255, 377–78
commas with nonrestrictive, 257, 298
creating, for concise sentences, 276
explanatory material, 314
phrase fragments, 237
pronoun case in, 255
Apps
APA reference list, 175
MLA works-cited list, 135
Argumentative essay(s), 32–40. *See also* Essay(s); Literary analysis; Thinking critically
model MLA-style essay, 34–40
organizing, 32–33

Art(s). *See also* Humanities
italicizing titles of works, 329
MLA works-cited list, 136
specialized databases, 77
Art history. *See also* Chicago documentation style; Humanities
composition overview, 364–65
Article(s) (grammatical), 375
definite, 375
indefinite, 327, 375, 395
in titles of works, 125, 200, 327, 328
use with nouns, 375
Article(s) (publications). *See* Journal article(s); Magazine article(s); Newsletter article(s); Newspaper article(s)
Artifact(s), 30
Artistic movements, capitalizing names of, 326
As
comparisons with, 254
parallel elements linked by, 280–81
As, like, 396
Ask.com, 84
Assignment(s)
analyzing, 16, 43
essay, 16
research project, 43
rhetorical situation and, 10
Association, prepositions and, 380
Asterisk (*), as search operator, 72
Astronomy. *See also* CSE documentation style; Natural and applied science(s)
composition overview, 364–65
Asynchronous communication, 348
At, as preposition, 380
At, to, 396
Atlases, CSE reference list, 225
Audience, 12–14, 347
academic, 12–14
checklist, 14
for digital documents, 347
for essay, 12–14, 16
identifying, 12–14, 16
peer-review, 12
for presentation, 356
in reading texts, 6
types of, 12
writing for, 12–14
Audio recording(s). *See also* Podcast(s)
APA reference list, 175
Chicago documentation style, 205
CSE reference list, 225
MLA works-cited list, 134, 137
Author name(s)
APA in-text citations, 166–68
APA in-text citations for authors with same last name, 167
APA reference list, 172–73, 182
CSE reference list, 221, 223–24
MLA parenthetical references, 115–18
MLA works-cited list, 119–20, 128–29
AutoCorrect tool, 325
Auxiliary (helping) verb(s), 369, 387–
to form present and past verb forms, 369
modal, 369, 387
Awhile, a while, 396
Awkward sentence(s), 277–79
faulty predication, 279
mixed constructions, 279
unnecessary shifts, 278–79

B

Bad, badly, 396
Base form, 245–48
BC, 334
Be, faulty predication, 279
Being as, being that, 396
Beside, besides, 396
Between, among, 395–96
Bible
capitalizing, 326
Chicago documentation style, 204
MLA parenthetical references, 116–17
MLA works-cited list, 132
no italics with, 329
numerals for divisions in, 337
periods for divisions in, 294
Bibliography(ies) (documentation styles)
APA reference list, 67–69, 108, 161–63, 169–79, 181, 182, 193
Chicago documentation style, 67–69, 108, 194–95, 196, 197–210, 213, 218
CSE reference list, 68, 69, 108, 219, 221–26, 227, 230
MLA works-cited list, 67–69, 108, 109–11, 118–38, 142, 157–60
Bibliography(ies) (reference tools), 81
Bibliography(ies) (student)
annotated, 45
preparing, 45, 67–69
working, 44–45
BibMe, 67
Bilingual writer(s). *See* Multilingual tip(s); Multilingual writers
Bing, 84
Biographical reference books, 81
Biology. *See also* CSE documentation style; Natural and applied science(s)
composition overview, 364–65
specialized databases, 78
Black, capitalizing, 326
Blackboard, 349
Block format, 351

Blog(s), 135, 349
APA reference list, 178
Chicago documentation style, 209–10
MLA works-cited list, 135
using, 349
Blogger, 349
Blu-ray
CSE reference list, 225
MLA works-cited list, 137
Body paragraph(s), 264–68
of business letter, 351
coherent, 265–66
of research project, 62–63
thesis-and-support essay, 18
unified, 264–65
well-developed, 266–67
Book(s)
APA in-text citations, 166–67
APA reference list, 171–74
Chicago documentation style, 200–04, 207
CSE reference list, 223–24, 226
italicizing titles of, 328
in library research, 70–73, 79–80, 83
locating missing, 80
MLA parenthetical references, 115–18
MLA works-cited list, 127–33
in online catalogs, 72–73, 79–80, 83
previewing, 2
quotation marks with parts of, 132
Book review(s)
APA reference list, 170
Chicago documentation style, 200
MLA works-cited list, 126
Bookmark, 86
Boolean search, 72–73
Borrowed words, 102, 103–04
Bracket(s), 317
APA reference list, 170, 171, 178
for comments within quotations, 317
ellipsis within, 98, 319
in formatting notes to self, 50
to indicate additions to quotations, 216
to indicate substitutions within quotations, 97, 317
to replace parentheses within parentheses, 317
Brainstorming, in idea generation, 17
Brand names, capitalizing, 327
Bring, take, 397
Bullets, 343
Business and economics. *See also* Social science(s)
composition overview, 364–65
specialized databases, 78
Business letter(s), 350–52. *See also* Workplace communication
format of, 314, 351
job application, 350–52
salutations, 314, 351
sample, 351
writing, 314, 350–52
Business name(s)
abbreviating, 294, 333–34
capitalizing, 327
By, MLA works-cited list, 129, 131

C

Call number(s), 79
Can, may, 397
Canvas, 349
Capitalization, 324–28. *See also* Proper noun(s)
of abbreviations, 327, 333, 334
APA reference list, 169, 170, 171
with colons, 314
editing misused, 328
of first word of sentence, 324, 325
of *I* (pronoun), 324
of important words in titles, 327
of lists, 343
MLA works-cited list, 119
MLA-style paper, 141–42
with parentheses, 316
of proper nouns, 325–27
Caption(s), 181, 192. *See also* Visual(s)
Cardinal number(s), as determiners, 376
Cartoon(s), MLA works-cited list, 136
Case, 253–56, 304–05, 306, 378. *See also specific types of case*
Catalog(s). *See* Online catalog(s)
Cause and effect
complex sentences to indicate, 271
compound sentences to indicate, 270
words and phrases to signal, 266
CBE documentation style. *See* CSE documentation style
CD(s)
APA reference list, 175
Chicago documentation style, 205
CSE reference list, 225
MLA works-cited list, 137
CD-ROMs
MLA works-cited list, 135
-ch endings, plurals with, 324
Chalkboards, 361
Chapter(s)
APA in-text citations, 167
Chicago documentation style, 203–04
CSE reference list, 224

numerals to identify, 337
quotation marks for titles, 311
Chart(s). *See* Graph(s)
Checklist(s)
adjectives in series, 296
APA-style paper, 180–82
audience in peer review, 14
Chicago-style paper, 211–13
computer printouts, 49
critical response writing, 8, 9
CSE-style paper, 226–27
document design, 342–43, 346
field research, 88
fragments, 239
highlighting symbols, 3
Internet research, 93–94
library research tips, 72–73, 80
for lists, 342–43
MLA-style paper, 141–42
note-taking, 49, 51
online database selection, 79
paragraphing, 22
photocopies, 49
plagiarism avoidance, 102, 104–05
previewing a text, 3
proofreading, 23–24
purpose of writing, 11
reading texts, 6
research project, 49
research projects, 42, 64, 69, 79, 80
restrictive and nonrestrictive modifiers, 299
revising conclusions, 268
revising introductions, 267
revising paragraphs, 22
revising sentences, 22
revising whole essay, 22
revising words, 22
search engine, 86
visuals, 142, 180–81, 211–12, 346
web searches, 86
writing assignment analysis, 16
writing portfolio, 31
Chemistry. *See also* Natural and applied science(s)
composition overview, 364–65
documentation styles, 230. *See also* CSE documentation style
specialized databases, 78
Chicago documentation style, 194–219
bibliography, 67–69, 108, 194–95, 196, 197–210, 213, 218
checklists, 211–13
Chicago humanities style, 196, 211–18
citation software, 67–69
directory, 194–95
endnotes and footnotes, 194–95, 196–97, 212, 217
manuscript guidelines, 211–13
Chicago humanities style, 196, 211–18
Chicago Manual of Style, The, 196, 196n. *See also* Chicago documentation style
Chronological order, 352
résumé, 352, 353
Circumlocution
avoiding, 275
defined, 275
Citation software, 67–69
Citation-sequence format, CSE documentation style, 220, 221, 227
Cite, site, 397
Cited in., APA-style paper, 167, 186
Civic groups, capitalizing names of, 327
Clause(s), 392–93. *See also specific types of clause*
misplaced, relocating, 283–84
nonrestrictive, 257, 298–99
restrictive, 257, 298–99
in series, 280
types of, 392–93
in varying sentence openings, 273
Clichés, 287–88
Climactic, climatic, 397
Clipped form(s), 294
CMS style. *See* Chicago documentation style
Coherent paragraph(s), 265–66
parallel structure in, 266
transitional words and phrases in, 265–66
Collaboration. *See also* Conference(s); Peer review
plagiarism avoidance, 101
writing in wired classroom, 347–50
Collection of work(s), MLA works-cited list, 132–33
Collective noun(s), 242, 385
as antecedents, 244
fixed amounts as, 242
subject-verb agreement with, 242
College writing. *See also* Documentation; Multilingual tip(s); Multilingual writers
audience for, 12–14
diction in, 348. *See also* Formal diction
euphemisms, 286
exclamation points in, 295
genre selection, 14–15
informal modifiers, 259
instructor comments in, 21, 64–65
peer review in, 13–14, 21, 65–66, 349
pronoun-antecedent agreement, 245
reading to write, 2–9
writing center in, 21, 101

Colon(s), 313–15
capitalization with, 314
in compound sentences, 270
editing misused, 314–15
with identifying tags, 309
to introduce lists, 238, 303, 313
to introduce quotations, 314
to introduce series, 313
in letters, 314
MLA parenthetical references, 115
quick guide, 292
with quotation marks, 312
to separate independent clauses, 292
to set off explanations, 292, 314
Color, in document design, 340–41
Comic strip(s), MLA works-cited list, 136
Comma(s), 295–302
in addresses, 301
with coordinating conjunctions, 269, 295–96
editing misused, 301–02
with identifying tags, 97, 300, 308–09
with independent clauses, 292, 295–96, 302
in interrupted quotations, 300
with introductory elements, 297
with nonessential material, 257, 292, 297–99, 300
with nonrestrictive modifiers, 257, 298–99
parentheses with, 316
with participial phrases, 374
with personal titles, 301
to prevent misreading, 301
quick guide, 292
with quotation marks, 300, 308–09, 311
in series, 292, 296–97, 302, 313
with transitional elements, 235, 239, 297, 299–300
Comma splice(s), 234–36
Command(s), exclamation points for, 295
Comment(s)
brackets with note to self, 50
of instructor, 21, 64–65
in peer review, 13–14, 65–66
within quotations, 317
Comment feature, 61, 64–65
Common knowledge, 101
Common noun(s), 385
Common sentence error(s), 234–45
agreement errors, 240–45
awkward sentences, 277–79
comma splices, 234–36
confusing sentences, 277–79
dangling modifiers, 284–85
faulty modification, 282–85
faulty parallelism, 281
faulty predication, 279
fragments, 236–39
fused sentences, 234–36
intrusive modifiers, 284
misplaced modifiers, 282–84
mixed constructions, 279
run-on sentences, 234–36, 303
shifts, unnecessary, 278–79
Communication, specialized databases, 77
Comparative form, 259–61
defined, 260
illogical, 261
irregular, 261
regular, 260
using, 260
Compare Documents feature, 21
Comparison(s)
with *than* or *as*, 254
words and phrases to signal, 265
Complement(s). *See* Subject complement(s)
Complement, compliment, 397
Complex sentence(s), 270–71, 394
as concise sentences, 276
constructing, 235–36, 270–71, 391, 392–93, 394
in revising comma splices, 235–36
in revising fused sentences, 235–36
in revising run-on sentences, 235–36
using, 270, 271, 394
Compound adjective(s)
defined, 331
hyphenating, 331–32
Compound antecedents, 244
Compound complement, detached, 237
Compound noun(s), 324
forming possessive case of, 305
Compound object, revising detached, 237
Compound predicate, revising detached, 237
Compound sentence(s), 269–70, 393. *See also specific types*
as concise sentences, 276
constructing, 235, 269–70, 393
excessive coordination, eliminating, 276
objective case in, 253–54
using, 270, 393
Compound subject(s)
joined by *and*, 241
joined by *or*, 241
Compound word(s), 331–32
adjectives, 331–32
dividing, 331
fractions, 332
numerals, 332
Compound-complex sentence(s), 394
constructing, 394
using, 394

Computer(s). *See also* Software; Word processor(s)
file management, 66
managing printouts, 49, 67–69
note-taking and, 48–49, 51, 67–69
working bibliography and, 44
Computer science. *See also* CSE documentation style; Natural and applied science(s)
composition overview, 364–65
specialized databases, 78
Computer software. *See* Software
Concession, words and phrases to signal, 266
Concise sentence(s), 273–77
adjective (relative) clauses, eliminating, 276–77
appositives, creating, 276
circumlocution avoidance, 275
complex sentences, creating, 276
compound sentences, creating, 276
deadwood elimination, 274
excessive coordination, eliminating, 276
passive construction, eliminating, 277
rambling, tightening, 276–77
redundancy deletion, 275
repetition elimination, 275–76
text messages, 273, 333
utility word elimination, 274, 286
wordiness, eliminating, 274–75
Concluding paragraph(s), 268
of argumentative essay, 33
of business letter, 351
of research project, 63
revising, 268
strategies for effective, 268
support, 33
of thesis-and-support essay, 18
words and phrases to introduce, 266
writing, 268
Concrete word(s)
abstract words *versus,* 286
defined, 286
Conditional relationships, complex sentences to indicate, 271
Conditional statements, 251
Conference proceedings, CSE reference list, 224
Conference(s), writing center, 21, 101
Confusing sentence(s), 277–79
faulty predication in, 279
mixed constructions in, 279
unnecessary shifts in, 278–79
Conjunction(s), 390–91. *See also* *specific types of conjunction*
types of, 390–91
using, 390–91
Conjunctive adverb(s), 389
in compound sentences, 389
list of, 389
Connotation
defined, 285
denotation *versus*, 285
Conscious, conscience, 397
Consistency, in document design, 342
Content note(s)
APA documentation style, 179
Chicago documentation style, 194–95, 196–97, 212, 217
defined, 139
MLA documentation style, 116, 139–40, 157
sample, 140, 157
Continual, continuous, 397
Contraction(s)
apostrophes to show omissions in, 305–06
formation of, 305–06
list of, 305–06
Contradiction, commas with contradictory phrases, 300
Contrast
complex sentences to indicate, 271
compound sentences to indicate, 270
words and phrases to signal, 265
Controversial statement, in introductions, 267
Coordinate adjective(s)
commas with, 296
defined, 296
Coordinate elements, 296. *See also* Coordination; *specific types*
commas between, 296
parallelism of, 280
Coordinating conjunction(s), 390
commas with, 269, 295–96
in compound sentences, 235, 269
list of, 269, 390
in revising comma splices, 235
in revising fused sentences, 235
in revising run-on sentences, 235
in titles of works, 327
Coordination, 271
to combine sentences, 271–72
excessive, eliminating, 276
Copyright page, 128, 172
Corporate author(s)
APA in-text citations, 167
APA reference list, 173
Chicago documentation style, 202
CSE reference list, 224
MLA parenthetical references, 117
MLA works-cited list, 129
Correlative conjunction(s), 390
commas with, 269, 295–96
in compound constructions, 269
list of, 280, 390
paired items linked by, 280
Could have, 397

Could of, should of, would of, 397
Council of Biology Editors. *See* CSE documentation style
Council of Science Editors (CSE), 220. *See also* CSE documentation style
Count noun(s), 374
Couple, couple of, 397
Course management software, 349
Courses. *See* Academic courses
Cover letters. *See* Letters of application
Creative Commons website, 64
Credibility, 89, 92
  of Internet sources, 92
  of library sources, 89
Credo Reference, 76
Criminal justice. *See also* Law; Social science(s)
  composition overview, 364–65
Criterion, criteria, 397
Critical response, 8–9. *See also* Thinking critically
  sample, 8–9
  writing, 8–9
Critical thinking. *See* Thinking critically
CSE documentation style, 219–30
  abbreviations, 222, 223, 225
  checklists, 226–27
  citation software, 68, 69
  citation-sequence format, 220, 221, 227
  CSE style, defined, 220
  directory, 219
  in-text, 220–21
  manuscript guidelines, 226–27
  model CSE-style research paper (excerpts), 227–30
  name-year format, 221
  in the natural and applied sciences, 220
  reference list, 68, 69, 108, 219, 221–26, 227, 230
Currency
  defined, 89, 93
  of Internet sources, 93
  of library sources, 89

D

-d, -ed ending
  in past participles, 373, 388
  spelling rules, 322
Dangling modifier(s), 284–85
  creating dependent clause, 284
  creating new subject, 284
  passive voice with, 285
  revising, 284–85
Dash(es), 315
  for emphasis, 315
  to indicate interruptions, 315
  with nonessential material, 292, 315
  quick guide, 292
  with quotation marks, 312
  to set off explanations, 292
  with summaries, 315
Data, 398
Database(s). *See* Online database(s)
Date(s)
  abbreviating, 222, 334, 335
  commas in, 301
  numerals in, 337
  parentheses with, 317
  questionable, marking, 294
Days of the week
  abbreviating, 335
  capitalizing names of, 325, 326
Deadwood
  defined, 274
  eliminating, 274
Decimal(s), numerals in, 337
Declarative sentences, 394
Definite article(s), 375
  omitting *the* from newspaper titles, 200, 328
Definition(s)
  faulty predication, 279
  in introductions, 267
  italics in, 330
Demonstrative pronoun(s), 376, 386
  as determiners, 376
  list of, 376, 386
Denotation
  connotation *versus*, 285
  defined, 285
Dependent (subordinate) clause(s), 392
  commas with introductory, 297
  in complex sentences, 270
  creating, to correct dangling modifier, 284
  as fragments, 236–37
  misplaced, revising, 283–84
  as modifiers, 283–84
Descriptive adjective(s), 388
Design. *See* Document design; Visual(s); Website(s)
Detached compounds, revising, 237
Determiner(s), 376, 389
  list of, 376
  using with nouns, 376
Diagram(s), 344
  in document design, 344–45
  sample, 345
Dialogue, 308
  interruptions in, 315
  pronoun-antecedent agreement, 245
  quotation marks with, 308
Diction
  for college writing, 348
  email, 333, 348, 355

formal, 287, 348, 355
informal, 245, 259, 295, 333
pretentious, 287
Dictionary(ies)
Chicago documentation style, 207
connotations and denotations, 285
italicizing terms being defined, 330
online, 286
quotation marks with definitions, 330
special, 81
Different from, different than, 398
Digital document(s), 347–50. *See also* Document design; Electronic source(s); Email; Internet research; Online database(s); Social networking sites
abbreviations in, 333
audience, 347
blogs. *See* Blog(s)
composing in digital environments, 347–50
diction in, 333, 348, 355
email. *See* Email
lists, 342
online forums. *See* Online forum(s)
podcasts. *See* Podcast(s)
purpose, 347
reading electronic texts, 6–7
synchronous/asynchronous communication, 348
text messages, 273, 333
wikis, 349
writing in wired classroom, 347–50
Digital Object Identifier (DOI)
APA documentation style, 175–79
Chicago documentation style, 206–10, 212
Diigo, 7
Direct address, commas with, 300
Direct object(s), 391, 392
objective case with, 253
Direct question(s), question marks with, 294
Direct quotation(s)
colons to introduce, 314
commas with, 300
identifying tags with, 96–97, 300, 308–09
Direction, prepositions and, 380
Directory of Open Access Journals, 81–82
Discipline(s). *See also* Humanities; Natural and applied science(s); Social science(s)
composing in, 362–65
other documentation styles, 230–31
plagiarism in, 105–06
writing in, 12
Discovery service, library, 71–72, 76, 79
Discussion list(s), 349
Disease(s), names of, 328
Disinterested, uninterested, 398
Dissertation(s), MLA works-cited list, 138
Document cameras, 360
Document design, 340–46
APA manuscript guidelines, 179–82
checklists, 342–43, 346
Chicago humanities manuscript guidelines, 211–13
CSE manuscript guidelines, 226–27
effective visual format, 340–41
email, 352, 355
headings in, 341–42
letter of application, 350–52
lists in, 342–43
memo, 352, 354
MLA manuscript guidelines, 141
model APA-style research paper, 182–93
model Chicago style research paper (excerpt), 213–18
model CSE-style research paper (excerpts), 227–30
model MLA-style essays, 25–30, 35–40
model MLA-style research paper, 143–60
résumé, 352, 353
Document names, capitalizing, 326
Documentation. *See also* Documentation style
to avoid plagiarism, 100–01. *See also* Plagiarism
defined, 113
of ideas, 13
importance of, 13, 100–01, 113
reasons for, 100–01
Documentation style
in the humanities, 113, 196, 365. *See also* Chicago documentation style; MLA documentation style
in the natural and applied sciences, 220, 230–31, 365. *See also* CSE documentation style
other styles, 230–31
in the social sciences, 165, 196, 365. *See also* APA documentation style
Dogpile, 85
Domain name, 86, 94
Don't, doesn't, 398
Double negative(s), 370

Drafting
file management, 66
final draft, 21–22, 25–30, 70
instructor comments in, 21, 64–65
peer review in, 13–14
research project, 61–64
revising drafts, 21–22, 64–69
rough draft, 20–21, 61–64
Dramatic work(s). *See also* Humanities; Literature
italicizing titles of, 329
MLA parenthetical references, 116
MLA works-cited list, 132
numerals for divisions in, 337
periods for divisions in, 294
DVD(s) (digital videodiscs)
Chicago documentation style, 205
CSE reference list, 225
MLA works-cited list, 137
DVD-ROMs
MLA works-cited list, 135

E

Each
with compound antecedents, 244
with compound subject joined by *and*, 241
-e endings, 323
Earth science(s). *See also* Natural and applied science(s)
composition overview, 364–65
documentation styles, 231. *See also* CSE documentation style
EasyBib, 67
EBSCOhost *Academic Search*, 76
Economic, economical, 398
Economics. *See* Business and economics
ed., eds. (editor, editors), 202
Edited work(s)
APA reference list, 173
Chicago documentation style, 201, 202
MLA works-cited list, 129–30
Editing, 23–24. *See also* Revision
essay, 23–24
research project, 70
Editorial(s)
APA reference list, 171
MLA works-cited list, 126
Eds. (editors)
Chicago documentation style, 201
Education. *See also* Social science(s)
composition overview, 364–65
specialized databases, 78
Effect, affect, 287, 395
e.g. (for example), 335, 398
ei, ie combinations, 322
Either...or, 241, 269, 270
Electronic address(es). *See also* URL (uniform resource locator)
divisions of, 176, 212, 294, 331
email, 348, 355
entering, 82, 348, 355
using correct, 348, 355
Electronic communication. *See* Digital document(s)
Electronic source(s), 70–81. *See also* Internet research; Online catalog(s); Source(s)
APA in-text citations, 168
APA reference list, 108, 175–79
Chicago documentation style, 108, 206–10
CSE documentation style, 108
CSE reference list, 225–26
evaluating, 91–95
italicizing names of, 328
in library research, 70–81
MLA parenthetical references, 118
MLA works-cited list, 108, 120, 122, 123–25, 133–35
online catalogs, 72–73, 79–80, 83
online databases, 74–79
Electronic texts. *See* Digital document(s)
Ellipses, 98, 318–19
within brackets, 98, 319
to indicate omissions within quotations, 98, 152, 318–19
for multiple authors in APA reference list, 173
Email
acronyms, 333
addresses for, 348, 355
APA in-text citations, 167
APA reference list, 177
Chicago documentation style, 209
diction in, 333, 348, 355
follow-up, 352
to instructor, 348
MLA works-cited list, 135
text messages, 273, 333
using, 348, 355
in the workplace, 352, 355
writing, 355
Embedding
to combine sentences, 272
defined, 272
Emigrate from, immigrate to, 398
Eminent, imminent, 398
Emojis, 333
Emoticon(s), 333
Emphasis
dashes for, 315
exclamation points for, 295
with interjections, 391
italics for, 330
through word order, 382
Encyclopedia(s), 81
Chicago documentation style, 207

MLA works-cited list, 127
online, 87, 91
End punctuation, 293–95. *See also* Exclamation point(s); Period(s); Question mark(s)
Endnote, 67–68
Endnote(s), 196
Chicago-style paper, 194–95, 196–97, 212, 217
MLA-style paper, 116, 139–40, 157
EndNote Basic/EndNote Web, 68
Engineering. *See also* CSE documentation style; Natural and applied science(s)
composition overview, 364–65
specialized databases, 79
English as a Second Language (ESL). *See* Multilingual tip(s); Multilingual writers
Enthused, 398
Entire work, MLA parenthetical references, 117
Environmental science. *See also* Natural and applied science(s)
specialized databases, 79
E-readers, MLA works-cited list, 132
-er endings, in comparatives, 260
ERIC, 209
ESL (English as a Second Language) writers. *See* Multilingual tip(s); Multilingual writers
Essay(s), 15–32. *See also* Argumentative essay(s); Literary analysis
audience for, 12–14, 16
checklists, 22, 23–24, 31
Chicago documentation style, 204
drafting, 20–21
editing, 23–24
final draft, 21–22, 25–30
idea generation for, 17
MLA works-cited list, 132
model MLA-style, 25–30, 35–40
outlines of, 20, 21
peer review of, 13, 21
planning, 15–17, 18–19, 20, 32–33
proofreading, 23–24
purpose of, 10–12, 16, 18
quotation marks for titles, 311
reading to write, 2–9
response, 8–9
revising, 21–22
shaping, 17–19
text reading and interpretation, 2–9
thesis-and-support, 17–19, 32–33
title selection for, 23
topic selection for, 16
writing process and, 15–24
-est endings, in superlatives, 260
et al. (and others)
APA documentation style, 166
Chicago documentation style, 202
MLA documentation style, 115, 129
etc. (and the rest), 335, 398
Ethics, in use of sources, 99–106. *See also* Plagiarism
Ethnic group(s), capitalizing names of, 326
Ethnic studies. *See* Social science(s)
Euphemism(s), 286
Evaluation, 89
in critical response, 8
instructor comments in, 21, 64–65
of library sources, 89–91
in peer review, 13–14, 65–66
of website content, 91–95
Evaluative writing, 11
Event names, capitalizing, 325, 326
Every
with compound antecedents, 244
with compound subject joined by *and*, 241
Everyday, every day, 399
Everyone, every one, 399
Exact time(s), numerals in, 337
Example(s)
punctuation to set off, 292
words and phrases to introduce, 266
Except, accept, 287, 395
Exclamation point(s)
with interjections, 391
with quotation marks, 309, 312
using, 295
Exclamatory sentences, 394
Expanded Academic ASAP, 76
Explanation(s)
colons to set off, 292, 314
dashes to set off, 292
Explicit, implicit, 399
Exploratory research, 43–44, 70–87
idea generation, 17
Internet, 81–87
library, 70–81
research question in, 43–44
working bibliography in, 44–45

F

Facebook. *See also* Social networking sites
using, 350
Farther, further, 399
Faulty modification, 282–85
dangling modifiers, 284–85
intrusive modifiers, 284
misplaced modifiers, 282–84
revising, 282–85
Faulty parallelism, 281
Faulty predication, 279
Favorites, 86
Fewer, less, 399
-f, -fe endings, plurals with, 323

Fiction. *See also* Literature; Prose
MLA parenthetical references, 116
Field research, 87–88
checklists, 88
interviews in, 88
observations in, 87–88
surveys in, 88
Fig. (Figure), with MLA-style visuals, 142
Figure(s)
APA-style paper, 181, 192
Chicago-style paper, 212
CSE-style paper, 226, 227, 229
MLA-style paper, 142, 148, 152
Film(s). *See also* Review(s)
APA reference list, 175
CSE reference list, 225
italicizing titles of, 137, 329
MLA works-cited list, 137
Final draft
essay, 21–22, 25–30
research project, 70
First person, 240, 254, 278, 324
Firstly (secondly, thirdly,...), 399
Fixed amounts, as collective nouns, 242
Flip charts, 361
Focused research, 46–48. *See also* Research project(s)
balancing primary and secondary sources, 47–48
defined, 47
reading sources, 47
Follow-up email(s), 352
Footnote(s)
APA-style paper, 179
Chicago-style paper, 194–95, 196–97, 217
Foreign words and phrase(s). *See also* Latin expression(s)
foreign plurals, 324
italics to set off, 329
Foreword
APA reference list, 173
MLA works-cited list, 131
Formal diction, 287, 348, 355
Formal outline(s), 57–61
parallelism in, 281
of research projects, 57–61, 64
sentence, 58, 60–61, 64
topic, 58, 59–60
Format. *See also* Genre
of APA-style research paper, 179–93
of business letters, 314, 351
of Chicago-style research paper, 211–18
of CSE-style research paper, 226–30
of follow-up emails, 352
of letters of application, 351
of long quotations within paper, 114, 116, 141, 165, 180, 309–10, 314, 329
of memos, 354
of MLA-style essays, 25–30, 34–40
of MLA-style research paper, 143–60
of résumés, 353
Forums, online. *See* Online forum(s)
Fraction(s), hyphenating, 332
Fragment(s), 236–39
correcting, 237–39
intentional use of, 239
recognizing, 236–37
Freewriting, in idea generation, 17
Further, farther, 399
Fused sentence(s), 234–36
Future perfect progressive tense, 251
Future perfect tense, 250
Future progressive tense, 250
Future tense, 249

G

Gender, 240
agreement in, 240–45, 378
pronoun, 378
sexist language, 24, 245, 288–89
General databases, 76–77
General science. *See* CSE documentation style; Natural and applied science(s)
General word(s), 286
Generally held beliefs, present tense to indicate, 249
General-purpose search engines, 83–85
Generic *he, him*, 245, 288–89
Genetics, documentation style. *See* CSE documentation style
Genre, 12, 15
in the humanities, 364
in the natural and applied sciences, 364
in reading texts, 6
selecting, 14–15
in the social sciences, 364
Geographical regions, capitalizing names of, 326
Geology. *See also* Natural and applied science(s)
composition overview, 364–65
documentation styles, 231. *See also* CSE documentation style
Gerund(s), 373, 388
possessive case before, 254
as verbals, 373, 388
Gerund phrase(s), 392
Good, well, 399
Google, 81, 83, 84
in detecting plagiarism, 100
resource summary, 85–86
Google Images, 64
Google Scholar, 81, 86
Got to, 399

Government agencies, capitalizing names of, 327
Government document(s)
APA reference list, 174
Chicago documentation style, 205, 208
documentation styles, 231
MLA parenthetical references, 117
MLA works-cited list, 138
Grammar, 240–61, 368–94. *See also* Parts of speech *and specific concepts; specific concepts*
Grammar checker(s), 24
Graph(s), 344
APA-style paper, 192
in document design, 344
MLA-style paper, 148, 152
sample, 345
Graphic(s). *See* Visual(s) *and specific types*
Graphic narrative
defined, 131
MLA works-cited list, 131

H

Hanged, hung, 399
He, she, 288, 399
Heading(s), 341–42
APA-style paper, 180, 184, 185, 342
consistency of, 342
in document design, 341–42
indentation of, 342
number of, 341
phrasing of, 341
previewing, 2
research project, 63
résumé, 353
typographical emphasis in, 342
using, 341–42
Helping verbs. *See* Auxiliary (helping) verb(s)
Highlighting, 3
of electronic texts, 7
symbols in, 3
of text, 3, 7
His or her, 245, 288–89
Historic, historical, 400
History. *See also* Chicago documentation style; Humanities
capitalizing historical periods, 326, 328
composition overview, 364–65
names of historical periods, 326
specialized databases, 77
Hits, 72, 83
Holiday(s)
abbreviating, 335
capitalizing names of, 326
Home page(s). *See also* Website(s)
course, 133
italicizing, 329
MLA works-cited list, 133
Homophone(s), 287, 395–405
Hopefully, 400
Humanities. *See also* Literature
composition overview, 364–65
disciplines within, 364
documentation styles, 113, 196, 395. *See also* Chicago documentation style; MLA documentation style
genres used in, 364
plagiarism in, 105
research methods and sources in, 47–48, 77–78, 365
specialized databases, 77–78
style and format of papers in, 113, 364
Hung, hanged, 399
Hyphen(s), 330–32
to break word at end of line, 330–31
to divide compound words, 331–32
in forming dashes, 315
MLA works-cited list, 129
with prefixes, 332
with suffixes, 332
suspended, 332

I

I. *See also* First person
capitalizing, 324
I, me, in compound constructions, 254
i.e. (that is), 400
Ibid. (in the same place), 197, 217
-ible, -able endings, 323
Idea(s)
documenting, 13
generating, 17
plagiarism avoidance, 103–04
for research project, 43
Identification number(s), 337
Identifying tag(s), 96–97, 308
at beginning of quoted passage, 308–09
colons with, 309
with direct quotations, 96–97, 300, 308–09
at end of quoted passage, 97, 309
integrating sources with, 63–64, 96–97
to introduce source material, 96–97
location of, 96–97, 308–09
in middle of quoted passage, 96, 308
for paraphrases, 96–97, 98–99
punctuating, 97, 300, 308–09
for quotations, 96–97, 308–09. *See also* Quotation(s)
for summaries, 98–99, 266

Identity, complex sentences to indicate, 271
Idiom(s), 380
prepositions in, 380, 381–82
ie, ei combinations, 322
If, whether, 400
Illusion, allusion, 395
Illustrated book
defined, 131
MLA works-cited list, 131
Illustration(s). *See* Figure(s); Table(s); Visual(s)
Image(s). *See also* Visual(s)
CSE reference list, 226
online resources, 64
Immigrate to, emigrate from, 398
Imminent, eminent, 398
Imperative mood, 251
Imperative sentence(s), 251, 295, 394
Implicit, explicit, 399
Imply, infer, 400
In, as preposition, 380, 381
Inappropriate language, 287–88
clichés, 287–88
jargon, 287
pretentious diction, 287
Indefinite article(s), 327, 375, 395
Indefinite pronoun(s), 241–42, 244, 377, 386
agreement errors, 240
as antecedents, 244–45
forming possessive case of, 304
list of, 242, 244, 377, 386
as subjects, 240, 241–42, 377
subject-verb agreement with, 241–42
Indefinite pronoun subjects, 241–42, 377
Indentation
APA-style paper, 180, 185
Chicago-style paper, 211, 212, 215
CSE-style paper, 228
of headings, 342
of lists, 342
of long poetry passages, 310
of long prose passages, 180, 309–10
MLA-style paper, 141, 143, 144
Independent (main) clause(s), 392
colons to set off, 292
commas to set off, 292, 295–96, 302
in complex sentences, 270
in compound sentences, 269–70
coordinating conjunctions with, 269, 292
in revising fragments, 237
semicolons to set off, 292, 300, 302–03
separating, 292, 295–96, 300, 302–03
transitional words and phrases to connect, 235, 300
Indicative mood, 251
Indirect object(s), 392
objective case with, 254
Indirect question(s), periods with, 293, 295
Indirect quotation(s), 313
Indirect source(s)
APA in-text citations, 167, 186
Chicago documentation style, 203
MLA parenthetical references, 115
Individual ownership, apostrophes to indicate, 305
Infer, imply, 400
Infinitive(s), 373, 388
split, 284
in titles of works, 327
as verbals, 373, 388
Infinitive phrase(s), 392
Informal diction
adjective forms in, 259
adverb forms in, 259
in digital documents, 333
exclamation points in, 295
pronoun-antecedent agreement, 245
Informal outline(s). *See* Scratch outline(s)
Informative writing, 10–11
-ing ending
in gerunds, 373, 388
in present participles, 373
spelling rules, 322
Inseparable phrasal verb(s), 371
Instagram. *See* Social networking sites
Instant messaging
acronyms in, 273, 333
text message length, 273
Instructor
comments of, 21, 64–65
email to, 348
Integrating source material, 63–64, 95–99
identifying tags, 63–64, 96–97
paraphrases, 53–54
quotations, 95–98
summaries, 52–53
visuals, 64, 142
Intensive pronoun(s), 377, 386
Intentional plagiarism. *See also* Plagiarism
avoiding, 101
defined, 100
Interjection(s), 391
commas with, 300
using, 391
Interlibrary loan, 79–80
Internet research, 81–87. *See also* Electronic source(s)
APA reference list, 108, 175–79
checklists, 93–94

Chicago documentation style, 108, 206–10
CSE documentation style, 108, 225–26
evaluating sources, 91–95
MLA works-cited list, 108, 133–35
online forums, 95
permalink URLs, 44
plagiarism avoidance, 102
plagiarism detection, 100
websites, 70–73, 81–87, 209
Interpretation, in critical response, 8
Interrogative adverb(s), 389
Interrogative pronoun(s), 383, 386
Interrogative sentences, 394
Interruption(s)
commas to punctuate, 300
dashes to indicate, 315
Interview(s), 88
APA in-text citations, 167
APA reference list, 175
Chicago documentation style, 204–05
conducting field research, 88
MLA works-cited list, 139
In-text citation(s)
APA documentation style, 161, 165–68
CSE documentation style, 220–21
MLA documentation style, 109, 113–18, 147, 294
quotation ending in ellipsis, 318
Into, as preposition, 381
Intransitive verb(s), 372–73, 391
Introductory element(s)
commas to set off, 297
dependent clauses, 297
paragraphs. *See* Introductory paragraph(s)
prepositional phrases, 297
transitional words and phrases, 297
verbal phrases, 297
Introductory paragraph(s), 267
of argumentative essay, 33
of research project, 62
revising, 267
strategies for effective, 267
thesis-and-support essay, 18
writing, 267
Intrusive modifier(s), 284
misplaced, revising, 284
split infinitives, 284
Inversion, of word order, 243
iPad, as teleprompter, 358
Irregardless, regardless, 400
Irregular plural nouns, 305
Irregular verb(s), 188, 246–48, 368, 388
Is when, is where, 279, 400
It
ambiguous antecedent, 256
with nonhuman nouns, 378
Italic(s), 328–30. *See also* Underlining
APA in-text citations, 167
APA reference list, 169, 170
for emphasis, 330
with foreign words and phrases, 329
for legal case names, 326
MLA-style papers, 116–18, 119, 131–32, 328–29
with titles of works, 116–18, 130, 131, 311, 328–29
with words as words, 329–30
Its, it's, 287, 400
Ixquick, 85

J

Jargon, 287
Job application. *See* Letters of application
Joint ownership, apostrophes to indicate, 305
Journal(s)
blogs as, 349. *See also* Blog(s)
in idea generation, 17
Journal article(s), 75
APA reference list, 169–70, 176, 177
Chicago documentation style, 198, 206, 208–09
continuous pagination, 169, 198, 222
CSE reference list, 222, 226
in library research, 74–79
MLA works-cited list, 120, 122–24, 133
previewing, 2
quotation marks for titles, 311
separate pagination, 169, 198, 222
in subscription databases, 74–79
Journalism, documentation styles, 231
JSTOR, 77
Justification, in document design, 340

K

Kartoo, 85
Key words and phrases
highlighting, 3
repeating, 281
in title selection, 23
Keyword search, 72–73, 82
abstracts in APA-style paper, 184
Boolean search, 72–73
conducting, 82–83
legitimacy of online sources, 94
library, 72–73, 83
of online catalogs, 72–73, 83
subscription database, 74–79
Web browser, 82–83
Kind of, sort of, 400

L

Label(s)
 APA-style paper, 181, 181, 192
 Chicago-style paper, 212
 in computer file management, 66
 CSE-style paper, 229
 for drafts, 66
 MLA-style paper, 142
 with visuals, 346
Language(s). *See also* Foreign words and phrase(s); Humanities; Latin expression(s); Multilingual tip(s); Multilingual writers
 capitalizing names of, 326
 composition overview, 364–65
 documentation style. *See* MLA documentation style
 use of native, 4, 21, 52
Latin expression(s)
 e.g. (for example), 335, 398
 et al. (and others), 115, 129, 166, 202
 etc. (and the rest), 335, 398
 Ibid. (in the same place), 197, 217
 i.e. (that is), 400
 plural forms, 324
 sic (thus), 317
Latino, Latina, 326
Law. *See also* Social science(s)
 abbreviating legal case names, 117–18
 capitalizing legal case names, 326
 documentation styles, 231
 italicizing legal case names, 326
 MLA parenthetical references, 117–18
Lay, lie, 248, 373, 401
-le endings, in comparatives, 260
Learning outcomes, 30
Least, in superlatives, 260
Leave, let, 400
Lecture(s)
 MLA works-cited list, 139
 presenting. *See* Oral presentation(s)
Length
 text message, 273
 varying sentence, 271–72
Less
 in comparatives, 260
 less, fewer, 399
Let, leave, 400
Letters (of alphabet)
 apostrophes for omitted, 305–06
 apostrophes in plurals of, 306
 as letters, setting off, 306, 329–30
 parentheses with, 316
 silent, 323
Letters (correspondence). *See also* Business letter(s); Letters to the editor
 APA in-text citations, 167
 APA reference list, 171, 174
 Chicago documentation style, 205
 MLA works-cited list, 126, 139
Letters of application, 350–52
 follow-up emails for, 352
 sample, 351
Letters to the editor
 APA reference list, 171
 Chicago documentation style, 200
 MLA works-cited list, 126
LexisNexis Academic Universe, 77
Library of Congress Subject Headings, 83
Library research, 70–81
 advantages of, 70–71
 books, 70–73, 79–80, 83
 circulating collection, 70–73
 databases, 74–79
 discovery service, 71–72, 76, 79
 electronic sources, 70–81
 evaluating sources, 89–91
 exploratory, 70–81
 in the humanities, 77–78
 library websites, 70–73
 in the natural and applied sciences, 78–79
 online catalogs, 72–73, 79–80, 83
 periodical types, 75
 reference sources, 80–81
 scholarly publications, 74–79
 in the social sciences, 78
 special services, 79–80
Lie, lay, 248, 373, 401
Life, lifestyle, 401
Life science(s). *See* CSE documentation style; Natural and applied science(s)
Like, as, 396
Limiting modifier(s)
 defined, 282
 placing, 282–83
Line number, MLA parenthetical references, 116
Line spacing, 341
 APA-style paper, 179, 185
 for business letters, 351
 Chicago-style paper, 211, 212, 215, 217
 CSE-style paper, 226, 227, 228
 in document design, 341
 MLA-style paper, 141, 143, 144
Linear documents, 6
Line/lines, MLA parenthetical references, 116
Linguistics, composition overview, 364–65
Link(s), 93–94

Linking verb(s), 243, 258, 387, 392
faulty predication, 279
incorrect use of *be*, 279
list of, 387
subject complements and, 258
subject-verb agreement with, 243
List(s)
APA-style paper, 180, 189
capitalization, 141–42
colons to introduce, 238, 303, 313
constructing, 342–43
in document design, 342–43
fragments as, 238
parallelism in, 281, 343
parentheses for points on, 316
previewing, 2
Listserv(s)
Chicago documentation style, 209
defined, 349
using, 349
Literary analysis. *See also* Review(s)
present tense in, 249
Literary movements, capitalizing names of, 326
Literature. *See also* Humanities; Literary analysis; Poetry; Prose
composition overview, 364–65
documentation styles. *See* Chicago documentation style; MLA documentation style
long quotations of, 114, 116, 141, 165, 180, 309–10, 314
MLA parenthetical references, 114, 116
MLA works-cited list, 132, 334
periods for divisions in, 294
specialized databases, 77
Location, complex sentences to indicate, 271
Long prose passages, 309–10
setting off in text, 114, 141, 165, 180, 309–10, 314
Long quotation(s)
colons to introduce, 314
of poetry, 114, 116, 141, 310, 319, 329
of prose, 114, 141, 165, 180, 309–10, 314
Loose, lose, 401
Lots, lots of, a lot of, 401
-ly endings
in comparatives, 260
in compound adjectives, 332

M

Magazine article(s)
APA reference list, 170
Chicago documentation style, 199, 206–07
CSE reference list, 222
MLA works-cited list, 124–25
previewing, 2
quotation marks for titles, 311
in subscription databases, 74–79
Magazine(s), italicizing titles of, 328
Main clause(s). *See* Independent (main) clause(s)
Main idea. *See* Thesis; Topic sentence(s)
Main verb(s), 387
Mamma, 85
Man, 401
Map(s)
CSE reference list, 225
MLA works-cited list, 136
Margin(s), 340
APA-style paper, 180, 185
Chicago-style paper, 211, 215
CSE-style paper, 228
in document design, 340
MLA-style paper, 141, 144
with visuals, 346
Mathematics. *See also* Natural and applied science(s)
composition overview, 364–65
documentation styles, 231. *See also* CSE documentation style
May be, maybe, 401
May, can, 397
Me, I, in compound constructions, 254
Media, medium, 401
Medicine. *See also* Natural and applied science(s)
documentation styles, 231. *See also* CSE documentation style
specialized databases, 79
Memo(s), 352
APA in-text citations, 167
format of, 354
sample, 354
Mendeley, 68
Metacognitive writing, 10
Metacrawler engine(s), 85
Metasearch engine(s), 85
Microsoft PowerPoint, 359
Microsoft Word, 24, 322
AutoCorrect tool, 325
Comment feature, 61, 64–65
Compare Documents feature, 21
grammar checkers, 24
Search and Find command, 24
spell checkers, 24, 322
thesaurus access, 286
Track Changes feature, 21, 65–66
Might have, might of, 401
Misplaced modifier(s), 282–84
dependent clauses, 283–84
limiting modifiers, 282–83

Misplaced modifier (*continued*)
modifying words, 282–83
phrases, 283
revising, 282–84
squinting modifiers, 283
Mixed construction
defined, 279
revising, 279
MLA documentation style, 109–60
abbreviations in, 116, 117–18, 125, 126, 128, 294, 334, 335
checklists, 141–42
citation software, 67–69
content notes, 116, 139–40, 157
directory, 109–11
in the humanities, 113
italics in, 116–18, 119, 131–32, 328–29
long quotations in, 309–10
manuscript guidelines, 141
MLA style, defined, 113
model MLA-style essays, 25–30, 34–40
model MLA-style research paper, 143–60
numerals in, 335, 336–37
parenthetical references, 109, 113–18, 147, 294
spelled-out numbers *versus* numerals, 336–37
works-cited list, 67–69, 108, 109–11, 118–39, 142, 158–60
MLA Handbook, 113n, 141
Modal auxiliary(ies), 369, 387
Modern Language Association (MLA), 113. *See also* MLA documentation style
Modifier(s), 282, 378. *See also* Adjective(s); Adverb(s)
dangling, 284–85
faulty modification, revising, 282–85
multilingual writers and, 378–79
nonrestrictive, 257, 298–99
phrases, 283
restrictive, 298–99, 301
squinting, 283
verbal phrases as, 283
Money amounts, numerals in, 337
Month(s)
abbreviating, 222, 335
capitalizing names of, 326
commas with, 301
Monument names, capitalizing, 325
Mood, 251–52. *See also specific types of mood*
shifts in, 278
types of, 251–52
More, in comparatives, 260
Most, in superlatives, 260
Movie(s). *See* Film(s)
MP3 file
APA reference list, 175
MLA works-cited list, 137
podcasts, 349–50
Multilingual tip(s). *See also* Multilingual writers
adjective use, 258, 297, 379
adverb use, 258
annotating text, 4
capitalization, 328
commonly confused words, 381
drafting, 21
embedding, 272
idea generation, 17
note-taking, 52, 54
planning essay, 17
reading text, 2
subordination, 272
using native language, 4, 21, 52
varying sentences, 272
Multilingual writers, 368–84. *See also* Multilingual tip(s)
adjective use, 378–79
adverb use, 378–79
modifier use, 378–79
noun use, 374–76
preposition use, 380–82
pronouns, 376–78
verb use, 368–74
word order, 382–84
Multiple author(s)
APA in-text citations, 166
APA reference list, 173, 182
Chicago documentation style, 201–02
CSE documentation style, 221, 223
MLA parenthetical references, 115
MLA works-cited list, 128–29
Multivolume work(s)
APA reference list, 173
Chicago documentation style, 203
MLA parenthetical references, 115
MLA works-cited list, 131
Music. *See also* Humanities
APA reference list, 175
Chicago documentation style, 205
composition overview, 364–65
CSE reference list, 225
documentation styles, 231
italicizing titles of long works, 329
MLA works-cited list, 137
quotation marks for titles of songs, 311
Musical(s). *See* Dramatic work(s)

N

Name(s). *See* Author name(s); Personal name(s); Place name(s); Proper noun(s); Publisher's name
Name-year format, CSE documentation style, 221
Narrowing of focus, words and phrases to introduce, 266
Nationalities, capitalizing names of, 326
Natural and applied science(s)
composition overview, 364–65
disciplines within, 220, 364
documentation styles, 220, 230–31, 365. *See also* CSE documentation style
genres used in, 364
plagiarism in, 106
research methods and sources in, 48, 78–79, 365
specialized databases, 78–79
style and format of papers in, 226–30, 364
N.d. (no date of publication)
APA documentation style, 177
Negative verb(s), 369–70
Neither...nor, 241, 244
News service(s), MLA works-cited list, 125–26
Newsletter article(s), MLA works-cited list, 127
Newspaper(s)
italicizing titles of, 328
the in titles of, 200, 328
Newspaper article(s)
APA reference list, 171, 179
Chicago documentation style, 200, 207
CSE reference list, 222–23
MLA works-cited list, 125–26
previewing, 2
quotation marks for titles, 311
in subscription databases, 74–79
No. (number), 335
No, commas with, 300
Noncount noun(s), 374–75
articles with, 375
list of, 374–75
Nonessential material, 297–99
commas to set off, 257, 292, 297–99, 300
dashes to set off, 292, 315
nonrestrictive modifiers, 257, 298–99
parentheses to set off, 292, 316
Nonexistent antecedent(s), 257
Nonfinite verb(s). *See* Verbals, verbal phrase(s)
Nonrestrictive modifier(s), 298–99
commas to set off, 257, 298–99
types of, 298–99
using, 298–99
Nor, with compound antecedents, 241, 244
Not, as search operator, 73
Note(s). *See* Content note(s); Endnote(s); Footnote(s); Note-taking
Notecards, for presentation notes, 358
Note-taking, 50–57
to avoid plagiarism, 61, 95
computer files/printouts, 48–49, 51, 67–69
paraphrases in, 50, 53–54
photocopies in, 48–49, 67–69
quotations in, 50, 55
source information in, 50–52
summaries in, 50, 52–53
synthesis in, 55–57
Noun(s), 374–76, 385. *See also specific types of noun*
capitalizing. *See* Proper noun(s)
compound, 305, 324
forming possessive case of, 304–05
multilingual writers and, 374–76
other determiners with, 376
plural, 323–24, 374, 375
possessive case, 304–05
prepositions to introduce, 389–90
singular, 374
types of, 385
using, 374–76, 385
using articles with, 375
verbs formed from, 374
we, us before, 255–56
Noun clause(s), 393
Noun phrase(s), 392
in rambling sentences, 277
wordy constructions, eliminating, 277
Number, 240, 278–79, 368. *See also* Numeral(s)
agreement in, 240–45, 368, 377
cardinal, 376
ordinal, 376
shift in, 278–79
Number, amount, 396
Numeral(s), 336–37. *See also* Number
apostrophes for omitted, 306
conventional uses, 337
as determiners, 376
with divisions in literary works, 337
hyphenating compound, 332
identification numbers, 337
in lists, 343
MLA-style paper, 335, 336–37

Numeral (*continued*)
- as numerals, setting off, 306, 329–30
- parentheses with, 316
- questionable, marking, 294
- spelled-out numbers *versus*, 336–37
- symbols with, 336, 337

Nursing. *See also* Medicine; Natural and applied science(s)
- composition overview, 364–65
- specialized databases, 79

O

-*o* endings, plurals with, 324
Obituaries, MLA works-cited list, 140
Object(s)
- compound, revising detached, 237
- direct, 253, 391, 392
- indirect, 254, 392

Object complement(s), 391
Object of preposition, 254, 389
Objective case, 253–54
Objectivity, 89, 93
- of Internet sources, 93
- of library sources, 89–90

Observation(s), 87
- in field research, 87–88
- in idea generation, 17

Offensive language, 288–89
- sexist language, 24, 245, 288–89
- stereotypes, 288

OK, O.K., okay, 402
Omission(s)
- apostrophes to indicate, 305–06
- commas to indicate, 301
- ellipses to indicate, 98, 152, 318–19
- of *the* from newspaper titles, 200, 328
- within quotations, 98, 152, 318–19

On, as preposition, 380, 381
One-page article(s), MLA parenthetical references, 115
Online catalog(s), 72–73, 79–80
- keyword searches of, 72–73, 83
- subject searches in, 73

Online database(s), 74–79. *See also* Online database(s)
- APA reference list, 177, 179
- Chicago documentation style, 208–09
- choosing, 75–76
- frequently-used, 76–77
- general *versus* specialized, 76–79
- in the humanities, 77–78
- italicizing titles of, 329
- MLA works-cited list, 108, 123–25
- multi search, 76
- in the natural and applied sciences, 78–79
- permalink URLs, 44
- searching, 74–79
- in the social sciences, 78
- subscription, 74–79

Online forum(s)
- APA reference list, 178
- Chicago documentation style, 209
- evaluating material from, 95
- listservs, 349
- MLA works-cited list, 135

Online magazines and journals. *See* Electronic source(s); Online database(s); Subscription services, library
Online publication(s). *See* Electronic source(s)
Online study guides, 75–76
Online video
- APA reference list, 178
- Chicago documentation style, 210
- MLA works-cited list, 134

Onto, as preposition, 381
Openings, sentence, 272–73
Open-source software, 87, 349
Opinion, unnecessary statement of, 274
Opposing Viewpoints Resource Center, 77
Or
- *and/or*, 396
- with compound antecedents, 244
- compound subjects joined by, 241
- *either...or*, 241, 269, 270
- as search operator, 73

Oral presentation(s), 355–62
- delivering, 362
- getting started, 356
- planning, 356–57
- presentation notes, 357–58
- presentations, defined, 355
- quotation marks to set off, 307–10
- rehearsing, 361–62
- visual aids, 358–61

Order, 376
Order of adjectives, 379
Ordinal number(s), as determiners, 376
Organization
- of argumentative essay, 32–33
- of research project, 61–64

Organization name(s). *See also* Corporate author(s)
- abbreviating, 294, 333–34
- capitalizing, 327
- CSE documentation style, 224

Outline(s). *See also* Formal outline(s); Scratch outline(s)
- essay, 20, 21
- parallelism in, 281
- presentation, 358
- research project, 57–61, 64

Overhead projectors, 360
-*ow* endings, in comparatives, 260
Ownership. *See* Possessive case

P

P., pp.
APA in-text citations, 165, 167
APA reference list, 169, 173
MLA works-cited list, 122
Page header(s), APA-style paper, 180
Page number(s)
APA parenthetical references, 165
APA reference list, 169, 170
APA-style paper, 180
Chicago-style paper, 196–97, 198, 211, 212
CSE-style paper, 222, 227, 228
MLA parenthetical references, 116, 118
MLA works-cited list, 120–21
MLA-style paper, 123, 141
numerals for, 337
Painting(s)
italicizing names of, 329
MLA works-cited list, 136
Paired items
linked by correlative conjunctions, 280
parallelism of, 280
Pamphlet(s)
italicizing titles of, 139, 329
MLA works-cited list, 139
Paper(s). *See* Documentation; Essay(s); Research project(s)
Par., pars., MLA parenthetical references, 118
Para., APA in-text citations, 168
Paragraph(s), 264–68
APA in-text citations, 168, 185
body. *See* Body paragraph(s)
checklists on, 22
coherent, 265–66
concluding. *See* Concluding paragraph(s)
introductory. *See* Introductory paragraph(s)
MLA parenthetical references, 118
parallel structure in, 266
revising, 22
topic sentences in, 63, 264–65
transitional words and phrases in, 265–66
unified, 264–65
well-developed, 266–67
Parallelism, 280–81
in coherent paragraphs, 266
effective use of, 280–81
faulty, 281
of headings, 341
items in series, 280
in lists, 281, 343
in outlines, 281
repeating key words in, 281
Paraphrase(s), 53–54
to avoid plagiarism, 103
identifying tags with, 96–97, 98–99
integrating, 53–54
MLA parenthetical references for, 114
in note-taking, 50, 53–54
sample, 54
Parentheses, 316–17
with commas, 316
with other punctuation, 316
within parentheses, brackets for, 317
with points on list, 316
question marks in, 294
quick guide, 292
to set off nonessential material, 292, 316
Parenthetical reference(s), 113
APA documentation style, 161, 165–68
MLA documentation style, 109, 113–18, 147, 294
placement of, 114
quotation ending in ellipsis, 318
Participial phrase(s), 374
commas with, 374
as verbals, 392
Participle(s), 373–74, 388. *See also specific types of participle*
recognizing, 373, 388
types of, 373–74, 388
as verbals, 374, 388
Parts of speech, 368–82, 385–91. *See also specific parts of speech*
Parts of works
APA in-text citations, 167
APA reference list, 173–74
Chicago documentation style, 203–04
CSE reference list, 224
MLA parenthetical references, 116–17
MLA works-cited list, 131, 132–33, 334
numerals with divisions, 337
periods to mark divisions, 294
quotation marks for titles, 311
Passed, past, 402
Passive voice, 252, 277, 372
with dangling modifiers, 285
eliminating, 277
intentional use of, 252, 372
in rambling sentences, 277
shift from or to active voice, 278, 285
transitive verbs with, 373
using, 252
Past participle(s), 373, 388. *See also* Verbals, verbal phrase(s)
formation of, 373
in principal parts, 246–48
Past, passed, 402
Past perfect progressive tense, 251

Past perfect tense, 250
Past progressive tense, 250
Past subjunctive mood, 251
Past tense, 249
in discussing own research, 188
in discussing research of others, 186
in principal parts, 246–48
using, 249
Patterns of development, 10–12
Peer review, 13, 21
audience in, 12
checklists, 14
comments in, 13–14, 65–66
drafts in, 13–14
refereed publications, 89, 92
of scholarly publications, 90
wikis in, 349
Percent, percentage, 402
Percentage(s), numerals in, 337
Perfect tense(s), 249–50
types of, 249–50
using, 249–50
Period(s), 293–94
with abbreviations, 293–94, 333–36
abbreviations without, 293–94, 333, 334
with divisions in literary works, 294
in electronic addresses, 176, 294
with ellipses, 318–19
to end a sentence, 293
with identifying tags for quoted passages, 308–09
in indirect questions, 293, 295
MLA works-cited list, 142
with quotation marks, 308–09, 311
in revising comma splices, 234–35
in revising fused sentences, 234–35
in revising run-on sentences, 234–35
Periodical(s), 75. *See also* Journal article(s); Magazine article(s); Newspaper article(s)
previewing text, 2
Permalink URLs, 44
Person, 240, 278, 368
agreement in, 240–45, 368
shift in, 278
Personal communication. *See also* Email
APA in-text citations, 167
APA reference list, 174
audience for, 12
Chicago documentation style, 204–05, 209
conveying information informally, 11
genre selection, 15
journals in, 17
MLA works-cited list, 135, 139
privacy in the workplace, 355
Personal name(s). *See also* Author name(s); Titles of people
capitalizing, 325
Personal pronoun(s), 377, 385
avoiding apostrophes with plural, 307
list of, 385
Personal title(s). *See* Titles of people
Persuasive writing, 11. *See also* Argumentative essay(s)
Pharmacy. *See also* Natural and applied science(s)
composition overview, 364–65
Philosophy. *See also* Humanities
capitalizing names of philosophic movements, 326
composition overview, 364–65
specialized databases, 78
Photocopies, managing, 48–49, 67–69
Photograph(s), 346
in document design, 346
MLA works-cited list, 136
sample, 346
Phrasal verb(s), 370–71
inseparable, 371
separable, 370–71
Phrase(s), 237, 392. *See also* Transitional words and phrase(s) *and specific phrase types*
contradictory, commas with, 300
fixed amounts in, 242
in headings, 341
misplaced, 283
as modifiers, 283
in narrowing focus, 266
nonrestrictive, commas with, 299
plagiarism avoidance, 103
in series, 280
to signal comparisons, 265
to signal contrast, 265
between subject and verb, 241
subject-verb agreement in, 240–43
types of, 392
in varying sentence openings, 273
wordy, revising or eliminating, 275
Phrase fragments
appositive, 237
prepositional phrase, 237
verbal phrase, 237
Phrasing, of headings, 341
Physical sciences. *See* Natural and applied science(s)
Physics. *See also* Natural and applied science(s)
composition overview, 364–65
documentation styles, 231. *See also* CSE documentation style
Physiology, documentation style. *See* CSE documentation style
Place name(s)
abbreviating, 294, 335

capitalizing, 326
prepositions and, 380
Plagiarism, 99–106
avoiding, 42, 49, 50, 51, 95, 99–106
checklist, 104–05
detecting, 100
examples, 102–04
intentional, 100, 101
other kinds of, 101
revising to eliminate, 102–05
self-plagiarism, 101
in specific disciplines, 105–06
unintentional, 99–101
Planning, 16
analyzing assignment in, 16
of essay project, 15–17, 18–19, 20, 32–33
idea generation in, 17
of research project, 62–63
synthesis, 56–57
topic selection in, 16
in writing process, 15–17
Planning Guides
argumentative essays, 32–33
oral presentation, 356–57
research project, 62–63
synthesis, 56–57
thesis-and-support essay, 18–19, 32–33
Play(s). *See* Dramatic work(s)
Plural(s)
of abbreviations, 306
apostrophes to indicate, 306, 307
foreign, 324
forming, 306, 323–24
possessive case of, 304–05
singular subjects with plural forms, 242–43
subject-verb agreement, 240–43
Plural noun(s), 323–24
articles with, 375
using, 374
Plus, 402
Plus sign (+), to indicate nonconsecutive pages, 125
Podcast(s), 349
APA reference list, 178
Chicago documentation style, 210
CSE documentation style, 226
MLA works-cited list, 134
using, 349–50
Poetry. *See also* Literature
indicating omissions in, 319
italicizing titles of long poems, 329
long quotations of, 114, 116, 141, 310, 319, 329
MLA parenthetical references, 114, 116
MLA works-cited list, 132
numerals for lines of, 116, 337
periods for divisions in, 294
quotation marks for titles, 311
slashes to separate lines of, 310, 318
Political science, composition overview, 364–65
Popular periodical(s), 75, 90. *See also* Magazine article(s)
evaluating, 90
scholarly publications *versus,* 90–91
Portfolios. *See* Writing portfolios
Positive form, 259, 261
Possessive case, 253, 254
apostrophes in, 304–05, 306
determiners, 376
forming, 304–05
Postal abbreviation(s), 223, 294
Posters, 361
PowerPoint. See Microsoft PowerPoint
Precede, proceed, 402
Predicate, 391–92
commas between subject and, 301
compound, revising detached, 237
Predication, faulty, 279
Prediction, in conclusions, 268
Preface
APA reference list, 173
MLA works-cited list, 131
Prefix(es), hyphens with, 332
Preposition(s), 380–82, 389–90
commonly confused, 381
in idiomatic expressions, 380, 381–82
lists of, 380–82, 390
multilingual writers and, 380–82
object of, 254, 389
repeating for parallelism, 281
in titles of works, 327
using, 380–82, 389–90
Prepositional phrase(s), 392
commas with, 297, 298, 299
list of, 380
misplaced, 283
as modifiers, 283
phrase fragments, 237
in rambling sentences, 277
wordy, eliminating, 277
Present participle(s)
defined, 373, 388
formation of, 373
Present perfect progressive tense, 250
Present perfect tense, 249–50
Present progressive tense, 250
Present subjunctive mood, 251
Present tense, 248–49
agreement errors, 240
in literary analysis, 249
in principal parts, 246–48
special uses of, 249
using, 248–49
Presentation(s). *See* Oral presentation(s)

Presentation notes, 357–58
Presentation software package(s), 358–59, 360
Pretentious diction, 287
Previewing, 2–3
  checklist, 3
  of electronic texts, 7
  of text, 7
Prezi, 359
Primary research. *See* Field research
Primary source(s), 47–48
  balancing with secondary sources, 47–48
  in the humanities, 47–48
  in the natural and applied sciences, 48
  in the social sciences, 48
Principal part(s), 245–48
  irregular verbs, 246–48
  regular verbs, 245–46
Principal, principle, 402
Print source(s). *See also* Source(s); *specific print sources*
  APA in-text citations, 166–67
  APA reference list, 169–74
  Chicago documentation style, 198–205
  CSE reference list, 221–24, 225
  MLA parenthetical references, 115–18
  MLA works-cited list, 122, 123, 124, 125, 126, 127, 128–133,138–139
Privacy, in workplace communication, 355
Proceed, precede, 402
Professor. *See* Instructor
Progressive tense(s), 250–51
  types of, 250–51
  using, 250–51
Project MUSE, 77
Pronoun(s), 376–78, 385–86. *See also* Antecedent(s)
  agreement with antecedent, 240, 243–45, 256–57, 278–79, 377
  case, 253–56, 304–05, 306, 378
  to eliminate unnecessary repetition, 275
  forming possessive case of, 304
  gender, 378
  lists of, 242, 244, 377, 386
  multilingual writers and, 376–78
  placement in sentence, 377
  prepositions to introduce, 389–90
  reference, 256–57, 377
  revising reference errors, 256–57
  sexist use of, 245, 288–89
  subject-verb agreement, 241–42, 243
  types of, 385–86. *See also specific types*
  using, 253–57, 376–78, 385–86
Pronoun reference, 256–57, 377
Proofreading, 23–24, 70
Proper adjective(s), hyphens between prefixes and, 332
Proper noun(s), 325–27, 385
  capitalization rules, 325–27
  commas with names of people, 301
  hyphens between prefixes and, 332
ProQuest Research Library, 77
Prose
  indicating omissions in, 318–19
  long quotations of, 114, 116–17, 141, 165, 180, 309–10, 314
  MLA parenthetical references, 114, 116
Psychology. *See also* Social science(s)
  composition overview, 364–65
  specialized databases, 78
Public writing. *See also* Website(s)
  audience for, 12
Publication date(s)
  APA reference list, 169, 170, 182
  Chicago documentation style, 201
  CSE in-text citations, 222
  MLA works-cited list, 120, 123
Publication Manual of the American Psychological Association, 165n
Publisher's name
  APA reference list, 169–74
  Chicago documentation style, 201
  colons to separate publication place from, 314
  CSE reference list, 171
  MLA works-cited list, 120, 121, 122, 126, 127, 128, 314, 334
Punctuation, 291–319. *See also specific punctuation marks*
  APA reference lists, 169
  Chicago bibliography, 213, 218
  Chicago documentation style, 196–97
  CSE reference lists, 222, 223
  end, 293–95
  for identifying tags, 97, 300, 308–09
  to indicate changes to quotations, 97–98
  of lists, 343
  MLA parenthetical references, 114
  overview/directory, 292
  quick guide, 292
Purpose, 10, 347
  determining, 11
  of digital documents, 347
  of essay, 10–12, 16, 18
  prepositions and, 380
  for presentation, 356
  in previewing, 2–3
  in reading texts, 6
  of research project, 70
  thesis statement and, 18

of writer, 10–12
in writing for audience, 12

Q

Qiqqa, 68
Qtd. in (quoted in), MLA parenthetical references, 115, 146
Question(s)
asking for information, 383
in idea generation, 17
indirect, periods with, 293, 295
interview, 88
in introductions, 267
pronoun case in, 255
research, 43–44
research question, 43–44
survey, 88
tag, 300, 383–84
types of, 88
word order in, 382–84
yes/no, 382–83
Question mark(s), 294–95
abbreviations with periods and, 293
editing misused, 295
at end of direct question, 294
other punctuation marks with, 294–95
with questionable dates or numbers, 294
with quotation marks, 309, 312
as search operators, 73
Quotation(s)
additions within, 97–98, 216
APA in-text citations, 165, 180
brackets to indicate changes in, 97–98, 216
capitalizing first word of, 324
colons to introduce, 314
comments within, 317
in conclusions, 268
identifying tags, 96–97, 308–09
indirect, 313
integrating, 95–98
interrupted, commas with, 300
in introductions, 267
MLA parenthetical references, 114
MLA-style paper, 141, 147
in note-taking, 50, 55
omissions within, 98, 152, 318–19
of poetry, 114, 116, 141, 310, 319, 329
of prose, 114, 116–17, 141, 165, 180, 309–10, 314
within quotations, 312
run in with text, 114
set off from text, 114, 165
substitutions within, 97–98
Quotation mark(s), 307–13
APA reference list, 169
for borrowed words, 102, 103–04
colons with, 312
with definitions, 330
double, 312
editing misused, 313
with long prose passages, 309–10
with other punctuation marks, 300, 308–09, 311–12
with poetry passages, 310
as search operators, 72
single, 312
for titles of essays, 311
for titles of periodicals, 167
for titles of unpublished dissertations, 138
for titles of works, 119, 123–24, 131–32, 167, 311, 328
for titles within titles, 123–24, 131–32
when to use, 102, 103–04
Quotation, quote, 402
Quote, quotation, 402
Quoted in, Chicago documentation style, 203
Qur'an
capitalizing, 326
Chicago documentation style, 204
MLA parenthetical references, 116–17
MLA works-cited list, 132
no italics with, 329

R

Race(s), capitalizing names of, 326
Radio program(s)
italicizing titles of, 329
MLA works-cited list, 134, 137
quotation marks for episodes, 311
Raise, rise, 402
Rambling sentence(s)
adjective (relative) clauses, 276–77
excessive coordination, 276
passive constructions, 277
tightening, 276–77
wordy noun constructions, 277
wordy prepositional phrases, 277
Ratio(s), numerals in, 337
Reading, 2–9
active reading, 2
of electronic texts, 6–7
in idea generation, 17
sources in field research, 47
to write, 2–9
Real, really, 403
Reason is that, reason is because, 279, 403
Reciprocal pronoun(s), 386
Recording(s). *See also* Podcast(s)
APA reference list, 175
Chicago documentation style, 205
CSE reference list, 225
MLA works-cited list, 134, 137
Redundancy
deleting, 275
redundant, defined, 275

Refereed sources, 89, 92
Reference list(s), 169. *See also* Bibliography(ies) (documentation styles); Works-cited list(s)
  APA-style, 67–69, 108, 161–63, 169–79, 181, 182, 193
  CSE-style, 68, 69, 108, 219, 221–26, 227, 230
Reference, pronoun, 256–57, 377
Reference source(s), 80–81
  APA reference list, 174
  Chicago documentation style, 207
  general, 83–85, 87, 91
  MLA works-cited list, 127, 133
  online, 87, 91, 286
  specialized, 81
Reflective statement, 31–32
Reflective writing, 10
Reflexive pronoun(s), 386
Refutation, in argumentative essay, 33
RefWorks, 68
Regardless, irregardless, 400
Regular plural nouns, 304–05
Regular verb(s), 245–46
Rehearsal, of presentations, 361–62
Relative clause(s). *See* Adjective (relative) clause(s)
Relative pronoun(s), 386
  as antecedents, 243
  in complex sentences, 270, 271
  in dependent clause fragments, 237, 238
  list of, 243, 271, 386
  subject-verb agreement with, 243
Reliability, 89, 92
  of Internet sources, 92
  of library sources, 89
Religion(s). *See also* Humanities; Sacred text(s)
  capitalizing names of, 326
  composition overview, 364–65
  specialized databases, 78
Remote antecedent(s), 256–57
Repetition
  eliminating unnecessary, 275–76
  of key words and phrases, 281
  parallelism and, 281
  unnecessary, 275–76
Republished work(s), MLA works-cited list, 130
Research guides, 75–76
Research project(s), 41–106. *See also* Documentation; Exploratory research; Focused research; Internet research; Library research
  assignment analysis, 43
  checklists on, 42, 51, 69
  drafting, 61–64
  editing, 70
  exploratory research, 43–44, 70–87
  field research, 87–88
  final draft, 70
  fine-tuning thesis statement, 57
  focused research, 46–48
  integrating source material, 63–64, 95–99
  managing source information, 48–49
  note-taking, 50–57
  outlines, 57–61, 64
  plagiarism avoidance, 99–106
  planning, 62–63
  research, defined, 42
  research process, 42
  research question, 43–44
  revising, 64–69
  search strategy, 70–87
  sources for, 63–64
  thesis statement, 44, 45–46, 57, 62
  topic selection, 43
  visuals in. *See* Visual(s)
  working bibliography, 44–45
Research question, 43–44
Response papers
  critical, 8–9
  sample, 8–9
Restrictive clause(s), 257, 298–99
Restrictive modifier(s), 298–99, 301
Résumé(s), 352
  chronological order, 352, 353
  designing, 352
  sample, 353
Review(s). *See also* Book review(s)
  MLA works-cited list, 126
Revision
  checklists for, 22, 69, 267, 268
  with Compare Documents feature, 21
  of dangling modifiers, 284–85
  to eliminate plagiarism, 102–05
  of essays, 21–22
  of faulty modification, 282–85
  of faulty parallelism, 281
  of faulty predication, 279
  of fragments, 237–39
  instructor's comments in, 21, 64–65
  of intrusive modifiers, 284
  of misplaced modifiers, 282–84
  of misused abbreviations, 335–36
  of misused apostrophes, 307
  of misused colons, 314–15
  of misused commas, 301–02
  of misused question marks, 295
  of misused quotation marks, 313
  of misused semicolons, 303
  of mixed constructions, 279
  of paragraphs, 22
  peer review in, 13–14, 21, 65–66
  of pronoun reference errors, 256–57
  of research projects, 64–69
  strategies for, 21–22

with Track Changes, 21, 65–66
of unnecessary shifts, 278–79
word-processing tools for, 21, 64–66
Rhetorical situation, 9–15
assignment and, 10
audience for writing, 12–14
considering, 10
defined, 10
genre selection, 14–15
for oral presentation, 356
purpose for writing, 10–12
Rise, raise, 402
Rough draft, 61–64. *See also* Revision
essay, 20–21
research project, 61–64
Running heads, APA-style paper, 180
Run-on sentence(s), 234–36, 303
comma splice, 234–36
correcting, 234–36, 303
fused sentences, 234–36
recognizing, 234

S

's
in forming plurals, 304–05, 306
in forming possessive case, 304–05
-s, -es endings
plurals with, 240, 304–05
possessive form of nouns with, 304–05
-s, -ss endings, plurals with, 324
Sacred text(s). *See also* Bible; Qur'an
capitalizing titles of, 326
Chicago documentation style, 204
MLA parenthetical references, 116–17
MLA works-cited list, 132
no italics in titles of, 329
Salutation(s)
business letter, 314, 351
punctuation of, 314
Sarcasm, 295
Scene number, MLA parenthetical references, 116
Scholarly journal(s), 75. *See also* Journal article(s)
italicizing titles of, 328
Scholarly publication(s), 75, 90. *See also* Journal article(s)
evaluating, 90
popular publications *versus*, 90–91
refereed, 89, 92
scholarly journals, defined, 75
Scientific Style and Format: The CSE Style Manual for Authors, 220n
Scientific writing. *See also* CSE documentation style; Natural and applied science(s); *specific sciences*
documentation styles, 231
passive voice in, 252, 372
present tense to indicate scientific truth, 249
Scope of coverage, 90, 94
of Internet sources, 94
of library sources, 90
Score(s), numerals in, 337
Scratch outline(s), 20
essay, 20
example, 20
Sculpture, italicizing names of, 329
Search and Find command, 24
Search engine(s), 82–87
Bookmark or Favorites, 86
Boolean searches, 72–73
checklists, 86
choosing the right, 83–85
entering electronic address, 82
general-purpose, 83–85
italicizing names of, 329
lists of, 84–86
search operators, 72–73
specialized, 85–86
Search operators, 72–73
Search strategy, 70–87
exploratory research, 43–44, 70–87
focused research, 46–48
Season(s), names of, 328
Second person, 240, 278
Secondary source(s), 47–48
balancing with primary sources, 47–48
in the humanities, 47–48
in the natural and applied sciences, 48
quotations in Chicago documentation style, 203
in the social sciences, 48
Second-language learner(s). *See* Multilingual tip(s); Multilingual writers
Section(s)
APA in-text citations, 167
quotation marks for titles, 311
-seed, -cede endings, 323
Selected bibliography. *See* Bibliography(ies) (documentation styles)
Self-plagiarism, 101
-self, with reflexive pronouns, 386
Semicolon(s), 302–03
APA in-text citations, 168
in compound sentences, 235, 269
editing misused, 303
MLA parenthetical references, 116
quick guide, 292
with quotation marks, 312
in revising comma splices, 235
in revising fused sentences, 235
in revising run-on sentences, 235, 303

Semicolon(s) (*continued*)
to separate independent clauses, 292, 300, 302–03
in series, 292, 303
with transitional elements, 235, 269, 300, 303
Sentence(s), 269–81, 391–94. *See also* Common sentence error(s); Complex sentence(s); Compound sentence(s); Compound-complex sentence(s); Punctuation; Simple sentence(s); Subject of sentence; Topic sentence(s)
basic patterns, 391–92
capitalizing first word of, 324, 325
checklists for, 22
classifying, 394
concise, 273–77
imperative, 251, 295, 394
indicative, 251
periods to end, 293
revising, 22, 234–45
within sentences, parentheses with, 316
tenses in, 248–51
types of, 251, 269–71, 393–94
varied, 269–73
wordiness, eliminating, 274–75
Sentence fragment(s). *See* Fragment(s)
Sentence outlines, 58, 60–61, 64
research project, 60–61
sample, 60–61
Separable phrasal verb(s), 370–71
Sequence, words and phrases to signal, 265
Series
adjectives in, 296–97, 379
colons to introduce, 313
commas in, 292, 296–97, 302, 313
MLA works-cited list, 130
parallelism in, 280
semicolons in, 292, 303
Set, sit, 248, 373, 403
Sexist language, 245, 288–89
eliminating, 289
Search and Find command to locate, 24
Shall, will, 403
Shaping, 17–19
-sh endings, plurals with, 324
She, he, 288, 399
Shift(s), 278–79
in mood, 278
in number, 278–79
in person, 278
in tense, 278
unnecessary, revising, 278–79
in voice, 278, 285
Ship(s), italicizing names of, 329
Short story(ies)
MLA works-cited list, 132
quotation marks for titles, 311
Should have, 397
Should of, could of, would of, 397
[Sic] (thus), 317
Signed work(s), 133. *See also* Anonymous/unsigned work(s)
Silent letter(s), 323
Simple sentence(s), 269, 393
constructing, 391–92, 393
using, 393
Simple, simplistic, 403
Simple tense(s), 248–49
types of, 248–49
using, 248–49
Since, 403
Singular noun(s)
forming possessive case of, 304
subject-verb agreement, 240–43, 368
using, 374
Singular pronoun(s), forming possessive case of, 304
Sit, set, 248, 373, 403
Site, cite, 397
Slang, quotation marks with, 313
Slash(es), 317–18
in electronic addresses, 176, 294, 331
in quotes of poetry, 310, 318
to separate options, 317
Slide projectors, 361
So, 403
Social networking sites
APA reference list, 178–79
Chicago documentation style, 210
conveying information informally, 11
MLA works-cited list, 135
using, 350
Social science(s)
composition overview, 364–65
disciplines in, 364
documentation styles, 165, 196, 365. *See also* APA documentation style
genres used in, 364
plagiarism in, 105
research methods and sources in, 48, 78, 365
specialized databases, 78
style and format of papers in, 364
Sociology and social work. *See also* Social science(s)
composition overview, 364–65
specialized databases, 78
Software. *See also* Apps *and specific software names and types*
APA reference list, 175
citation tools, 67–69

course management, 349
file management, 66
grammar checkers, 24
for highlighting and annotating Web-based texts, 7
italicizing titles of, 329
MLA works-cited list, 135
open-source, 87, 349
plagiarism-detection, 100
presentation, 358–59, 360
in revision process, 21, 66
spell checkers, 24, 322
word processing. *See Microsoft Word;* Word processor(s)
Sometime, sometimes, some time, 403
Songs, quotation marks for titles, 311. *See also* Music
Sort of, kind of, 400
Source(s). *See also* Documentation; Electronic source(s); Print source(s)
citation tools, 67–69
ethics in using, 99–106. *See also* Plagiarism
evaluating, 89–95
in exploratory research, 43–44
integrating into paper, 63–64, 95–99
paraphrasing. *See* Paraphrase(s)
primary. *See* Primary source(s)
quoting. *See* Quotation(s)
reading, 47
in research notebook, 44–45
secondary. *See* Secondary source(s)
summarizing. *See* Summary(ies)
synthesizing, 55–57
visuals in Chicago-style paper, 211–12
in working bibliography, 44–45
Spacecraft, italicizing names of, 329
Special dictionary(ies), 81
Special event names, capitalizing, 325, 326
Specialized databases, 76, 77–79
Specialized search engines, 85–86
Specific word(s), 286
Speech(es). *See* Oral presentation(s)
Spell checker(s), 24, 322
Spelling, 322–24
-able, -ible endings, 323
editing, 23–24
final consonants, doubling, 322
homophones, 287, 395–405
ie/ei combinations, 322
plurals, 323–24
-seed, -cede endings, 323
silent *e* before suffix, 323
silent letters, 323
spell checkers, 24, 322
suffixes, 323
y before suffix, 323
Split infinitive(s), 284
Squinting modifier(s), 283
State names, abbreviating, 294
Statistic(s)
documenting source of, 103
numerals in, 337
Stereotypes, types of, 288
Street name(s), abbreviating, 335
Structure names, capitalizing, 325
Style
document design. *See* Document design
in the humanities. *See* Chicago documentation style; MLA documentation style
in the natural and applied sciences. *See* CSE documentation style
in the social sciences. *See* APA documentation style
Subject complement(s), 258, 387, 392
with adjectives, 258
compound, detached, 237
in subjective case, 253
Subject of sentence, 391–92
agreement with verb, 240–43, 368
collective nouns as, 242
commas between predicate and, 301
compound, 241
creating new, to correct dangling modifier, 284
indefinite pronouns as, 240, 241–42, 377
inverting subject-verb order, 243
lack of, in fragments, 236, 238–39
singular subjects with plural forms, 242–43
Subject of verb, subjective case with, 253
Subject search, 73
online catalog, 73
subscription database, 74–79
Subjective (nominative) case, 253, 255
Subject-verb agreement, 240–43, 368
Subjunctive mood, 251
eliminating need for, 252
forming, 251–52
using, 251–52
Subordinate clause(s). *See* Dependent (subordinate) clause(s)
Subordinating conjunction(s), 390–91
in complex sentences, 270
in dependent clause fragments, 237, 238
list of, 270, 390–91
Subordination
defined, 272
in varied sentences, 272
Subscription services, library, 74–79

Subsequent edition(s)
  Chicago documentation style, 203
  MLA works-cited list, 130
Subsequent references, Chicago documentation style, 197, 217
Subtitles, colons to separate titles from, 314
Suffix(es)
  -able, -ible, 323
  doubling final consonants before, 322
  hyphens with, 332
  -seed, -cede, 323
  silent *-e* before, 323
  spelling rules, 323
  -y before, 323
Summary(ies), 52–53. *See also* Abstract(s)
  in critical response, 8
  dashes to set off, 315
  identifying tags with, 98–99, 266
  integrating, 52–53
  MLA parenthetical references for, 114
  in note-taking, 50, 52–53
  sample, 52–53
Superlative form, 259–61
  defined, 260
  illogical, 261
  irregular, 261
  regular, 260
  using, 260
Superscript(s), 139, 196
  APA documentation style, 179
  Chicago documentation style, 196, 211, 215
  CSE in-text citations, 220, 228
  MLA documentation style, 139–40, 146, 149
Supposed to, used to, 404
SurfWax, 85
Survey(s)
  conducting, 88
  defined, 88
  field research, 88
Suspended hyphen(s), 332
s.v. (under the word), 207
Symbol(s)
  in highlighting text, 3
  numerals with, 336, 337
Synchronous communication, 348
Synonym(s)
  defined, 285
  in thesaurus entry, 285–86
Syntax, plagiarism avoidance, 103
Synthesis, 55–57
  in critical response, 8
  in note-taking, 55–57
  planning, 56–57
  sample, 56
  of source material in paper, 55–57
  understanding, 56
Synthesizing source(s), 55–57

T

Table(s), 344
  APA in-text citations, 168
  APA-style paper, 181, 190
  Chicago-style paper, 211–12
  CSE-style paper, 227
  in document design, 344
  MLA-style paper, 142
  sample, 344
Tag question(s)
  commas with, 300
  defined, 383–84
Take, bring, 397
Taking notes. *See* Note-taking
Technical terms
  abbreviating, 334, 335
  quotation marks with, 313
Technical writing
  abbreviations of technical terms, 334, 335
  APA reference list, 174
  CSE reference list, 224
  documentation styles, 231
  passive voice in, 252, 372
  present tense to indicate scientific truth, 249
Telephone communication
  APA in-text citations, 167
  text messages, 273, 333
Teleprompt+, 358
Television program(s)
  APA reference list, 174–75
  italicizing titles of, 329
  MLA works-cited list, 134–35, 137
  quotation marks for episodes, 311
Temperature(s), abbreviating, 334
Tense, 248–51, 368–69
  perfect tenses, 249–50
  progressive tenses, 250–51
  shift in, 278
  simple tenses, 248–49
Tentative thesis, 45–46, 57
Text message(s), 273, 333
Than
  comparisons with, 254
  parallel elements linked by, 280–81
Than, then, 404
That
  ambiguous antecedent, 256
  commas with, 97, 257, 299
  in restrictive clauses, 257
That, which, who, 257, 404
The
  omission from newspaper titles, 200, 328
  use as article, 375

The number, a number, 242
The reason...is because, faulty predication, 279, 403
Their
in eliminating sexist language, 288–89
pronoun-antecedent agreement with, 244
Their, there, they're, 404
Themselves, theirselves, theirself, 404
Then, than, 404
There, their, they're, 404
Thesauri, 285–86
Thesis, 18
Thesis statement
argumentative, 33
characteristics of effective, 18–19
defined, 18
essay, 18–19, 33
fine-tuning, 57
in reading texts, 6
research project, 44, 45–46, 57, 62
in shaping essay, 18–19
structure of, 18–19
tentative, 45–46, 57
Thesis-and-support essays, 17–19, 32–33
model MLA-style essays, 25–30, 34–40
Planning Guides, 18–19, 32–33
They
in eliminating sexist language, 288–89
their, there, they're, 404
Thinking critically, 13
in annotating text, 4–5
critical response to text, 8–9
in research process, 42
in writing process, 13
Third person, 240, 278
This, ambiguous antecedent, 256
Till, until, 'til, 404
Time measure(s)
abbreviating, 334–35
capitalizing, 325, 326, 328
colons in expressions of, 314
commas in dates, 301
complex sentences to indicate relationships, 271
numerals in, 337
prepositions and, 380
present tense to indicate future time, 249
words and phrases to signal time, 265
Title page(s)
APA-style paper, 183
Chicago-style paper, 211, 214
CSE-style paper, 226
MLA-style paper, 143
Titles of people
abbreviating, 333
academic degrees, 301, 325
capitalizing, 325
commas with, 301
periods with, 293
sexist use of, 288
Titles of work(s)
APA-style paper, 183
articles in, 125, 200, 327, 328
capitalizing important words in, 327
Chicago-style paper, 211, 214, 215
colons to separate subtitles from, 314
CSE-style paper, 228
essay title selection, 23
italicizing, 116–18, 130, 131, 311, 328–29
MLA-style paper, 143, 144
omitting *the* from newspaper titles, 200, 328
quotation marks to set off, 123–24, 129, 131–32, 167, 311, 328
research project, 70
shortened, in MLA parenthetical references, 114, 115, 117, 118, 334
within titles, in MLA works cited list, 123–24, 131–32
To
in forming infinitives, 373, 388
as preposition, 381
To, at, 396
To, too, two, 404
Topic outlines, 58
research project, 58, 59–60
sample, 59–60
Topic selection
essay, 16
idea generation and, 17
presentations, 356
research project, 43
topic, defined, 16
Topic sentence(s)
at beginning of paragraph, 264–65
implied, 265
placement of, 264–65
research project, 63
in unified paragraphs, 264–65
Track Changes feature, 21, 65–66
Train(s), italicizing names of, 329
Transcription(s), APA reference list, 175
Transitional words and phrase(s), 265–66, 299
at beginning of sentence, 297
in coherent paragraphs, 265–66
commas with, 235, 239, 297, 299–300
in compound sentences, 269

Transitional words and phrase(s) (*continued*)
  to connect independent clauses, 235, 300
  fragments introduced by, 239
  frequently-used, 265–66
  list of, 265–66, 269
  semicolons to introduce, 235, 269, 300, 303
  to separate independent clauses, 292
Transitive verb(s), 372–73, 391, 392
Translation(s), MLA works-cited list, 130
Try to, try and, 404
Turabian documentation style, 196n. *See also* Chicago documentation style
Turnitin.com, 100
Twitter. *See also* Social networking sites
  using, 350
Two, to, too, 404
Type size, in document design, 341
-type, 404
Typeface, in document design, 341, 342

U

Underlining, in highlighting text, 3
Unified paragraphs, 264–65
Unintentional plagiarism. *See also* Plagiarism
  avoiding, 42, 49, 50, 51, 100–01
  defined, 99–100
Uninterested, disinterested, 398
Unique, 405
Unnecessary repetition, 275–76
Unnecessary shifts, revising, 278–79
Unsigned work(s), 133. *See also* Anonymous/unsigned work(s)
Until, till, 'til, 404
URL (uniform resource locator), 82
  APA reference list, 175–79
  Chicago documentation style, 206–10
  division of, 176, 212, 294, 331
  domain name, 86, 94
  entering electronic address, 82, 348, 355
  legitimacy of online sources, 94
  MLA works-cited list, 133–35
  pasting, 44, 82
  permalink, 44
Us, we, before a noun, 255–56
Used to, supposed to, 404
Utility word(s), 274, 286
Utilize, 405

V

Vague wording, 19
Vandalism, 87
Varied sentence(s), 269–73
  length in, 271–72
  sentence openings in, 272–73
Verb(s), 245–52, 387–88. *See also* Tense; Verbals, verbal phrase(s); Voice; *specific types of verbs*
  action, 258–59
  agreement with subject, 240–43, 368
  base form, 245–48
  formed from nouns, 374
  to introduce source material, 96
  inverting subject-verb order, 243
  irregular, 188, 246–48, 368, 388
  lack of, in fragments, 236, 238–39
  mood, 251–52, 278
  multilingual writers and, 368–74
  negative, 369–70
  phrasal, 370–71
  principal parts, 245–48
  regular, 245–46
  simplest verb forms, 369
  types of, 387–88
  using, 368–74, 387–88
  voice, 252, 277, 372. *See also* Active voice; Passive voice
Verb phrase(s), 387, 392
Verbals, verbal phrase(s), 388, 392. *See also* Past participle(s); *specific types of verbal*
  commas with, 297, 298, 299
  as fragments, 236
  infinitives in, 373, 388
  misplaced, 283
  as modifiers, 283
  phrase fragments, 237
  recognizing, 388
  types of, 388
Video games
  italicizing names of, 329
Video recordings. *See* DVD(s) (digital videodiscs); DVD-ROMs; Online video
Visual(s), 64, 344–46. *See also* Document design; Website(s)
  APA-style paper, 180–81, 190, 192
  checklists, 142, 180–81, 211–12, 346
  Chicago-style paper, 211–12
  CSE-style paper, 227, 229
  integrating, 64, 142
  MLA-style paper, 142
  online resources of images, 64
  presentation software, 358–59, 360
  in research projects, 64, 142

Visual aid(s), 358–61
chalkboards, 361
computer presentations, 358–59, 360
document cameras, 360
flip charts, 361
overhead projectors, 360
posters, 361
slide projectors, 361
whiteboards, 361
Visual cues, 2
annotating text, 4–5
highlighting text, 3
in previewing texts, 2, 3
in writing, 4–5
Voice, 252, 277, 372. *See also* Active voice; Passive voice
shifts in, 278, 285

W

Wait for, wait on, 405
Warning, in conclusions, 268
We, us, before a noun, 255–56
Weather, whether, 405
Web, 81–87
MLA works-cited list, 133–35
plagiarism avoidance, 102
plagiarism detection, 100
search engines, 72–73, 82–87, 329
URLs, 82
Web browsers, 82–87, 329
Web browser(s), 82–87
checklist, 86
italicizing names of, 329
keyword search, 82–83
Web page(s). *See* Home page(s)
Website(s), 71
APA reference list, 177
Chicago documentation style, 209
evaluating content of, 91–95
italicizing names of, 329
library, 70–73
MLA works-cited list, 133–35
Website design. *See* Document design; Website(s)
Well, good, 399
Well developed paragraphs, 266–67
Were, we're, 405
Whether, if, 400
Whether, weather, 405
Which
ambiguous antecedent, 256
commas with, 257, 299
in nonrestrictive clauses, 257
Which, who, that, 257, 404
White, capitalizing, 326
White space, in document design, 340
Whiteboards, 361
Who, which, that, 257, 404
Who, whom, 254–55, 405
Whoever, whomever, 254–55
Who's, whose, 405
Wikipedia, 87
Wikis, 349
using, 349
Will, shall, 403
Wired classroom. *See* Digital document(s)
Word. See Microsoft Word
Word(s), 285–89. *See also* Parts of speech; Transitional words and phrase(s); Word order
abstract, 286, 385
borrowed, 102, 103–04
breaking at end of line, 330–31
capitalizing first, 324, 325
checklists for, 22
choosing right, 285
clichés, 287–88
commonly confused, 287, 381, 395–405
compound, 331–32
concrete, 286
connotation, 285
denotation, 285
euphemisms, 286
general, 286
hyphens to divide, 330–32
inappropriate language, 287–88
jargon, 287
key, repeating, 281
in narrowing of focus, 266
offensive, 24, 245, 288–89
order of. *See* Word order
plagiarism avoidance, 102, 103–04
pretentious diction, 287
repeating, 281
revising, 22
in series, 280
sexist language, 24, 245, 288–89
to signal comparisons, 265
to signal contrast, 265
specific, 286
stereotypes, 288
between subject and verb, 240–41
utility, eliminating, 274, 286
in varying sentence openings, 273
as words, apostrophes in plurals of, 306
as words, setting off, 306, 311, 329–30
Word order, 243, 382–84
inverting, 243
multilingual writers and, 382–84
position of adjectives, 378–79
position of adverbs, 378–79
in questions, 382–84
standard, 382
subject-verb agreement, 243

Word processor(s). *See also Microsoft Word*
file labels, 66
file management, 66
grammar checkers, 24
in revision process, 21
spell checkers, 24, 322
thesaurus access, 286
Wordiness, eliminating, 274–75
circumlocution, 275
deadwood, 274
excessive coordination, 276
noun constructions, 277
passive constructions, 277
prepositional phrases, 277
utility words, 274, 286
wordy phrases, revising, 275
Wording
of thesis statement, 19
vague, 19
WordPress, 349
Working bibliography, 44–45
assembling, 44–45
computer file, 44
Workplace communication, 350–55. *See also* Business letter(s)
audience for, 12
emails, 352, 355
memos, 352, 354
privacy issues, 355
résumés, 352, 353
Works-cited list(s), 44, 118. *See also* Bibliography(ies) (documentation styles)
checklists, 142
MLA-style, 67–69, 108, 109–11, 118–39, 142, 158–60
preparing, 67–69
working bibliography as basis for, 44–45
World Wide Web. *See entries beginning with* "Web"
WorldCat/WorldCat Local, 73
Would have, 397
Would of, should of, could of, 397
Writing. *See also* College writing; Essay(s); Multilingual tip(s); Multilingual writers; Personal communication; Research project(s)
audience types, 12
composition overview, 364–65
patterns of development, 10–12
public, 12
reading to write, 2–9
rhetorical situation, 9–15, 356
stages of writing process, 15–24
workplace communication, 12, 350–55
Writing center
conferences, 21
plagiarism avoidance, 101
Writing portfolios, 30–32
assembling, 30–31
checklist, 31
purpose of, 30
reflective statement, 31–32
Writing process
stages of, 15–24
word-processing tools for, 24

X

-x endings, plurals with, 324

Y

Yahoo!, 84
-y endings
in comparatives, 260
plurals with, 323–24
suffixes with, 323
Yes, commas with, 300
Yes/no question(s), 382–83
Yippy, 85
Your, you're, 405
YouTube
APA reference list, 178
Chicago documentation style, 210
MLA works-cited list, 134
with presentation software, 359

Z

-z endings, plurals with, 324
Zoo, 85
Zoology, documentation style. *See* CSE documentation style
Zotero, 69

Correction Symbols

abbr Incorrect abbreviation: **37a–c**; *editing misuse,* **37d**
adj Incorrect adjective: **19a; 44d**; *comparative/superlative forms,* **19c**
adv Incorrect adverb: **19b; 44d**; *comparative/superlative forms,* **19c**
agr Faulty agreement: *subject/verb,* **16a**; *pronoun/antecedent,* **16b**
aud Audience not clear: *identifying audience,* **2c; 40a**
awk Awkward: **23a–c**
ca Incorrect case: **18a**; *case in special situations,* **18b**
cap Incorrect capitalization: **34a–b**; *editing misuse,* **34c**
coh Lack of coherence: *paragraphs,* **20b**
con Be more concise: **22a–c**
cs Comma splice: *correcting,* **14b**
d Inappropriate diction: *appropriate words,* **26a**; *inappropriate language,* **26b**; *offensive language,* **26c**
dead Deadwood: **22a1**
det Use concrete details: **26a3–4**
dev Inadequate development: **20c**
dm Dangling modifier: **25c**
doc Incorrect or inadequate documentation: *MLA,* **10a**; *APA,* **11a**; *Chicago,* **12a**; *CSE,* **13a**
exact Use more exact word: **26a**
frag Sentence fragment: *correcting,* **15b**
fs Fused sentence: *correcting,* **14b**
ital Use italics: **35a–c**; *for emphasis or clarity,* **35d**
mix Mixed construction: **23b**
mm Misplaced modifier: **25a**
ms Incorrect manuscript form: *MLA,* **10b**; *APA,* **11b**; *Chicago,* **12b**; *CSE,* **13b**
num Incorrect use of numeral or spelled-out number: **37c; 38a–b**
p Punctuation error: **Pt. 6**
par *or* **¶** New paragraph: **20a–d**
no ¶ No paragraph: **20a–d**
¶ coh Paragraph not coherent: **20b**
¶ dev Paragraph not developed: **20c**
¶ un Paragraph not unified: **20a**
plan Lack of planning: **3a; 42b**
purp Purpose not clear: *determining purpose,* **2b; 40a**; *purpose checklist,* **p. 11**
ref Incorrect pronoun reference: **18c**
rep Unnecessary repetition: *eliminating,* **22b**
rev Revise: **3d; 9e**
run-on Run-on sentence: *correcting,* **14b**
shift Unnecessary shift: **23a**
sp Spelling error: **33a–g**
sxt Sexist or offensive language: **26c2**
thesis Unclear or unstated thesis: **3b; 5d; 5h**
var Lack of sentence variety: **21a–c**
w Wordiness: *eliminating,* **22a**
ʼ Apostrophe: **30a–d**
[ ] Brackets: **32d**
: Colon: **32a1–3**; *editing misuse,* **32a4**
, Comma: **28a–f**; *editing misuse,* **28g**
— Dash: **32b**
. . . Ellipsis: **32f**
! Exclamation point: **27c**
// Faulty parallelism: *using parallelism,* **24a**; *revising,* **24b**
- Hyphen: **36a–b**
( ) Parentheses: **32c**
. Period: **27a**
? Question mark: **27b**
" " Quotation marks: **31a–c**; *with other punctuation,* **31d**; *editing misuse,* **31e**
; Semicolon: **29a–b**; *editing misuse,* **29c**
/ Slash: **32e**

Contents

Ten Habits of Successful Students (insert)
How to Use This Book v
Teaching and Learning Resources viii

PART 1 Approaching Texts 1

1 Reading to Write 2
a Previewing a Text 2
b Highlighting a Text 3
c Annotating a Text 4
d Reading Electronic Texts 6
e Writing a Critical Response 8

2 Understanding the Rhetorical Situation 9
a Considering the Rhetorical Situation 10
b Determining Your Purpose 10
c Identifying Your Audience 12
d Selecting a Genre 14

3 Developing Essay Projects 15
a Planning 15
b Shaping 17
c Constructing a Scratch Outline 20
d Drafting and Revising 20
e Editing and Proofreading 23
f Model Student Essay 25
g Creating a Writing Portfolio 30

4 Writing an Argumentative Essay 32
a Organizing an Argumentative Essay 32
b Model Argumentative Essay 34

PART 2 Conducting Research 41

5 Developing a Research Project 42
a Moving from Assignment to Topic 43
b Doing Exploratory Research and Formulating a Research Question 43
c Assembling a Working Bibliography 44
d Developing a Tentative Thesis 45
e Doing Focused Research 46
f Managing Photocopies, Scans, and Downloaded Material 48
g Taking Notes 50
h Fine-Tuning Your Thesis 57
i Outlining, Drafting, and Revising 57
j Preparing a Final Draft 70

6 Finding Information 70
a Finding Information in the Library 70
b Finding Information on the Internet 81
c Doing Field Research 87

7 Evaluating Sources 89
a Evaluating Library Sources 89
b Evaluating Internet Sources 91

8 Integrating Source Material into Your Writing 95
a Integrating Quotations 95
b Integrating Paraphrases and Summaries 98

9 Using Sources Ethically 99
a Defining Plagiarism 99
b Avoiding Unintentional Plagiarism 100
c Avoiding Intentional Plagiarism 101
d Avoiding Other Kinds of Plagiarism 101
e Revising to Eliminate Plagiarism 102
f Understanding Plagiarism in the Disciplines 105

PART 3 Documenting Sources 107

10 MLA Documentation Style 113
a Using MLA Style 113
b MLA-Style Manuscript Guidelines 141
c Model MLA-Style Research Paper 141

11 APA Documentation Style 165
a Using APA Style 165
b APA-Style Manuscript Guidelines 179
c Model APA-Style Research Paper 182

12 Chicago Documentation Style 196
a Using Chicago Humanities Style 196
b Chicago Humanities Manuscript Guidelines 211
c Model Chicago Humanities Research Paper (Excerpts) 213

13 CSE and Other Documentation Styles 220
a Using CSE Style 220
b CSE-Style Manuscript Guidelines 226
c Model CSE-Style Research Paper (Excerpts) 227
d Using Other Documentation Styles 230

PART 4 Writing Grammatical Sentences 233

14 Revising Run-Ons 234
a Recognizing Comma Splices and Fused Sentences 234
b Correcting Comma Splices and Fused Sentences 234